Our Language and Our World

Also edited by S. I. Hayakawa
Language, Meaning and Maturity
Selections from ETC.: A *Review of General Semantics*, 1943–1953

Our Language and Our World

Selections from
ETC.: *A Review of General Semantics*
1953–1958

Edited by
S. I. HAYAKAWA

Illustrations, except as noted, by
William H. Schneider

H|B

Harper & Brothers, Publishers, New York

*George F. Johnson Library
St. Peter's College
Jersey City 6, N. J.*

OUR LANGUAGE AND OUR WORLD
Copyright © 1959 by S. I. Hayakawa
Copyright © 1953, 1954, 1955, 1956, 1957, 1958 by The International Society for General Semantics
Printed in the United States of America

All rights in this book are reserved. No part of the book may be used or reproduced in any manner whatsoever without written permission except in the case of brief quotations embodied in critical articles and reviews. For information address Harper & Brothers, 49 East 33rd Street, New York 16, N. Y.

FIRST EDITION

C-I

The Library of Congress catalog entry for this book appears at the end of the text.

Contents

FOREWORD — vii

I COMMUNICATION IN PUBLIC AFFAIRS

A Gospel-True Fable	Louis B. Salomon	3
Semantic Difficulties in International Communication	Edmund S. Glenn	12
Shall We Sit Idly By?	Herbert A. Thelen	35
The Meanings of "Democracy": Puerto Rican Organizations in Chicago	Lester C. Hunt, Jr. Nicholas von Hoffman	52
Intensional Orientation and National Unity: A Case Study from Pakistan	John J. Honigmann	66
The Process of News Reporting	Ken Macrorie	75
The Milk of Human Kindness?	Stanley Diamond	88
How to Attend a Conference	S. I. Hayakawa	103

II EDUCATION AND RE-EDUCATION

The Art of Psychoanalysis	Jay Haley	113
Reality, Possibility and Children	David Smillie	126
Semantic Play Therapy	Salvatore Russo Howard W. Jaques	133

A Semantic Approach to Counseling William H. Pemberton 141
The Significance of Being Unique Earl C. Kelley 152
Toward a Theory of Creativity Carl R. Rogers 172
Toward a Humanistic Psychology A. H. Maslow 186
The Fully Functioning Personality S. I. Hayakawa 202

III THE ARTS: HIGHBROW AND LOW

Design as Metaphor Weller Embler 221
Sexual Fantasy and the 1957 Car S. I. Hayakawa 235
Why the Edsel Laid an Egg: Motivational Research vs. the Reality Principle S. I. Hayakawa 241
The Language of Pictures Paul R. Wendt 247
A Grammar of Assassination Martin Maloney 256
Communication in Science Fiction Robert Plank 272
Popular Songs vs. the Facts of Life S. I. Hayakawa 279

IV LANGUAGE AND THOUGHT

The Blind Men and the Elephant: Three Ends to One Tale Raymond J. Corsini 295
A Chinese Philosopher's Theory of Knowledge Chang Tung-sun 299
What Phonetic Writing Did to Meaning Richard Dettering 325
Technological Models of the Nervous System Anatol Rapoport 343
The Psychology of Heresy Hans H. Toch 358
Language and Truth Weller Embler 371

Index 387

Foreword

This is the second collection of articles from the quarterly *ETC.: A Review of General Semantics* to appear in book form. The first, *Language, Meaning and Maturity* (Harper, 1954), was chosen from *ETC.'s* first ten volumes, 1943-1953. The present collection, with the exception of one article from an earlier volume, is selected from issues of *ETC.* published from 1953 to 1958, Volumes XI to XV.

The unity of this collection, as in the case of the earlier anthology, lies in the fact that all the contributors are concerned with problems of communication in ways that are meaningful from the point of view of general semantics. Most of the contributors may be termed "general semanticists," in that they derive a considerable portion of their insights and theoretical apparatus from the formulations of Alfred Korzybski (1879-1950), whose book *Science and Sanity: An Introduction to Non-Aristotelian Systems and General Semantics* (Lancaster, Pa., 1933; 4th ed., Lakeville, Conn., 1958) gave a name to this area of concern and intellectual capital with which to start business. The remaining contributors (except for Chang Tung-sun, whose views on the matter are not known) are friendly to the Korzybskian point of view—at least friendly enough to contribute to a journal which represents it.

The Korzybskian point of view is simply stated. It is that assumptions about the nature of our knowledge which underlie modern science are the assumptions essential to sanity. Prescientific assumptions are embedded in language itself, to some extent in vocabulary, but even more significantly in its structure. As Korzybski wrote:

> ... a language, any language, has at its bottom certain metaphysics, which ascribe, consciously or unconsciously, some sort of structure to this world. ...
>
> We do not realize what tremendous power the structure of an habitual language has. It is not an exaggeration to say that it enslaves us through the mechanism of semantic reactions and that the structure which a language exhibits and impresses upon us unconsciously, is *automatically projected* upon the world around us. (*Science and Sanity*, pp. 89-90)

General semantics was conceived of by Korzybski as a discipline to improve human functioning and to reduce the propensity of human beings to talk themselves into trouble. It seeks these goals by striving to increase awareness of the extent to which the way in which we talk about the world shapes our perceptions of that world. " 'Mental' therapy," wrote Korzybski in *Science and Sanity* in the course of his discussion of Freud, "always has the semantic aim and method; namely, to discover the unconscious material and make it conscious, and so make proper evaluation possible." The "unconscious material" of general semantics is the linguistic unconscious. And the goals of general semantics, like those of psychoanalysis, are therapeutic as well as scientific.

As the present collection reveals, general semantics has had a broad influence. Although Korzybski himself stressed principally the usefulness of general semantics in education and psychotherapy, he also insisted that as a *general* theory of human symbolic functioning, it would prove suggestive and valuable in almost every kind of human activity. Twenty-five years after the publication of *Science and Sanity*, it looks as if he might yet prove to have been right. The essays herein—on international communication, community organization, communication in business, education, psychotherapy and personality theory, art and design, popular culture, general linguistics and philosophy—represent only some of the many directions in which general semantics has stimulated inquiry and provided insights.

The following are other developments which are not mentioned in this book. *Western Reserve Law Review* (March, 1958) devoted an entire issue to general semantics and the law. Almost a thousand executives of the Pacific Telephone and Telegraph Company were given forty-hour training courses in general semantics in the early months of 1957, using a discussion manual prepared by the late Irving J. Lee (later published as *Handling Barriers in Communication*, by Irving J. and Laura L. Lee, Harper, 1957). A unit of general semantics is required of all cadets in the U.S. Air Force Academy in Denver. Classes in general semantics are being conducted in a number of penal institutions, some initiated by the educational or custodial staff (as at San Quentin) and some by the inmates themselves (as at Leavenworth). Psychological tests to measure evaluative well-being and evaluative disorder have been devised on general semantics principles.

Books and articles on general semantics—original works as well as translations from U.S. sources—have appeared in the past ten years in German, Swedish, Italian, Spanish, Japanese, Chinese (in Taiwan and Hong Kong), and Korean. Two rival organizations, with differing interpretations of general semantics, are reported to exist in Tokyo. Critical discussion of general semantics has appeared in philosophical and linguistic circles in the Communist nations. A sober evaluation of general semantics and its limitations as judged from a Thomist point of view is now to be found in Mother Margaret Gorman's monograph, *The Educational Implications of the Theory of Meaning and Symbolism of General Semantics* (Catholic University of America Press, 1958). An International Conference on General Semantics sponsored by Mexico City College in August, 1958, attracted two hundred and fifty participants from many nations and many fields of endeavor—education, government, business, diplomacy. *The Saturday Evening Post* (December 27, 1958) introduced its readers to general semantics through an article, "How Words Change Men's Lives," by the present writer.

While students of general semantics have reason to be gratified at the spread of their ideas (and I have far from exhausted the list of indications of interest), they have no reason for complacency. The wide diffusion of Korzybski's ideas is clear indication that they "sound right" to people in many fields of activity. But general semantics, like any other brilliant and ambitious synthesis, contains much that is only half-proved, much that is conjectural. Hence, much that sounds right still has to be proved right—or wrong. Much that is theoretically attractive still has to undergo the tests of experimental validation as well as practical application.

Dr. Anatol Rapoport once wrote that the value of a theory lies not so much in the questions it answers as in the fruitful questions it raises. Dr. Hans Selye, the great pioneer in research into the effects of stress on the organism, has expressed a similar thought: "My theories are not infallibly true—and, to my mind, a theory, to be valuable, need not be true but fertile, fertile in leading us to important new facts. When a theory has been fully proved, it has run its course."

Are the questions raised by general semantics fruitful? Are its theories fertile? We who feel that they are can establish our case only by further research and further thought. It is hoped, therefore, that this collection will raise at least as many questions as it answers— questions that will lead to new theories and new interpretations as well as to new facts.

The important questions raised by general semantics are urgent ones, having to do, as Korzybski insisted, with the sanity of the human race. Dr. G. Brock Chisholm, former Director General of the World Health Organization and now president of the World Federation for Mental Health, has said:

> We find that rarely is it possible to discuss intelligently, without striking prejudices which have been inculcated in childhood, such ordinary commonplace things as health, clothes, Negroes, politics, patriotism, conscience, Jews, superstitions, war and peace, money, sex, property, marriage, religions, some diseases, India, wage scales, socialism, communism, trade unions, political parties, and so on through a long list which varies from place to place, time to time, family to family. Very few people can think clearly and honestly about many of these things; and yet these, and such as these, are the things which make up the life of man and which, misunderstood, mishandled, and fought over, have caused most of the fear and misery of the world. ("Can Man Survive?" *ETC.*, IV [1947], 107.)

Such being the human condition, the tasks of general semantics, both scientific and therapeutic, are as urgent as they are enormous. We know all too little about the health and pathology of human communication and symbolic functioning—and what we know, we largely fail to apply. At all levels, therefore, the theoretical as well as the practical, students of general semantics have work to do. I earnestly hope that this volume will to some degree stimulate that work.

It remains for me to acknowledge my indebtedness to the many people who, by helping to keep *ETC.* going and growing, have made the present volume possible. The Board of Directors of the International Society for General Semantics, which has continued to honor me with the editorship of *ETC.*, has guided me in innumerable ways, by consultation and correspondence, in the performance of my tasks, at the same time allowing me genuine editorial freedom. My colleagues, Dr. Anatol Rapoport (associate editor since 1945), Dean Russell F. W. Smith (assistant and associate editor, 1951-1955), Dr. John R. Kirk (assistant editor, 1953-1956), Dr. Richard Dettering (assistant editor since 1956), and Dr. Walter E. Stuermann (assistant editor since 1957) have shared with me the pleasures and burdens of editorial work, as well as the recurrent embarrassment caused by spring issues that appear in July and summer issues that appear in October.

Jean Taylor (later Mrs. David M. Burrell) was executive secretary of the International Society for General Semantics for five years, from 1950 to 1955. Her untimely death in July, 1958, was deeply mourned by all members of ISGS who knew her, whether personally or through her lively correspondence. The ingenuity and effort and personal warmth which she expended in steering ISGS through these difficult years had much to do with its survival and growth.

Evelyn Rochetto (Mrs. Paul A. Rochetto), membership secretary from 1950 to 1955 and executive secretary since 1955, has continued throughout the years to serve ISGS with an energy and devotion beyond the call of duty. Her work in initiating services for chapters of ISGS, which are scattered in many cities throughout the U.S. and Canada, has been especially helpful to the organization. I am also indebted to Miss Nancy Baker of San Francisco for her assistance in preparing the present manuscript for publication.

Grateful acknowledgment is made for permission to quote brief selections from the following:

The Science of Culture by Leslie A. White (Farrar, Straus & Cudahy, 1949)

Science and Sanity by Alfred Korzybski (4th ed., Lakeville, Conn., 1958)

The Public Arts by Gilbert Seldes (Simon and Schuster, Inc., 1956)

"The Philosopher and His Words," by Warner Fite in *The Philosophical Review*, March, 1935

"Mowing," by Robert Frost from *Complete Poems of Robert Frost* (Henry Holt and Company, Inc., 1930, 1949)

"The Hollow Men" and "Burnt Norton" by T. S. Eliot from *Collected Poems, 1909-1935* (Harcourt, Brace and Company, Inc., and Faber and Faber Limited)

"Cold in Hand Blues" by Gee and Longshaw (C. R. Publishing Co.)

"Young Woman's Blues" by Bessie Smith (Empress Music Inc.)

Because of difficulties of communication with continental China, I have not attempted to get in touch with Mr. Chang Tung-sun or his translator in order to get permission to reprint his article, "A Chinese Philosopher's Theory of Knowledge," which appeared in the *Yenching Journal of Social Studies* (Peking), Vol. I, No. 3, 1939, translated by Mr. Li An-che from the Chinese original, which had appeared in the *Sociological World*, Vol. X, July, 1938, under the title, "Thought, Language and Culture." This note, if it ever comes to the attention of Mr. Chang or Mr. Li, is to thank the former for having written the article and the latter for having translated it, to apologize to them both for thus unceremoniously appropriating their work, and to look forward to the time when, with the alleviation of some of the present difficulties in international communication, exchanges of scholarly courtesies will once again be possible.

S. I. HAYAKAWA

San Francisco State College

I. Communication in Public Affairs

Among the lower primates there is little co-operation. To be sure, in very simple operations one ape may co-ordinate his efforts with those of another. But their co-operation is limited and rudimentary because the means of communication are crude and limited; co-operation requires communication. Monkeys and apes can communicate with one another by means of signs—vocal utterances or gestures—but the range of ideas that can be communicated in this way is very narrow indeed. Only articulate speech can make extensive and versatile exchange of ideas possible, and this is lacking among anthropoids. Such a simple form of co-operation as "you go around the house that way while I go around the other way, meeting you on the far side," is beyond the reach of the great apes. With the advent of articulate speech, however, the possibilities of communication became virtually unlimited.

LESLIE A. WHITE, *The Science of Culture*

A Gospel-True Fable

LOUIS B. SALOMON

There once grew up, on a plain in the land of Shinar, a city in which no two people spoke the same tongue. Each one had a language of his own with a rich vocabulary, as useless as a drinking cup in the desert, because if you lived here you soon found that no matter how clearly you enunciated—even if you shouted till you were red and angry— you were answered only by a deprecatory smile and hands outspread; and though you wrote in large capital letters you could see that they conveyed as little to your neighbor as his absurd scrawlings did to you. If you wanted to borrow a handful of salt, or invite a neighbor to potluck, or seduce his wife, or threaten to push his face in, or call his attention to a poisonous serpent at his heel, or remind him that he needed a bath, you had to do a good deal of pointing and gesticulating, supplemented by noises indicating approval or disapproval.

While this effectually blocked discussions about consistency, the allness of the all, wit vs. humor, and kindred subjects, it worked for practical business; and if ever you felt you just *had* to comment on a relationship too abstract to be stated in terms of sticks and stones, the bystanders would simply look at you with puzzled curiosity, make some of *their* noises in an interrogative tone, hoping somehow to hit on a common denominator of meaning, and finally go their ways shaking their heads in frank acknowledgment that they had no idea what you were trying to tell them. And you in turn would go home to carry on a wordless conversation with your wife about a leaky roof or weeds in the garden, but never to answer such questions as whether your feeling for her depended more upon love, adoration, affection, or respect.

In short, there were no misunderstandings.

Oh, there were *disagreements,* of course. A woman might slam down a plate of tripe before her husband for the eighth successive day and

have it flung, all hot and soggy, straight in her face; and unless she felt a positively morbid fondness for tripe she must have resented it—but she knew what he meant, all right, just as surely as if he could have told her in plain English, or Russian, or Aramaic: "I'm fed up with tripe." Possibly more so. This same man, while taking a little mixed wine (proportions: three to one) for his stomach's sake, might fall out seriously with a crony who felt that anything less than a five-to-one mixture was sissified; but if they ended up drinking sullenly apart it was not because either of them thought the other had slandered the honor of his grandmother or coddled subversives or doubted the existence of God. Communication-wise, it couldn't have been dreamier.

Now, one afternoon a resident of this happy district, out for a stroll, stopped to watch a neighbor pottering away near a huge pile of brick. The worker had already laid out a row in the shape of a rectangle and was busy building up a second row on top of the first, carefully buttering each brick with the slimy mud of the countryside, lining it up and tapping it firmly into position with the butt end of his trowel. When he looked up he nodded a friendly greeting, then waved his hand in an unmistakable invitation to pitch in and help. The newcomer, having nothing better to do, gave a grunt of assent, whereupon the bricklayer with another gesture indicated a number of piles of brick stashed at strategic points around the perimeter of his masonry rectangle, as well as a liberal supply of extra trowels. Of mud there was God's plenty. What more could one need? In a few minutes there were two bricklayers buttering, lining up, tapping home; each thinking his own thoughts but refraining from comment that would obviously have been useless. And the work, of course, went twice as fast.

The new helper, in fact, soon became so absorbed in the rhythm of his labor that he failed to notice when a third man happened by and was also quickly inveigled into lending a hand. By the time dusk forced a halt, the busy *chink-chink-slap-clink* of over a dozen workmen blended into a very pleasant little chorus of industry. When they stepped back to look at their handiwork they were genuinely astonished to see how much they had accomplished: from the bare earth now rose a brick wall enclosing a space perhaps fifty feet square, and, though it was not finished evenly along the top, it was everywhere at least waist-high and in some spots higher.

The next day most of them returned to the job, some of them even accompanied by friends who sociably doffed their coats and went to work, the supply of brick being apparently inexhaustible. What with this force and new recruits picked up during the day, the walls rose at a truly astonishing rate; by noon it was necessary to start erecting scaffolding, and the noise of the hammers attracted even more helpers. By evening of that day the project had become the talk—in a manner of not speaking—of the whole community. People came in droves to watch, and most of them lent a hand, so that even though an ever-increasing share of the total energy had to be spent in raising the bricks to working level, the top moved skyward day after day without any appreciable slackening. The builders got a real thrill from looking at the progress of a structure which no one of them could ever have undertaken by himself.

Naturally, a prime cause for this harmonious efficiency was the absence of disputes. There were some irrepressible extroverts who chattered whenever they felt like it and even made up little songs, not always flattering, about their fellow laborers; yet no one had wounded feelings or tried to interfere with anyone else's freedom of gibberish. The nearest approach to a flare-up came when a burly citizen named Eben upset a bucketful of gooey mud onto Arphaxad, a new volunteer, some fifteen feet below. The recipient came swarming noisily up the scaffolding, but when he noticed the way a brick in Eben's beefy paw looked hardly bigger than a bar of soap, Arphaxad suddenly recollected that only cuts and bruises can't be washed away. And so the work went on apace.

And the Lord came down to see the city and the tower, which the children of men builded. And the Lord, who was frankly angry, said, "This they begin to do: and now nothing will be restrained from them which they have imagined to do."

And the Lord bethought himself of a way to curb and punish the pride of the children of men. "Go to," he said. "Let us go down, and consolidate their language, that they may understand one another's speech." And it was done.

And the whole earth was of one language, and of one speech.

In a bustling group around one of the stockpiles of brick, a worker who had paused to rest for a moment looked up at the towerlike structure. "Going up pretty fast, isn't she?" he remarked complacently to another, who, loaded hod on shoulder, was about to mount the scaffolding.

"Oh, I don't know. Seems to me it could go a lot faster."

"Well, maybe, but you've gotta admit it's going up pretty fast."

"All depends on what you mean by 'fast.'"

"Why, I mean fast, just like I said. What do you think I mean—slow?"

"I know. I heard you. But where I come from they put up buildings so fast it makes this look like a government project."

"Well, if you don't like it here—" but the other had already moved off, and there was no use trying to shout after him through the clamor of the place.

On a plank of scaffolding forty or fifty feet above the ground, were

A GOSPEL-TRUE FABLE   7

two men who for some days had been operating as a team, one serving as hod carrier, the other laying the brick, with the visible result that the masonry at their station rose higher than anywhere else.

"I'm getting ahead of you," said the bricklayer. "If you don't get moving I'll be ready for another load before you get back."

The other man good-humoredly shouldered his hod. "O.K., here I go again. I didn't want you to think I was stepping on your heels."

The bricklayer flushed slightly. "That's a good one! You just keep 'em coming and see if I complain."

"I wouldn't complain either if all I had to do was stay up here and lay 'em out. You know how much a load of brick weighs?"

"Now, let's be fair. You agreed to this the same as I did. It's not my fault you happen to be stronger and I have a knack for the skilled work. That's just the way things are."

The other man lowered his hod slowly, portentously. "Just a minute," he said. "What was that crack about the *skilled* work?"

"That's what I said. I admit I couldn't do as much carrying as you do. I just want you to be fair."

"Fair—that's just what I want *you* to be! You think a man can carry a hod just any old way? Why, I've seen men—"

"Don't make me laugh. I'm talking about skill, *real* skill, not just a strong back and enough sense not to fall off the planks."

"Is that so! Well, I'm going to show you a little skill right now so you'll know what it is."

"Look out, now. Don't you push me! Look out, or I'll—"

A scuffle. A scream. A crunching thud. The bricklayer stared down in consternation as men started running toward the body below. It was the first blood of the enterprise.

Everyone agreed to suspend work for the rest of the day because of the tragedy, but actually building operations remained at a standstill for several days, because by nightfall an argument over whether to call the occurrence an accident or use a harsher word had drawn in practically everyone except the conscience-stricken hod carrier, and even threatened to split the community permanently into irreconcilable factions. Only the persuasive tongue and tireless efforts of the originator of the enterprise finally succeeded in drawing together a mass meeting, at the building site and with himself presiding, at which he steered through a resolution pledging renewed loyalty and co-operation in prosecuting the task so gloriously begun and so unfortunately interrupted.

"My good friends," he said after the motion had been overwhelmingly carried, "I want to thank you for your unselfish devotion and give you my personal assurance that I will keep supplies moving when and where needed, until the last brick has been laid to complete this monument—which, as the tallest man-made structure in the world, will be a credit to our community and attract everyone's attention to the livest, most wide-awake, fastest-growing, biggest little town in all Shinar."

There was a scattering of applause, together with a restless stir and mutter. An elderly, prosperous-looking man in the back rose to his feet.

"Did I understand you to say, sir," he inquired, "that this building is just a monument?"

The chairman smiled ingratiatingly. "I'd hardly say *just* a monument, sir. Surely a monument means a great deal, a symbol of—"

"I'm sure it means a great deal to you. But I'm a practical man, and I've assumed all along that the structure when finished would serve a practical purpose. It was only with that understanding that I put in my time working on this project of yours, and frankly, sir, I feel I've been taken in."

"That goes for me too!" exclaimed a martial voice near the front. "It never occurred to me for a moment that this wasn't a watchtower and a fortress. Why, properly armed and provisioned it could command the countryside for miles around and give us just the edge of practical superiority we need against the Syrians."

"Just a minute!" cried the first speaker. "You've got me wrong; I'm a businessman, and I'm not interested in tying up capital in armaments that will be outmoded in two years. When I talk about practical I mean something useful, productive, like a store or a warehouse or a factory."

"My friend," said the military man in a voice heavy with irony, "I'm sure you will be allowed to do something useful, like scrubbing latrines, when the Syrian army takes over your factories and warehouses. There's a war on, and we're dealing with a ruthless foe that knows exactly what he wants—that may have secret agents in this very gathering sowing seeds of—"

A long-haired young man sprang to his feet. "Mr. Chairman!" he shouted, "I want to protest against calling the venture our armed forces are now engaged in, a war. It's a police action, as everybody knows, and calling it war is only a trick of the military big brass to grab powers they're not entitled to!"

"Now that you mention it," said the military man grimly, "why aren't you in uniform? You look pretty healthy to me."

Boos and confused shouts drowned out further interchange for several minutes before the chairman could restore order.

"Gentlemen, gentlemen!" he pleaded. "I'm sure our differences can be ironed out. The monument—the structure—call it what you will—may be adapted for a number of different uses. The important thing is to get back to work on it as quickly as possible so that we can truly take pride in the tallest, the greatest, the most awe-inspiring—"

"Stop!"

The deep, commanding voice drew all eyes to a tall, gaunt, cloaked figure with hand upraised. A hush fell upon the crowd.

The tall man spoke slowly. "This is blasphemy. God has set his judgment against pride. He has punished it before, and he will punish it again. Let us abandon pride before it is too late."

"Now you just hold on there!" exclaimed the chairman, for the first time showing irritation. "I don't see anything wrong in being proud of our town. I'm ready to tell the world I'm proud of belonging to the snappiest, peppiest, up-and-comingest burg in this country or any other."

"That is the very pride I mean!" the solemn one thundered. "Not the humble pride of a good citizen, ever ready to acknowledge his errors, but the false and sinful pride of superiority, of being the tallest, strongest, best."

"Then all I can say, brother, is, you've got a mighty strange notion about pride," retorted the chairman sharply. "What you're trying to tell this meeting is, there's a lot of things wrong with this town, and we ought to go around apologizing for living here instead of boosting it every chance we get. Is that right?"

"In a sense, yes," said the other, sadly.

"What do you mean, in a sense? I believe in plain language, and when I see a knocker and a troublemaker I let him know what I think of him. Am I right, neighbors?"

A many-throated growl replied, and fists were shaken. The military man jumped onto a brick pile and raised his hand for attention. "I told you the enemy would be in your midst!" he shouted. "Now maybe you'll listen to me!"

"That's right," cried the young man who had clashed with him before, and who was now anxious to make up for his discomfiture. "They're trying to provoke us into an all-out war. They'll stop at nothing!" He pointed an accusing finger at the cloaked man. "I dare you to tell us where you're from!"

Many voices in the crowd took up his demand, but there was no answer. "You see?" screamed the youth. "He's afraid to tell us who sent him here!"

The other shook his head slowly. "If you know not who has sent me, then indeed you are lost."

The brick was fatally handy. The young man didn't even realize he had thrown it till he saw it strike the shoulder of the cloak, staggering its wearer. By himself he would certainly not have flung a second one. But there were others.

The fury died as suddenly as it had burst forth. Someone drew a corner of the cloak over the bloody face. Amid a shocked silence the chairman, his voice shaking with emotion, called upon them all to renew their pledge of co-operation and mutual trust; and although previously some of the crowd had abstained from voting there was now a full-throated, unanimous assent as they solemnly promised to carry the tower to its completion, though it should cost their lives, their fortunes, and their sacred honor.

But each man knew in his heart that it was a lie, and that the work would never be resumed.

Autumn, 1954. Dr. Salomon is professor of English, Brooklyn College, Brooklyn, New York, and Fulbright lecturer in American literature in Turku, Finland, 1958-59.

Semantic Difficulties in International Communication

EDMUND S. GLENN

It is too often assumed that the problem of transmitting the ideas of one national or cultural group to members of another national or cultural group is principally a problem of language. It is likewise assumed that that problem can always be solved by the use of appropriate linguistic techniques—translation and interpretation. A constant and professional preoccupation with the problem of international communication has convinced me of the fallacy of this point of view.

Patterns of Thought

Both an eminent professional philosopher, Professor Max Otto, and a very prominent layman, President Eisenhower, have recently stated that each man has a philosophy, whether or not he is aware of that fact. This means of course that people think in accordance with definite methods or patterns of thought. The methods may vary from individual to individual and even more from nation to nation.

Philosophical controversy is a historical fact. It is a mistake to believe that philosophical differences of opinion exist only at the level of conscious and deliberate controversies waged by professional philosophers. Ideas originated by philosophers permeate entire cultural groups; they are in fact what distinguishes one cultural group from another. The individuality of, for instance, Western culture, or Chinese culture, cannot be denied. The fact that when speaking of the English, the Americans, the French, or the Spanish, we tend to use expressions such as "national character" should not blind us to the fact that what is meant by "character" is in reality the embodiment of a philosophy or the habitual use of a method of judging and thinking. Thus the French describe themselves as Cartesian; the English and the Americans seldom describe themselves, but still they act consistently in such a manner as to be described by others as pragmatic or empirical. Professor Karl Pribram writes,

Mutual understanding and peaceful relations among the peoples of the earth have been impeded not only by the multiplicity of languages but to an even greater degree by differences in patterns of thought—that is, by differences in the methods adopted for defining the sources of knowledge and for organizing coherent thinking.

No mind can function to its own satisfaction without certain assumptions regarding the origin of its basic concepts and its ability to relate these concepts to each other. These assumptions have undergone significant changes in the course of time and have varied more or less among nations and among social groups at any given time. These differences in methods of reasoning have generated tension, ill-feeling, and even hatred.

The determination of the relationship between the patterns of thought of the cultural or national group whose ideas are to be communicated, to the patterns of thought of the cultural or national group which is to receive the communication, is an integral part of international communication. Failure to determine such relationships, and to act in accordance with such determinations, will almost unavoidably lead to misunderstandings.

Soviet diplomats often qualify the position taken by their Western counterparts as "incorrect" *nepravilnoe*. In doing so, they do not accuse their opponents of falsifying facts, but merely of not interpreting them "correctly." This attitude is explicable only if viewed in the context of the Marxist-Hegelian pattern of thought, according to which historical situations evolve in a unique and predetermined manner. Thus an attitude not in accordance with theory is not in accordance with truth either; it is as incorrect as the false solution of a mathematical problem. Conversely, representatives of our side tend to propose compromise or transactional solutions. Margaret

Mead writes that this attitude merely bewilders many representatives of the other side, and leads them to accuse us of hypocrisy, because it does not embody any ideological position recognizable to them. The idea that there are "two sides to every question" is an embodiment of nominalistic philosophy, and is hard to understand for those unfamiliar with this philosophy or with its influence.

Or again, on a slightly different plane: a simple English "No" tends to be interpreted by members of the Arabic culture as meaning "Yes." A real "No" would need to be emphasized; the simple "No" indicates merely a desire for further negotiation. Likewise a nonemphasized "Yes" will often be interpreted as a polite refusal.

Not all patterns of thought, or rather not everything in patterns of thought, is due to the influence of well-defined methodologies. Association of ideas plays a great part in thought; thus, clearly, each man's thought is to a large extent a function of this man's past.

Thus for instance, the word "colonialism" carries particularly irritating connotations to most Americans whereas it carries no such connotations to most Englishmen, Frenchmen, or Dutchmen. The reason for this is obviously anchored in history. It may not necessarily be, on the part of the Americans, the effect of a fully thought out political theory, but may be a simple association of ideas based on verbal habits which describe the American Revolution as the rising of "colonies" against an "empire."

Denotation and Connotation

Problems of this type appear in a much more complicated form whenever two words in two different languages have the same denotation but different connotations.

Thus for instance, the French word *"contribuable"* and the English word "taxpayer" denote the same thing, but their connotations are not identical. "Taxpayer" is a word descriptive of physical action, of something which might have been seen with the eyes. It evokes the image of a man paying money at, for instance, a teller's window. "*Contribuable*," on the contrary, embodies an abstract principle. It evokes not an image but a thought, the thought that all citizens must contribute to the welfare of the nation of which they are a part.

Let us consider for a moment the connotations of these two words in the context of the North Atlantic Treaty Organization. A normal reaction on the American side will be: Does the man who pays get a fair return on his money? Or, in other words, is the Mutual Assistance Program really the best way of getting the most security for the least cost? A typical reaction on the French side will be quite different: Does everyone contribute equally to the common cause? Are the Americans as deeply and personally involved as the French? I would not be surprised if some of the differences of opinion which arose at various moments within NATO between the United States and France were not due to a large extent to this particular semantic difficulty.

The Role of Language

The preceding paragraph showed how patterns of thought may influence language and in turn be influenced by it. Both "taxpayer" and *"contribuable"* are comparative neologisms. If a certain method of word formation—by intension—was chosen by the French, it is because it corresponded to the pattern of thought prevalent in France. If another method of word formation—by extension—was chosen by the English, it is because it corresponded to their most general pattern of thought. Thus, peculiarities of language may constitute good indications of the prevalent manner of thinking.

However, once created, words and expressions assume an active role and contribute to the fashioning of thought. Thus two types of situations arise:

1. Cases where a given language is capable of expressing various shades of meaning and where the pattern of expression selected by given individuals provides a clue for the determination of their pattern of thought.

2. Cases where a certain combination of denotation and connotation cannot be obtained in a simple manner in a given language.

An example of the first case may be found in the following expressions: "What should we do under the circumstances?" and "What does the situation require?" Although the denotations of these two questions are just about identical, the answers, influenced in part by connotations, may tend to be different. The point is that although one of these two forms will appear more natural than the other, the English language is capable of using both.

The following occurrence may be presented as an example of the second case: At an international conference which took place a few years ago and in which both the United States and the Soviet Union participated, it became rapidly apparent that the Soviet Union would not sign the agreement in preparation. The reason for it was a disagreement in substance, which would not be overcome. The Russians, however, continued to participate in the work of the various committees, and in particular of the drafting committee, mainly it seemed in order to preserve diplomatic niceties. Their representatives were seldom heard from.

Thus, considerable surprise was created when a seemingly unimportant proposal by the U.S. delegate resulted in an outburst of violent Soviet opposition. Even more surprising was the attitude of most Europeans and in particular of the French who publicly sup-

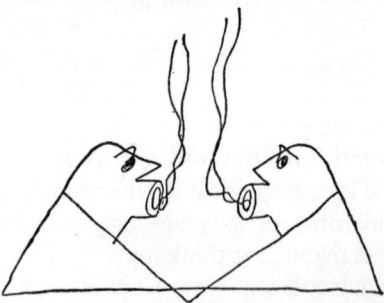

Disputants Unscathed after a Volley of Semantic Blanks at Close Range

ported the United States but privately stated that it was a mistake to have backed the Soviets against the wall by an attitude which they described as rigid and overbearing. The proposal of the U.S. delegate consisted in inserting in the preamble to the proposed agreement a clause taken from another instrument and containing the expression "expanding economy."

I would suggest the following explanation for this incident: the expression "expanding economy" is neutral with respect to the Aristotelian categories of accident and essence. An "expanding economy" may be an economy which happens to be expanding because of various outside influences, or else an economy which is expanding because of characteristics inherent to its nature.

In Russian "expanding economy" becomes *rasshiryayushchiyasya ekonomiya*" in which the reflexive form is used. Although it would be incorrect to say that *"rasshiryayushchiyasya"* has the denotation of the English expression "self-expanding" it unquestionably carries a connotation which will lead a Russian-speaking listener to conclude that "expanding economy" means an economy expanding for reasons inherent to its nature.

Thus in this case language itself directed the attention of the listener away from one possible explanation and in the direction of another. To compound the confusion the difference between accident and essence is much more important to a person whose mind follows the Marxist-Hegelian patterns than to a person whose mind follows an empirical or pragmatic bent. The fact that an economy is expanding may warrant a certain type of action in the eyes of the empiricist, whichever be the cause of the expansion of the economy. To a Hegelian an economy expanding for accidental causes is bound to reverse itself unavoidably and rapidly.

Now it so happens that Marxist theory rules that the economy of the Western world must contract and cannot expand. Thus the recognition of an inherently expanding character in this economy, and this is an official document, could not fail to appear completely unacceptable to a Soviet delegate.

Classification of Patterns of Thought

The problem of defining, describing and analyzing patterns of thought is not the only one which needs to be faced in the field of international communications. Questions such as translation *proprio motu*, choice of media and levels of approach, etc., also deserve attention. However, as they have been less neglected than were the problems of basic philosophical, ethnical, anthropological and linguistic determinations, they will be considered outside the scope of this paper.

I will deal here only with the analysis of pronouncements made by persons belonging to the Western cultural world and using one of the European languages. I do not feel competent at the present moment to do any work which would extend beyond the boundary defined above. In consequence, the classifications suggested below will be such as to help in analyzing a field limited to one culture, albeit an important one. Three basic groups of criteria will be used in the sample analysis at the end of this paper.

1. PATTERNS OF REASONING. Professor Karl Pribram, who has pointed out the importance of linguistically determined assumptions in the

formation of concepts, distinguishes, in his book *Conflicting Patterns of Thought*, the following four patterns of reasoning.

A. *Universalistic reasoning.* Universalistic reasoning is based on the premise that the human mind is able to grasp directly the order of the universe. Reason is credited with the power to know the truth with the aid of given general concepts and to establish absolutely valid rules for the organization of human relationships in accordance with these concepts. Universalistic reasoning proceeds from the general to the particular; it believes that general concepts, or universals, possess a reality independent from those of their components or constituents. The best way to determine what will happen in a given case is to know what happens in a more general category and then to determine what particular modifiers make the case in question a slight exception to the general rule.

B. *Nominalistic, or hypothetical, reasoning.* Nominalistic philosophy rejects the belief that general concepts have a reality of their own; instead it considers them merely as names, as convenient categories, more or less arbitrarily established by human minds. Reasoning proceeds from the particular to the general. Any exercise in pure reason establishes merely a hypothesis which must be verified by concrete experience.

Although these descriptions of patterns of thought may give the impression of dealing with abstract and complex reasonings, the influence of the patterns of thought described above may be found also at very concrete levels. Thus, for example, French visitors to New York are in general highly critical of the New York subway. What repels them is not the dirt or the crowding, but the evident lack of comprehensive planning in the geographical distribution of lines. For instance, there is no subway line which would take one from the business district around Wall Street to the new business district around Rockefeller Center, or from the Cloisters to the Metropolitan Museum of Art. The argument that the New York subway is the one which carries the greatest number of persons the most rapidly over the greatest distances from home to work and from work home does not impress the French visitors overly much.

On the contrary, the Paris Métro covers all of Paris like a spider web. Convenient changeover stations make it possible to go from any monument to any other. At the same time the Métro strikes the

American visitor as almost unbelievably slow. It does not reach very far into the suburbs, where many people live, and its routes do not necessarily follow the pattern of home-to-work and work-to-home connections.

I will put it that the Paris Métro is based on the universalistic concept of a means of transit designed to provide for the needs of a city, considered as such, or as a universal, a collective noun. Lines run from one point of interest to another, no part of the city being deprived of a means of communication with all of the other parts; at the same time considerations such as the density of traffic are almost completely disregarded. On the contrary the New York subway is nominalistic; there is no network planned to cover a collective entity, the city; on the contrary, lines are built in such a way as to do the most possible good to the greatest possible number of individuals considered as such. It is not much help to those who want to go from one residential area to another—but then people go fairly seldom from one residential area to another. On the contrary, it is every day that people go from home to work and from work home, and the New York subway is planned according to this consideration.

The names selected in each case by popular usage express the same preoccupation as the planning. "Métro" is an abbreviation of *"métropolitain"* or "metropolitan." The French language has resources which would have enabled Parisians to have selected a name such as "subway," but they did not choose to do so. Likewise English has the word "metropolitan," and the official titles of the various subway organizations in New York include words such as "transfer," "transit," and "system," yet the names chosen by the public are "subway," "el," or in Britain, "underground" or "tube."

It might be noted that *"chemin de fer"* is etymologically as well as factually similar to "railroad." But then, French railroads have the same characteristics from the point of view of planning as does the New York subway. Rail lines follow lines of probable maximum density which in France means that they radiate from Paris to the provinces. At the same time the network is not completed by transversal roads; the shortest way of getting from one provincial town to another may very often be the long way through Paris. This state of affairs was always considered illogical by the French and was violently criticized by them. As a result of this criticism it has been corrected to a large extent. The same criticism might have been leveled against

American railroads. I remember being told that the best way to get from Sheridan, Wyoming, to San Francisco was through Seattle. Yet the criticism which might have been leveled at the American roads are in fact never heard. The American public understands that it is not economical to provide trains for occasional travel along low-demand routes.

Now it so happens that the French railroads were started by English capital and planned under English inspiration: they even run on the left whereas everything else in France runs on the right. Thus even this exception seems to confirm the rule: the fact that France is by and large a universalistic country does not mean that nominalism is entirely without influence there.

C. *Intuitional or organismic reasoning.* This type of reasoning stresses intuition rather than systematic cogitation. It is thus in a position to ignore some of the basic opposition between nominalism and universalism. It considers that the relationship between a collectivity and its members may be compared to the relationship between a biological organism and its component cells. Organismic reasoning opposes intuitive to discursive consciousness and claims that reliance on one's intuition enables man to be "independent yet subject to one's duties" (Joel). It is often associated with extreme nationalism and is prevalent in Germanic and Slavic Central Europe.

D. *Dialectic reasoning.* Hegelian dialectics are derived from universalism and, like universalism, believe in the possibility of a full understanding of the universe through reason. "But, according to the principles of dialectics, comprehension of the ever-changing nature of the phenomena and the flux of events can not be achieved with the aid of rigid concepts, alleged to be implanted in the human mind. The course of events is believed to be determined by the operation of antagonistic forces and must be understood with the aid of concepts adjusted to the contradictions logically represented by these forces" (Pribram).

Marxist dialectic materialism follows the Hegelian pattern which it modifies by the dogma of the predominance of materialistic factors.

2. THE VERB "TO BE" AND THE VERB "TO DO." The classification described above has been used very successfully by Professor Pribram in the analysis of a broad historical evolution of the patterns of

thought. Other types of classification may be useful in supplementing it in cases of a more concrete nature.

One such method of classification may be found in the difference which separates the logic of the verb "to do" from the logic of the verb "to be."

The logic of the verb "to be" is basically two-valued: things are either thus or not thus. Propositions are either true or false. Meaningless propositions may generally be eliminated and reasoning presented in such a way that a two-valued logic applies.

Discussion: *Peaceful Resolution of International Conflicts*

On the contrary the logic of the verb "to do" is essentially multivalued: one does not do things truly or untruly, one does them more or less well.

All men are confronted with situations in which they tend to reason in terms of the verb "to be" and with other situations in which they tend to reason in terms of the verb "to do." There are, however, still other situations which may be studied by either of the methods correlated with these two verbs. Choices made by various individuals are indicative of the patterns of thought followed by them.

Quite obviously a prevalence of reasoning in terms of the logic of the verb "to do" ties in with nominalism, while a prevalence of reasoning in terms of the logic of the verb "to be" ties in with universalism. Thus an analysis undertaken in terms of these two verbs will be helpful in detecting patterns of thought. More than that, such an analysis will also show why it is that in some cases nominalists and universalists reach different conclusions even when starting from identical premises.

Let us take as examples the two concepts of compromise and intervention. If A wishes to paint the wall black and B wishes to paint it white, they may reach an honorable compromise by painting it gray. If A now states that the wall is black, and B states that the wall is white, they may not compromise by calling it gray, as this would make liars of both of them. They may try to convince one another, they may try to fight it out, or they may drop the subject.

I believe that the instability of the French cabinets is due to the fact that, when faced with an issue, the French tend to ask themselves, "What is right?" That is why there are so many issues which often come up for debate and seldom reach the stage of solution. That is also why action can be undertaken only at the expense of excluding from the cabinet for the time being those who do not agree with the majority and who can compromise only by being absent, even temporarily.

It may be noted that the verb "to compromise" has a dual meaning both in French and in English, as for instance in "compromise the difference" and "compromise one's integrity." The first of these two meanings is by far the more frequent in English, the second one by far the more frequent in French.

Let us turn now to the concept of intervention. A and B intend to have lunch together but have not agreed on the choice of a restaurant. They discuss the question in terms of their likes and dislikes, one saying that he would like to go one place and the other that he would like to go to another. C, who has not been invited, overhears the conversation, steps in and tells them what to do. C's attitude would be unanimously considered extremely rude: the action taken by a group to which he doesn't belong, in a case when this action does not affect him, is none of his business.

Once more A and B intend to have lunch but are not in agreement on the choice of a restaurant. This time, however, they conduct their discussion in terms of the verb "to be," A saying that food is better at one place and B that it is better at another. C, who still has not been invited, again overhears their conversation, again steps in offering some factual information about either or both of the two places. This time C's attitude will probably be quite acceptable.

Yet in fact there is no difference between the two situations. If a person wants to have lunch at a certain restaurant, it is probably because the person in question believes that the food is good there. Conversely, to say that food is good at a place means simply that one likes what is served there. As for factual information, one might do well to remember Goethe's saying: that which we call facts are nothing but our own pet theories. Thus again the difference is not in the situation, but in the patterns of thought.

It may be noted that French has several words which more or less mean intervention, for instance *"intervention," "immixion," "ingérence."* The two latter have a pejorative meaning. If now we pass from the nouns to the verbs, we see that the verbs corresponding to the pejorative nouns take the reflexive form, thus: *"s'immiscer," "s'ingérer,"* but *"intervenir.* Thus clearly what brings in the pejorative meaning is an insistence on the intervener, the doer, as opposed to an insistence on the situation.

Let us now consider the hypothetical case of the country A which wishes another country B to take a certain step of a very controversial nature. Country A is basically nominalistic, country B is basically universalistic. Country A will not try to influence public opinion in country B; its government thinks of intervention in terms of the verb "to do" and considers it *a priori* as an unfriendly gesture. Country A will try to negotiate directly this issue at government level, offering perhaps some inducements in another field as basis for a compromise, which being nominalistic, it considers honorable. Unfortunately country B, being universalistic, cannot accept a barefaced compromise. At the same time it would not necessarily have resented an intervention, even addressed directly to its own public opinion, if such intervention were made in sufficiently theoretical and impersonal terms.

3. DENOTATION AND CONNOTATION. Of the two methods of classification suggested above, only one may be qualified as linguistic. Yet language may influence thought or else be used as an indication of an existing pattern of thought correlated with a pattern of expression in many more ways than one. Unfortunately the field of the mutual influence of language and thought is as yet largely unexplored. In conse-

quence purely linguistic manners of classification will need to be developed slowly, through experience.

It appears clear, nevertheless, that a search for connotation as distinct from denotation may clarify many concrete situations. Some examples of situations of this kind have been given previously, some others will be found below.

In seeking to systematize the influence of connotations particular attention will have to be paid to the formation of names of sets or classes, or of representatives of sets, either through extension or through intension. Extensive or descriptive formation will generally indicate the prevalence of nominalist patterns and of multivalued logic. On the contrary, intensive formation will indicate the prevalence of universalistic patterns. Both types of word formation will be found in most languages. Areas in which words are formed by one or the other system will in general correspond to areas in which a corresponding type of reasoning is prevalent.

Analysis of connotations should go beyond simple words. It should also embrace sentence structure, set expressions made up of several words, current metaphors, proverbs, and manners in which groups of words may be formed around the same root.

For instance an expression such as *"faire faire,"* which can never be properly translated into English—"to have something done" lacks both spontaneity and generality—is in itself an indication of a certain contempt toward action and at the same time is an expression of respect toward the thought which precedes action; in other words it is an expression of universalistic thinking.

The use of the verb "to do" as the principle auxiliary verb in English is also a program in itself.

The systems of classification suggested above are not intended to cover the entire field. They are, rather, examples of lines which can be followed. No analysis should neglect the possibility of finding other explanations such as the ones which may be derived from the implications of history, even where those implications cannot be expressed in terms of semantic or philosophical categorization.

Thus, for instance, of all the great democracies the United States is the one which shows the greatest intolerance of domestic Communism. I believe that an explanation of this fact may be found in the very tradition of the beginnings of an American nationality. Most European countries are founded on a tradition of indigenous ancestry.

There are naturalized Frenchmen and Britons, and other Frenchmen and Britons who are descendants of immigrants, but people of these descriptions constitute very small minorities of the citizens of their respective countries. In consequence it is difficult for European countries to consider unwelcome the exponent of any political ideology as long as he can point out a long line of indigenous ancestry. On the contrary, the United States as a nation was created by men and women who had come to a new continent in order to establish a society based on certain definite ideals. It may be interesting to note in that connection how much more important is for American tradition the settlement of the Pilgrims in 1620 than is the settlement of the gentlemen adventurers of Virginia in 1607. The United States thus bases its tradition on the establishment of an ideology on virgin soil. It is thus quite normal for Americans to think that those who wish to establish some other ideology should go and do it somewhere else.

A Day in the Security Council

In the paragraphs below I will try to analyze the complete stenographic record of the first part of the one-hundredth meeting of the Security Council. The record used is in three languages—English, French, and Russian. Analysis will start in all cases with the consideration of statements in the original language, then pass on to the translations.

In that connection it should be noted that (1) the differences of opinion of the various representatives are due primarily to questions of a political nature the discussion of which falls outside the scope of the present paper. At the same time the type of arguments chosen by the participants and the manner in which those participants present their arguments are considered indicative of patterns of thought and will be the subject of the present analysis.

(2) The translations by linguists of the United Nations Secretariat are invariably excellent. Although I have spent many years in work of this type, there is not one single aspect of these translations on which I feel I could improve.

In order to facilitate reading the various points being analyzed will be numbered consecutively.

1. The President, a Belgian, says, "*Aucune proposition n'étant faite dans ce sens, j'en déduis....*"

The last word becomes "I assume" in the English translation. "I deduce" would have been stiff, "I conclude" almost impolite, implying that no change of opinion or of interpretation on the part of the Assembly would be welcome. "I assume" is correct because that is the word which an English-speaking chairman would have chosen in all probability, and also because, in a nominalistic or hypothetical reasoning, one acts upon assumptions. Assumptions become certainties only after action has resulted in their verification.

The President could not have used the French equivalent of "I assume." If one considers that reason is capable of reaching entirely valid conclusions one does not act upon assumptions. *"Je suppose"* would have implied that the members of the Council have not made

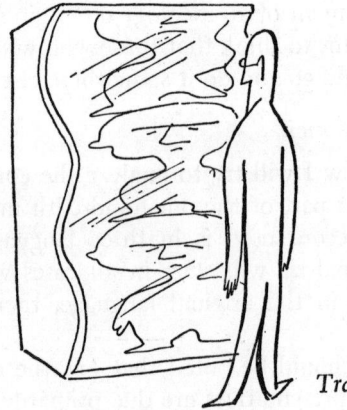

Translation

their positions sufficiently clear to allow the President to reach a clear conclusion.

The Russian translation uses *"zaklyuchaiyu"*—"I conclude." The strength of this word may be best evaluated if one realizes that the participle form *"zaklyuchonnyi"* means a prisoner and is often used in the subsequent remarks of the Russian delegate.

In that respect it may be interesting to note that Slavic languages tend to create groups of words using the same root with different prefixes and suffixes. Thus for instance *"zaklyuchit' "* to conclude, *"izklyuchit' "* to exclude, *"vyklyuchit' "* to switch off, *"vklyuchit' "* to switch on or to include. A still better example is found in the Polish verbs "to read." There is one such verb in English, and twelve in Polish, to wit:

czytać	to read
czytywać	to read habitually
przeczytać	to read completely
przeczytywać	to read completely and habitually
odczytać	to read aloud to a group, to communicate a written text
odczytywać	the same thing habitually
wyczytać	to read excerpts, to interpret (a meaning)
wyczytywać	the same thing habitually
wczytać	to read a meaning into a text
wczytywać	the same thing habitually
zaczytać się	to bury oneself in one's reading
zacytywać się	the same thing habitually

It is not difficult to imagine how such a manner of expression would encourage a manner of thinking prone to a certain subtlety in distinctions and to a certain rigidity of categorization. Situations should fall into one of several clearly defined patterns; whenever they fail to do so, they would be considered with disbelief or at least skepticism.

2. An intervention of the Australian delegate, who alludes to the need of investigating "the situation which is before us."

"Which is before us" becomes *"qui nous est soumise"* in French and *"rassmatrivayemym nami"* in Russian. "Which is before us" is neutral. *"Qui nous est soumise"* means literally "which is submitted to us" and implies the assumption of authority of a body of men—the Security Council—over a situation. The Russian expression means "which is under consideration" but with the connotation of "which is being taken apart" or "in regard to which the precise category into which it falls has to be determined." Both the establishing of a hierarchy and that of fixed categories are characteristic of universalism.

3. Where the Australian delegate says that the situation needs to be investigated, the Soviet delegate says that the question is already decided. It is the "same" situation as the one which was discussed before. The difference of opinion between the two delegates is due to the fact that the Australian looks at it from the point of view of procedure while the Soviet delegate looks at it from the point of view of substance. (Once again it is realized that they may have political reasons for adopting the attitude which they have taken. Nevertheless

the manner of argumentation remains indicative of the pattern of thought.) An insistence on the procedural aspect is well in keeping with the nominalist attitude, as after all it is procedure which will determine the manner of action—if not necessarily the direction of such action—of a body such as the Security Council. On the contrary an insistence on the broad substantive aspects of the situation is well in keeping with a manner of thinking according to which historical development falls in a predetermined course, and the main task of the statesman is to recognize and diagnose correctly a substantive situation. The "correct" action to be undertaken will follow more or less automatically from a correct diagnosis.

4. The Soviet delegate claims that the present situation is part and parcel of a more general situation and should not be discussed separately. In doing so, he uses the expression *"opryedyelyennaya stadiya"* which becomes *"phase nouvelle"* and "another aspect" in English. Literally it means "a well-defined phase." Even such an expression as "another phase" might have conveyed to an English-speaking listener the idea that special measures should be taken, as it is perfectly normal to treat each phase of a situation separately. An expression such as "a well-defined or well-determined phase" would have even accentuated this idea of separateness from the more general question, and thus expressed an intention exactly contrary to that of the speaker. *"Phase nouvelle"* is faithful to the meaning but *"phase bien determinée"* would have again given the impression that this phase should be separated from the broader aspects of the problem. As a matter of fact the expression *"opryedyelyennaya stadiya"* would have conveyed an intention somewhat contrary to that of the speaker even to a non-Communist Russian listener. If used by the Soviet delegates it is because it fits in with the Marxist interpretation of history according to which evolution proceeds necessarily from one "well-determined phase" to another; the fact that the phase is well determined, and not merely vaguely outlined, proves that it is indeed an integral part of a correctly diagnosed and described over-all situation.

5. In the same intervention the Soviet delegate said that the decision of the Council *"dolzhen reshat'sya avtomaticheski."* As "should be reached automatically" is ambiguous in English, it becomes "the question settles itself automatically" in the English translation, and *"pouvons trancher d'office"* in the French translation. The English translation is a wee bit stronger than the original Russian,

the French quite a bit weaker. But both convey clearly the dialectical meaning: once the correct diagnosis is reached, the manner of action is determined automatically.

6. The Australian delegation again takes the floor and spells out his meaning: the substantive situation is irrelevant for a moment as the Council must first of all settle a question "concerning the operations" of one of its subsidiary organizations.

7. The President, speaking in French, states that a commission has requested a certain government *"de faire ajourner"* certain measures. This becomes "requested to postpone" in the English translation. In French, a government acts directly only at a very high level. In regard to questions of a less exalted nature, it merely causes an action to be taken. Thus a clear hierarchy between principle and mere action is established. (In Russian this becomes "a request in regard to postponement.")

8. The United States delegate finds that the situation is clearly one of procedure. The question is "simple" because the "only concrete" action which may be taken is a procedural one. The procedural situation should not be "seized upon" in order to introduce long arguments about substance.

9. It might be noted that the expression "draft resolution" becomes *"projet de résolution"* in French and *"proyekt rezolyutsiyi"* in Russian. A draft is something you work upon and try to perfect. The implication is that it is only the final product which will be judged. A project is something which may be rejected *in toto*; the implication is that the desirability of such a project should be decided upon theoretically before any work is spent in trying to reach perfection.

10. The Soviet delegate reiterates that *"otvyet mozhet byt' tol'ko"* —there is but one answer to the question. Once again the Soviet delegate asks how is it possible to consider a question of procedure— about which nothing is said in the theory of historical evolution— independently from the question of substance, which is the one to which an answer can be found through dialectics.

11. The Russian *"utvyerzhdyeniye"* appears as "assertion" in English and as *"avis"* in French. *"Avis"* means in this context merely "opinion." "Assertion" is stronger, but not as strong as "affirmation" which would be the closest to the original Russian. However the very strength of "affirmation" would tend to give it an ironical or even pejorative connotation. *"Utvyerzhdyeniye"* is very strong; it derives

etymologically from *"tvyerdyi"*—"hard" and the obsolete *"tyerdynya"* —"fortress." The contrast between the weakness of the French expression and the strength of the Russian one is particularly striking, the more so that we tend to consider both nations as following a more or less universalistic bent. Incidentally, it is quite as easy to express the meaning of "opinion" in Russian as that of "affirmation" in French. The present choice of words, on the part of the Russian delegate and on the part of the very competent French translators, is probably due to the absence in pure universalism and to the presence in Hegelianism of an element of systematic strife: thesis versus antithesis.

12. The Soviet delegate further states that he "cannot understand" how his opponents can consider a procedural aspect as being distinct from the more general question of substance.

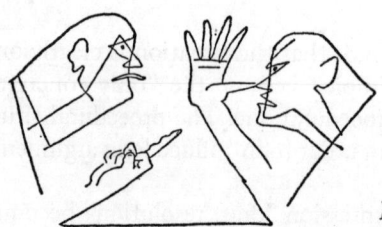

Language of East-West Diplomacy

13. The Russian *"sootvyetstvovat'"* becomes "to signify" in English and *"appeler"* in French. It literally and also etymologically means "to correspond" (*so-otvyet, cum—respondere*). This again shows a predilection for rigid categories.

14. The representative of France takes the floor. For obvious reasons he sides with the Australian and the American and gives his own very brief restatement of their position. The only thing which he introduces and which was not contained in the earlier speeches of the Western delegates is one little word: *"donc"*—"therefore." The effects of this little word will be seen in some of the subsequent remarks.

15. For the French delegate the question is *"la question dont il s'agit."* This is translated into Russian by the equally impersonal *"ryech idyet,"* but becomes in English "the question with which *we* are concerned" with a shift of emphasis from the situation *per se* to the people dealing with it.

16. *"Il est naturel"* remains "it is natural" in English but becomes *"yestyestvenno"* in Russian. This word derives from the root *"yest-*

yestvo" meaning "substance" and itself deriving from the word "to be." It is much closer in its connotations to the Aristotelian original than is "natural."

17. There are two French words which correspond to the English word "probable." These are *"probable"* and *"vraisemblable,"* the latter containing the connotation of a judgment as to truth value which is absent from the first. It might be interpreted as meaning "something similar to the established scheme of truth." The one Russian word translating "probable," *"vyeroyatno,"* corresponds to the French word *"vraisemblable."*

18. The delegate of the United States takes the floor to "concur with the opinion expressed by the delegate of France." Now, as we have mentioned before, the delegate of France merely restated the position taken by the delegates of Australia and of the United States. He did, however, add the little word "therefore," which made the position so much clearer and more forceful that it becomes from now on known as the French position.

19. The delegate of the United States presents a draft resolution for the purpose of "giving concrete form" to opinion and to enable "the Council to dispose of this matter." It would be "the acme of futility" to discuss questions of substance when there is need for an immediate procedural decision.

20. The President says, *"Je ne voudrais préjuger en rien la décision que le Conseil de securité va prendre."* *"Préjuger"* remains *"pryedugadyvat'"* in Russian (etymologically, "to guess before my turn") but becomes "to prejudice" in English, thus implying that prejudging by a President could not fail to influence the action of the Council. Once again emphasis is shifted from situation to action.

21. The delegate of Australia also expresses his agreement with the delegate of France.

22. "To have no claim" becomes *"ne pas pouvoir prétendre"* in French and *"nye imyeyet' prava,"* "to have no right," in Russian. The English word "claim" is extremely difficult to translate, as it expresses an entirely nominalistic idea: that of a juridical situation which is neither clearly white nor clearly black, but which on the contrary takes into account the legitimacy of practical adjustment.

In trying to present an over-all evaluation of the meeting described above, one should remember that the various delegates were faced indeed with difficult political problems. On the other hand, however, the men who engaged in the debate described were unquestionably far above the average in preparation for and experience in handling international communication.

The impression obtained is that whereas the French and the Belgian members of the Assembly on the one hand and the American and the Australian on the other have retained their individuality, communication between them has been established; in particular the Frenchman and the Belgian have conclusively shown that they understood not only the position, which would be a political matter, but also the reasoning, which is a semantic matter, of the Australian and the American. On the contrary, the degree of communication between the Soviet delegate and the delegates of Australia and of the United States appears to be nil. Once again political situations may not be disregarded. When the Soviet delegate states that he does not understand the attitude of his opponents, he may be simply seeking to gain some rhetorical advantage. At the same time, however, the very fact that this form of argumentation should have occurred to him shows that he genuinely believes that it is at least conceivable that people of good will might find the attitude of the Australian and the American delegates difficult to understand.

At the same time no attempt is made by anyone to explain the basis of his manner of thinking; all that the various speakers do is to present arguments which appear pertinent once a certain manner of thinking is accepted.

Thus for instance nobody has made a speech along these lines: "It is true that the basic problems which we are supposed to discuss here are the political problems of the world. Those problems, however, are complex, and their solution cannot be expected to be reached rapidly. In consequence we must separate from those problems questions pertaining to our day-to-day operations within the Council. If we did not do so, we would be unable to accomplish any useful work whatsoever."

The converse was not heard either: "Operations can be fruitful only if they are in agreement with the substance of the situation to which they pertain. Thus it is better to postpone any action than to undertake an action which might make it more difficult for us to analyze the situation correctly and to take in the end such measures as the situation dictates."

The precise point under dispute in this meeting was whether the delegates of certain nonmember countries should be invited to participate in the debate. This participation was at first opposed by the Australian delegate in extremely conciliatory terms. It does not appear to be necessary "for the present." The Council should however be ready to reconsider in accordance with possible developments. After the Soviet delegate has taken the floor to suggest that an invitation be extended, this invitation is again opposed by the delegates of the United States and Australia in terms much stronger than those used previously. The Soviet delegate had based his arguments on the subordination of the procedural aspects to substantive ones; as the nonmember nations are interested in the substantive aspects, they should participate in all the discussions, and in fact the debate should bear on substance principally. The Western delegates reply that the question is one of procedure over which only members of the Council have jurisdiction. The increasing acrimony of the debate leads to the impression that the Australian and the American delegates oppose more the pattern of thought of the Soviet delegate, with his insistence on discussion and inaction, than they do the actual invitation which he champions.

To sum up, it appears that all difficulties of international communication have not been solved in the case above. The purely linguistic problem was solved superbly, insofar as translation and interpretation may solve it, by the staff of the United Nations Secretariat. The question of patterns of thought, however, does not appear to have been given any attention whatsoever.

Conclusion

In presenting this paper I do not wish to say that it is possible to arrive at a rigid classification of patterns of thought which would apply in all cases. Neither do I wish to imply that national or cultural groups are characterized by a rigid and constant adherence to definite patterns of thought. Nor again do I wish to imply that there is a rigid correspondence between languages and patterns of thought.

What I hope to have shown is:

1. That there exist correlations between patterns of thought and patterns of expressions and that those correlations may be used in the analysis of patterns of thought.

2. That patterns of thought will be more easily recognized through

the connotations appearing in the patterns of expression than in the denotations of statements.

3. That forms taken by language tend in many cases to encourage certain patterns of thought and to discourage others.

4. That connotations appearing in language have at least as much a part in influencing thought as do denotations.

5. That even an imperfect method of classification may greatly help in analyzing patterns of thought as they appear in concrete cases, and thus to make it easier to overcome some of the obstacles inherent in international communications.

Words—Returning from an International Conference

Spring, 1954. Edmund S. Glenn, who has studied in Europe and the U.S., received in 1954 a Rockefeller Foundation Grant for research in languages and patterns of thought. This research, conducted at Georgetown University, resulted in the foregoing paper, which was originally presented at the Second Conference on General Semantics, Washington University, St. Louis, 1954. It also formed the basis of the Scientific Conference on Interpreting and Intercultural Barriers of Communication which was held in Washington, D.C., on January 4, 1956, under the auspices of the U.S. Department of State and the Josiah Macy, Jr. Foundation. Since 1950 Mr. Glenn has been chief of the Interpreting Branch of the U. S. State Department.

Shall We Sit Idly By?

HERBERT A. THELEN

The Second World War created a vast number of jobs in Chicago's industry. Labor was attracted from all over the country, but especially from the South. During the decade beginning in 1940, there was an increase of 42 per cent among the nonwhite population in Chicago. The construction of houses and other dwelling units did not keep pace with the increase of population, and the resulting shortage of housing became Chicago's number one problem. Two-thirds of the new dwelling units created between 1940 and 1950 failed to meet minimum legal standards of quality. Overcrowding developed, and, with it, the decline of morale and communication among neighbors.

The population increase strained the available city services to the utmost. The conditions accompanying overcrowding aggravated still further the problems of maintaining police, fire, and health protection. The average cost of maintenance per citizen increased far beyond what the city budget provided. Many areas were slighted altogether by one or another of the city's services.

The solution of these civic difficulties was vastly complicated by the Supreme Court ruling that bailiffs of Federal Courts could not be used to enforce restrictive covenants. People began to react not only to the grim facts but also to all sorts of racial fears and fantasies.

In some neighborhoods there was panic or rioting when the first Negroes moved in. As residents fled, their places were taken by Negroes, whose need for housing was most desperate—and who were willing to make desperate bargains for property. In some areas, the Negro in-migration "took over" one block after another, thus in effect simply extending the "black belt."

Social Disorganization

The skyrocketing prices of property, the limitation of property income by rent control, the pressure for housing of any kind—these caused individuals in all parts of the city to decide to sublet or to create new, smaller units in their buildings. In many cases this decision ushered into neighborhoods an unfamiliar kind of person: the tenant. With increased mixing of apartments, rooming houses, kitchenette flats, and single-family residences came greater mixing of people who differed in their class levels, social backgrounds, values, and ways of life. And these changes were most visible when the incomers were Negroes.

The mixing of class and caste resulted not only in the breakdown of communication on the block but also in the feeling that communication would now be impossible. Neighbors were no longer seen as people one could identify with; the sense of common cause was lost. People felt more and more reluctant to talk with the neighbors, and their concerns accordingly turned inward on themselves rather than being directed outward as in the past. The deterioration of the physical community created only personal problems for individual residents, rather than problems for the block or the community as a whole to deal with.[1]

The feeling of apathy and frustration of neighbors was assimilated into "official" attitudes toward neighborhoods where changes were occurring. There was increasing reluctance of city servants to meet the needs of these areas—and this added fuel to the flames of resentment and frustration. The result was, in effect, that all the usual channels by which citizens normally can get at least some action were gradually blocked off.

[1] It is true, however, that some neighborhoods contained many groups with regular meetings. But these were nonaction groups which provided, perhaps, some feeling of escape from the frustrations of the role of citizen. They contributed very little to the rectification of conditions or to the adjustment of individuals to the conditions.

Finally, as if to complete this sorry picture of disorganization, there was flight; people moved out, sometimes in blind panic and sometimes to find the better living their war prosperity made possible. In either case, the flight was on the part of people who had enough money to flee; and these people tended to belong to the group which had provided leadership and vigilance in the past. Thus flight was not only the symbol of panic and of defeat in the face of anxiety; it was also the creator of a vacuum in the power structure of the city. And there was no lack of people ready and able to turn civic disorder into personal wealth. Most notable was the alliance between crime and politics: during the decade it changed from a hothouse plant, delicately and blushingly nurtured by a few, into a rank prairie weed openly and knowingly nurtured by the many.

Most citizens were part, parcel, and carrier of the social disorganization. They felt lonely, isolated, "cut off" from the "group." Some felt that they had been singled out for special persecution. Feelings of helplessness became widespread and with these feelings came a stifling blanket of fears. It was, for example, not uncommon for people to be afraid at night to put their autos in the garages on the alley. Along with fear came anxiety and anger at feeling fearful. Out of this arose interpretations that were mostly projections of hostility onto convenient target groups (scapegoats): the Negroes, the cops, the landlords, yes, even the Democrats.

The fears were expressed in rumors of all sorts; nothing was too silly to be handed on: the Urban League has a million dollars to "break" white blocks for Negro occupancy; the syndicate wants to convert all the big homes in the Fourth Ward into rooming houses. Fears and anxieties snowballed because there were no channels for constructive action to relieve frustration. Apathy and defeatism set in, and with these, hypocrisy and guilt feelings, because when one is lonely he thinks it is his fault; he blames himself and at the same time tries to put up a front both to himself and to the "group" which he does not realize exists no longer. These conditions are clearly revealed, for instance, in an interview with a lovely lady who said that she had lived in the neighborhood all her life and intended to finish her days there. In the midst of this painted picture of security and comfort a man in overalls interrupted by ringing the doorbell. He said, "I'm from Ace Moving Company. Is this the house where I am to pick up the furniture?" People would often protest they were going to stay in the neighborhood and that they loved it—right up to the point where they melted away into the suburbs.

A general interpretation of all these events is that individual behavior became more and more determined by self-concern. It expressed reaction to anxiety insufficiently controlled by contact with the world of objective facts.

Facing Facts

By November, 1949, the flight of people along Drexel Avenue, where the Negroes had moved in, threatened serious depletion of the congregations of certain churches. At their request, the late Tom Wright, director of the Chicago Commission on Human Relations, began preliminary discussions with the 57th Street Meeting of Friends. From this, came a meeting of forty concerned citizens from various organizations in the Hyde Park-Kenwood area. The meeting was stormy, and it faced some very sobering facts:

1. The fact that sociologists and planners predicted that the area would be a slum in ten years;

2. The fact that nobody knew of any examples of a community which, when once started on the path of deterioration, had worked its way back out;

3. The fact that a whole dynamic pattern of forces toward deterioration was practically unopposed; and that the reversal of these forces would require all-out action on a staggering array of fronts.

The group saw that there were logically just three alternatives:

1. Citizens could flee from the area, leaving it to exploiters and others to profit from social deterioration;

2. The group could sit tight and do nothing on the grounds that the problems were too big or that they did not have the required resources;

3. The group could start to work.

I think that this group recognized that going to work did not necessarily mean success, but that successful or not one must try. Following this feeling of commitment, the group planned a program, and talked about what it could do rather than what it couldn't do to get started. Half of the resulting program was concerned with pinpointing specific objectives: enforcing the law; bettering the schools; getting recreation facilities; establishing relations with the building commissioner's office; planning for future development; running a survey of the area to find the extent of deterioration; and so on. For each of these objectives, working committees were recruited and set up, and many of these committees became influential in mobilizing pressures strategically to get decisions changed or improved for the benefit of the community.

The second half of the program was concerned with what has been sometimes called the "grass-roots" aspects. Basically, the origin of this part of the program was the realization, in general terms, that no one group of forty dedicated individuals could possibly provide the man-hours, skill, time, and energy required to reverse the whole pattern of social action in the community. A veritable army—co-ordinated, active, and energetic—would be required.

Also, it was further recognized that (by definition) a conservation area is one which is unstable in the sense that its ultimate fate is in doubt. The positive forces of growth appear to have been halted but deterioration has not yet progressed to the point of slum conditions. For slum conditions, incidentally, there is a pat answer: this is to bring in the bulldozer to knock everything down, relocate the citizens, build new buildings, then move some of the people back in. This area had not reached that point. Progress or deterioration in the area was seen to depend upon the wisdom of the individual actions of the citizens. Thousands of decisions made by citizens every day add up to a cumulative impact, a dynamic, tending toward improvement or toward deterioration.

Some of the kinds of individual acts and decisions which would forecast the community's future are:

1. Decisions about how extensively and how adequately to keep up property;

2. Decisions about the use to which property will be put, particularly with respect to the type of dwelling units and number of people living in each;

3. Initiation of actions and follow-up requests for city services;

4. Engagement with others in neighborly conversation so that individuals could test ideas about new uses of property before trying to put them into effect;

5. Expression of attitudes of friendliness or indifference or hostility which foster concern for the welfare of all or which indicate only concern for oneself;

6. Maintenance of an attitude of objectivity toward rumors; the

tendency to make objective inquiry and the feeling of trusting other people's common sense, so that one does not rush off always believing the worst.

Since these and many other everyday behaviors of citizens seem to determine the fate of the community it was necessary to try to reach everybody if possible under conditions which would result in the most intelligent behavior possible. The program of organizing citizens block by block on a quasi-social basis was set up to provide the social psychological conditions under which neighbors would tend to make intelligent decisions based on diagnosis of objective realities rather than to make decisions in panic based on unrealistic fears or to make exploitative decisions based on immediate rather than long-range self-interest.

Before finally adopting the program of block organization it was decided to try the idea of neighborly meetings in one block first. A certain block on Drexel Avenue had the first meeting in January, 1950. This meeting illustrated many of the principles and characteristics of most subsequent block meetings.

It just happened that this block meeting was planned at a strategic time, namely, when rumors were sweeping the block that a house was about to be sold to exploiters who would pack a Negro family into each room. People were concerned and knew that each of the others was concerned. In other words, there was something to discuss and no question about that! As soon as the rumor swept the block, four people put their houses up for sale. Everybody in a row of fifteen owner-occupied houses was invited to the meeting by a small planning group of four. These four personally visited the families with whom they were already acquainted—it was easier that way.

As the people came into the meeting, it was clear that they had different expectations, ranging from the notion that we were met to consider strategies to keep the Negroes out to the feeling that we ought to invite Negroes in and turn the neighborhood into an interracial paradise. These attitudes were expressed fairly readily by people in small discussion groups which had formed before the meeting started.

After about twenty minutes, the feeling arose that we should get started, and there were many glances toward the chairman and host. An old man, about eighty, climbed upon the stair landing and opened the meeting with, "What do you want me to tell you about those damn niggers?" There was a decidedly awkward pause, and the leader replied that while listening to the informal conversations before the meeting opened, he discovered that we had a wide range of feeling about Negroes among us. And he suggested that we might as well accept this as the fact about ourselves that we could do nothing about. He pointed out, however, that Negroes had bought the apartment across the street and he felt that the block faced certain objective possibilities:

Sweeping Generality Followed by Private Opinion

It could form a pitchfork mob to try to drive the Negroes out;
It could attempt to ignore them;
It could attempt to establish communication with them with the idea of explaining the block's determination to prevent physical deterioration and to make the block a pleasant place in which to live.

Posed this way, that is, with the objective reality orientation based on alternative action possibilities, the group quickly decided to get into communication. A committee was appointed to go calling; attention was given to the problem of avoiding the use of people who had strong feelings either for or against Negroes. The committee that did call was a strange combination of investigating committee and friendship group. The Negroes, fortunately, could see the committee's embarrassment and were mature in helping them to establish communication.

Three other actions were taken from the first meeting; the second meeting started with the reporting of these actions, introduction of new people, and the setting up of an agenda consisting of the things people on the block thought were problems to be looked into.

Objectives of Block Meeting

As the neighbors left the first meeting they felt considerable relief from anxiety. The meeting had not yet done anything very important by way of taking action, but the neighbors had found out something that they "knew" intellectually but could never have really felt if they had not been called together to enter into action. They had found out that there were a lot of people just as concerned, just as disturbed, and just as frustrated as they were. Instead of feeling that "everybody else is perfectly able to cope with the situation but I am not," the individuals found that everybody was equally *unable* to cope with the situation, so that the feeling of inadequacy was dissolved and was replaced by the much more objective perception that the group as a whole had problems. Thus feelings of being an outsider, of being unable to cut the mustard in the community—feelings which had led individuals to turn in on themselves and feel lonely—were replaced by a complete reversal of the relationship to the group. The group of neighbors was felt now to be supportive; one was no longer alone. Under these conditions of establishment of communication and support the individual could feel free to act intelligently rather than out of anxiety.

The restoration of communication thus started through the need for reducing anxiety, but it continued as a new pattern on the block. The neighbors had become acquainted at the block meeting, and each day, as they passed one another on the block, they would say hello. The network of communication on the block was reinforced and grew because it became a part of the way of life on the block. Aside from reduction of anxiety, this meeting also illustrates a second dynamic and a second objective: namely, the setting up of processes of co-operative problem-solving. These are important for two reasons. First, it is only through working together that people acquire meaning for each other, and the meaning people have for one another makes the neighborhood one's home. In other words, the relationships developed under conditions of co-operative working are also the relationships that will stabilize the neighborhood. Second, the solving of problems on the block makes its own contribution to the restoration or maintenance of the block. The moving of abandoned cars; the installing of porch lights to dispel darkness; the prompt reporting of movements of materials into houses so that conversion plans can be checked; the development of tot-lots and recreational space; the collective buying and sharing of garden implements—all these things are not only the

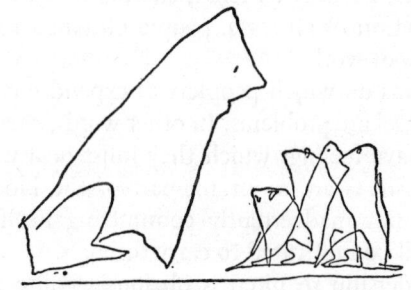

A Vague Question Gives Birth to a Litter of Vague Answers

foci for neighborly communication but positive acts of neighborhood improvement in their own right.

And finally, the third objective is one of collective enlightenment to develop a pressure against civic slothfulness. Through the recognition and formulation of problems, the discussion of alternative action possibilities, the seeking of necessary information, the clarification of ideas of why conditions are as they are and what can be done about them—all of these things lead to greater enlightenment, greater acceptance of realities as they are, and to the understanding of the broader significance of the co-operative work. In a sense, then, participation in the block program is also an educational experience with, we hope, some transfer value to many situations of everyday living.

Principles for Block Leaders

In running meetings to obtain these objectives a number of important principles have been identified. These have become, in effect, the bases for the training of leadership for community action. Let us take a look at some of these principles, not necessarily in the order of their importance.

1. For the neighbors to remain involved and interested over a long period of time, they must receive rewards at a sufficient rate. The two kinds of rewards possible are *gratification* of individual need for such things as dominance, friendship, intimacy with certain people, and the opportunity to test ideas; and *satisfaction* in the group accomplishment of tasks. Particularly at the beginning it was evident that the reward for task accomplishment would not be sufficiently great and frequent to avoid discouragement and to maintain involvement. Therefore, the meetings by design developed a quasi-social character so that through parties, friendly chitchat, sharing of hobbies, games, and informal conversation of all sorts, people obtained rewards over and above the rewards of work.

2. The only problems on which people will expend energy are the problems which they feel are problems. In other words, they are things about which people have feelings which they must deal with. Therefore, the problem census is an important part of the block meeting so that the group is not inadvertently committing itself to action along lines nobody will be motivated to carry through.

3. The kind of leadership required is obviously going to be both permissive and work-oriented. We have found from experience that a leadership team is far more effective than a single leader. A team will make a more objective analysis of how the last meeting went, and it will have more information and understanding to use in planning the next meeting.

4. A concomitant of the initial attitudes of people in disorganized areas is the feeling of lack of trust and suspicion of each other. We have found that meetings can be organized much more successfully when friends call on friends so that the initial hurdle of distrust does not have to be jumped over or burrowed under.

5. The basis of participation in block meetings is merely that one lives on the block. There is no test of ideology because it is not what people say they believe that is important so much as their willingness to work on problems. As long as there is willingness to work on problems, ideological differences can be settled or avoided. Moreover, the people who are out of sympathy with the movement are very likely

to be the ones whose actions are most likely to be damaging to the block; therefore special effort is put forth to involve them in the meetings.

6. A widespread fear often expressed by certain types of people is that citizens might decide to take a wrong action and if so the block organization would become an instrument of evil. There are two relevant principles that make this an unnecessary worry. The first is, that under reasonably "democratic" leadership, the socially desirable side of people's ambivalence has a tendency to get reinforced and to govern decisions. In plain English, what this means, is that if the group is torn between the desire, let us say, to keep Negroes out and also the desire to accept their coming, then under good leadership conditions, they are much more likely to decide on the socially approved course of action rather than the disapproved one. The second principle involved here is that whatever decision is made should be regarded as tentative and open for review. Presumably if the decision to keep Negroes out is a bad decision, then acting on it will produce evidence to that effect; the evidence will be in the form of discomfort, difficulties in selling property, and the like. By adopting an experimentalistic approach to decision-making, the decision can always be changed when further relevant evidence becomes available.

7. Each block group is seen as having the right to decide for itself just how autonomous it ought to be. While the parent organization puts a great deal of effort into getting blocks organized and rolling, it avoids stirring up problems of divided loyalty. Everybody in the block can feel loyalty to his own neighborhood group, but many people may not wish to affiliate with the parent organization. Moreover, by the time a block group has, through its own efforts achieved a degree of satisfaction and success, it sometimes resents any kind of interference, large or small, by a central organization. The principle, then, is that each block determines its own degree of autonomy.

8. In many cases it is very difficult to know what course of action is the "right" course of action to solve the problem. In such cases, the criterion of good decision-making is that there is mature co-operation through which all relevant facts and feelings are expressed and soberly considered. Under these conditions we can assume that the decision arrived at is the best one the group is capable of making; it is to be accepted as sound until further evidence comes in.

Kinds of Problems Worked On

It is clear that there are certain kinds of problems that every block works on. There are, in addition, many types of projects which seem to be congenial to certain blocks but not to others.

Thus, the problems all blocks are encouraged to deal with include:

1. Setting up block standards—e.g., of quality for dwelling units, or a code of behaviors that the block expects from its residents. Through participation in the development of such standards through discussion, a coercive preventive force arises which prevents many selfish impulses from finding expression.

2. There is a whole range of city services available to citizens for maintaining and servicing the neighborhood. Continual alertness in checking these and if necessary, complaining about them, might be thought of as vigilance functions. The most important vigilance functions from a community standpoint are probably those centering around the reporting of suspected illegal conversions and the reporting of crime.

3. The typical improvement projects, such as putting in tot-lots, planning parking space, and so on, have been discussed above.

In addition to these three basic kinds of effort, some of the following types of projects have been undertaken:

4. Joining with other blocks on an area job, such as cleaning up the length of a business street or digging out all the fire plugs in the area when they are covered with snow.

5. Collective private enterprises, such as equipping a shop or running hobby nights and sharing tools.

6. Recreational or social activities, such as parties, square dancing, and poker festivals to raise money for tot-lots and the like.

7. Educational programs, using speakers who can tell the neighbors what they can do to make their homes less attractive to burglars; what to do about auto larcenies; how to have a beautiful lawn.

Supportive Mechanisms for Recruitment, Training, and Spread

The most significant dynamics and ideas about citizen participation through the block program have been presented. But having significant ideas and getting them into widespread action throughout the community require a great many supportive devices and a great deal of effort. The total action program includes not only the use of block meetings and of working committees stemming from such meetings, but also the use of mass meetings, mass media, and interviews with a large number of individuals.

Mass meetings do a great deal to produce a climate favorable for block meetings within the community. The typical pattern of the mass meetings can be described about as follows:

Block people invite all of their neighbors to come, and, in some cases car pools are arranged. The meeting opens with socio-dramas of a variety of typical perplexing incidents, and the general aim is, through these socio-dramas, to identify and express most of the different attitudes held by members of the audience. In effect, this sets the limits for emotional expression, and tends to be highly involving of the audience. Following the socio-dramas, there is usually a period of discussing facts. This may be done by a panel of experts or by informed resource people. Here the aim is to place the emotionalized problem into a cognitive context. How widespread are these conditions? What are the forces causing them? What sorts of solutions are there? The third step is one of audience participation in identifying the problems they see in the neighborhood. This is ordinarily done through the division of the meeting into smaller groups ("buzz groups") followed by a problem census on the blackboard, and deciding on problem priorities through voting or interpretation.

By this time the meeting has a clear sense of problem, and also some sense of gratification through the recognition of community of concern. The next step is to outline the plans for action, for the training of block leaders, and for the involvement of more people. A training session for leaders is announced. Finally, each person in the audience has a card on which to check one of some eight ways of participating further. These range from being a block leader to volunteering for secretarial work.

The most effective meeting of this kind was in an area where Negroes were moving in, so that there was plenty of affect to be channeled. At this meeting out of 230 people, 45 volunteered to attend the announced training sessions, with the understanding that they might very well become block leaders.

Some meetings, which are more frankly aimed at immediate organization of blocks, set up the all-important buzz groups in somewhat different fashion. The floor of the meeting hall is laid out like a map of the community, and there are street corner signs placed in their proper spatial relationship to each other. The people are then asked to find their own "neighborhood" and join with their neighbors to discuss problems and elect someone from their own group to be a leader. This person then comes in for training and takes responsibility either for carrying on or for finding someone to take his place.

For the purpose of helping people who are interested in being block leaders but are not quite sure they are "ready" for the responsibility, a type of training session which we have called the "community clinic" has been invented. These are held every three weeks. They start with a statement of the objectives of the block program. This is followed by a report summarizing the various activities of the working committees of the conference, in an effort to help people realize the extent of the resources they can draw upon, and also to feel a part of the total program. After this comes the reporting of block meetings held since the last clinic. Actions, issues, and attitudes are reported by someone from the block; and these are exciting stories indeed. Next the group is divided into small practice groups which are variously concerned with practicing calling on people to invite them to meetings; strategies for finding leadership in blocks and getting them organized; skills and techniques for leading meetings; and finally, a session devoted to giving authoritative information about how various kinds of problems can be worked on.

The people coming to these meetings are recruited through the local Hyde Park *Herald*, through a mimeographed newsletter, through personal arm-twisting of acquaintances, and through the executive secretary of the conference who notes every person who calls in with a problem as a potential organizer of a block.

In addition to these devices, there is a steering committee for block operation composed of leaders from the various organized blocks. These meetings are concerned with developing program ideas, training of leaders, swapping experiences, and planning recommendations to the conference as a whole.

Consultation is available to individuals who wish it through the conference office which has a part-time block worker; through the University which has funds from the Wieboldt Foundation to maintain a consultant service; and through the block steering committee whose experienced block leaders are willing to help others.

During the summer there is a workshop, jointly sponsored by the Human Dynamics Laboratory at the University and the Chicago

Commission on Human Relations. It spends three weeks in bringing people together from action organizations in the Chicago area with the findings, techniques, and methods of urban sociology and group dynamics. Block leaders are welcomed in this workshop, and have demonstrated considerable skill in applying their training to the development of block programs.

One of the most effective methods for spreading the program to other blocks is through the use of observers who attend the meetings and then go home and do likewise.

Significance and Accomplishment of the Block Program

1. The pattern of action through citizen participation with supporting services has been taken over with appropriate modifications by groups in other parts of Chicago: Woodlawn, Park Manor, Chatham-Avalon, and in Oakland.

2. There is no question that the city hall attitude toward these areas as being beyond redemption and not worthy of servicing has changed in proportion to the activities of these neighborhood conferences.

3. There is no question either that the active, quiet groundwork of these neighborhood conferences is making a real contribution to involving major institutions in their areas in the work. This brings in power people of the community who are capable of dealing directly at political and economic levels with some of these problems.

4. There is no question that the areas with active block organizations have improved physically and stabilized themselves psychologically. Illegal conversions have stopped, flight from these areas is well nigh stopped, and there is much more tendency to regard the neighborhood as home.

Speaking personally, as a methodologist in the field of social action, I should say the most exciting demonstration made by the block program is that there is a vast, almost limitless source of power that can be tapped for improvement of the community. This source of power is the individual's own need for security and adequacy channeled into constructive community activity. If this power can be mobilized and involved in community work, there seems to be almost no limit to what can be accomplished.

A second significant feature for me has been the gradual spelling out of the role of the citizen in urban society. It is a much larger role than merely putting a ballot in the box every few years. It involves exercise of responsibilities, knowledge, and will to use available resources for problem-solving. So far as I know at the present time there is no place where these important aspects of the citizen role are specifically taught except in the action of the neighbors on the block. From one standpoint, the block program can be regarded as a vast adult education program in learning the operational meaning of democracy.

The third generalization that emerges from our experience is that the rules of discourse recommended by general semantics take on extremely practical significance when seen in the context of block meetings, which, especially at the early stages, are often fraught with anxieties. The avoidance of ideological discussion at high levels of abstraction, the avoidance of sweeping generalities, the substitution of observable fact in place of rumor and unchecked inference, the insistence on the concrete and specific in discussion, the making of accurate "maps" of the community "territories" prior to decision-making—these are rules of discourse which govern the way in which group leaders try to conduct their meetings. They also govern largely the discussion of mature groups. This is not to say that group leaders or members have studied or are consciously applying the principles of general semantics. But the student of general semantics who finds himself in a block organization quickly sees ample confirmation of semantic principles in the successes of the group. As fears and prejudices are unblocked and extensionalization begins, communication becomes richer in content and relevancy, resulting in the sharing of knowledge and therefore in realistic problem-solving behavior.

The final major demonstration is that there is a close relationship between the concepts of scientific method and democracy. Avoiding for the moment the arguments about what democracy is, still I am impressed by such parallels as the fact that you can relate the requirement of scientific method for all relevant information to the democratic concept of respect for individuals. You can equate the need to test ideas apart from people, using objective criteria, as the major condition for obtaining freedom for expression in a group. You can equate the testing of hypotheses as the basic instrument for consolidating knowledge with the step-wise planning of action in which each step is based on the effects of the previous step. It is my feeling that these and other parallelisms between democracy and scientific method are by no means accidental. I see these, along with some common teachings of most religious creeds, as evidence that man, through various avenues of interpretation of experience, is gradually beginning to nail down a fairly basic set of ideas about human interaction, its control, and its possibilities for the achievement of a better world.

Autumn, 1953. Dr. Thelen is professor of educational psychology and director of the Laboratory for Study of Teaching and Learning Processes, University of Chicago. His article is based on a speech given before the Chicago Chapter of the International Society for General Semantics, March 27, 1953. He is author of The Dynamics of Groups at Work *(1954) and co-author of* Emotional Dynamics and Group Culture *(1958).*

POSTSCRIPT, *November, 1958. By 1954 the Conference had changed the climate of the community to one of determination to rebuild the area. The Southeast Chicago Commission was formed, which, under the leadership of the University of Chicago, mobilized almost every major institution in the power structure of the community. The Conference, with its grass-roots approach, and the Commission, with its power-oriented, technical approach, have fought together—with a good deal of friction engendered by their different ways of life—for urban renewal. Together they have approached agencies at all levels, from city council to the President of the United States. As of now, 40 per cent of the slums in the area have been torn down and rebuilding has begun. About $30,000,000 of federal money has been earmarked for the project, which is the first urban renewal (as distinguished from slum clearance) project in the United States. A similar amount will be invested by private redevelopers. Furthermore, it is expected that improvements by homeowners to existing properties will total $40,000,000 within a few years. Without the action described in this article, it is doubtful that any of these developments would have occurred. The full story of the Hyde Park–Kenwood Conference, written by Julia Abrahamson, its executive director for the first seven years, is to be found in* A Neighborhood Finds Itself *(Harper, 1959).*

The Meanings of "Democracy":
Puerto Rican Organizations in Chicago

LESTER C. HUNT, JR.
NICOLAS VON HOFFMAN

In the long battle of the cold war the question of what democracy is and in what countries it is to be found has taken a place of great importance in our foreign policy and the foreign policy of all other nations. China is refused admittance to the United Nations because it is not democratic; Germany and Japan keep us up at night as we wonder if they can ever be democratic. In our concern we have begun to think of democracy as a kind of mechanism which only needs to be put down in the right place to be operative. Yet democracy involves more than laws and formal political structures. A better example of the fact cannot be found than one which exists right within our own nation.

Since 1954 the authors have been closely associated with the small though growing Puerto Rican colony in Chicago. The experience has been enjoyable, and it has also been instructive, in that it has provided them with an opportunity of looking at some old ideas like "democracy" and "the democratic process" in some new ways.

Coming as they have from the farms and hills of backwoods Puerto Rico, the newly arrived have found Chicago a strange and frightening place. They have not been fortunate enough to come with the education or knowledge that could help them out of their dilemma of being country folks in the big city. Almost none of them speaks English well, many can hardly be thought of as speaking it at all, nor do they have the advantage of being well educated in their own mother tongue. Their Spanish vocabulary is small, writing in it comes hard. Their general education is about on the same level, fourth or fifth grade, we estimate.

The Chicago adventure is a shock for many of the Puerto Ricans not only because the city is so large and complicated, but also because their contact with our typical continental institutions had been so superficial prior to their arrival here. Some of the men of course had been in the army, but, it is to be hoped, a tour of duty in an infantry platoon does not represent the best introduction to the life of civilian America. When we use the term "Puerto Rican" in this article it is the Puerto Rican of this background we have in mind, not the wealthier cultivated Puerto Rican, the doctor, the lawyer, or the man who spent time studying at schools outside his native island.

Shortly after the Puerto Ricans' first establishment in Chicago they began to combine in organizations, as have so many other foreign-language immigrant groups. The organizations they have formed have a multiplicity of purposes. Some seek to promote financial security through welfare and insurance schemes, others are purely social in nature, others religious, and many have mixed all these purposes and others besides. Not all the Puerto Rican organizations have been successful or even partly so in what they have set out to do, and as a matter of simple fact very few have ever lived long enough to attempt to achieve their purposes. The histories of their birth, life, and death is a history of suspicions, quarrels, feuds, struggling ambitions, enraged resignations, and seldom anything harmonious. Nevertheless, whatever the outcome, each organization has claimed in common with all the others one characteristic, that of being "*democratico.*" It would be no exaggeration to say that the Puerto Ricans almost to a man are passionate believers in "democracy."

Amid suffocating billows of forensic cliché on the sublimity of "democracy," Puerto Rican organizations are conducted in what would appear to us continentals the most "undemocratic" fashion. The casual passer-by might ascribe this to ignorance of what real democracy is and thereby reduce the question to one of "educating," to use the word now in vogue, the Puerto Rican in democracy. Such an analysis might justify itself if they were people so foreign to our ideas of self-rule that the ideas could come to them as something entirely fresh and new. This is not the case. Puerto Rican culture has given them a distinct idea of democracy and their language has reinforced the idea. The word *"democracia"* is commonplace among Puerto Ricans, but their idea of democratic conduct is not ours by any means. Thus the words, *"democracia"* (democracy), *"presidente"* (president), *"comité"* (committee), have different definitions for them and for us. The effect is twofold for it not only maintains them in their own ideas, but makes it exceedingly difficult for them to understand our meaning. Again it should be clearly understood that when the authors refer to Spanish words we are contemplating the Puerto Rican migrant's Spanish, not the Spanish language of Spain. It is the value they assign words which we are examining in this article and which accounts for the differences in their behavior and the continentals'.

Usually we are able to look with some equanimity on a democratically controlled group that we have membership in, whether it be a small local one or the government itself. On the whole our experience with such organizations has been pleasant and at least not completely disappointing. That there should be one or many minority opinions is not disturbing; once the decision is reached we are sure our group will go through with it, the minority as well as the majority. The Puerto Ricans' approach is far less relaxed.[1]

Historically the successful groups the Puerto Rican has been associated with have not made any pretense of being democratic. Until a scant fifty years ago his island was a Spanish crown colony and one of Spain's few that never revolted. During the hundreds of years of Spanish rule it became implicit in the culture that the relationship between men was essentially one of superiority and inferiority, that is, of strong man, weak man, not aristocracy. The notion persists even in the Puerto Rican clubs and organizations of Chicago, where he who has a little more than most is addressed as "Don José" or "Don Miguel." There is a case on record of a total stranger who walked into a Puerto Rican meeting and was nominated as an officer without his saying a single word (he could speak no Spanish) because of the expensive-looking suit he was wearing.

[1] The reader ought to bear in mind that we are contrasting Puerto Rican practice with the continentals' ideal type of behavior. Sociologists and historians have long since demonstrated the existence of some rather sizeable gaps between what we like to think we do and what we do.

The advent of American rule brought no real change for a long time. Undisguised tutelage had been exchanged for a tutelage with the mumbo-jumbo, though not the substance, of democracy. Today, under the so-called Commonwealth system, Puerto Rico does enjoy a real measure of democratic self-rule, but the experience is very recent and has not had time to drop its roots into the language, customs, and life of the island's people. Puerto Ricans cannot look back on a tradition of lay justices of the peace, juries, or town meetings. It would be a mistake to assume that with the granting of limited autonomy by the U.S. Congress the transition to modern parliamentary democracy was smoothly accomplished. Many Puerto Ricans had been made cynical watching the forms of self-government manipulated to circumvent the majority will while the island was an American possession. The presence of the *Nacionalista* party with its attendant belief in violence shows there are other Puerto Ricans who reject or cannot understand our idea of democratic procedure. One Puerto Rican tells that in a frantic effort to prevent fraud every voter in his village was locked up in the town hall after he had cast his ballot until the polls were closed.

No wonder that many Puerto Ricans are possessed of mixed feelings when they find themselves members of a democratic group. On the one hand they have not escaped being fired by the word "democracy" as it has made its way around the world, but on the other hand once they are in a "democratic" situation they are very pessimistic about the group's chances of success. They are seized by apprehensions that the group will disintegrate, that the membership will quit, or that in spite of the democratic process it will fall victim to the will of a small clique or a single individual who will run it against the wishes of the majority. In time an implicit definition of a group or any self-governing body has shaped itself in Puerto Ricans' minds which differs quite radically from our own. Instead of seeing it as a union flexible enough to arrange itself according to varying circumstance, they are prone to view an organized group as something whose rigidity and unanimity endows it with the power to make headway. A good group is characterized by singleness of purpose, by many people of identical will.

The Puerto Rican has no word with which to express our word "speaker" or "chairman." For us the word "president" suggests someone who exercises executive authority, and the thought of a "president" presiding over any deliberative body strikes us as being somewhat unusual.[2] In that case a "president" would be doing the job customarily assigned to another English-speaking cultural type, the chairman or speaker. None of this is so with the Puerto Rican who not only lacks the word "chairman" but the role of chairman too. The role does not exist in his culture and it is very hard for him to conceive of it, as anyone who has tried to explain to a Puerto Rican what a chairman is will certainly testify. If you try to show him a chairman is the elected head of a deliberating body who must not speak one way or another on a matter that is being discussed on the floor, the Puerto Rican is apt to consider the notion illogical. For him it is inconsistent to think of a *"presidente"* being restricted to interpreting rules of procedure so that every opinion may be aired and the majority's will fairly and speedily arrived at. The Puerto Rican's view of the group and the president suggests that one is supplement and the other complement. No group is a really democratic group without both. The rigid unity of purpose the Puerto Rican expects from the membership calls forth and is reflected in the figure of the ascendant, nonparliamentary image of the president.

It should now be somewhat easier to understand what experiences Puerto Ricans have in mind when they use the word *"democracia."* It is what we would probably call "popular dictatorship," to be distinguished from fascism or totalitarianism. The group which elects the president is seen as one giving a wide mandate to a man who is the symbol and executor of the majority's will, and the group itself henceforth becomes a kind of collective tribunate ratifying or vetoing the president's acts. Should the president lose favor, he is out. A president may command 51 per cent of the votes but in this scheme of things bare voting majorities count for little since he has ceased to represent a united will. Our notion that deliberative groups can successfully initiate action, day by day ironing out different kinds of policies and passing them on to the administrator, is more or less absent.

The depth of these definitions in the Puerto Rican mind is demonstrated in the case of a Puerto Rican club which had been given an "English" type constitution that conferred most of the real power on the *"reunión de los miembros"* (membership meeting) and made the *"presidente"* what we could call a chairman. The newly elected president was most unhappy after he had read the constitution, claiming

[2] Even though the presiding officer in the U.S. Senate is addressed as "Mr. President."

he was a president in name only, and the membership, mistrustful of itself and unable to realize how a president could have so little power, was confused. The situation was only resolved after the constitution was amended so that no vote could be taken until the president had delivered himself of a *"pronunciamento"* (opinion). Once the members knew what the president thought, they felt comfortable in approving or disapproving it.

Democracy for us carries within it the idea that all have an important day-to-day part to play in the process. To express the idea we use phrases like "working at it," "participating in it." Among Puerto Ricans, whose history is so different, such notions do not exist as part of the idea of democracy. There is no expectation that, once banded together, people will try and stick together using their organization as a means of solving the difficulties they are faced with; on the contrary, the Puerto Rican immediately commences to fear the membership will vanish even before the ink is dry on the new constitution. In order to prevent what he is afraid will come to pass he relies on the written words in a document, which is to say, he falls back on his ancient heritage of statutory law. He cannot appeal to his peers on the basis of their sharing an unwritten code of conduct in these matters as an English-speaking person might do with his background of common law. His listeners would not understand him; unless it is so written they cannot see that an obligation exists. As you might expect the result is that no Puerto Rican organization can exist for very long without the cement of a constitution.

By our lights the Puerto Rican approach to democratic organization is very impractical. Swept away by the sensation the word "democratic" creates in his head, he is apt to expect impossible things from his organization, and in fact many Puerto Rican groups begin with grandiose designs that are hopelessly too ambitious. In part inexperience in handling their own affairs is to blame for that, but only in part. Since the individual member does not think he is responsible for realizing such designs, he is unable to look at them from the point of view of the man whose job it is. How to conclude the task successfully is the leader's worry. It ought to be emphasized these understandings are not the result of sloth or stupidity, but of an amalgamation of a culture and a set of abstract ideas.

Americans, and English-speaking people generally, often think of a constitution as a set of governing by-laws that work by virtue of certain tacit understandings. Puerto Ricans do not think of a constitution in that way. For them nothing can be assumed and what the constitution does not say is irrelevant. So it is not surprising that we use a number of key words in very different senses. We associate rights and obligations, rights being what we may do providing we do not impinge on others' rights, and obligations being what we ought and ought not to do. *"Derecho"* is the word for rights in Puerto Rican Spanish; its meaning is to be relieved of the obligations of objective law. In other words it contains a notion of privilege which is entirely absent from our definition. Obligation—it is interesting to note there is no word the Puerto Ricans use consistently for the term—is the duty to do something for them but holds no idea of refraining from doing something.

Another term we hear used in connection with our democratic organizations is the phrase "sense of responsibility," by which we mean a person's spontaneous recognition of the part he must play if the process is going to work. It might not be inaccurate to say we consider "responsibility" our expression for the proper attitude toward our rights and obligations; however, it is impossible to give these definitions too precise a meaning since they refer more to a state of mind, a spirit, than to concise legalisms. By contrast the Spanish word *"responsibilidad"* is not associated in the Puerto Rican head with the democratic process nor does any term exist for him that describes the assumption of a role of action regardless of whether it is written down or not. Puerto Rican culture is profoundly nonpuritan, and the Puerto Rican views Man as an animal who does not follow the commands of the guardian of his soul, the conscience. The Puerto Rican view of human nature assumes that people will do anything that is not specifically made illegal or they are not physically prevented from doing. (Young girls are chaperoned because, were they not, they would do what they are not supposed to do, but unlike us, Puerto Ricans do not blame the girl if she falls. She could not be expected to act as if she had a chaperone when she did not; that would be expecting her to act contrary to her nature. We on the other hand attempt to build chaperones who can never be absent right into ourselves.)

Although institutions like chaperonage have fallen on bad times among the poorer Puerto Ricans who live in the countryside and migrate to the North American cities, the view of man and his nature which inspired them continues to exist as strong as ever. That view is the one which determines the Puerto Rican definition of words like "right," "obligation," and "responsibility."

Consequently, it is inaccurate to speak of the rights and obligations of the majority and the minority in Puerto Rican groups as we do in our own. After a vote has been taken and one party sees it is in the minority, it feels no compunction about walking out and leaving the rest of the group entirely. That is a "right." On the other side of the fence the majority is not restrained by the fear that reprisals against the minority can be carried too far. Just the reverse. The need to be sure in its own mind of the group's solidity may actually provoke the majority to drive out a minority because to the Puerto Rican there is always something subversive about a dissenting opinion. The thought of a "loyal opposition" is an incomprehensible contradiction of terms, and indeed many Puerto Rican groups find one of their gravest problems is the fierce factionalism that allows no quarter and is constantly inciting the majority to disenfranchise the minority, or on the other side finds the minority quitting.

The antiquity of the growth of the democratic procedure among the English-speaking people is attested to by the number of idioms in our language which describe it. Thus we "address the chair," "we have the floor," we "sit" as a committee of the whole, we "table" a motion. To "address the chair" in Spanish with Puerto Ricans present is to talk to a seat of some kind and invoke much laughter. He who would *"tener el sueldo,"* our "hold the floor," would only suggest the comic image of somebody trying to hold a floor. In case it seems we are asking a lot of the Puerto Ricans when we say they have no procedural terms in common use, recollect the millions of English-speaking people, with great education and very little, who are aware of this kind of language albeit their use of it is not nicely precise. Senators in Congress make "motions," as labor union members and children in grammar school do. In our culture there is no other way to conduct any kind of a public meeting, and it is almost impossible to be brought up here without absorbing these expressions and their meanings. No continental American could make the mistake of the Puerto Rican who rose to his feet in a meeting in order to make an *"emoción."* He meant a *"moción"* of course, but where he came from no one had ever heard of anything like that, but they all had heard of an emotion —everybody has them—so used the word that sounded like "motion" and was more familiar.

An American assumes the various procedural usages are a necessary part of the "democratic way of doing things." They are in his mind a distinct cluster of devices, of means to an end, democracy. His Puerto Rican opposite number makes a much hazier distinction of these means ensuring the goal (which is only natural if his definition of democracy, popular dictatorship, is recalled). *"Votación"* (voting) is what Puerto Ricans think of as the necessary procedure, but it is a mistake to think they look at procedure as a means to an end, the end being democracy in this case. It would be more proper to say a *"votación"* is a sign that whatever business is at hand is being attended to in a democratic way. In effect the Puerto Ricans do not share our idea of what democracy is, their culture lacking the tools to realize it, although their *"votación"* serves them very well for what they want.

"Votación" and voting present another example of two similar words in Spanish and English that have different referents. In a Puerto Rican group a vote on any issue, regardless of how inconsequential it may be, can take on the appearances of a bitter test of strength by which pride and power are won and lost, and this is quite understandable since in the Puerto Rican scheme of popular dictatorship, voting must mean a vote of confidence. Certainly the vote of confidence idea exists among us as well, but it is a secondary definition. Our first definition of voting is a canvass to determine the prevailing opinion, and that is the Puerto Rican secondary definition.

Although it would be impossible to reach a consensus as to what would be the ideal type of formal structure for any body or group, we do have certain widely held ideas about the composition, function and interrelation of the various subgroups our organizations contain. A committee is a fact-finding, recommendation-making group of small size; a "board" is an overseeing group composed of the top executives in an organization as well as men who are removed from its day-to-day existence. We think of many such ideas as very logical and more or less self-evident. Puerto Ricans do not find them so. As an example the Puerto Ricans will translate our word "committee" by the Spanish word *"comisión"* until they have been corrected a sufficient number of times to remember the, strange to them, Spanish word *"comité,"* but whatever word they use, they mean some sort of quasi-juridical body. The idea of a committee which goes out and gathers information to be acted on by the mother group is one they have great initial difficulty sympathizing with, and it is only after they have had to work with it a long time that they are able to operate within our design. One Puerto Rican organization, out of fear a small clique would dominate it, decided upon having a board of directors to look out for the majority's interests, but it forbade a single officer to sit on it or appear before it, thus so isolating it from the running of the organization that it was completely useless. The idea was highly "un-Puerto Rican," and involved the employment of units of organization foreign to Puerto Rican culture and experience. Significantly the scheme was suggested by a man who had attended a university. He had assimilated our terminology but its application was still as mysterious to him as when he had left the island.

The continental will invariably make a sharp distinction between a man and his office. Likewise he is prone to think of each office in an organization as the seat of certain functions. The Puerto Rican has other ideas. "*Directiva*" is a word he uses to signify the sum total of an organization's officers and their power. When he uses the expression he has a broad embracing thought in mind which is quite different from our narrow one when we use the term "officers" of an organization. Characteristically he first thinks of power as we of function. Doubtless the continental must always keep a weather eye cocked to know where the real power lies but we are also accustomed to balancing considerations of that kind off against the traditional limitations our organizations hedge the use of power with, and it is here we part company with our Puerto Rican brothers. Most Puerto Rican arrivals here on the continental United States are fundamentally rural people who may have spent a couple of years in San Juan at the most. Puerto Rican country life has never developed any institutions analogous to the village communes of some European countries that gave the farmer a degree of self-determination and a structure to fight powerful men's maraudings. Centuries of experience have brought the Puerto Rican to the conclusion a man is more limited in what he can do by the amount of money and power he possesses than anything else. Even at the present time his contact with labor unions and other organizations which propose any other standard but the one of power is tenuous, and while his government offers him all kinds of protections and guarantees, it is nonetheless one whose form and shape he did not reason out, but one that was given him.

During the course of a group's meeting when its chairman was being hotly attacked, an indignant Puerto Rican woman rose to shout at the attacker, "You can't talk to my chairman like that!" Her choice of the word "my" is significant. An English-speaking person would rarely say "my chairman" lest he be thought very condescending or naïve, but the woman was being neither. She was using the word chairman as a synonym for *"presidente,"* and *"presidente"* is a word Puerto Ricans use almost interchangeably with *"jefe,"* meaning leader, boss, or chief. "You can't talk to my leader that way" is a sentiment a person speaking any language and in any culture can understand. Leadership is seen as a *sine qua non* of headship, so to speak of a weak president or one who does not display the qualities of leadership is asking the Puerto Rican to change a cultural definition.

Among English-speaking Americans there is some difference of opinion as to what leadership may be, some holding it to be the manipulation of techniques, others holding it to be a personal attribute. Puerto Ricans overwhelmingly agree with the latter definition. Leadership is personal, the leader commands a personal following and a personal loyalty. What is more, he sees it in himself as a personal quality, witness the president of a Puerto Rican organization who explained his duty as a leader required him "to enforce discipline." Or else, "What would happen to my leadership?"

During World War II Americans found the German *"mein Fuehrer"* very funny, suggestive of a pack of wooden-headed little men hopping around at the beck and call of a ranting megalomaniac. They seemed to have assumed *"mein Fuehrer"* was not a term that could be applied to any German leader but only the one, Adolf Hitler. Now to the American the assumption comes quite naturally because we analogize from our idea of the Presidency. Save in times of the worst national peril the President is thought of only as a leader in his peculiar capacity as the head of a political party. As the President he is first and foremost the chief magistrate whose power is dependent only on his tenure in office. Puerto Ricans would probably find that *"mein Fuehrer"* joke a little strained. The term *"mi jefe,"* "my leader," is in common use. They dispose themselves at the leader's beck and call, and give him an authority and power we would never give.

The Puerto Rican leader may find he will have a very difficult time of it. He is accorded power which can justly be called dictatorial, but it is not totalitarian. He may never falter or lose his way because the opposition, real or potential, is always waiting for him, and his opposition is bound by no constitutional restraint. It is not the loyal opposition, for by the very terms under which he holds office all opposition is disloyal. So long as the leader can keep the majority happy, his mandate will be renewed, and the opposition's constant sabotage will be frustrated, but when the clouds gather and darken, a Puerto Rican organization is faced with a crisis of magnitudinous proportions.

From time to time a leader in an organization will cease to be the embodiment of the group's will, and his popular dictatorship will become unpopular or tyrannical in the Puerto Rican's eyes. The succession of leadership is no mechanical action in a Puerto Rican organization; the falling leader retains his hard core faction, and above all his pride. Defeat is personal repudiation, just as elevation was once personal approval. The battle is always ferocious (like so many of our own) but the result is not so often the continuance of the organization, but mitosis or disintegration. A mild sensation was created in Chicago Puerto Rican circles upon a Puerto Rican leader's fall when he announced he had no intention of withdrawing, but was content to maintain his membership in a subordinate capacity. Such acts are rare and very much the exception. In most organizations the succession of power remains what it has always been, a sort of bloodless revolution.

Democracy as we know it is a form alien to the Puerto Rican culture and new to the society. Time and experience will unquestionably prevent too many repetitions of tangles like the one a Puerto Rican organization got itself tied up in when, looking for a constitution, it adopted without change a replica of the Elks'. Yet sophistication may only bring with it a smoothness in style instead of a shift in the basic Puerto Rican understanding of continental democracy.

To date there are half a million or more Puerto Ricans in New York, in excess of ten thousand in Chicago, and smaller numbers in cities like Philadelphia and Cleveland. The Puerto Rican population in these places cannot be counted on to diminish, but, on the contrary, to increase. In the opinion of most experts who have visited the island of Puerto Rico itself, its economic plight is so acute, its population so large that only by exporting people can it reasonably hope to win solvency some day. The Commonwealth of Puerto Rico has recognized the validity of this conclusion by establishing large and well-staffed offices in both New York and Chicago whose job it is to secure employment and render other services to the newly arrived

Puerto Rican. For the first time in the history of the migration of foreign-language groups to our cities one of them is being served at the place of its destination by the government of its origin.

Mr. Clarence Senior, who is in charge of the Commonwealth of Puerto Rico's continental program, writes in favor of what he calls "cultural pluralism," by which he means "preserving cultural traits, of dignifying qualities and practices different from our own and of creating a feeling of pride in the folkways, mores, customs, conventions and social patterns, characteristic of the immigrant in his homeland." Occupying the official position he does, it must be concluded he voices the Commonwealth of Puerto Rico's policy with regard to its operation within the United States.

The writers raise no question about the right of any citizen to live any way he pleases, but what is the wisdom of one government encouraging certain culture patterns on the part of people who live in another political jurisdiction? Can Puerto Ricans continue to live in New York and Chicago without undergoing profound changes in languages and culture, whether they like it or not? The question is not asked in the spirit of theoretical speculation, but because on it should hinge some important decisions in the realm of public policy. Understanding of and participation in democracy, as continentals recognize it, is contingent on the knowledge and implicit definitions which belonging to a culture imparts. Perhaps it might be better if the Commonwealth did *not* pursue a policy calculated to prolong those particular cultural patterns which impede their participation in continental democracy.

Is it not possible that ambitious leaders might exploit Puerto Rican cultural patterns to the disadvantage of national unity in areas of public policy where unity is needed? (Critics of ex-Congressman Vito Marcantonio, who became a leader of many of New York's Puerto Ricans and whose rise was viewed with alarm by a majority of Republicans and Democrats alike, would be quick to say that this is precisely what he did.) Before we accept a broad program of encouraging cultural diversity, we should be sure that we know to what extent our political system uses our culture as a base. We should be selective enough in our encouragement of diversity not to encourage those patterns which make the functioning of democracy even more difficult than it is. And needless to add, what holds true for the

Puerto Rican minority can be safely borne in mind in thinking about all our minority problems.

Spring, 1956. Lester C. Hunt, Jr., formerly of the staff of the Catholic Charities Bureau of the Roman Catholic Diocese of Chicago, and Mr. von Hoffman, formerly of the research staff of the Industrial Relations Center of the University of Chicago, are now field representatives of the Industrial Areas Foundation of Chicago.

Intensional Orientation and National Unity: A Case Study from Pakistan

JOHN J. HONIGMANN

Modern nations consist of extremely heterogeneous assortments of people. Religious and occupational organizations, for example, are split by many racial and tribal categories whose mutual sentiments are often antagonistic. Where these antagonisms are strong they may interfere with the goals of the nation itself. The groups or organizations comprising the nation may embody mutually incompatible goals or maintain themselves, in part at least, through mutual distrust of one another. While some of these intranational loyalties decline with time, or with the extension of communication systems (tribal loyalties may remain strong in the marginal regions of a country that lacks extensive central control), other forms of separatism actually increase with growing size and increasing specialization. The anthropologist, Robert Lowie, points out that "nationalism cannot extinguish the primeval separatism of men who feel thoroughly at home only with a minute group of kindred, camp mates, or fellow villagers. The larger the population consolidated, the greater is the chance of diverse sympathies and interests, the likelier the growth of centrifugal tendencies." However, even the small, isolated, tribal units traditionally investigated by anthropologists do not always reveal perfect homogeneity, although whatever divisive loyalties and incompatible goals exist among them are less evident than in nations like France or the United States.

Some degree of homogeneity of sentiment is sought in any domestic national policy. Nations, in order to be nations, must develop and maintain national sentiments that will override provincial, sectarian, and other partisan loyalties. One way of doing this is through political ceremony. Probably in every country a majority of the population, directly or through mass communications, participates in one or more ceremonies that stress the assimilation of disparate interests to a few overriding values. W. Lloyd Warner, in the concluding chapter to his book, *Democracy in Jonesville*, describes how Memorial or Decoration Day ceremonies in the United States operate "to integrate the whole community, with its conflicting symbols and its opposing, autonomous churches and associations." At the same time these ceremonies serve the manifest purpose of commemorating the war dead. "The unifying and integrating symbols . . . are the dead," says Warner, and their graves "are the most powerful of the visible emblems which unify all the activities of the separate groups of the community."

Although the functions of ceremony in political life deserve more study than they have hitherto received, this paper will describe another process that also relies on symbols in order to assimilate diversity within a national community. To this process the name "intensional orientation" may be applied.

In semantics the concept "intensional orientation" refers to the tendency to use words without applying them to explicit, empirical referents. Some words, of course, lack immediately inspectable empirical referents. The physical sciences nevertheless manage to use such words (for example, "electron") unambiguously by rigidly specifying the indirect consequences from which the existence of postulated entities may surely be known. Intensional orientation refers to the employment of ambiguous, loosely defined concepts, the precise meaning of which it is difficult or impossible to pin down. Semanticists deplore this tendency to use words "meaninglessly." With any such normative attitude this paper remains unconcerned. We are interested in the empirical political functions and dysfunctions of intensional orientation. Examples of intensional orientation are abundantly available. Our discourse is replete with words that are employed without any clearly explicit meaning, words like "Christianity," "freedom," "democracy," "coexistence," "justice," and "rights." Hundreds of thousands of pages have been written defining some of these concepts logically with the use of other words but very little attempt has been made to specify the observable conditions designated by, say, "freedom." Semanticists insist that extensional definition is essential for "proper" use of words but an anthropologist doubts such a blanket judgment. Surely, people who have used words in this fashion for several hundred years must be deriving reward from their intensional orientation. The semanticist's insistence on the rigorous use of words fails to show the adjustments in social life sometimes provided by intensional orientation.

A striking case study providing insight into the role of intensional orientation in public affairs comes from Pakistan. Founded with the

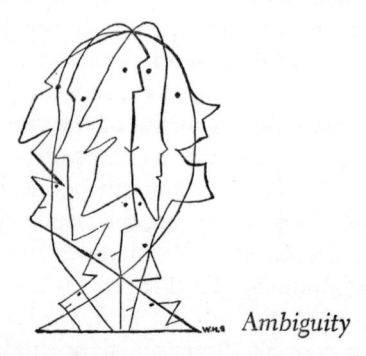

Ambiguity

departure of the British from India in 1947, Pakistan is a nation divided into two physical regions separated by over a thousand miles of the Indian subcontinent. In this geographical separation lies Pakistan's first challenge to national unity. Most of the eighty million Pakistanis are Muslims. As a matter of fact, during the agitation against British rule following World War I, Pakistan was conceived as a future dominion where "the vast majority of the followers of Islam [would] be uninhibited in the development of their culture and free to follow their own way of life . . . and to worship God in freedom."[1]

A nation speaks through its publicists, people in or out of government office who are moved by a spontaneous sense of responsibility for national organization and goals. Since 1947 publicists in Pakistan

[1] Liaquat Ali Khan, *Pakistan, Heart of Asia* (Cambridge: Harvard University Press, 1950), p. 5.

have reiterated that in Pakistan some sixty million Muslims will follow their Islamic way of life. The presence of about thirteen million Hindus in the nation as well as several million Christians has not been ignored but the proposed title of the country, "Islamic Republic of Pakistan," indicates the influence of the Muslim majority. "The guiding force for us in Pakistan is Islam and our unalterable and irrevocable objective is an Islamic State," according to Ghyasuddin Pathan, Minister of State and Finance. A letter to the editor of the English-language daily, *Dawn*, recalls that "The All-India Muslim League, under the leadership of . . . Qaid-i-Azam [Muhammad Jinnah] gathered and organised ten crores [i.e., 100 million] of scattered Muslims of the sub-continent under the banner of the Muslim League, with the guarantee that the new State of Pakistan shall be governed by an Islamic Constitution." A Minister of Education promises to "see to it that every aspect of our national activity is animated by this ideology [Islam]. . . ." Here and there, however, more secular notes have been struck as when, shortly after the founding of the nation, Qaid-i-Azam Muhammad Ali Jinnah, told the newly formed Constituent Assembly: "You may belong to any religion or caste or creed—that has nothing to do with the business of the State."[2] Begum Liaquat Ali Khan, wife of an assassinated Prime Minister, stated that "The welfare of the common man was the only sound basis of any State." There have also been attempts to reinterpret Islam with the heritage deriving from nearly two hundred years of liberal-secular British administration. For example, an editorial in *Dawn* (Karachi) on the occasion of the Prophet's birth anniversary says:

> Today lip-service is paid to the example of Mohammad, but ignoramuses parading as philosophers and imposters passing for messiahs pretend to find his principles unsuited to modern conditions. . . . The evolutionary

[2] Quoted in *Report of the Court of Inquiry Constituted Under Punjab Act II of 1954 to Enquire into the Punjab Disturbances of 1953*. The Court of Inquiry itself declared that the average Muslim was living in the past and yearning for a return of the golden age of Islam. "He finds himself standing on the crossroads . . . with the dead weight of centuries on his back, frustrated and bewildered and hesitant to turn one corner or the other. . . . Little does he understand that the forces which are pitted against him, are entirely different from those against which early Islam had to fight, and that on the clues given by his own ancestors human mind has achieved results which he cannot understand. . . . Nothing but a bold reorientation of Islam to separate the vital from the lifeless can preserve it as a World Idea and convert the Musalman into a citizen of the present and the future world from the archaic incongruity that he is today."

ideal of Islam is quite compatible with all forms and manifestations of political and social progress. . . . Secularisation, which constitutes a fundamental departure from the postulates of Islam and the social set-up envisaged by the Holy Prophet is not the answer to our social and political problems.

An acceptable middle course has not been easy to discover between fundamentalism and outright, Western secularism.

The undeniable sincerity with which Pakistani publicists reiterate the central place of Islam in national life does not obscure the reality that the Muslims of Pakistan do not constitute a homogeneous people. Some of the most pronounced economic differences in the world color the interests of Pakistanis who follow Islam. It has been alleged that the leaders of the country are Punjabis, Bengalis, or Sindhis first and Pakistanis only as an afterthought. Whether exaggerated or not, provincial rivalries or conflicting loyalties helped to hold up the making of the constitution for seven years and in October, 1954, contributed to the dismissal of the Constituent Assembly by the Governor-General. The insistence on Pakistan constituting an Islamic state is quite self-consciously designed to overcome some of the divisive forces implied by these and other alignments. The use of a religious label as a symbol of national unity is facilitated in a country where great emotional fervor characterizes religion, and that was ostensibly sought and founded on the basis of a religious ideology.

Study quickly reveals how use of Islam as a national symbol exemplifies intensional orientation. The doctrine and practice of Islam are not formalized like the religion of the Roman Catholic Church. No central authority exists with potential power to define the obligatory beliefs of Muslims. Hence, Islam comprises a number of sects. The bulk of Pakistanis are Sunni Muslims but a few are Shia, Ahmadi, or belong to even smaller splinter groups. Such divisions, generally speaking, have not directly sought to influence policy along sectarian lines. There is, however, another division among Pakistani Muslims, one that is involved in the struggle to determine the implications of an Islamic state in Pakistan. We refer to the opposition existing between fundamentalists on the one hand and Muslims of a more liberal or neo-orthodox persuasion on the other. In 1953 the latter, who held most of the important posts in government, thus controlling military and police power, found themselves confronted by a popular agitation endorsed by fundamentalist theologians. Nearly naked power came to be pitted against the Government in an attempt to force acceptance of a fundamentalist conception of Islam. In putting down this attempt the Central Government only reluctantly and equivocally revealed its own antifundamentalist position. The situation is an instructive one to show that practical difficulties as well as advantages may be connected with intensional orientation. It will, therefore, be examined in greater detail. The following description of the 1952-53 agitation is based on the *Report of the Court of Inquiry*.

In July, 1952, some sixty *ulama*, or Muslim theologians, gathered in Lahore, the capital of Punjab Province. After listening to speeches they formed a twenty-man Council of Action to press for an official declaration of policy on three demands: (1) the Ahmadi (or Qadiani) Muslims must be declared a minority community with a limited and distinct status relative to the majority of the Muslim population; (2) the Foreign Minister, Chaudhri Zafrullah Khan, an Ahmadi, must be dismissed from the Cabinet of the Pakistan Government; (3) other Ahmadis occupying key government positions must also go. These issues had originally been raised by a minor political party, the Majlis-i-Ahrar-i-Islam, presumably as part of a movement to attract popular support away from the dominant Muslim League party, which was solidly entrenched in Central and Provincial Government offices. Once the demands won support from the leaders of religious bodies the latter could be expected to promote wider mass support for the whole movement. The official position of the Central Government in the face of these demands held simply that all groups, including the Ahmadis, had the right to propagate their religious beliefs and hold office. That stand expressed not only the 1935 Government of India Act, parts of which served as an interim constitution, but also the spirit which the British had bequeathed to the Subcontinent. Many *ulama* would have been more willing to accept such a position as far as the Christians and even the Shia Muslims were concerned than for the hated Ahmadis.

Differences between the relatively more orthodox followers of Islam and the Ahmadis had begun in 1882 when Mirza Ghulam Ahmad in Qadian, Punjab, declared himself to have been entrusted by God with a special mission. He related several other revelations to a growing body of followers until 1901, when he proclaimed himself a prophet. That was the last straw for his also growing opposition. Most

Muslims believe that the *Qur'an*—the word of God—explicitly states that following Muhammad there would be no further prophets. Theologians therefore branded Mirza Ghulam Ahmad and his followers as infidels. Yet the sect continued to grow until, in 1954, forty-six years after the leader's death, some two million Ahmadis lived in Pakistan.

To implement their demands the *ulama* and Ahrarists resorted to agitation in the form of public meetings and propaganda of other sorts in which the Ahmadis and their doctrines were often vilified and abused. In January, 1953, a body of distinguished *ulama* conferred in Karachi, the national capital. They appointed another Council of Action which, on January 21, delivered an ultimatum to the Prime Minister of Pakistan that threatened "direct action" if the demands failed to win official acceptance. Exactly what the threat of direct action connoted was ambiguous. The members of the Council, who later testified before a Court of Inquiry appointed by the Punjab Government, stated they meant only peaceful agitation. The Court disputed that this was actually their intention. Direct action began a little more than a month later when the Council decided to send forth volunteers to court arrest by picketing the houses of the Governor-General and Prime Minister. At that point the Government moved into action and ordered the arrest of all prominent leaders of the agitation, even members of the *ulama*. Newspapers fanning the movement were banned.

Until this time the Central Government had refused to make any clear and forthright pronouncement on the validity of the *ulama's* demands. The Punjab Government, administering the province where much of the agitation centered, took the position that answers to the demands could only come from the Center. Both governments had acted to control any use of force against Ahmadis or Ahmadi property, although the perpetrators of such acts often escaped serious punishment. In February, 1953, the Center's deep reluctance to declare national policy finally ceased. In a secret, coded telegram to the Punjab Government the Administration said that "The Ahmadis or indeed any section of people cannot be declared a minority community against their wishes" and persons "cannot be removed from key positions under Government only on the ground that they are Ahmadis." But, the telegram went on, the Central Government did not want to have the first point publicized as its own "unless the situation demands." In other words, the Muslim Government of Pakistan still feared to become publicly associated with a position which many of its members endorsed but which might turn out to be very unpopular.

In the Punjab the police proved unable to control the growing violence of the agitators which, however, had quickly been quelled in the federal district of Karachi. The Pakistan Army offered assistance on March 2 but still disturbances continued in Lahore and elsewhere. A surprising thing happened on March 6, after a week of violent upheaval. The Prime Minister of the province, Mian Mumtaz Muhammad Khan Daultana, broadcast a statement offering to negotiate with the *ulama* and to place their demands before the Central Government. Within an hour after this offer the Center declared martial law in Lahore. Four days later Daultana publicly withdrew his statement about which, he told the Court of Inquiry, he had never been sincere. On the surface it appears that the strong show of naked power organized by the fundamentalists nearly brought the Punjab Government to its knees.

The case of the Punjab Disturbances has been detailed in order to illustrate how intensional orientation involving the concepts of Islam and an Islamic State opened the way for a threat to the stability of Pakistan. The generality of the symbol was intended to hold together Muslims of varying degrees of orthodoxy and shades of opinion. Such generality, the essence of intensional orientation, might have worked in a country where only slight importance attached to religious beliefs and values and in which violent agitation played a small part in public life. It did not succeed where ego involvement with the tenets of religion was pronounced and with a population that holds to a belief in the rightness of popular direct action. Direct action in India and Pakistan seems to imply that under certain circumstances any authority may properly be coerced. The agitation, originally fanned by the Ahrarists and supported by the *ulama*, constituted an attempt to end the official policy of a loosely defined concept of Islam in favor of a narrower (but presumably not less intensionally oriented) definition. According to the report of the Court of Inquiry, the very vagueness concerning the implications of an Islamic nation "created in the mind of the *ulama* and the citizens of Pakistan the belief that any demand which could be established on religious grounds would not only be conceded but warmly welcomed by the people at the helm of the State who had during the last several years been crying themselves hoarse over their intentions." But, of course the last thing the Government desired was to pattern the new nation after the shape of a medieval Islamic community,[3] which was the manifest intention of some of the *ulama*. Yet, some "people at the helm of the State" experienced considerable conflict on this point. The Prime Minister of Pakistan, Khwaja Nazimuddin, held many conferences with the *ulama*. He impressed the Court of Inquiry as "a devoutly religious man, and since he did not straight away reject the demands, he must have been impressed by their plausibility."

Leaving the Pakistan incident, we may generalize, saying that although a condition of intensional orientation can foster a degree of national unity in a heterogeneous nation it may not suffice by itself to control sectarian and other differences of opinion. Intensional orientation refers to using words in such a way as to leave a situation relatively unstructured. Sometimes it is useful to speak intensionally in order to tuck under a single blanket-symbol as wide a variety of bedfellows as possible. But to leave unstructured the meaning of concepts which are subjectively perceived to possess vital importance invites organized subgroups in a community to attempt to replace vagueness and ambiguity by their own meanings.

Winter, 1955-56. Dr. Honigmann, author of Culture and Personality, *is professor of anthropology at the University of North Carolina.*

[3] According to the *Report,* "*the ulama* were divided in their opinions when they were asked to name some precedent of an Islamic State in Muslim history. . . . Most of them, however, relied on the form of Government during the Islamic Republic from 632 to 661 A.D. . . ."

The Process of News Reporting

KEN MACRORIE

In February, 1949, Joseph T. Klapper and Charles Y. Glock published in *The Scientific American* an incisive content analysis of the newspaper reporting in the case of Edward U. Condon, head of the Bureau of Standards, who was called a weak security risk by the House Committee on Un-American Activities. In their study, entitled "Trial by Newspaper," Mr. Klapper and Mr. Glock said:

Bias may be shown . . . in the manner in which a paper reports an event and in its selection of which events to report and which to omit. An outside observer, lacking the newspapers' access to the events on which they based their reporting, can only judge their treatment of the Condon case by comparing the way in which the various newspapers dealt with the same events.

But must an outside observer lack the newspapers' access to events on which they base their reporting? Can he judge reports fairly when he has no notion of how they emerged through the complex process of modern reporting?

A communicative act may be thought of as a *transaction*, involving manifold relationships between persons, their pasts, and their present situations—as suggested by the explorations of John Dewey and Arthur F. Bentley in *Knowing and the Known* and Adelbert Ames,

Jr. and his followers in perception experiments.[1] Looked at in this way, one of the most crucial elements in a communication becomes the very selection of subjects, which Mr. Klapper and Mr. Glock suggest is outside the content analyst's purview.

Surely a description of the whole process of a news report in the making will tell more than a mere examination of printed reports in the paper. Here is an example of how an actual news report may be studied *in process*.

At 11:15 A.M., Friday, May 21, 1954, in the newsroom of the *New York Times*, Robert E. Garst, assistant managing editor, told me that I could probably accompany Peter Kihss, a city reporter, on a news assignment. Marshall E. Newton, assistant city editor, got in touch with Mr. Kihss, who agreed to meet me that afternoon at the Customs House annex at 54 Stone Street in lower Manhattan.

The hearing of the Senate Subcommittee of the Judiciary Committee took place in a locked room containing hundreds of canvas mailbags piled in rows, stacks of packages wrapped in brown paper, and dozens of magazines spread on a large table. About fifteen people were present, some looking over the literature on the table, which proved to be foreign Communist publications, many printed in English. A few rows of folding chairs were lined up, facing the table. The place looked more like the back room of a post office than a setting for a Senate investigative hearing.

Soon a man wearing a gray-blue suit and black-and-white shoes entered and loudly greeted several men, his entourage following him. He was addressed as "Senator." Someone said his name was Welker [Idaho]. He told one of his assistants, who had been awaiting him, that he wanted someone to make a call for him to a hotel. He gave instructions for getting in touch with one or another of two men connected with the Pittsburgh baseball club who he said would get him some tickets to a game the Pirates were playing. "If you can't get him," he said, "ask for Vernon Law." The Senator moved to the back of the room where a man began to brief him, saying, "Now, Senator, what we have here on the table is . . ."

A few minutes later, at 1:25, Mr. Peter Kihss, the *Times* reporter, arrived. We introduced ourselves and I explained my purpose. He said he was going to introduce himself to the Senator, adding that he used

[1] See *ETC.*, Vol. XII, No. 4 (Summer, 1955), "Special Issue on Transactional Psychology."

to know the members of this committee. He talked to a number of the principals, including the Senator and Deputy Collector Irving Fishman, who knew most about the details of handling the Communist propaganda coming through Customs to the Port of New York. One of the officials said that approximately three-quarters of a million pieces of Communist propaganda were in the room and that they represented just two days' accumulation. Mr. Kihss greeted other newspapermen who arrived, and they exchanged what information they had on the purpose and personnel of the hearing. It was scheduled to begin at 2 P.M. At approximately 1:45, photographers began to take pictures. First they shot stills of the Senator and his associates looking at magazines on the table. They asked him to take one that was boldly titled *Soviet Union* and hold it as if he were reading, yet so they could see his eyes and the title. Then a Telenews crew, after rigging lights, blowing a fuse or two, and rearranging the principals at the table as well as the news reporters sitting nearby, photographed the Senator while he made a statement about the purpose of the hearings. Without explaining the issues, he emphasized the increasing flood of propaganda that was "pouring" into the United States.

Since, as the cameraman put it, the Senator "fluffed" some of his lines while partially improvising his speech and looking up into the camera, a retake was necessary on one lengthy part of his statement. He uncomplainingly posed for all the cameramen, while they maneuvered and rearranged him and his associates like mannequins. Finally, on one cameraman's insistence that he again hold up a piece of literature, he showed some irritation and said that that was enough. About forty-four minutes after picture-taking had started, the camera crew packed up and left. At 2:32, the hearings began.

In his opening statement, Senator Welker said there were 34 million pieces of propaganda in the room (perhaps he had read "¾ million" as "34 million"). No one corrected him although his words were being recorded both by a stenotype operator and a tape recorder. The Senator swore in as the first witness the Collector of Customs, Robert W. Dill, who said that the room held a two-day supply of mail. From this point on, I had difficulty following the details of the hearing.

Witnesses from the Customs House testified and discussions of the laws under which they were operating were carried on, seldom to any clear resolution. At one point, Senator Welker dramatically asked the members of the press to pick out any sack of mail in the room for inspection. The reporters said they were content to have any one of them opened which was handy. One of the Customs workers cut the seal on one bag and spilled the contents on the table before everyone. The principals and the reporters began looking over the addresses on the packages. Under Senator Welker's questioning, Deputy Collector Fishman read off the names on several of the packages, saying that he recognized one as that of a man at the Soviet United Nations delegation, who frequently received such mail. All of these comments were being made a part of the record.

At 2:59, when the reel of tape in the recorder needed to be changed, Senator Welker arose, announced that the hearings would be suspended for a few minutes, and went out to complete his call about baseball tickets.

When the hearings resumed, Deputy Collector Fishman asked permission to correct his sworn testimony about the name on the package. He said that on further check he had found that the man named was not the person he had identified as belonging to the Russian UN delegation. Other names from packages were read off. One of these, that of a library, and another, of a committee, later appeared, accompanied by addresses, in the tenth paragraph of an Associated Press account of seventeen paragraphs sent over the AP wire. Mr. Kihss later implied to me that he did not approve of reading names in this way. The public might infer that those named were Communist sympathizers when perhaps they were simply students of Communism. Mr. Kihss examined more packages than anyone else at the table. At times throughout the hearing, he asked questions, confirmed or corrected factual statements made by officials, and showed such an active knowledge of the proceedings, past and present, that one reporter chided him for having so much interest in them.

When one of the principals spoke of labeling material "Communist propaganda," Mr. Kihss attempted to straighten him out on the wording of the 1938 Alien Registration Act, which he said did not require the labeling of mailed material as "Communist propaganda," but simply as "political propaganda." Mr. Arens, the committee counsel, and Mr. Fishman, Deputy Collector of Customs, discussed this point further and read portions of the McCarran Act ordering labeling of material. From time to time, Mr. Kihss consulted papers he carried in a brown envelope, including a printed copy of the proceedings of the executive session hearings of the subcommittee headed "Communist Underground Printing Facilities and Illegal Property, March 6—July 11, 1953." Mr. Kihss had said earlier that because that day was his father's birthday, he would have preferred not to work, but he was the logical choice for the story since he had covered this subject on November 12 and 13, 1952, and October 11, 1953. At that time, he said, he had been concerned about the problem of the Federal law preventing the mailing of Communist propaganda to recognized anti-Communist scholars at such centers as Columbia and Harvard universities. As the law stood, the Customs officials were only supposed to let mail go through to people registered as foreign agents or to embassies, consulates, etc. Yet those same agents might, if they wished, distribute the material to book shops which could sell it to any individual in the country who cared to buy it. Customs officials had let some of the mail go through to university scholars—as anyone can see by visiting libraries and centers for Russian study—but they knew they were disobeying the letter of the law in doing it, even though they were acting in the best interests of the United States. Both officials of the Customs and the Post Office in the past, Mr. Kihss said, had made recommendations for legislation legalizing such distribution, but no legislation had resulted.

This point was never raised at the hearing. Instead, Senator Welker and his counsel made much of the bill the Senator said he had proposed for the stamping of "Communist propaganda" on the material so that readers would know what they were getting. Under Mr. Kihss's questioning, the Senator admitted that actually his bill did not provide for this. Rather it applied to propaganda coming from any country, including England or France, for example, and provided for that material to be labeled "political propaganda" only. Mr. Kihss complained to a reporter friend that the point about the scholars receiving the material was one of the central issues in the whole affair, and yet it had never been taken up during the hearing.

Under persistent questioning by the counsel, one of the Customs officials testified that the bags in the room at the time were in part mail that had been there for a month. Under further questioning, he said that about 30 per cent of it had been there a month and the rest was current—had come in the last few days and would be moved out as soon as possible. The reporters, especially Mr. Kihss, were irritated by the shifting statistics that were being given on the amount of mail coming in, especially since the increase was being made one of the important points in the hearing. One of the women who testified for the Customs said that for the two-week period, May 5 to 18, about 600 bags of mail, or 100,000 pieces of published material, reached the port. The Associated Press and United Press dispatches later said that such mail was arriving in New York at the rate of 300 bags a

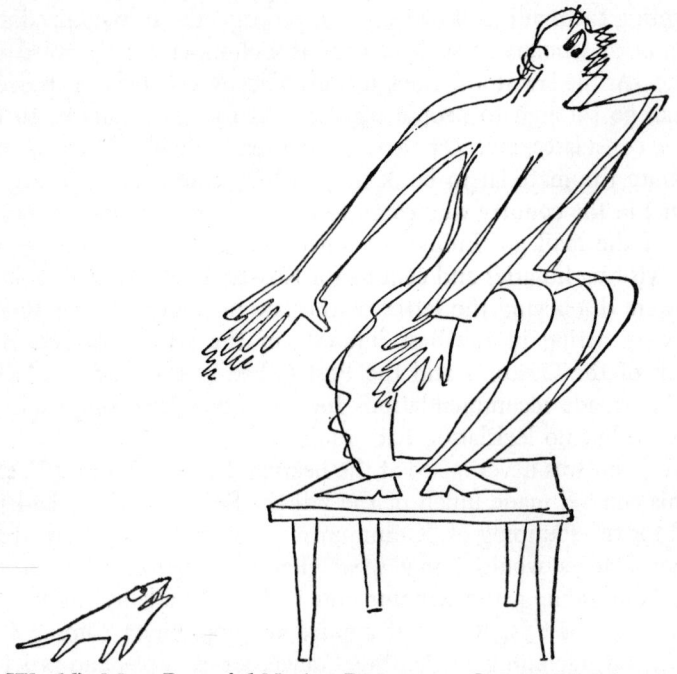

The World's Most Powerful Nation Reacts to a Certain Word

week. Apparently the reporters or editors had averaged the 600 bags for two weeks, which was probably not a long enough period to yield a representative average. Mr. Kihss, when he later wrote his story, stuck to the more precise statement: "From May 5 to 18, 100,000 pieces of published material . . ."

Senator Welker asked the Customs officials what they thought of his proposed legislation requiring all political propaganda to be so stamped. Mr. Fishman, the Deputy Collector, agreed that it would be helpful in reducing the volume of mail they received from foreign countries. Earlier, witnesses had testified at length on the inadequacy of the Customs House staff to process the mail. Some of it was in Russian and Chinese and had to be interpreted before it could be judged for propaganda content. Mr. Fishman told of an inspection trip he had made of American ports handling such material. He said that in St. Paul one official who did not know Russian was attempting to process the flood of propaganda with the aid of a Russian dictionary and his own efforts to learn the language.

The hearing, I gathered, was designed to put down for public record the salient facts of the matter of propaganda mailings into the Port of New York. It often confused rather than enlightened me. For example, when Collector of Customs Robert W. Dill testified as the first witness, he said that about sixty ships were coming or going every day at the port, but he did not say that all of them carried Communist propaganda. The wire story sent out by the United Press included these words, "Communist propaganda is arriving here from behind the Iron Curtain on 60 ships daily." It further stated:

Any material addressed to individuals, institutions or any other addressee not on the list of registered agents supplied the customs service by the Department of Justice, it was testified, are returned to the Postmaster designated as material which cannot be forwarded and which is to be returned to the sender.

The New York *Herald Tribune* story, "300 Bags Weekly of Red Mail Here," on page 4, and the *Daily News* story, "Reveal Red Literature Flooding U.S.," page 5, and the New York *Journal-American* story, "Bare Flood of Red Propaganda Here," page 4, repeated this assertion in different words. Mr. Kihss said that the mail which was not forwarded was actually confiscated rather than returned to the sender, a fact which he had reported in an earlier article.

At one point, a Customs House film reviewer was interrogated about Communist propaganda films. He read some of the reviews he had prepared, and under questioning admitted that he knew some of these films were being shown at the Stanley Theater in Times Square, New York City. Mr. Kihss told me that this fact had been brought out at preceding hearings and was "old stuff." I knew that any reader of the *Times* could examine daily advertisements for the Stanley Theater, read reviews of its films, and like me, trot over to the Stanley and see a film on ballet—or even a faked-up propaganda film—without being converted to the Communist party.

At 3:47 Senator Welker officially concluded the hearing, but not before he and Customs officials had exchanged elaborate compliments, the Senator praising the officials' co-operation and the officials assuring him that he was always welcome. Earlier in the afternoon the Senator had complimented Mr. Dill and his "gallant men" of the Customs.

When the principals arose from the table, the reporters sought them for further questioning. Mr. Kihss asked the Senator and his counsel for specific information about his bill which they had mentioned. When asked for a copy of it, the Senator and his counsel said they had none with them, but the counsel said it was "S-37," and the Senator nodded in agreement. After talking with others, Mr. Kihss again returned to the Senator, who was about to leave, and asked him whether he had been considering including in his bill anything to clear up the trouble the Customs encountered in being legally denied the right to send these important Communist documents to recognized American scholars. The Senator said that it did not. Mr. Kihss asked whether he could say in his story that the Senator was aware of this problem—that he was working on it. The Senator reflected and answered yes.

Mr. Kihss, another reporter, and I left the building. On the way to a drugstore telephone, Mr. Kihss emphasized what a poor story this was. When the other reporter left, Mr. Kihss called the *Times*. Then we headed for the nearest subway, and boarded a train. After one stop, I noticed that the subway car was identified as the Lexington Avenue line. We realized that in our absorption with the story—Mr. Kihss had been poring over his finely written personal shorthand in his notebook—we had boarded the wrong train. He suggested that we could get off at Grand Central and shuttle across to Times Square. On the way, he told me that this was the kind of story he liked to think about a long time before he wrote, to let it jell. It had him stumped, he said, because the most important issue was not even taken up in the hearings. He had two alternatives, he thought: to write a short, straight story giving the facts, which were really old stuff except for the increased flow of material, or to write a long article in which he editorialized constantly in order to explain to the lay reader the significance of the whole controversy, and he would not be allowed to do that. He really did not know what he would do, he said. He looked over his notes, which he held in a secretary's stiff notebook. He underlined in pencil the portions he thought important.

When he arrived at the newsroom, he found in his mailbox an office memorandum stating that, "Space requirements make it necessary that stories should run 15 to 20 per cent shorter than they have been recently. Our goals should be simplicity and clarity, through the use of short sentences, careful organization and the elimination of unnecessary details." He went to the newspaper's library and with the help of a librarian found that "S-37," the bill the counsel had said was Senator Welker's, was in reality one introduced by Senator McCarran. Further checking in congressional records shed no light. Next he went to the morgue and checked quickly through recent clippings on Senator Welker. Again no light. He got out his own notes and files on past Customs stories he had done, and again said he did not know what to do with the story, adding that perhaps no story at all would be best. Then he went to the desk of the national editor. Later, he wrote me what happened there:

When I reported to Ray O'Neill, who handled the written story as the national news editor, the substance of the conversation as I recollect it now [one week later] went like this. I said:

"Ray, I was assigned to the Welker Senate Internal Security subcommittee hearing on Communist propaganda. The story today was that we're getting an increasing flow of Communist propaganda. We had some new statistics, about 100,000 pieces coming in by mail alone between May 5 to 18, and there was a show of about hundreds of mail bags piled up in the Customs House annex where the hearing was held. But otherwise, the hearing didn't get very far. I asked Welker after the hearing about the problem of the scholars who need this stuff—you know we studied this in 1952 and 1953. He said he was studying it. The customs fellows tell me their legislative recommendations seem to be stalled in Washington. The scholar issue didn't come up in the hearing itself."

"How much space do you need—we don't have much tonight," he rejoined.

"Anything from one paragraph up—it wasn't too important," I said.

"All right, 400 words, but we may have to cut it back to an M head," he said. (An M head runs 200-250 words.)

At 5:15, he began typing a summary of the story, which the *Times* requires to help editors see what they have to work with. When he finished, he began typing a scratch version of the story itself. He looked this over, made some changes, and then began writing the story on special copy paper with attached carbons. He bent over the typewriter, typing quickly. At 5:32, when he was on page 3, a man dropped on his desk the first "take" of the Associated Press wire report on the story. He stopped typing, read the dispatch, and told me that it was pretty close to what he was writing. When he finished, he had more than three pages, with his copy triple-spaced. He penciled out several sentences. "Still too much," he said, and slipped a new set of copy sheets into the typewriter. On the edge of the unoccupied next desk, a telephone—almost touching the one on his desk—began to ring insistently. He never looked up, but clattered on with his story, his head bent over the keyboard.

By 6 P.M., he had finished the final version, six paragraphs, which ran to exactly 321 words, 79 under his prescribed limit. I told him that the fifth paragraph, which included Senator Welker's comments on scholars, made the story valuable because it showed what his knowledge brought to the story. He said that it was an important paragraph, but that he couldn't justify putting it any higher in the story. He checked over his copy and dropped it in a box at the national desk.

A few minutes later, he went over to the copy desk, where several men kidded him about coming over to protect his story from cutting. "If it's 405 words," one copyreader said to me, "we'll cut it." The story had come from the national desk with no changes. Mr. Kihss left after introducing me to men on the copy desk. I sat down next to Jack Randolph, a copyreader, who let me look over his shoulder. He went through the story quickly, and without hesitation drew two diagonal lines through the sixth, and last, paragraph. He broke the first paragraph into two. Then, spending only about five minutes, he made minor changes to conform to *Times* style, such as changing "United States" to "Federal" and the phrase: "In the last two weeks from May 5 to 18, 100,000 pieces of published material . . ." to the simpler and easier to read: "From May 5 to 18, some 100,000 pieces of published material . . ."

Then he crossed out the last clause in the fifth, and now last, paragraph: "but legislative recommendations on this point have been pending in Washington for months." He looked over the whole story again. "Still too much," he said, and marked diagonals through the rest of the fifth paragraph, which contained the scholars' issue. Before cutting, it had read:

After the hearing, Senator Welker said he was studying the need of responsible scholars for such material for research on Communism. At present, the Customs Service and Post Office Department use their own discretion to forward material addressed to these quarters, but legislative recommendations on this point have been pending in Washington for months.

This paragraph differentiated Mr. Kihss's story from accounts by other reporters who had not had his acquaintance with the controversy.

After Mr. Randolph puzzled out a headline for the story, I went back to Mr. Kihss's desk and told him the sad news. He was angry that his story had been cut to 194 words, when he had written 321 for a 400 limit. He told me that he had worked on many papers, some of which had always been tight for space, and that he had learned to write for word limits, which he carefully observed, usually writing fewer words than the limit. In this story, he knew how important the fifth paragraph was. After talking out his feeling for a while, he said he would try to do something about it. At 6:58, he intercepted Mr. Randolph at the drinking fountain. Later he wrote me what happened:

I told Jack Randolph that for two years in a row, the *Times* had made studies of this problem of Communist propaganda from the viewpoint of the difficulties encountered by scholars and research men, including our own Harry Schwartz. I contended we ought to record what, if anything, was happening on that phase. I said I had been ordered to write up to 400 words, and had stayed in that space—if I'd known the story was to have been less, I could have geared it accordingly. But in any case, I said I could get the scholars' phase into twenty-five words, as a minimum, and that the story had now been cut so hard that it was already well below the 250-word maximum for M heads.

Mr. Randolph agreed to add these two sentences, which Mr. Kihss hurriedly composed:

Afterward, Senator Welker said he was studying scholars' need for such material. The Customs and Post Office now use their own discretion in research cases.

Mr. Kihss had cut his original paragraph considerably, but he had made the important point. Mr. Randolph said the story had left the copy desk, but that they would send along the "add" and hope that it would get in. The story appeared in the late city edition of the *Times* on Saturday morning, May 22, 1954, on page 6. It was identical with Mr. Kihss's edited copy, except for one misspelling: *progoganda*, a typographical error.

After the story was in, Mr. Kihss and I sat at his desk discussing reporting problems. I said that I thought what a reporter decided to emphasize in a story made a great difference—no matter how fair or impartial he was trying to be. Mr. Kihss agreed, and as examples, typed off two possible "leads" for the story he had done. A reporter on one paper, he said, could understandably have written this lead:

> United States' failure to recognize the menace of Communist propaganda was shown today when the Senate Internal Subcommittee brought out that Communist publications were entering the country on a vastly increased scale.

A reporter for another paper could have written this lead, he said:

> The Senate Internal Security Subcommittee got into a competition for anti-Communist headlines with Senator Joe McCarthy's circuses today, when it staged a hearing on Communist propaganda—the first half hour being devoted entirely to posing for television cameras.

Mr. Kihss did not judge the committee one way or the other. He reported what Senator Welker wanted him to report—the increase of mail from Soviet sources, but he went on to suggest the need for Americans to read and study Soviet publications.

In the light of what goes on before a news story reaches print, of which the foregoing is only one illustration, the "objective" content analysis of finished news stories seems to miss the point so completely as to be us unreal as a game—a playing with words as with counters, with no regard for what they stand for or what was omitted before those particular words were chosen. Understanding the perceptual frameworks of those who supply the story and those who write and edit it is infinitely more important than staring at, counting, and otherwise analyzing the little black marks on paper that finally result. "The word is not the thing," we say. How true this is! And the news *report* is not the repor*ting*, which is a *process*—complex, perplexing, and human.

Summer, 1956. Dr. Macrorie is assistant professor in the department of communication skills, Michigan State University. This article is based on a doctoral study at Columbia University.

RED MAIL INCREASING FROM FOREIGN PORTS

A Senate Internal Security subcommittee heard yesterday that the volume of Communist propaganda coming here from abroad had increased "very materially" since 1951.

From May 5 to 18, some 100,000 pieces of published material in various languages reached the Port of New York by mail alone.

The Customs House annex at 54 Stone Street was heaped with mail bags containing perhaps 750,000 pieces of material still to be studied to determine its mailability under Federal laws, as a task force composed of Senator Herman Welker, Republican of Idaho, and Richard Arens, counsel, held the hearing.

Senator Welker said he was proposing legislation to require that material be labeled as "Communist propaganda" before being shipped here. Deputy Collector of Customs Irving Fishman, in charge of restricted merchandise, said such a move would probably reduce the admissible flow sharply, on his theory that shippers would refuse to label it.

Collector of Customs Robert W. Dill, Assistant Collector Francis B. Laughlin, Mr. Fishman and three subordinates testified that such material was now admitted when addressed to a registered foreign agent. It may be seized, however, if found to be political progoganda addressed to a non-agent.

Afterward, Senator Welker said he was studying scholars' need for such material. The Customs and Post Office now use their own discretion in research cases.

RUMANIAN LEGATION PUT OFF AIR WAVES

WASHINGTON, May 21 (*P*)— The United States has silenced a short-wave radio operated by

From New York Times, *Saturday, May 22, 1954, p. 6*

The Milk of Human Kindness?

STANLEY DIAMOND

On October 16, 1956, at Dr. Hayakawa's English 239 Communications Workshop at San Francisco State College, for the second time in three years I heard him say: "Now notice, what I am suggesting is that you view the daily problems in your work, in your social activities, in your homes, as problems of communication. If this way of looking at problems is helpful—if it provides for you one means of dealing with these problems—fine. If not, well, there are always the Great Books." Now what I'm thinking that the Doc meant was, "Let your imagination soar, boy, broaden and deepen it and let that old communication include just about the whole damned works, at least *your* whole damned works."

As I say, this was the second time I'd heard the holy words—holy because I was one of the early converts. I rushed back to my apartment after class to check my 1954 notes to see if I could find the date when first I'd been given the word. It took some searching but there it was—on a day in July, 1954. "Notice," the notes read, "I am not suggesting that communication is *all* there is. I am suggesting that you try thinking of just about everything in terms of communication." Dr. Hayakawa continued, "Consider communication perhaps in another sense; consider it as a fundamental ethic. And see if any of this is meaningful for you after you've thought about it for a few years."

At the time I was not operating at this altitude but that one little sentence, *think of just about everything in terms of communication*, was like a lost love come home, and I embraced it with a "Kid—have I been waiting for you a long time." What I mean is that I'd had these vague feelings about understanding and communicating, but they'd never quite made it to the conscious. And that's why the explosion of July, 1954, triggered by the good doctor, was a booming one which reverberates still in the rat race which is my neuron net. It all made particular sense to me at the time because I was meeting with economists and various trade association representatives throughout California—trying to make a series of pricing and fair trade programs workable for the milk industry. In certain areas, the industry at that time was directly violating a large number of these regulatory programs that it was my job to administer.

Talk about communication foul-up at these economists' meetings! Talk about monotonous yak at highly abstract levels—except when the abstraction level dropped a couple of notches unintentionally, which only helped stir up the meaninglessness. In the economics business, where confusion is easy to come by, some of these boys were so glib, so articulate in defending the confusion, that the whole mess seemed momentarily clear only in the anesthetizing mist of the fourth in line of ten Scotches on the rocks. And do you think I was any help? Hell, I remember saying things like, "Why don't we think about stabilizing conditions with some new ideas?" What the "new ideas" would be and what I meant by "stabilizing" perhaps an astrologer might know. I didn't. If anyone had made me climb down the abstraction ladder to lower levels from that altitude, the pratfall would have matched a sonic boom. There was nothing, you see, to break the fall.

At every meeting I thought, "Man, a multiordinaliteur would have a ball here." "Stability," "economic laws," "private enterprise," "American way," "freedom" were hurled around and bounced off the walls. By using these words, you see, the boys could clear their consciences and a lot of other things, for the record, for all the citizens to see. It's a solid survival technique.

Well, the findings of the economists and trade association representatives finally reached the level of the "Committee." The Committee was one of those mysterious bureaucratic huddles in Sacramento whose members I didn't ever clearly identify. They would meet in one of the echoless corner offices—you know—the kind lined with acoustic tile, a rug (which is the badge of a bureau chief), and several leather chairs—all enshrouded in the bluish smoke of expensive cigars.

The Committee didn't have any extraordinary difficulty in reaching a decision. The general semanticists would have been proud of the decision though. "Let's have a pilot experiment," they said. "We'll let Diamond work out a program for one of our really troublesome areas. How about C-W & H in Northern California? They've been among the worst in California for a couple of years."

So that's how it started—late in '54. I'd been living between SF and LA so I moved up to SF more or less permanently. Let me give you some background so we can all wallow in this mess for a while and try to relate the action to general semantics, communication, etc. As some of you may know, milk production and dairy product sales are rigidly regulated in California. Set by the state, for example, are the minimum prices paid to producers at the ranches; minimum prices paid by the stores and restaurants for their purchases from the milk distributors; the minimums when you buy milk at the store, and when you have it delivered to your home. Some of you didn't know that, did you? Well, it's true. Now, one of the questions involved in the administration of these price control programs is to what degree are these prices being observed. And the degree of compliance varies. When the Committee said the C-W & H area was pretty beat up, what they meant, as I found out later, was that practically all distributors, and there were fourteen of them, were ignoring the legal prices established for home deliveries. For example, if the price was twenty-two cents a quart plus a four-cent service charge for delivery, most milk companies would not collect the service charge if the customer took more than four quarts of milk per delivery. So my job was to get the prices raised to comply with the minimum prices. Imagine my popularity with the distributors and especially the consumers, and especially specially with the mother with the four kids whose husband's take-home pay was $68.75 each week!

I've mentioned the service charge of four cents per delivery. Without going into the economic justification for the charge, it was considered a nuisance by some customers and by some milk distributors.

Milk distributors who wanted an illegal competitive advantage could easily find some ways of not collecting the delivery charge. We'll discuss those means later. The point I wish to make is that violations were reported to be widespread in this area. If we could not obtain compliance with the pricing program, we wanted to remove this area from controls. To try to get compliance in this situation could be quite an experiment, couldn't it—a real communication laboratory?

I asked that an auditor, Fred, and an investigator, Leo, be made available to me for the experiment. I'd known these men and something of their work throughout the state for the past year. It occurred to me later that a credit was due Dr. J. Samuel Bois, another famed general semanticist, for helping me to choose Fred and Leo. Dr. Bois would certainly say, "You have to think about individuals as well as functions, so try to make the functions fit the people." My point is that Fred enjoyed sitting at a desk all day, making accounts balance and pursuing decimal points with fierce tenacity. Leo could only do this kind of a job if one section of his brief case was kept adequately supplied with Miltowns. Leo, on the other hand, loved yakking with people and especially, it seemed, if they were strangers. Fred and Leo were extraordinarily well suited for their jobs.

Making the decision for the first step was easy. Extensionalize, boy. We would ring doorbells, talk to housewives, and later we would audit distributors' records and then talk to distributors. What we were saying, of course, was, "Let's get some accurate information"— right? We split up, each assigned to a group of distributors to copy lists of names and addresses of customers. We decided to copy the names and addresses of the larger customers because they would be the most likely to be getting price concessions.

At our first meeting in San Francisco we reviewed the reports on the C-W & H area. They were fascinating in a stormy sort of way. They said competition was savage in this area. Most distributors accused their competitors of being lying, thieving, double-crossing s.o.b.'s. Bottles and cases were broken and stolen, bottle caps were punctured, and truck tires occasionally were slashed.

The reviewing of the reports took three days. Then came the big doorbell-ringing campaign. Leo and I would both call on a sample of 150 customers, and Fred would start to audit the records of the distributors to determine whether or not they were properly accounting for their daily put-up, i.e., the total products bottled or packaged each day. We agreed to meet each evening to exchange information, discuss technique, etc.

Now, I don't know how many of you have ever rung doorbells and yakked it up with the housewives—but it's an experience, it's an experience! I don't ever need any additional proof about "never stepping in the same stream twice." You never knew when a door opened whether it would slam back on you with your mouth still open, or whether a kid would open the door and take a healthy belt at you. Maybe a bosomy *hausfrau* in pin curlers and without make-up would say, "Come in and have a glass of the red, cousin." A husband might answer the door, listen to you for fifteen seconds and bellow, "Christ, what'll they want next!" Or if you were invited into the house— kids would tug at your papers, or maybe you'd hold a couple of them while the mother talked on the phone. Sometimes you rang just in time to help move the piano, take a kid to school, call a doctor for someone ill, or any of a dozen other unpredictables. Now and then I had an opportunity to practice my nondirective techniques and there are some gals in the C-W & H area who will never forget that odd little character who rang the bell, said he was getting some information about milk and asked a lot of questions. Some of these gals still ask themselves, "What in the hell made me talk so much that day about things I've never told anyone about?"

We learned a lot punching those doorbells. We learned that about only one out of five of the housewives knew what she paid for her milk; that the driver was frequently the key to the distributor's popularity; that time of service was important; that things like credit given when the husband was on strike were important; that some people preferred buying from a small company; that some people liked to change distributors because they were just bored. Some had cousins who sold insurance to the distributor and were doing him a favor. And some drivers gave the kids ice cream.

After all our information gathered from the doorbell ringing had been broken down and analyzed, we did find that price violations were indeed widespread and that these were handled in many interesting ways. Free products were given to make up the service charge; sometimes drivers returned the sixty cents in cash to the customers and were repaid by their companies. Sometimes the customer was billed but the sixty cents was not collected; sometimes one bill, deducting the sixty cents, was given the customer, but the correct bill would be turned in to the office with the driver making up the difference by showing "breakage," which had not, in fact, occurred. Well, there were lots of little cover-up gimmicks used in the conspiracy. It was especially interesting because so many people were involved. Drivers, foremen, managers, owners—all knowingly part of this conspiracy.

Other interesting things evolved from our survey. Distributors had never made any surveys as such. The distributors' information came to them from their salesmen and drivers. The distortion of information was sometimes due to the tensions and anxieties of holding a job. For example, if a salesman had a bad day, i.e., had not written any new accounts, he would tell his boss, "You've got to give me a chance to compete, boss. Everybody out there has me beat on price. Nobody is collecting the service charge." And if a driver lost a customer and he was questioned about it, he might well say, "It's that cheap Jew outfit down the street, boss, they've got us beat a cent a quart. I'll get the customer back if I can meet that price." Now, one very important factor was involved at this point. The supervisor, manager, or owner would rarely, if ever, go out and check the salesmen's and drivers' reports. This is how most of the difficulties started, I believe. They started on unverified reports. Supervisors didn't observe a most elementary general semantics principle—extensionality—"go out and check it, man." The drivers' and salesmen's reports were exaggerations, distortions, and frequently just goddam lies.

Our team, with this basic information, now went separate ways. Leo, the investigator, continued talking to the housewives, only this time he obtained statements from some of them and made a tentative evaluation as to whether they might be satisfactory witnesses if we wished to proceed legally against the distributors. The auditor, Fred, continued his audits of the distributors' records. My job was to interview each owner or branch manager, to talk with them about their illegal activities and get their feelings about correcting them.

The three of us continued to meet each night and exchange experiences and views. At the end of the third week we were ready to make a number of generalizations and determine our next major step. Leo had enough statements from the housewives to assure our being confident of winning any civil suits we might initiate. Fines in excess of $50,000 could have been sought through the courts against the distributors. Leo's statements could also have been used to suspend or revoke the licenses of these distributors if we chose this type of action.

Fred's audits disclosed that accounting practices were loose; that products especially could not be traced accurately. Where drivers received monies to cover illegal rebates they had given, these charges were posted to a miscellaneous expense account and called "incentive plan."

In my discussions with the owners and managers some said in

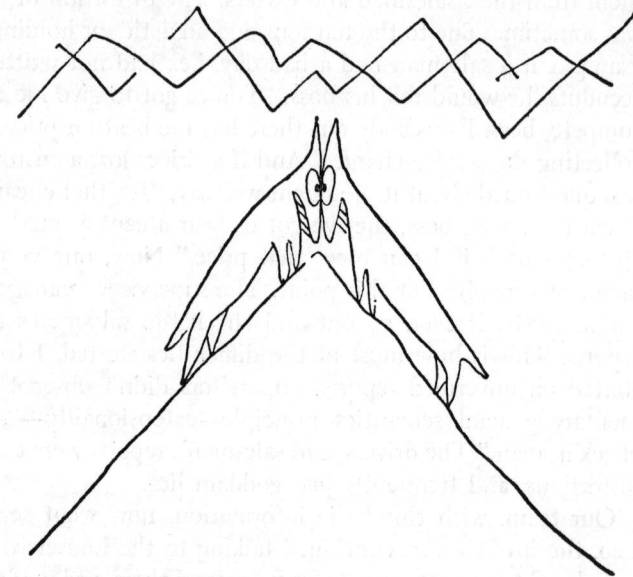

Mounting Tensions Reach an Impasse

off-the-record conversations that the situation was hopeless, that controls in that area should be removed and the boys should be permitted to "slug it out." A few distributors had very few illegal sales and did not wish to get into the bloody arena. Several branch managers of major distributors said they would make no admissions; that they were going to hold and increase their business, and those who got in their way, including our team, had better be prepared for the consequences. "Look," one manager said, "you're talking about my job. I've been with the company seventeen years. If I don't hold my own in this rat race I'm through—I'm forty-two years old, I have a wife and two kids, a plaster on the house and $750 in the bank. You think I'm going to be caught draggin' at the end of this battle, with district and division managers beating on my back with raised quotas! Hell, man, if my volume falls off the guys in San Francisco just smile and say, 'We're sure sorry, Mike, but you know how it is—why don't you try the beer business?' You characters, you bureaucrats think you can sit around with your feet on a desk, look out at the bay and run a milk business. Christ, you should have to meet a payroll, a sales quota, etc., etc."

And Mike wasn't the only one. And I'm not condemning Mike. The poor guy lived under this crushing pressure every waking hour and most of his dreams were probably a purplish pool of his competitors, district and general sales managers at the head office, all of them in a boiling, bubbling stew. Mike would be turning the fire up a little higher and drooling.

Raymond interested me too. He was the thirty-two-year-old cardiac with a Harvard Graduate School of Business Administration diploma for '48 on the wall. He was a local branch manager of one of the main companies. He worked in his shirt sleeves. "Sure," he said, noticing my examination of his diploma, "Sure, I'm a Cambridge boy but this one wears brass knuckles. Nobody in this valley has better statistics than I have, but these numbers on paper, these graphs don't mean a goddam thing. What counts is what's going on out there—the battle in new tracts, on the street, at the doors of the customers. Do you know," he went on, "this is a war. I have guys watching my competitors' trucks, following their salesmen. I try to hire their men—they try to get mine. They break my bottles—I break theirs. My drivers tangle, and it gets bloody. Sometimes the tires on my trucks are slashed, and sometimes my competitors' tires get slashed. You know, if I ever run into that real special bastard, Mike, I'll kill the s.o.b."

"Have you ever seen this special guy, Mike?" I asked.

"Sure, I've seen him," Ray yelled. "It's my business to know my competition."

"Ever talk to him?"

"Yeah, about a year ago we met in a bar. He said hello. He offered to buy me a drink. I told him to stuff it."

"Never talked to him since?"

"No, why?"

"He says he thinks you're probably a nice enough guy, underneath. He knows you're a Cambridge boy. He's older than you. He's from

Pennsylvania—Business Administration Graduate School, 1941. Believe he was a Phi Delt."

"I was a Zeke. Only knew one Phi Delt worth the powder to blow him to hell."

"Well, think about it and I'll be back in a few days."

"By the way, what was your house?"

"I was an Alpha Delt."

"Hmm, my brother-in-law is an Alpha Delt."

"Maybe you'll let me meet him sometime. I'll see you next week, Ray, and think about how we can improve things around here, especially with Mike."

"Now, look, don't start me on the kick again. Knock it off!"

One real inspiration came to me through Art, an owner and operator of one of the smaller plants. Art said, "I don't have much trouble. I know a lot of people in the valley, lived here all my life. Nobody gets my old customers, and I get a little bit of the new move-ins."

"Do you think we can do much about this situation here in the valley?" I said.

"You know what I'd do, if I were you?"

"No, tell me, Art."

"I'd find out if the San Francisco and Oakland headquarters of these outfits would allow the local managers to meet and discuss local conditions by themselves. If they'd do this, I'd set a deadline for having all deals cut off. After that date, I'd make these local managers call each other on any illegal deals their drivers or salesmen report. I think these guys would work together if they'd only talk to each other."

"Thanks, Art," I said, "I think you've given me an idea."

Now, was anything ever more obvious? Art's comments crystallized this situation for me. This was really a simple problem of communication. I was just positive that Hayakawa, Lee, Johnson, et al., were at my ear, nodding knowingly and saying, "This is what we try to keep telling you, cousin, it's a simple matter of communication."

Now in the third week, I talked to head office sales and administration executives of major distributors in Oakland and San Francisco, and presented them with this plan. Effective September 1, let's eliminate all sampling. Effective September 1, let's cut off all illegal deals. Effective September 1, on any reports of illegal sales, the local manager receiving the report will phone the local manager of the company complained against. The manager of the company complained against will investigate the complaint and report back to the manager making the complaint. If this tentative plan was agreed upon, I would call a meeting of all distributors in the area. I would outline the plan and answer any questions. I held a nasty club all this time, of course. The club was the rarely mentioned threat of civil penalties and license suspension or license revocation. That club played its sinister role well.

In any event, the head office executives agreed to let us try our plan and a meeting was called. Thirty-two owners and managers with various assistants appeared at the meeting. Like any solid old Rotary, Kiwanis, or Exchange club, we opened the meeting by everyone giving his name, company, and position. Then I read extracts from about fifteen violations which Leo had picked up. The customers and milk distributors' names were not disclosed. The feedback cues indicated to me that every distributor present felt all fifteen violations were his. He was seeing, I felt, the embarrassment and humiliation of a first-page spread in the local press, plus $7,500 in penalties, plus an expensive defense if he wished to resist.

Then I read our plan, with the September 1 target date. And then came the questions.

Question: "How the hell do I know what my drivers do out there?" Answer: "First, see that your drivers pay for everything they take out. Second, why do you pay route supervisors? Make *them* supervise. Third, who's running your business, you or your drivers? How about you controlling your show? Fourth, simplest of all, just go out and check your drivers' stories—take the driver along."

Question: "Suppose somebody doesn't want to go along with this program?" Answer: "Every day of every violation is a $500 fine. We would prefer not to take any action against anyone. We are asking you to give this a try."

Question: "How much service can we expect from the state?" Answer: "For three months we'll give you twenty-four-hour service—i.e., you call our office about any complaint or problem. Someone will see you the next day."

Then each man in the room was called upon by name, first name, of course, for any comment he might wish to offer. And there were a lot of those. Mike and Ray shook hands—still chilly though. But it was a start. September 1 was two weeks away.

I tell you, it was the damnedest thing you ever saw, those two weeks before September 1. Ray knocked off thirty-five cases of milk, all illegal. Bill, another manager, who we thought was rather clean, knocked off nineteen cases of illegal sales. Mike, who we thought was one of the worst, only had ten cases to knock off. It was a soul-searing torture for these sales-minded managers to tell customers, "Sorry, either you pay the new prices or I can't serve you." And I had some thoughts about homesteading a few acres on the moon if the plan goofed.

September 1 arrived. Leo, Fred, and I were on hand. We split up, each to contact five distributors during the day and to find out whether the program was starting out as agreed upon by the distributors and by us. Distributors were tense and wary. Everything seemed O.K. for the first day. The next two days we each took part of the area to stop drivers and talk with them about the situation. Everything was quiet. Still O.K. Everyone was on the ball. No violations were reported. There were no fights, no tire-slashings, no broken bottles. Pretty good, but still, only the third day.

We moved back to SF on the fourth day. I asked Leo to spend one day each week for the next month back in the area talking with the distributors, stopping a few drivers; just let them know we're around. The second month Leo was to spend two days in the area, again just checking, just being around and available. He reported that the local managers were all calling one another on activities in the field, that credit managers had scheduled a meeting for a discussion of their mutual problems, and conditions generally were looking up.

At the end of three months we called another meeting of all distributors to see if our luck was holding out. Everyone was cautiously confident that conditions would remain stable. The comments went like this: "I have no complaints. I've called five of my competitors. I believe they've told me the truth each time. I have never lied to any competitor who's called me. I like this." Another: "My volume is down a hundred gallons a day but I run my show now—my drivers and salesmen don't run it. I can sleep nights now. I used to have nightmares about my men getting slugged, my trucks wrecked, and my milk poisoning kids. What's more important, in a couple of months, when I get my routes reshuffled, I'll have a black figure at the end of the month—and I haven't had one of those in a long time." Another: "You know what I think? A man just has a hell of a job sitting across from a guy at a table or talking to him on a phone and telling him a lie. I think that's what's making this thing work." Another: "You know what I do sometimes? When one of my drivers says, 'Those bastards down the highway are wheeling and dealing in the new tract outside of town,' I ask, 'Who told you, Bob?' He says, 'Two of my customers told me.' I say, 'Hop in the car. Bob, let's go talk to your customers.' Why, hell, nobody ever told Bob nothin'. And that's stopped a lot of squawking around my place." Another: "We're getting along fine but the state has to have somebody around here. I can tell you my competitor is a thieving chiseler, but I can't tell him that. Of course, he can say the same thing about me. My point is, we've gotta have a third party without an ax to grind." Another: "As long as I can talk to the local manager here and don't have to call his SF office to report anything, I'll get along fine." And so it went. Everybody had something to say—all of it encouraging.

I went back to Los Angeles to complete some work and returned to the Bay area in July, 1955. We worked out a similar program in another area in Northern California. It was a breeze. Extensionalize, push like hell to prevent confusion of abstractive levels; listen, listen, listen; remember the *et cetera*. There's always more. Reduce the threat to communication, reduce the threat, reduce the threat.

Reviewing these two experiences, let me think through again the very conscious application of some aspects of communication study to the problem. There are plenty of credits for everyone but star billing for this low-budget who-done-it should be given to the general semantics boys. If I find out later that I'm wrong. I'll make 'em bloody villains in my next article for *ETC*.

First we went out to get "information." "How extensional can you get?" Leo asked after I'd explained extensionality to him. "Any more extensional and I'd have moved in with some of the dames I talked to."

When Leo said he talked to these dames, he meant he listened, and so did I. We listened and we listened. Not empathically, of course, all the time, but carefully just about all the time and, by and large, understandingly. "Watch your projections, boy," we cautioned.

Our focus, our orientation, I think, was most important. By that I mean we were not out for some quick, smashing victory in battle. We were prepared to be patient, to listen, and to evaluate what we heard in a speaker's context, if possible. For example, it just didn't mean too much to me at the time to have the distributor Mike bellow, "You bastards are wrecking our American system. This country was built on freedom—and that's what you guys will never understand. You'll never understand that." As Leo put it, "We just sit around and let 'em run down." In this case, all I saw was poor Mike getting a little relief from the tensions and frustrations of daily, inconclusive battle. After Mike had quieted down, I did ask in my silkiest Rogerian, "You feel then, Mike, that the state's interfering with your freedom to operate?" And Mike took off again on another three-minute tirade. So I said, "The hell with it, I'll slip Mike the Rogerian some other time."

My point here is that we wouldn't dream of arguing with Mike; he was just inaccessible at this point. What was important with Mike was that we could always enter his plant and we could always talk with him. Don't argue, debate, or talk for a victory, is the way we thought about it. If we lost contact with anyone, if they refused to see us, this we would have considered catastrophic. I put it to you, as long as that communication is open, you'll work it out. You'll work out just about anything.

For our industry meetings we arranged things like having a trade association secretary give a lunch for all the local managers and owners. Later, at our meeting, we sat around a table—no authoritarian line-up for us. Every man's name, his company, and his position were written on a blackboard. Every man introduced himself.

We watched details at the meeting. Fred, with his coat off, tugged occasionally at his frayed but sturdy, faded blue suspenders. Leo had stuffed his tie in his pocket and hung his coat over his chair.

My opening at our first meeting was something like, "I think, men, we are all on the same side. I think we all have the same goals. We want you to operate in the black; we want to prevent wide price fluctuations; we want to prevent price wars; we want the present number and kinds of distributors to remain in competition; we want increased efficiencies, with savings passed on to the consumers. What I'm saying, I suppose, is, let's have the same competition but let's play according to the rules." This was intended as a kind of shared perception at an industry rather than an individual plant level.

We'd get back to the lowest abstractive level from time to time by reminding the distributors of our customer survey. I'd read from a report, "Here's Mrs. W. H. on Happy Valley Lane, who says, 'A salesman named H called on me about July 19, three months ago. He said he represented X Company. He said he'd give me a rebate in cash of one dollar each month if I'd change to his company. I did change and he's been giving me the one-dollar rebate each month.'" This was intended to reestablish our position as knowing what the hell we were talking about.

Each man present was called on by first name for his comments on any questions. This was our feedback. And anyone who said, "Nothing to say, now," or "Let me think about it," we noted and saw later, privately. It's interesting that when you think of a feedback and its purpose you tend to listen differently, to hear differently.

Another aspect of communication which I'd been interested in utilizing and now had the opportunity to use was the "grapevine." For example, we were quite sure that one driver who had been stopped and spoken to became five drivers by the time the information was reported back to his supervisors. So Leo would stop and interview drivers of three companies in one part of the county, race to another part of the county fifteen miles away and stop several more. Then he would speed away another fifteen miles and do the same thing. What distributors told us was, "The county is crawling with you state guys and full of guys visiting customers." We suggested that the housewives discuss our visits with their drivers. And that reached the distributors as "guys going up and down the streets ringing every doorbell in the county."

Remember our discussions of the "self-fulfilling prophecy"? One thing that flipped us and to which we gave the highest priority for action was when a manager or supervisor said, "Look, this is all pretty talk and you guys are trying, but I'll give this deal three months, and it'll fall apart." This guy had to have the program "fall apart" in three months. His self-concept, in a sense, was under attack. These characters were often tough to handle. One method that worked in one case was to phone this distributor each week for several weeks to check on local conditions, and Leo would see him on his visits in the area. Because we gave him a kind of responsibility for reporting conditions, he took on a sense of responsibility for maintaining our program.

I also recall one supervisor, Ashworth, who said, "I've been working in this valley for fifteen years and I'm telling you, in four months these guys will be back with their axes. You guys don't understand. It'll never, never, never work. Right now, I could get you twenty violations in twenty minutes." After an hour of discussing this situation with this Ashworth, I felt he could not be reached; there probably wasn't much I could do with him. You know what I did do later though? I told his boss, "For Christ's sake, Art, do me a favor and tell that guy Ashworth to just shut up. He'll kill our program before it starts." When I next saw Art, I asked what he'd done about Ashworth. "Ashworth? I did like you said, I told him, 'Goddam it, Ashworth, if you want to work here, just shut up—if the state's program doesn't work, you'll be the first one to go.'" Rough? Sometimes this is what it takes—if it works. As far as I know, it worked with Ashworth.

I think of our either/or discussions, too. We didn't ever expect immediate and enduring stability. We expected difficulties to develop on prices from time to time. We expected some distributors to assist us aggressively in achieving stability and we expected others to drag along. We expected to and did give more attention to the "draggers." My point is that we would not abandon the program with an "either you guys are all with us or out this deal goes." We thought in terms of degrees of co-operation and compliance.

Now don't you think because we came out of this conquerors and kings, ear-weary and hoarse, but haloed, that we therefore packed up our Korzybski, Hayakawa, Johnson, Rapoport, and Lee, stuffed their worn and fingered pages into the saddlebags, and rode off along the dusty trail, steely eyes searching the hills for smoke signals and the trails for moccasin prints—seeking out more of the dreaded Sioux. We hadn't that much reason for self-congratulation.

We did what we managed to do because the distributors were ready for it, and we knew it. They were losing money; they were sick and tired of the violence, the daily tension, the daily anger, waiting for competitors' tricks, actual and imagined. So we threw every general semantics theory and communication technique known to us into this steaming, savage, stinking mess.

I put it to you kids. Didn't general semantics come up smelling like a nonverbal rose?

Summer, 1957. Mr. Diamond is district supervisor for the Bureau of Milk Control, California State Department of Agriculture. A graduate of the University of California, he says he has also been a professional musician, an undernourished writer, and an even more undernourished actor.

How to Attend a Conference

S. I. HAYAKAWA

The purpose of a conference is, of course, the exchange of ideas, the enrichment of our own views through the support or the challenge provided by the views of others. It is a situation created specially for the purposes of communication.

Since I am a student of semantics, I am going to venture some observations on the process of communication in the hope that, whether my observations are correct or not, the very fact that I make them may at least help to make the reader aware of the problems of communication that confront participants at any conference in addition to the problems inherent in the subject matter.

There are two aspects to communication. One is the matter of output—the speaking and writing, involving problems of rhetoric, composition, logical presentation, coherence, definition of terms, knowledge of the subject and the audience, and so on. Most of the preoccupation with communication is directed toward the improvement of the output, so that we find on every hand courses in composition, in effective speaking, in the arts of plain or fancy talk, and how to write more dynamic sales letters.

But the other aspect of communication, namely, the problem of intake—especially the problem of how to listen well—is relatively a neglected subject. It does not avail the speakers to have spoken well if we as listeners have failed to understand, or if we come away believing them to have said things they didn't say at all. If a conference is to result in the exchange of ideas, we need to pay particular heed to our listening habits.

A common difficulty at conferences and meetings is what might be called the *terminological tangle,* in which discussion is stalemated by conflicting definitions of key terms. Let me discuss this problem using as examples the vocabulary of art criticism and the discussion of design. What do such terms as "romanticism," "classicism," "baroque," "organic," "functionalism," etc., *really* mean? Let us put

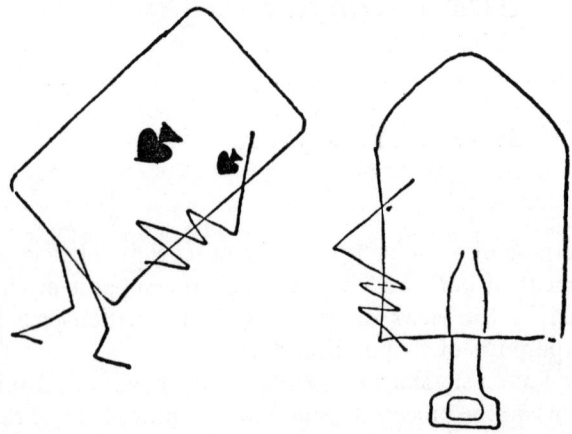

A Spade Calling a Spade a Spade

this problem into the kind of context in which it is likely to occur. For example, a speaker may talk about "the romanticism so admirably exemplified by the Robey House by Frank Lloyd Wright." Let us imagine in the audience an individual to whom the Robey House exemplifies many things, but *not* "romanticism." His reaction may well be, "Good God, has he ever *seen* the Robey House?" And he may challenge the speaker to *define* "romanticism"—which is a way of asking, "What do *you* think 'romanticism' really is?" When the speaker has given his definition, it may well prove to the questioner that the speaker indeed doesn't know what he's talking about. But if the questioner counters with an alternative definition, it will prove to the speaker that the questioner doesn't know what *he* is talking about. At this point it will be just as well if the rest of the audience adjourns to the bar, because no further communication is going to take place.

How can this kind of terminological tangle be avoided? I believe it can be avoided if we understand at the outset that there is no ultimately correct and single meaning to words like "romanticism" and "functionalism" and "plastic form" and other items in the vocabulary of art and design criticism. The same is true, of course, of the vocabularies of literary criticism, of politics and social issues, and many other matters of everyday discussion. Within the strictly disciplined contexts of the languages of the sciences, exact or almost exact agreements about terminology can be established. When two physicists talk about "positrons" or when two chemists talk about "diethylene glycol," they can be presumed to have enough of a common background of controlled experience in their fields to have few difficulties about understanding one another. But most of the words of artistic and other general discussion are not restricted to such specialized frames of reference. They are part of the language of everyday life—by which I mean that they are part of the language in which we do not hesitate to speak across occupational lines. The artist, dramatist, and poet do not hesitate to use the vocabularies of their callings in speaking to their audiences; nor would the physician, the lawyer, the accountant, and the clothing merchant hesitate to use these words to one another if they got into a discussion of any of the arts.

In short, the words most commonly used in conference, like the vocabulary of other educated, general discussion, are public property—which is to say that they mean many things to many people. This is a fact neither to be applauded nor regretted; it is simply a fact to be taken into account. They are words, therefore, which either have to be defined anew each time they are seriously used—or, better still, *they must be used in such a way, and with sufficient illustrative examples, that their specific meaning in any given discourse emerges from their context.*

Hence it is of great importance in a conference to listen to one another's statements and speeches and terminology without unreasonable demands. And the specific unreasonable demand I am thinking of now is the demand that everybody else *should* mean by such words as "romanticism" what I would mean if I were using them. If, therefore, the expression, "the romanticism of the Frank Lloyd Wright Robey House" is one which, at first encounter, makes little sense to us, we should at once be alerted to special attentiveness. The speaker, by classifying the Robey House as "romantic," is making an unfamiliar classification—a sure sign not that he is ill-informed but that he has a way of classifying his data that is different from our own. And his organization of his data may be one from which we can learn a new and instructive way of looking at the Robey House, or at "romanticism," or at whatever else the speaker may be talking about.

Since a major purpose of conferences is to provide ample opportunity for conversational give-and-take, perhaps it would be wise to consider the adoption, formally or informally, of one basic conversational traffic rule which I have found to be invaluable in ensuring the maximum flow of information and ideas from one person to another, and in avoiding the waste of time resulting from verbal traffic snarls. The rule is easy to lay down, but not always easy to follow: it is that *we refrain from agreement or disagreement with a speaker, to refrain from praise or censure of his views, until we are sure what those views are.*

Of course, the first way to discover a speaker's views is to listen to him. But few people, other than psychiatrists and women, have had much training in listening. The training of most ororverbalized professional intellectuals (which would include most people who attend conferences) is in the opposite direction. Living in a competitive culture, most of us are most of the time chiefly concerned with getting our own views across, and we tend to find other people's speeches a tedious interruption of the flow of our own ideas. Hence, it is necessary to emphasize that listening does not mean simply maintaining a polite silence while you are rehearsing in your mind the speech you are going to make the next time you can grab a conversational opening. Nor does listening mean waiting alertly for the flaws in the other fellow's arguments so that later you can mow him down. Listening means trying to see the problem the way the speaker sees it—which means not sympathy, which is *feeling for* him, but empathy, which is *experiencing with* him. Listening requires entering actively and imaginatively into the other fellow's situation and trying to understand a frame of reference different from your own. This is not always an easy task.

But a good listener does not merely remain silent. He asks questions. However, these questions must avoid all implications (whether in tone of voice or in wording) of skepticism or challenge or hostility. They must clearly be motivated by curiosity about the speaker's views. Such questions, which may be called "questions for clarification," usually take the form, "Would you expand on that point about...?" "Would you mind restating that argument about....?" "What exactly is your recommendation again?" Perhaps the most useful kind of question at this stage is something like, "I am going to restate in my

The Speakers Are Prisoners of Their Vocabularies

words what I think you mean. Then would you mind telling me if I've understood you correctly?"

The late Dr. Irving J. Lee of Northwestern University has suggested another form of questioning which he describes as "the request for information concerning the uniqueness of the particular characteristics of the condition or proposal under consideration." I shall simply call these questions "questions of uniqueness." All too often, we tend to listen to a speaker or his speech in terms of a generalization, "Oh, he's just another of those progressive educators," "Isn't that just like a commercial designer?" "That's the familiar Robjohn-

Giddings approach," "That's the old Bauhaus pitch," etc. It is a curious and dangerous fact—dangerous to communication, that is—that once we classify a speech in this way, we stop listening, because, as we say, "We've heard that stuff before." But *this* speech by *this* individual at *this* time and place is a *particular* event, while the "that stuff" with which we are classifying this speech is a *generalization* from the past. Questions of uniqueness are designed to prevent what might be called the functional deafness which we induce in ourselves by reacting to speakers and their speeches in terms of the generalizations we apply to them. Questions of uniqueness take such forms as these: "How large is the firm you work for, and do they make more than one product?" "Exactly what kind of synthetic plastic did you use on that project?" "Are your remarks on abstract expressionism and Jackson Pollock intended to apply equally to the work of De Kooning?"

Something else that needs to be watched is the habit of overgeneralizing from the speaker's remarks. If a speaker is critical of, let us say, the way in which design is taught at a particular school, some persons in the audience seem automatically to assume that the speaker is saying that design shouldn't be taught at all. When I speak on the neglected art of listening, as I have done on many occasions, I am often confronted with the question, "If everybody listened, who would do the talking?" This type of misunderstanding may be called the "pickling in brine fallacy," after the senior Oliver Wendell Holmes's famous remark, "Just because I say I like sea bathing, that doesn't mean I want to be pickled in brine." When Alfred Korzybski found himself being misunderstood in this way, he used to assert with special forcefulness, "I say what I say; I do not say what I do not say." Questions of uniqueness, properly chosen, prevent not only the questioner but everyone else present from projecting into a speaker's remarks meanings that were not intended.

All too often, the fact that misunderstanding exists is not apparent until deeper misunderstandings have already occurred because of the original one. We have all had the experience of being at meetings or at social gatherings at which Mr. X says something, Mr. Y believes Mr. X to have said something quite different and argues against what he believes Mr. X to have said. Then Mr. X, not understanding Mr. Y's objections (which may be legitimate objections to what Mr. X didn't say), defends his original statement with further statements.

These further statements, interpreted by Mr. Y in the light of mistaken assumptions, lead to further mistaken assumptions, which in turn induce in Mr. X mistaken assumptions about Mr. Y. In a matter of minutes, the discussion is a dozen miles away from the original topic. Thereafter it can take from twenty minutes to two hours to untangle the mess and restore the discussion to a consideration of Mr. X's original point. This is the kind of time-wasting which I should like to help avoid.

All this is not to say that I expect or wish conferences to avoid argu-

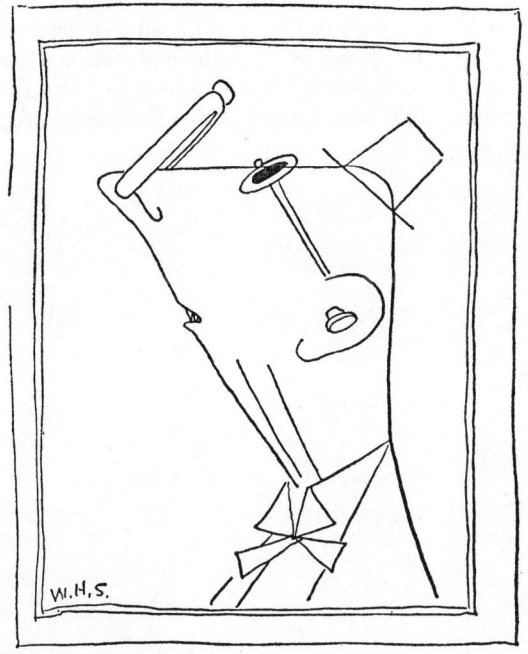

Prejudice Listening to Reason

ment. But let us argue about what has been said, and not about what has not been said. And let us discuss not for victory but for clarification. If we do so, we shall find, I believe, that ultimately agreement and disagreement, approval and disapproval, are not very important after all. The important thing is to come away from a conference with a fund of information—information about what other people are doing and thinking and why. It is only as we fully understand opinions and attitudes different from our own and the reasons for them that we better understand our own place in the scheme of things. Which is but another way of saying that while the result of communications successfully imparted is self-satisfaction, the result of communications successfully received is self-insight. Let us attend conferences and take part in them not only for the sake of increased self-satisfaction, but also for the sake of increased self-insight.

Autumn, 1955. Dr. Hayakawa is professor of language arts, San Francisco State College; editor (and founder), ETC.: A Review of General Semantics, 1943 to present; author, Oliver Wendell Holmes *(1939),* Language in Action *(1941),* Language in Thought and Action *(1949), (ed.)* Language, Meaning and Maturity *(1954). His paper was presented at the opening session of the International Design Conference, Aspen, Colorado, June 13, 1955.*

II. Education and Re-education

It is obvious that in the human organism the field for stimulations is vastly greater than in animals. We are subjected not only to all external stimuli but also to a large number of permanently operating *internal* semantic stimuli, against which we have had, as yet, very little protective psychophysiological means. Such structurally powerful semantic stimuli are found in our doctrines, metaphysics, language, attitudes, etc. These do not belong to the objective external world. . . . As our inquiry has shown, in practically all "mental" ills, a confusion of orders of abstractions appears as a factor. When we confuse the orders of abstractions and ascribe objective reality to terms and symbols, or confuse conclusions and inferences with descriptions, etc., a great deal of semantic suffering is produced.

Obviously, in such a delusional world, different from the actualities, we are not prepared for *actualities*. . . . [T]he general preventive psychophysiological discipline in all such cases of confusion of orders of abstractions is found in "consciousness of abstracting." . . .

A fundamental difference between "man" and "animal" is found in the fact that a man can be conscious of abstracting, and an animal cannot. . . . Our human world is more complex; the number of stimuli is enormously increased. Against this excessive stimulation we need protection, which is found in consciousness of abstracting. One adjusts oneself by increasing the field of "consciousness," and by giving it properly evaluated content as against the vast "unconscious" which covers the animal's life and our own past. . . . "Mental" therapy always has the semantic aim and method; namely, to discover the unconscious material and make it conscious, and so make proper evaluation possible.

ALFRED KORZYBSKI, *Science and Sanity*

The Art of Psychoanalysis

JAY HALEY

Enough research has been done by social scientists to corroborate many of Freud's ideas about unconscious processes. Yet there has been surprisingly little scientific investigation of what actually occurs during psychoanalytic treatment. Fortunately this situation has been remedied by a scholar on the faculty of Potter College in Yeovil, England. Assigned a field trip in America, this anonymous student spent several years here studying the art of psychoanalysis both as a patient and a practitioner. His investigation culminated in a three-volume work entitled *The Art of Psychoanalysis, or Some Aspects of a Structured Situation Consisting of Two-Group Interaction Which Embodies Certain of the Most Basic Principles of One-upmanship*. Like most studies written for Potter College the work was unpublished and accessible only to a few favored members of the clinical staff. However, a copy was briefly in this writer's hands and he offers here a summary of the research findings for those who wish to foster the dynamic growth of Freudian theory and sharpen the techniques of a difficult art.

Unfamiliar terms will be translated into psychoanalytic terminology throughout this summary, but a few general definitions are necessary at once. First of all, a complete definition of the technical term "one-upmanship" would fill, and in fact has filled, a rather large encyclopedia. It can be defined briefly here as the art of putting a person "one-down." The term "one-down" is technically defined as that psychological state which exists in an individual who is not "one-up" on another person. To be "one-up" is technically defined as that psychological state of an individual who is not "one-down." To phrase these terms in popular language, at the risk of losing scientific rigor, it can be said that in any human relationship (and indeed among other mammals) one person is constantly maneuvering to imply that he is in a "superior position" to the other person in the relationship. This "superior position" does not necessarily mean superior in social status or economic position; many servants are masters at putting their employers one-down. Nor does it imply intellectual superiority as any intellectual knows who has been put "one-down" by a muscular garbage collector in a bout of Indian wrestling. "Superior position" is a relative term which is continually being defined and redefined by the ongoing relationship. Maneuvers to achieve superior position may be crude or they may be infinitely subtle. For example, one is not usually in a superior position if he must ask another person for something. Yet he can ask for it in such a way that he is implying, "This is, of course, what I deserve." Since the number of ways of maneuvering oneself into a superior position are infinite, let us proceed at once to summarize the psychoanalytic techniques as described in the three-volume study.

Psychoanalysis, according to the Potter study, is a dynamic psychological process involving two people, a patient and a psychoanalyst, during which the patient insists that the analyst be one-up while desperately trying to put him one-down, and the analyst insists that the patient remain one-down in order to help him learn to become one-up. The goal of the relationship is the amicable separation of analyst and patient.

Carefully designed, the psychoanalytic setting makes the superior position of the analyst almost invincible. First of all, the patient must voluntarily come to the analyst for help, thus conceding his inferior position at the beginning of the relationship. In addition, the patient accentuates his one-down position by paying the analyst money. Occasionally analysts have recklessly broken this structured situation by treating patients free of charge. Their position was difficult because the patient was not regularly reminded (on payday) that he must make a sacrifice to support the analyst, thus acknowledging the analyst's superior position before a word was said. It is really a wonder that any patient starting from his weak position could ever become one-up on an analyst, but in private discussions analysts will admit, and in fact tear at their hair while admitting, that patients can be extremely adroit and use such a variety of clever ploys[1] that an analyst must be nimble to maintain his superior position.

Space does not permit a review of the history of psychoanalysis here, but it should be noted that early in its development it became obvious that the analyst needed reinforcement of the setting if he was

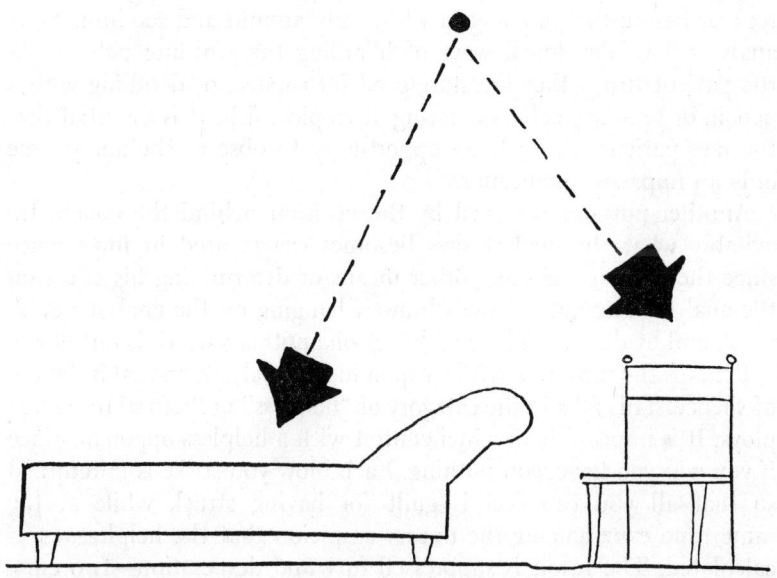

Freud's Ploy ". . . was the use of a couch for the patient to lie down upon."

to remain one-up on patients more clever than he. An early reinforcement was the use of couch for the patient to lie down upon. (This is often called "Freud's ploy," as are most ploys in psychoanalysis.) By placing the patient on a couch, the analyst gives the patient the feeling of having his feet up in the air and the knowledge that the analyst has both feet on the ground. Not only is the patient discon-

[1] A "ploy" is technically defined as a move or gambit which gives one an advantage in a relationship.

certed by having to lie down while talking, but he finds himself literally below the analyst and so his one-down position is geographically emphasized. In addition, the analyst seats himself behind the couch where he can watch the patient but the patient cannot watch him. This gives the patient the sort of disconcerted feeling a person has when sparring with an opponent while blindfolded. Unable to see what response his ploys provoke, he is unsure when he is one-up and when one-down. Some patients try to solve this problem by saying something like, "I slept with my sister last night," and then whirling around to see how the analyst is responding. These "shocker" ploys usually fail in their effect. The analyst may twitch, but he has time to recover before the patient can whirl fully around and see him. Most analysts have developed ways of handling the whirling patient. As the patient turns, they are staring off into space, or doodling with a pencil, or braiding belts, or staring at tropical fish. It is essential that the rare patient who gets an opportunity to observe the analyst see only an impassive demeanor.

Another purpose is served by the position behind the couch. Inevitably what the analyst says becomes exaggerated in importance since the patient lacks any other means of determining his effect on the analyst. The patient finds himself hanging on the analyst's every word, and by definition he who hangs on another's words is one-down.

Perhaps the most powerful weapon in the analyst's arsenal is the use of silence. This falls in the category of "helpless" or "refusal to battle" ploys. It is impossible to win a contest with a helpless opponent since if you win you have won nothing. Each blow you strike is unreturned so that all you can feel is guilt for having struck while at the same time experiencing the uneasy suspicion that the helplessness is calculated. The result is suppressed fury and desperation—two emotions characterizing the one-down position. The problem posed for the patient is this: how can I get one-up on a man who won't respond and compete with me for the superior position in fair and open encounter? Patients find solutions, of course, but it takes months, usually years, of intensive analysis before a patient finds ways to force a response from his analyst. Ordinarily the patient begins rather crudely by saying something like, "Sometimes I think you're an idiot." He waits for the analyst to react defensively, thus stepping one-down. Instead the analyst replies with the silence ploy. The patient goes further and says, "I'm *sure* you're an idiot." Still silence in reply. Desperately the patient says, "I said you were an idiot, damn you, and you are!" Again only silence. What can the patient do but apologize, thus stepping voluntarily into a one-down position? Often a patient discovers how effective the silence ploy is and attempts to use it himself. This ends in disaster when he realizes that he is paying twenty dollars an hour to lie silent on a couch. The psychoanalytic setting is calculatedly designed to prevent patients using the ploys of analysts to attain equal footing (although as an important part of the cure the patient learns to use them effectively with other people).

Few improvements have been made on Freud's original brilliant design. As the basic plan for the hammer could not be improved upon

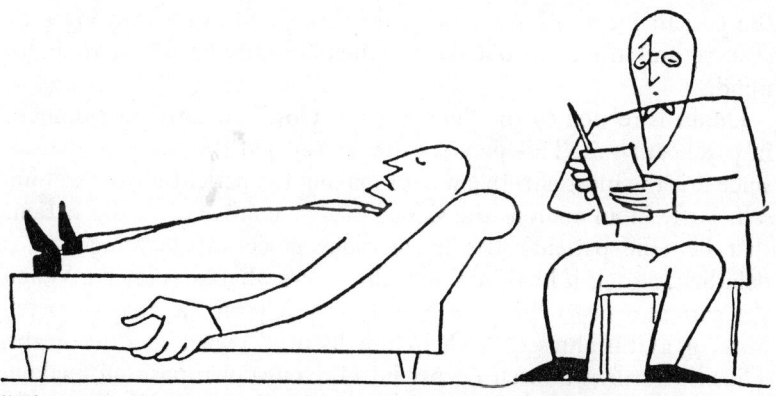

"*The analyst gives the patient the feeling of having his feet up in the air and the knowledge that the analyst has both feet on the ground.*"

by carpenters, so the use of the voluntary patient, hourly pay, the position behind the couch, and silence are devices which have not been improved upon by the practitioners of psychoanalysis.

Although the many ways of handling patients learned by the analyst cannot be listed here, a few general principles can be mentioned. Inevitably a patient entering analysis begins to use ploys which have put him one-up in previous relationships (this is called a "neurotic pattern"). The analyst learns to devastate these maneuvers of the patient. A simple way, for example, is to respond inappropriately to what the patient says. This puts the patient in doubt about everything he has learned in relationships with other people. The patient may say, "Everyone should be truthful," hoping to get the analyst to agree with him and thereby follow his lead. He who follows another's lead is one-down. The analyst may reply with silence, a rather weak ploy in this circumstance, or he may say, "Oh?" The "Oh?" is given just the proper inflection to imply. "How on earth could you have ever conceived such an idea?" This not only puts the patient in doubt about his statement, but in doubt about what the analyst means by "Oh?" Doubt is, of course, the first step toward one-downness. When in doubt the patient tends to lean on the analyst to resolve the doubt, and we lean on those who are superior to us. Analytic maneuvers designed to arouse doubt in a patient are instituted early in analysis. For example, the analyst may say, "I wonder if that's *really* what you're feeling." The use of "really" is standard in analytic practice. It implies the patient has motivations of which he is not aware. Anyone feels shaken, and therefore one-down, when this suspicion is put in his mind.

Doubt is related to the "unconscious ploy," an early development in psychoanalysis. This ploy is often considered the heart of analysis since it is the most effective way of making the patient unsure of himself. Early in an analysis the skilled analyst points out to the patient that he (the patient) has unconscious processes operating and is deluding himself if he thinks he really knows what he is saying. When the patient accepts this idea he can only rely on the analyst to tell him (or, as it is phrased, "to help him discover") what he really means. Thus he burrows himself deeper into the one-down position, making it easy for the analyst to top almost any ploy he devises. For example, the patient may cheerfully describe what a fine time he had with his girl friend, hoping to arouse some jealousy (a one-down emotion) in the analyst. The appropriate reply for the analyst is, "I wonder what that girl *really* means to you." This raises a doubt in the patient whether he is having intercourse with a girl named Susy or an unconscious symbol. Inevitably he turns to the analyst to help him discover what the girl really means to him.

Occasionally in the course of an analysis, particularly if the patient becomes obstreperous (uses resistance ploys), the analyst makes an issue of free association and dreams. Now a person must feel he knows what he is talking about to feel in a superior position. No one can maneuver to become one-up while free associating or narrating his dreams. The most absurd statements inevitably will be uttered. At the same time the analyst hints that there are meaningful ideas in this absurdity. This not only makes the patient feel that he is saying ridiculous things, but that he is saying things which the analyst sees meaning in and he doesn't. Such an experience would shake anyone, and inevitably drives the patient into a one-down position. Of course if the patient refuses to free-associate or tell his dreams, the analyst reminds him that he is defeating himself by being resistant.

A resistance interpretation falls in the general class of "turning it back on the patient" ploys. All attempts, particularly successful ones, to put the analyst one-down can be interpreted as resistance to treatment. The patient is made to feel that it is *his* fault that therapy is going badly. Carefully preparing in advance, the skillful analyst

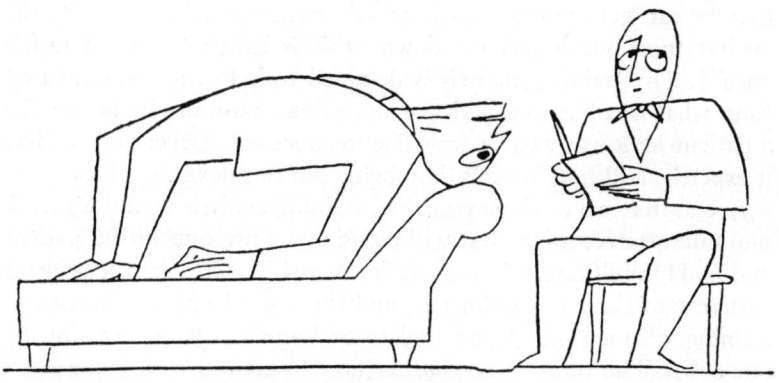

"It is essential that the rare patient who gets an opportunity to observe the analyst see only an impassive demeanor."

informs the patient in the first interview that the path to happiness is difficult and he will at times resist getting well and indeed may even resent the analyst for helping him. With this background even a refusal to pay the fee or a threat to end the analysis can be turned into apologies with an impersonal attitude by the analyst (the "not taking it personally" ploy) and an interpretation about resistance. At times the analyst may let the patient re-enter the one-down position gently by pointing out that his resistance is a sign of progress and change taking place in him.

The main difficulty with most patients is their insistence on dealing directly with the analyst once they begin to feel some confidence. When the patient begins to look critically at the analyst and threaten an open encounter, several "distraction" ploys are brought into play. The most common is the "concentrate on the past" ploy. Should the patient discuss the peculiar way the analyst refuses to respond to him, the analyst will inquire, "I wonder if you've had this feeling before. Perhaps your parents weren't very responsive." Soon they are busy discussing the patient's childhood without the patient ever discovering that the subject has been changed. Such a ploy is particularly effective when the patient begins to use what he has learned in analysis to make comments about the analyst.

In his training the young analyst learns the few rather simple rules that he must follow. The first is that it is essential to keep the patient feeling one-down while stirring him to struggle gamely in the hope that he can get one-up (this is called "transference"). Secondly the analyst must never feel one-down (this is called "countertransference"). The training analysis is designed to help the young analyst learn what it is like to experience a one-down position. By acting like a patient he learns what it feels like to conceive a clever ploy, deliver it expertly, and find himself thoroughly put one-down.

Even after two or three years in a training analysis seeing his weak ploys devastated, an analyst will occasionally use one with a patient and find himself forced into a one-down position. Despite the brilliant structure of the analytic fortress, and the arsenal of ploys learned in training, all men are human and to be human is to be occasionally one-down. The training emphasizes how to get out of the one-down position quickly when in it. The general ploy is to accept the one-down position "voluntarily" when it is inescapable. Finding the patient one-up, the analyst may say, "You have a point there," or "I must admit I made a mistake." The more daring analyst will say, "I wonder why I became a little anxious when you said that." Note that all these statements *seem* to show the analyst to be one-down and the patient one-up, but one-downness requires defensive behavior. By deliberately acknowledging his inferior position the analyst is actually maintaining his superior position, and the patient finds that once again a clever ploy has been topped by a helpless, or refusal to do battle, ploy. At times the "acceptance" technique cannot be used because the analyst is too sensitive in that area. Should a patient discover that this analyst gets embarrassed when homosexual ideas are discussed, he may rapidly exploit this. The analyst who takes such comments personally is lost. His only chance for survival is to anticipate in his diagnostic interviews those patients capable of discovering and exploiting this weakness and refer them to analysts with different weaknesses.

The most desperate ploys by patients are also anticipated in analytic training. A patient will at times be so determined to get one-up on his analyst that he will adopt the "suicide" ploy. Many analysts immediately suffer a one-down feeling when a patient threatens suicide. They hallucinate newspaper headlines and hear their colleagues chuckling as they whisper the total number of patients who got one-up on them by jumping off the bridge. The common way to prevent the use of this ploy is to take it impersonally. The analyst says something like, "Well, I'd be sorry if you blew your brains out, but I would carry on with my work." The patient abandons his plans as he realizes that even killing himself will not put him one-up on this man.

Orthodox psychoanalytic ploys can be highlighted by contrasting them with the more unorthodox maneuvers. There is, for example, the Rogerian system of ploys where the therapist merely repeats back what the patient says. This is an inevitably winning system. No one can top a person who merely repeats his ideas after him. When the patient accuses the therapist of being no use to him, the therapist replies, "You feel I'm no use to you." The patient says, "That's right, you're not worth a damn." The therapist says, "You feel I'm not worth a damn." This ploy, even more than the orthodox silence ploy, eliminates any triumphant feeling in the patient and makes him feel a little silly after a while (a one-down feeling). Most orthodox analysts look upon the Rogerian ploys as not only weak but not quite respectable. They don't give the patient a fair chance.

The ethics of psychoanalysis require the patient be given at least a reasonably fair chance. Ploys which simply devastate the patient are looked down on. Analysts who use them are thought to need more analysis themselves to give them a range of more legitimate ploys and confidence in using them. For instance, it isn't considered proper to encourage a patient to discuss a subject and then lose interest when he does. This puts the patient one-down, but it is a wasted ploy since he wasn't trying to become one-up. If the patient makes such an attempt then of course losing interest may be a necessary gambit.

Another variation on orthodox psychoanalytic ploys demonstrates a few of their limitations. The psychotic continually demonstrates that he is superior to orthodox ploys. He refuses to "volunteer" for analysis.

He won't take a sensible interest in money. He won't lie quietly on the couch and talk while the analyst listens out of sight behind him. The structure of the analytic situation seems to irritate the psychotic. In fact when orthodox ploys are used against him, the psychotic is likely to tear up the office and kick the analyst in the genitals (this is called an inability to establish a transference). The average analyst is made uncomfortable by psychotic ploys and therefore avoids such patients. Recently some daring therapists have found they can get one-up on a psychotic patient if they work in pairs. This is now called

"The patient finds himself hanging on the analyst's every word."

the "it takes two to put one down" therapy, or "multiple therapy." For example, if a psychotic talks compulsively and won't even pause to listen, two therapists enter the room and begin to converse with each other. Unable to restrain his curiosity (a one-down emotion) the psychotic will stop talking and listen, thus leaving himself open to be put one-down.

The master one-upman with psychotics is a controversial psychiatrist known affectionately in the profession as "The Bull." When a compulsive talker won't listen to him, the Bull pulls a knife on the fellow and attracts his attention. No other therapist is so adroit at topping even the most determined patient. Other therapists require hospitals, attendants, shock treatments, lobotomies, drugs, restraints, and tubs to place the patient in a sufficiently one-down position. The Bull, with mere words and the occasional flash of a pocket knife, manages to make the most difficult psychotic feel one-down.

An interesting contrast to the Bull is a woman known in the Profession as "The Lovely Lady of the Lodge." Leading the league in subtle one-upmanship with psychotics, she avoids the Bull's ploys which are often considered rather crude and not always in the best of taste. If a patient insists he is God, the Bull will insist that *he* is God and force the patient to his knees, thus getting one-up in a rather straightforward way. To handle a similar claim by a patient, the Lady of the Lodge will smile and say, "All right, if you wish to be God, I'll let you." The patient is gently put one-down as he realizes that no one but God can *let* anyone else be God.

Although orthodox psychoanalytic ploys may be limited to work with neurotics no one can deny their success. The experienced analyst can put a patient one-down while planning where to have dinner at the same time. Of course this skill in one-upmanship has raised extraordinary problems when analysts compete with one another at meetings of the psychoanalytic associations. No other gathering of people exhibits so many complicated ways of gaining the upper hand. Most of the struggle at an analytic meeting takes place at a rather personal level, but the manifest content involves attempts to (1) demonstrate who was closest to Freud or can quote him most voluminously, and (2) who can confuse the most people by his daring extension of Freud's terminology. The man who can achieve both these goals best is generally elected president of the association.

The manipulation of language is the most startling phenomenon at an analytic meeting. Obscure terms are defined and redefined by even more obscure terms as analysts engage in furious theoretical discussions. This is particularly true when the point at issue is whether a certain treatment of a patient was *really* psychoanalysis or not. Such a point is inevitably raised when a particularly brilliant case history is presented.

What happens between analyst and patient, or the art of one-upmanship, is rarely discussed at the meetings (apparently the techniques are too secret for public discussion). This means the area for debate becomes the processes within the dark and dank interior of the patient. Attempting to outdo one another in explanations of the bizarre insides of patients, each speaker is constantly interrupted by shouts from the back of the hall such as, "Not at all! You're confusing an id impulse with a weak ego boundary!" or "Heaven help your patients if you call *that* cathexis!" Even the most alert analyst soon develops an oceanic feeling as he gets lost in flurries of energy theories, libidinal drives, instinctual forces, and superego barriers. The analyst who can most thoroughly confuse the group leaves his colleagues feeling frustrated and envious (one-down emotions). The losers return to their studies to search their minds, dictionaries, science fiction journals, and Freud for even more elaborate metaphorical flights in preparation for the next meeting.

The ploys of analyst and patient can be summarized briefly as they occur during a typical course of treatment. Individual cases will vary depending on what maneuvers the individual patient uses (called "symptoms" by the analyst when they are ploys no sensible person would use), but a general trend is easy to follow. The patient enters analysis in the one-down posture by asking for help and promptly tries to put the therapist one-down by building him up. This is called the honeymoon of the analysis. The patient begins to compliment the therapist on how wonderful he is and how quickly he (the patient) expects to get well. The skilled analyst is not taken in by these maneuvers (known as the "Reichian resistance" ploys). When the patient finds himself continually put one-down, he changes tactics. He becomes mean, insulting, threatens to quit analysis, and casts doubt upon the sanity of the analyst. These are the "attempts to get a human response" ploys. They meet an impassive, impersonal wall as the analyst remains silent or handles the insults with a simple statement like, "Have you noticed this is the second Tuesday afternoon you've made such a comment? I wonder what there is about Tuesday," or "You seem to be reacting to me as if I'm someone else." Frustrated in his aggressive behavior (resistance ploys), the patient capitulates and ostensibly hands control of the situation back to the analyst. Again building the analyst up, he leans on him, hangs on his every word, insists how helpless he is and how strong the analyst, and waits for the moment when he will lead the analyst along far enough to devastate him with a clever ploy. The skilled analyst handles this nicely with a series of "condescending" ploys, pointing out that the patient must help himself and not expect anyone to solve everything for him. Furious, the patient again switches from subservient ploys to defiant ploys. By this time he has learned techniques from the analyst and is getting better. He uses what insight (ploys unknown to laymen) he has gained to try in every way to define the relationship as one in which the analyst is one-down. This is the difficult period of the analysis. However, having carefully prepared the ground by a thorough diagnosis (listing weak points) and having instilled a succession of doubts in the patient about himself, the analyst succeeds in topping the patient again and again as the years pass. Ultimately a remarkable thing happens. The patient rather casually tries to get one-up, the analyst puts him one-down, and the patient does not become disturbed by this. He has reached a point where he doesn't *really* care whether the analyst is in control of the relationship or whether he is in control. In other words, he is cured. The analyst then dismisses him, timing this maneuver just before the patient is ready to announce that he is leaving. Turning to his waiting list, the analyst invites in another patient who, by definition, is someone compelled to struggle to be one-up and disturbed if he is put one-down. And so goes the day's work in the difficult art of psychoanalysis.

Spring, 1958. Mr. Haley is a communications analyst on the Project for the Study of Schizophrenic Communication, which is directed by Gregory Bateson at the Veterans Administration Hospital, Palo Alto, California.

Reality, Possibility and Children

DAVID SMILLIE

Children think not of what is past, nor what is to come, but enjoy the present time, which few of us do.—JEAN DE LA BRUYÈRE

The conventional patterns of language and thought in our culture implicitly assume the importance of possibility, potentiality, and expectation. That is, we view the world in terms of what it might be, what it ought to be, or what it will be, looking beyond what is—the here and now. In industry we look for people who have *potentiality* and promise, *forward-looking* young men and women. We say of a child in school that, "You can *expect* a lot from that young man." We talk of education as *preparation*. We assume that the really significant patterns of life are in the realm of possibility, the immediate or distant future, and through these assumptions we becloud and obscure our vision and our realization of what is, of present and immediate existence.

True understanding of children must take into account the reality of the immediate and present. But first of all, we must see children in their reality, that is, perceive them for what they are.

When the psychologist speaks of perception, very often he is concerned with the problems of expectation, prediction, comparison, etc., rather than with the immediate act of seeing. In fact, there is a widespread notion that "seeing" is quite impossible without the concomitant processes of comparison, expectation, and prediction. Studies that have been done recently involving "perception and personality" or "motivation and perception" have asked such questions as whether more valued objects are seen as larger than less valued objects (comparison) or have asked subjects to indicate the nature of a word which is flashed on a screen for a fraction of a second (expectation) or to indicate the movement of two stationary lights in a dark room (prediction). While it may be true that much perceiving is infused with cognitive and emotional judgments, it becomes confusing to assume that perception and judgment are the same.

The failure to distinguish between the experience of perceiving and the judgments and evaluations which are applied to the experience, has resulted in the use of the hallucination as an example of faulty perception. It is generally claimed that the person who hallucinates has a false or unreal perception. However, the hallucination is no more unreal than the very clear memory or eidetic image in the absence of the remembered object. The hallucination is a clear perception with an unconventional judgment, namely, that the perceived entity is "out there" rather than "in here." The hallucination is to be explained (if it must be explained) in terms of faulty or unconventional *judgment*.

No matter what the perception (and I refer here to all or any sense modality, not solely to vision), it is possible to "see" without the mediation of concepts. Perception need not involve categorization, so that the *chair-that-I-perceive* need not have the categorical or conceptual properties of the *word* "chair" that I use to denote it. The percept need have none of the qualities which are necessary for the language that I use to describe it. I am referring here to what Korzybski has called "the territory" and to what A. H. Maslow calls "raw experience."

Because our world is permeated by expectation and possibility we find value in such qualities as foresight, predictability, analytic ability, etc. We teach our children to view the world in this way and we measure their growth toward maturity (intellectually and emotionally) by their ability to respond sensitively to the general expectations of others, to live in terms of future goals rather than present satisfactions and in general to adopt conventional adult orientations. In fact we require children to adopt our expectations as their own, as a prerequisite to our acceptance of them. We surround them with the idea that it is better to be big than to be small and then find in their response to this comparison a justification for characterizing the child as striving for omnipotence.

Because we strive ourselves after that which is not present—the goal —we see all life as goal-directed. When we find no goal in the life experience of a person we make up a goal of our own and call this an "unconscious" aim. We force and squeeze with our language, with our concepts, until we have obscured in our own life as well as that of others the presence of the immediate perception, the existence of goalless, purposeless activity.

It might seem, as we begin to classify and categorize all the world and all our own experiences, that we would completely lose our immediate perceptions. But the world can never be completely transformed into categories of cultural convention. The uniqueness of the individual and of his experience is persistently and pervasively there even as it is denied and obscured by language and reason. There are moments on a warm spring morning when we feel the warmth of the sun filtering through the soft green leaves, when we smell the damp moistness of the earth, and we realize at that moment that we are not striving for a goal. We know that we are living, in that moment, in the unanalyzed present and that our perceptions are real and unclassified. But these moments become lost in our hurry to become oriented once more to the world of an "almost present" reality.

The child is, however, less tangibly caught up in this striving for the unattainable. Surely it is necessary to go along with many of the requirements of the adult world, but these requirements are often entered into as though in a game.

The child's world is primarily and basically the world of the immediate, and only secondarily does he respond to the possible and the potential. Close observation and study of children always reveal this "presentness" of their reality, but it is usually seen as a lack of growth, intelligence, or socialization, rather than as a primary quality of their experience. Piaget, for instance, who has spent a long life in careful observation and analysis of children's thought, comes to the conclusion that the child's life is dominated by egocentricity—the lack of an ability to adopt the "as if" attitude ("I can see that mountain as if I were standing somewhere else"; "I can look at the world as if I were you"). That is, from Piaget's point of view the child is restricted and limited by an inability to adopt a broad orientation which takes into account the many more varied aspects of the world from multiple points of view rather than from a single point of view. While this is certainly true from the initial premises adopted by Piaget, I am suggesting here that the converse is also true. As one adopts the point of view of the "generalized other,"[1] one loses the freshness and spontaneity of the here and now. It is only as we see the world from the immediate that the true self of the individual comes into primacy. As the generalized other becomes the medium of cognizing the world, our perceptions become inextricably mingled with our conceptions, and we "see" the world in terms of bigger and smaller, of what might be or what ought to be or what must be.

An awareness of the freshness of a child's point of view came to me in a testing situation where I was asking four-year-old Michael to give me a definition of the word "dress."

"What is a dress?"
"A dress is a dress."
"Yes, I know. But I want you to tell me in your own words what a dress is."
"A dress is a dress."
"Can you tell me about it? You know what a dress is. Tell me what a dress is."
"It's already told."

The experience with Michael bothered me because I felt that he was telling *me* something important, and I didn't know what it was. Terman says, "The purpose of this test is . . . to see whether he can define [the word], either by expressing a usage, giving a description of the object, giving the material of which it is made, or categorizing it."[2] Michael failed to do any of these things in responding to the item, but in his failure he affirmed a wisdom which the test had no way to measure. As adults we come to believe that the dress is "cotton" or *is* "a garment" rather than seeing that the dress may be *described as* made of cotton or constituting one of a class of "garments." In raw and simple fact, however, *the dress is a dress*. In Michael's affirmation

[1] George Herbert Mead, *Mind, Self and Society* (Chicago: University of Chicago Press, 1934).
[2] Lewis M. Terman and Maud Merrill, *Measuring Intelligence* (Boston: Houghton Mifflin, 1937).

of that fact he was drawing upon his own experience and his own wisdom rather than utilizing the adult expectations involving description and categorization.

The testing psychologist finds a simple way to deal with the response of Michael since this sort of response is not unusual on an intelligence test. The psychologist says that this represents a failure in the conceptual sphere. Michael has failed to see that a dress is not only a dress but also a member of a class or category. At a verbal level this is certainly true. Dress may be classified as a "garment" or as "clothing." On the other hand, it may be broken down into further classifications such as blue dress, party dress, etc. The psychologist is thus suggesting that children must inevitably come to "see" dress in this way. For the child, however, the perception of the dress is a matter of sight and touch and immediacy. It is this dress or that dress. Because it is this and no more, the dress has an existence which is rich and full and immediate.

We become so involved in the "purpose" of ourselves and the world about us that we lose sight of the original purposelessness of our life and our perception. If we meet someone on a path we may ask, "Where are you going?" as though everyone was necessarily walking in order to get somewhere. While we may be able to accept the answer, "I'm just walking for pleasure," we then make the pleasure the goal. Because of this persistent and ubiquitous assumption we come to learn to give answers which fulfill the expectations of others ("Everything I do has a purpose") and then we come, as a part of the same process, to believe in the purposes themselves. Children who are partially caught up in this process, since it is important and even essential to relate to others in the culture, will often answer "why questions" with the simple word, "because." In this answer they have struck the heart of the matter. If your answer has a "because" in it, it satisfies the necessity for a purpose.

Experimental psychologists with their neat experimental designs have shunned the use of children as subjects in favor of rats and college students. I suspect it is because children will not be manipulated as will rats nor will they be conceptually directed as will adults and, therefore, force some of their own personality into the impersonal design, discouraging the psychologist from further experiments involving them. Child development and child psychology are scattered unsystematic fields, perhaps because children will not remain still enough to be systematized. Piaget's work stands as a monumental exception to this. This must be Piaget's genius.

As children have a way of "spoiling" the neat experimental designs of psychologists, so also they have a way of using language to fit their own situation rather than following the form prescribed by adult convention. Because children have not ordered their world in "lineal" fashion using each word as a step in the direction of a final goal (say "communication"), their language may express something in their experience simply and beautifully and directly. The following is an excerpt from a play therapy interview.[3] The therapist's comments have been omitted. The four-year-old boy is drinking water from a nursing bottle:

> You know,
> To get this room filled with this
> It takes millions and trillions of days.
>
> A very long time.
>
> It would take near to the end of counting
> And I would get so tired.
> It would take so long
> That I couldn't stay alive that long.
>
> On the fifteenth day I'd be a father
> And on the fiftieth day I'd be an old man.
>
> Like my neighbor.
> You know, he died last week.
> He died.
> The last day on the calendar he died.
> Just last week he died.

One may ask, I suppose, as those in psychoanalysis do, "What is the purpose or goal which is being expressed here?" One might answer within the psychoanalytic framework that this boy is expressing a desire to regress to the comfort and seclusion of his mother's womb, that he is expressing the desire to return to the undifferentiated unity of inorganic existence. While it is clear that this four-year-old is concerned with the passage of time and his own existence in this passage, we do not come any closer to an understanding through a spelling out of a motive or a goal. We come closer to his experience through listen-

[3] Clark Moustakas, *Children in Play Therapy* (New York: McGraw-Hill, 1953).

ing and even more broadly "awaring," not through explaining, these words.

It is this quality of "listening," not just with the ears but with our whole selves, that is necessary if we are to understand children. It is this total listening that has led me to the coining of the word "awaring." It is perhaps what Korzybski meant by "extensionality."

By "awaring," I do not mean a passive attitude expressed by such a phrase as "being aware." I am referring to an active participation in the event but one which does not transform or change the nature of the event being "awared" but enhances it as a bright-colored backdrop enhances the flame of a candle. It is this listening that we have lost in our conceptual and analytic ability. We feel we must take each event and compare it to other events (conceptualization) or we feel it necessary to break down the event into its component parts, looking at the pieces (analysis). Sadly, we lose our ability to "see" because the conceptualizing enters into and permeates the vision. I am claiming that we can "see," "listen," that we can "aware" events without limiting and stifling our intelligence or our thinking process.

Spring, 1958. Dr. Smillie is a staff member of the Merrill-Palmer School in Detroit, doing teaching and research in developmental psychology.

Semantic Play Therapy

SALVATORE RUSSO
HOWARD W. JAQUES

Several articles on the use of semantics in psychotherapy were included in *Papers from the Second American Congress on General Semantics*,[1] published in 1943. Psychiatrists, psychologists, counselors, and social workers reported on their use of general semantics in their therapeutic work and gave the impression that we were on the threshold of a new era in psychotherapy. This approach that seemed so promising thirteen years ago, however, has borne very little fruit, for a perusal of the *Psychological Abstracts* did not disclose a single semantic article on individual therapy since the Congress was held in Denver.

The lack of development in this field may be due in part to the expressed attitude of many of the therapists who pioneered this work that, while all therapists use semantics to some extent, general semantics is not an adequate or even a useful method by itself. Douglas G. Campbell, M.D., wrote, "As a general statement one can say that general semantics is emphatically not a psychotherapy in itself. It is an adjuvant, an accessory method." He also said that the principles of general semantics are best used piecemeal according to the progress

---

[1] M. Kendig (ed.), *Papers from the Second American Congress on General Semantics* (Chicago: Institute of General Semantics, 1943), p. 133.

of the case rather than "employing them as a system." Their indirect and auxiliary use, nevertheless, he believed, was valuable since it materially shortens the length of psychotherapy. This attitude that general semantics cannot be fashioned into a sufficient or complete mode of psychotherapy may have discouraged interested therapists from trying to develop actual techniques.

The accounts of semantic therapy that were presented at the Congress were sketchy and fragmentary. The writers usually gave hints or general suggestions, rather than actual details of their work. One got the impression that the therapist was experimenting and had not arrived at definite methods. The general principles or aims were clearly stated, such as training in map-territory or language-fact relationship, levels of abstraction, extensional devices, etc., but the actual procedures were absent. In those instances where some substantial account of the case was given, much more space was devoted to the results achieved than to the details of the method employed.

None of the cases reported apparently dealt with general semantics in the psychotherapy of children. Two cases of children with problems were discussed, but the semantic treatment was with the parents and not with the child. Our article deals with the direct use of semantic play with a child and may be the first case of its kind to be reported. The use of semantics was direct and became the basic mode of treatment rather than an auxiliary one; thus we found the need to coin the expression "semantic play therapy." The details of each play session are summarized so that one can follow our work step by step.

When the child whose treatment will be the subject of this article was accepted for treatment we had no intention of using semantic play. We resorted to it because we were desperate and felt that we needed a treatment out of the ordinary. The boy had been diagnosed in the usual fashion, as will soon be discussed, and given the usual permissive type of play that is used in many child guidance clinics. After ten sessions of play therapy we were confronted with the strong possibility that the parents would terminate the case if we could not produce results in the near future. The following account touches briefly on the first ten play sessions and deals mostly with our experiment with semantic play therapy. It might be noted that the semantic play sessions have a rationale. In the first one Larry was presented with an objective and impersonal situation unrelated to his immediate problem; in the last one he had arrived at a point where he had to deal with a problem parallel to his own on a human basis.

Larry was just eleven years of age and in the sixth grade when he was brought to the Wichita Guidance Center. He had been referred the summer before by a school counselor, who had described the boy as unhappy in school, not achieving, shy, unwilling to recite in class, and showing his resentment of school by crying and fretting.

The mother described him as quiet, serious, and worried about people's faults and world problems. He worried so much about school-work that he developed insomnia. He was very critical of himself and easily discouraged. When he was criticized, he "cried like a baby" and then complained that he was afraid that people knew he cried. He liked to paint and draw, was not interested in sports, and was too sensitive to swim in the nude at the YMCA.

Larry was jealous of his younger brother's academic achievement and brooded a lot over insults and injuries. He had taken a profound dislike to a man who was a neighbor and transferred his hate to the man's daughter, who played daily with the younger brother and visited the home often. Despite his hostility the neighbor girl remained friendly and tried in vain to win him over.

A diagnostic study was made. The study indicated that the parents had established very high and rigorous standards which caused him to develop a feeling of failure and inadequacy. His tests showed that he had made some compulsive attempts to achieve and had reacted to failure by being hypercritical of himself and others, and had learned to avoid threatening situations by childish means, such as negativism, weeping, and begging to be excused from the situation. He was not considered to be a seriously disturbed boy, but an unhappy one who was dissatisfied with everything and everyone, and who would respond favorably to play therapy with a male figure.

A conventional play therapy was used for ten consecutive weeks. He seemed very agreeable during these sessions and engaged in a variety of self-chosen activities: he made model planes, a bean shooter, a bracelet; played with water guns, modeling clay, mumble-peg; he accompanied the therapist to the drugstore for a soda. But while he was quiet, passive, noncommunicative in play sessions, at home he resisted coming to the Center as violently as he resisted going to school.

The mother had been seen concurrently by another member of the therapeutic team. She reported weekly his refusal to go to school and to come to the Center. He said that they weren't going to get anywhere because he didn't want them to make him better, and that they didn't ask him anything sensible or important, and that they could never make him like going to school or to the Center. In defense of his position he said that the mother's therapist did not like him, and that his own therapist was nice to him just so that he could do his work. He said that if his parents expected him to be nice at home by coming to the Center they were just wasting their time, for he would never be that way. At home he had become more antagonistic to the neighbor girl, and began to chase her away from the home.

While Larry had never intimated his great resistance to the Center to his therapist, he resisted so much at home that his family asked for help in this matter. Should they continue to force him despite his growing refusal, or should they allow his treatment to be terminated? The decision to terminate is usually left to the child, and in such instances most of them choose to continue when they are given the right, but in this case it was decided that he needed help and that he should be brought to the Center even against his will.

It was at this point that the therapeutic team felt that the boy might profit by some form of training in semantic play, since his problem appeared to us as basically a semantic one. It seemed that his difficulty lay in his pervasive dichotomy of the world and his allegiance to his categories. He clung so rigidly to his categories that he was enslaved by them. *Everything to him was either good or bad, everyone was either for or against him.* He couldn't understand how his parents, who liked him, could punish him or make him unhappy. When his stubborn use of categories became frustrating or painful, he could not realistically reconsider the situation, but resorted to sulking, crying, or temper tantrums.

It was apparent to us that he was reacting not to the realistic environment but to the world created by his own faulty and pervasive generalizations. He was projecting his preconceived dichotomy on the world and forcing all experience to fit it. Larry had no insight into his problem. We felt that we would have to help him escape from his perceptual chains, for unless he could be freed from his harmful thinking, improvement was not likely. Hence the decision was made to have him continue to come to the Center and get some basic experience in the classification of experiences and abstracting to arrive at a more realistic manipulation of his world. This need for semantic play therapy arose from a consideration of his conduct outside of the playroom.

For the next seven weeks he was given experience in a prearranged, highly structured situation. These seven sessions are described below. At the end of that time he was given the opportunity to decide for himself whether he wanted to terminate or continue his activities at the Center.

FIRST SESSION. Larry entered the playroom and found an object-sorting test scattered on a table. The therapist commented that someone must have left them out but that he knew what they were for. He said it was some sort of game and that they could play it if they wanted to. Larry sat on one side of the table and the therapist on the other. He was asked to select an object and place it in front of him. He selected a pair of pliers. Then he was asked to put all the objects with it that belong with pliers. He selected all the tools, and was told it could be called the tool pile, since they were all tools. He was then asked in what other way he could sort them, and he replied that he didn't know. It was suggested that he could choose all the metal ones. He agreed to this and the sorting continued. After a while the therapist chose an object, and Larry added all those that belonged with it; the next time Larry chose the master object, and the therapist chose those that went with it. Larry caught on very rapidly to the different ways objects could be classified and vied with the therapist to see if he could find more classifications than the therapist did. At the end the therapist put all the objects together and had him classify all of them in several groups, which the boy did successfully.

SECOND SESSION. The next week the therapist brought in three large wooden boxes that were used to store toys in the playroom. They contained a great diversity of toys, such as dolls, blocks, cars, planes, and tanks. Larry was asked if he recalled the game he had played last week; he replied that he did. He was told that they were going to continue it, but that it was going to be a little more difficult. Each day they would play with something more advanced. The problem was to classify all of the objects into *three* groups, one group for each box; the objects must be so classified that each box could be labeled. Larry dumped the material out of the boxes and began to sort them into three groups. He discussed the classification while he worked. He first divided them into metal, rubber, and wood. But this broke down. Then he tried to classify them by the nature of the toys. This broke down too, partly because he needed a classification for "junk" consisting of parts of objects. Then he used classifications of those that run on land, fly in air, or go in water. After many attempts and compromises he arrived at three large categories that seemed practical. The therapist printed the labels and they were pasted on the boxes.

THIRD SESSION. The therapist brought the same three boxes. Larry examined them and discovered that the contents had been mixed up. The therapist commented on this fact. Larry separated the objects and sorted them out and put them back into the boxes according to the old classification. When he had finished this, he went to all the other playrooms and brought out the boxes and worked on them. This time he made the labels and put them on the other boxes and worked on them. Thus he classified all the toys for all of the playrooms.

FOURTH SESSION. Larry asked what they were going to do that day. Therapist had brought a large stack of cards with pictures of animals on them cut from various magazines. He explained that this was a more advanced study of classification. Larry started the classification by making two piles, those that had fur and those that didn't. He put most of the birds and insects and four-legged animals in the fur class. The therapist discussed the fitness of placing both pigs and birds in the fur category. Larry argued that birds had fur under the microscope. This was the first time that he defended his sorting. He was told that since we didn't have a microscope we couldn't use that argument, thus pigs and birds wouldn't fit. Then he divided the animals into those that were edible and those that weren't; then into birds and non-birds. He had trouble with bats and insects. They could fly but weren't in the class of birds. At this point for the first time he talked to the therapist about not wanting to come to the Center. He asked how much longer he would have to come. He said that he didn't like to come to the Center because he preferred to play at home. He also preferred home to school.

FIFTH SESSION. The same cards were used again for classification. This time he sorted the cards into four piles. He still ran into a lot of trouble in his fourfold classification. Early in the hour he said he didn't want to come to the Center. He was told that the therapist would meet him anywhere Larry wanted to go. Larry replied that he just wanted to be with his friends. The therapist set up the classification of friends and nonfriends. Larry insisted that everyone was either his friend or not his friend. He discussed a couple of boys who were his friends and some who were not. Did the therapist come under the category of friend? He answered that he did not know. He was asked if he had ever acted like one of his nonfriends who disliked to bathe; he denied it.

SIXTH SESSION. Larry came in with tears in his eyes and his usual persecuted air. When asked what was wrong, he said that he did not want to come. The therapist discussed his usual method of resisting, and asked him why he persisted in using the same method if it didn't work. Therapist talked to him about the things he could do here. Larry replied that he could do things at home. But it was only once a week. Larry replied that he could have a good time at home once a week. Therapist talked to him about his wanting his own way. Larry said he always wanted it. He was asked if his younger brother always had his own way. No. Did his parents always get their own way? No. Did he want to be different from everyone else? He didn't answer. It was suggested that if his parents didn't let him do everything he wanted to do, it was because they liked him. If they didn't care about him they would have ignored him. This made him thoughtful and he suggested they go to the drugstore for a soda.

SEVENTH SESSION. Showed him the film *Angry Boy*. Larry said that it was a good movie but there wasn't any resemblance to him. When the similarity was pointed out he agreed. The film has two admirable scenes of play therapy. In one of them the child is provoked into shooting the therapist on the head with a dart gun because of persistent questioning. The child apologizes by saying that he was sorry, the gun slipped. But the therapist ignores the proffered reason and uses this as an occasion to discuss the relationship of people and their acts. He gets the boy to see that an instance of anger or hostility is not coextensive with the whole person, because people who like you sometimes hurt you, and you sometimes hurt people you like. Both the people in the film had just acted that way. Larry was able to understand this argument as well as the boy in the film.

When asked if he put up the usual fight coming, Larry said he hadn't, or he would have gotten a real spanking. He talked about the problem while he pounded modeling clay. When asked if he would continue to come if given a choice, he said no.

The mother was told of the boy's decision, and she agreed to the termination. She felt that he had improved greatly, and said the neighbors had spontaneously commented on the fact. An aunt who had visited the home had spoken of the difference in the boy. The mother thought that Larry had a better sense of responsibility and was talking more freely about his feelings to his parents. The strong antagonism he had had for the neighbor girl had lessened considerably. The mother felt that they had the situation well in hand, and would like to see if it wouldn't continue to improve without forcing him to come to the Center.

This case is reported in order to encourage the use of semantic play therapy with children. It may be that there have been other attempts similar in nature that have not been published. The reviewing of this case has caused this team to wonder why we hadn't used this method more often, and it has stimulated us to want to use it again in the future. We plan to start using this method from the very beginning by selecting at intake cases that we feel would profit by such a method. We realize that it falls far short of a complete example of semantic therapy, and has some of the limitations of the other cases reported, but we have confidence that it could be developed into a therapeutic device that might have wider application in psychotherapy with children.

Readers may have thought of—and some may even have had experience with—other ways in which the principles of general semantics can be actualized in the form of therapeutic techniques. If this paper stimulates the publication of descriptions and results of other experiences with general semantics in psychotherapy, it will have achieved its main purpose.

Summer, 1956. Dr. Russo is clinical psychologist and Dr. Jaques is staff psychologist at the Wichita Guidance Center, Wichita, Kansas.

A Semantic Approach to Counseling

WILLIAM H. PEMBERTON

The questions of those seeking counseling or therapeutic help are generally of three kinds. They ask *why* they or other people of their acquaintance think, feel, and act as they do. They ask the *meaning* of their own and other people's behavior. And they ask *what can be done* about it. In short, they seek information. The reassuring answer in practically every instance is that something *can* be done about it, that there is information which increases understanding of ourselves and others.

Therapy begins therefore with the suggestion that counselor and counselee engage in a joint search for this information, that they operate together as a "research team," structuring a program to ask as well as answer meaningful questions, to discuss methods and techniques for solving problems, to understand the mechanisms of human evaluation and misevaluation.

To create an atmosphere of exploration, a useful step in the early phases of therapy is for the counselor to introduce some axioms of research. The counselor suggests that the patient's questions, *why? what does it mean? what can be done?* cannot be fruitfully investigated except in the light of the following axioms:

1. There is no single why. (Causation is multiple.)
2. There is no single meaning. (Meanings also are multiple.)

3. There is no single thing to be done. (There are many alternative courses of action.)

Utilizing these axioms helps to avoid the tendency of maladjusted people to search for *the* cause, *the* meaning, *the* answer; to develop instead an understanding and appreciation of scientific problem-solving. The joint inquiry of counselor and counselee, then, moves in the direction of finding out *what* happened (rather than why), what are the possible meanings, and a search for constructive alternative courses of action from which decisions can be made.

Another aspect of what I call the "self-corrective" approach which gives a feeling of hopefulness to the counselee has been the early introduction of the counselor's faith, namely, the assumptions underlying therapy. These assumptions are that everyone has within himself the mechanisms of self-correction and self-direction, that everyone has a potential for growth and maturity, and that everyone has the capacity to improve his communicability, and so relate—to love and be loved—more effectively.

The first role, then, of the counselor-therapist is to create an environment, an atmosphere, so that growth and relatedness can be promoted. This means acceptance of individuals *as they are*, whether fearful, agitated, evasive, withdrawn, or otherwise. Nor is this acceptance an artifice, for experienced therapists are aware that unsuccessful defense and adjustment mechanisms are self-perpetuating attempts to protect oneself from and cope with vulnerabilities largely carried from childhood. These mechanisms or patterns of evaluation are clung to, and the thinking which accompanies them appears both logical ("true") and necessary ("right"). Defensiveness may be due to actual rejections or to errors in evaluation. In either circumstance the results are inflexibility, communication failures, and lowered self-esteem. Paradoxically, those who value themselves least are the most preoccupied with themselves, continuously asking, "What about me?"

Thus the first task in counseling research is to accept persons as they are, whatever the limitations, lacks, distortions, or inappropriate responses. Once the counselee feels accepted, he becomes less defensive, therefore more flexible, therefore better able to communicate and evaluate. This growth in self-fulfillment does not lead to disregard of others. Sensitivity to the needs of others becomes differentiated from defensive sensitivity, in which one uneasily protects and defends himself against his vulnerability to the values of others.

Simplifying medicine, physicians sometimes state that there is but one disease, congestion; and one cure, circulation. According to information theory, an organism adapts and survives in proportion to its ability to receive, retain, modify, use, and transmit information. From a semantic point of view, disease may be looked upon as a congestion of information; its cure, the free flow or circulation of information. Thus the second task of the counselor-therapist is that of becoming the counselee's "research associate" in the study of the communication process. Special emphasis is given to the study of the barriers to communication. Talking and thinking of the kind that prevents adaptation and predictability are reviewed and examined.

An effective way of presenting such information has been the use of the office blackboard. The remainder of this paper will describe the use of three of these blackboard diagrams. The first sketch to be drawn is the fictional "normal distribution curve" (or "bell curve," which is familiar enough so that it need not be reproduced here), used in this case to show degrees of sanity. The distribution suggests that only a small minority can be considered "sane" or "insane"; that the large average, the statistically "normal" group (the hump of the bell curve), is made up of the unsane, the partially sane, or the sane only part of the time. This distribution curve also can illustrate developmental characteristics; for instance, we can indicate what we call the emotionally infantile and the emotionally mature at the statistical extremes, and the emotionally adolescent as constituting the so-called normal group. Still another characteristic can be described for the distributed groups: for the insane (the infantile) insistence on absolute certainty; for the sane (the mature) acceptance of the principle of uncertainty or a search for degrees of probability and predictability. Among the large middle group there are found attitudes of bewildered ambivalence and confusion of direction; a reaching out for more irrational certainty with increasing degrees of threat. A final characteristic that can be charted on this curve is the degree of dependency: for the infantile, involuntary dependency; for the emotionally adolescent, rebellion against and denial of dependency by talking and acting *as if* independent; for the mature, voluntary dependency or interdependence.

We observe this grasping for certainties in psychological testing with projective techniques where, for example, unstructured stimuli such as ink blots are *really* something to the maladjusted, whereas for the more mature there is an attitude of *it might be,* or stated semantically, an awareness of the processes of abstracting and projecting. For the deeply pathological there is collapse of the perceptual organizing process.

A second useful diagram emerging from therapeutic research is the Defensiveness Scale by which one may estimate the degree of threat or defensiveness in oneself or others, and which may also describe the characteristic style or pattern of coping with stress situations. The six-level scale indicates *degrees of volition* or its opposite, in both behavior and talk. The top half (levels 1, 2, 3) indicates "threatening" and "threatened" behavior or talk, the bottom half (levels 4, 5, 6) is called "nonthreatening" and "nonthreatened" behavior. Level 1 represents the most reflex-like behavior, the most threatening, the most maladaptive; and level 6 the most reflective and considerate behavior.

In general, those operating on levels 1, 2, and 3 are, as indicated, threatened or defensive to the point of lacking choice in their behavior; thus judgments about them implying choice, though expected, are in error. Asking questions is placed on the border next to threatening behavior, since many questions can lead to threatening behavior and talk, especially the "why" question. An example of a threatening question may be seen when a wife says, "What's the matter with him?" which is but another way of saying, "There is something the matter." In many such instances, "Why did you do that (silly, stupid, unreasonable, foolish) thing?" and similar utterances, there is no request for information—only a release of affective judgments. Herein lies tragedy, for in addition to the involuntary character of the threatening behavior and talk, if one person uses these mechanisms, others will almost certainly reply in kind. The problem situation is aggravated. These mechanisms also operate in *intra*personal communication; for instance, evaluations such as "I'm no good" (judgment) and "I ought to change" (advice) seem to increase guilt and lead to further maladjustment.

The role of the counselor, working with the counselee as a partner in a "research" enterprise, is to present predominantly the nonthreatening role toward the counselee, namely, to ask for information, especially about how one feels, and to provide feedback and to act as reflector, without correcting, advising, or judging the counselee's attitudes. An aim in counseling is to get the counselee, too, to adopt "nonthreatening" in place of "threatening" language behavior. With the ventilation of feelings on the part of the counselee, tensions diminish, and the self-corrective process continues. The predictable results are changes in attitude and approach, and apparent increase in the capacity for choice—choice even of appropriate "threatening" behavior—the difference being that as improvement progresses, the behavior is determined by the individual rather than by the situation.

INVOLUNTARY SPEECH AND BEHAVIOR

"Threatened" and "threatening" (non-acceptance)	1. Ignoring—withdrawing: sullen silence.
	2. Attacking—criticizing:
	  (a) judgments: approval, disapproval;
	  (b) advice: "ought," "shall," "must."
	3. Deceiving—lying—joking—"pep talks."

"Non-threatened" and "non-threatening" (acceptance)	4. Asking questions:
	  (a) for information (what, where, when);
	  (b) by silence (observing, listening, inviting further communication).
	5. Stating feelings honestly:
	  (a) describing one's own feelings;
	  (b) understanding those of others.
	6. Providing feed-back: re-stating others' evaluations.

EXERCISE OF CHOICE IN SPEECH AND BEHAVIOR

So far the roles played by the therapeutic "research team," the tasks described, are not dissimilar to those found in other therapies. A third role in counseling which I wish to describe is more directly related to general semantics, namely, the presenting of a technique for evaluating and understanding the verbal processes of threatened persons. This presentation is facilitated by the use of Alfred Korzybski's diagram, the Structural Differential, by means of which the "natural order of evaluation" (from experiences to descriptions to higher order inferences and abstractions) is diagramed, and by which departures from this natural order can also be graphically pointed out. (Diagram.)

On the blackboard, a simplified version of the Structural Differential is drawn to represent (A) experiences, perceptions, observations; and (B) talk about experiences, perceptions, etc.

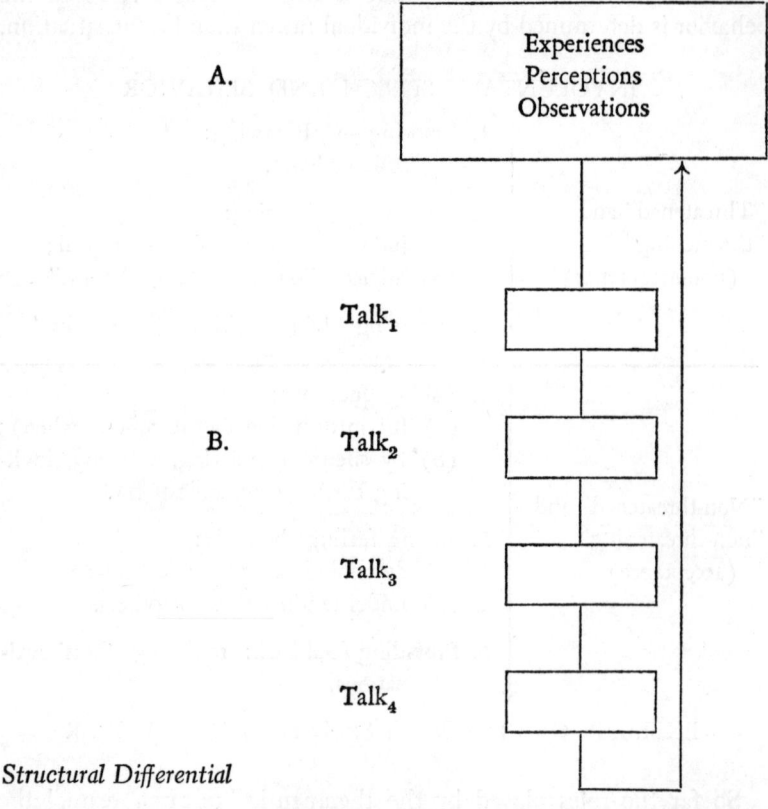

A. Experiences Perceptions Observations

B. Talk₁

Talk₂

Talk₃

Talk₄

Structural Differential

People react more to thoughts about things than to the things themselves. One aim of semantic therapy is to help to differentiate between events and thoughts about them. The maladjusted appear to lack this differentiating ability. For instance, we think of the neurotic as having no predictability, no foresight, and so behaving inappropriately. Actually these maladjusted individuals predict continuously, but they react to their thoughts as if they were identical with the things thought about. The results seem to be (whether with a forward look: "This might happen, or this, or this. . . ." or with a backward look: "I should have done this, no this, no this, no this. . . .") mobilization, overmobilization, and immobilization, with consequent fatigue and various earnest attempts to "stop thinking," "to get rid of my thoughts." The inappropriate behavior follows.

For our statistically normal man, the unsane, talk is rarely structured in an orderly way. The maladjusted not only fail to differentiate between experiences and thoughts about experiences (identification), but confuse the levels of talk. To be descriptive about the maladjusted: (1) they tend to assume that everyone is having the same experience on the perceptual level as themselves, or in other words, that there is only one "right" way to look at or feel about anything; (2) they tend to assume that if they talk long enough, loudly enough, "reasonably" enough they will be able to influence others to their way of evaluating; (3) they tend to assume that the characteristic by which something is named, labeled, or judged is *in* the object— that what they say about it is the "right" characteristic, the "real" name, the "real" meaning; (4) they tend to make generalized conclusions from very few experiences in such a way that new experiences have to fit old conclusions or remain ignored; (5) they tend to shut out further consideration of a problem with, "That's all there is to it."

The following are three practical examples of the use of the Structural Differential in understanding and coping with communication barriers. For the first example: after drawing the diagram, a cookie is held up (experience level) and described ($talk_1$). The question is asked, "What is it?" "What is it called?" The usual response is "cookie." Then it is pointed out that in England it is called a "sweet biscuit," and that other cultures have still other names for it. Then we ask, "What is its *real* name?" This is the point at which arguments begin—arguments as to who is "right" and who is "wrong" ($talk_3$— opinions, judgments). It is then pointed out that $talk_3$ is often treated as $talk_1$ ("fact"), which sometimes results in major disturbances in some individuals, such as defending, attacking, and "proving who is *really* right."

Next we imagine that the cookie has been broken and divided and eaten. Again opinions are asked: "It is good," "It is stale," etc. ($talk_3$).

Here again the attention of the participant is called to the possibility of arguments about "who is right."

From here we go to a clinical example. During sexual intercourse, there is, let us say, an incompleted act (talk$_1$—descriptive fact). The wife says, "You don't love me" (talk$_3$—inferential statement, but reacted to by the speaker as if it were a descriptive fact). When the husband denies this, she goes on, "There must be another woman" (further inference). He replies, "There is no other woman!" "You're a liar!" she cries (talk$_3$ again reacted to as talk$_1$). And so on . . . into the counselor's office!

Further examples can be found in many everyday assertions: "Your tastes in art are atrocious," "Your political opinions are stupid." Denials, accusations, quarrels, and withdrawals are the usual consequences. To attempt to achieve agreement on the facts at the descriptive level which underlie such judgments is a laborious process, but treated as a "research problem" by the disputing parties, with the help of the counselor, it can be most rewarding. For example, with the couple where one tells the other, "Your taste in draperies is terrible," the task of a joint search for draperies suitable to both can usually bring results, since this involves translating opinions (talk$_3$) into hypotheses (talk$_4$), then these into experiences at the subverbal level.

With such cases it is possible, through the use of diagraming, to see the reversal of the natural order of evaluation involved in disputes over "fact" and "opinion," "right" and "wrong," "truth" and "falsehood." The mechanisms of such disputes can be talked about in the counseling situation without alienating the person or persons being counseled. With awareness of the mechanisms, with this more scientific approach to talking, assertions become probability statements and predictive hypotheses, leading to the quest for further information and to testing, rather than finalities to be defended. An attitude of inquiry, an open-mindedness to new experience, is brought about, with consequent revisions of beliefs, theories, and conclusions. There also develops from visualizing the abstracting process with the Structural Differential an awareness of the uniqueness of individual experiences, the uniqueness of individual needs and values, and, more importantly for therapy, an awareness of the uniqueness of an individual's defense and adjustment mechanisms or characteristic styles of problem-solving. Thus there develops a respect for the other's way as being *another* way, rather than the insistence on "my way" as the *only* way, which is the source of so much difficulty in daily domestic life.

Apprehensiveness and phobic reactions are another area in which the Structural Differential has proved useful. The overapprehensive display certain time disorientations, for example, treating their feelings and predictions (talk$_3$, talk$_4$) as "fact" (talk$_1$) *before* the event. The diagram helps people translate apprehensions into predictive hypotheses, which may then be compared with earlier experiences. A "wait and see" attitude is induced. Talking and thinking become more orderly, and apprehensiveness becomes an inference-checking game, leading to increased predictability.

In problems of a more serious kind, in which the individual's experiences have resulted in defense and adjustment mechanisms inaccessible to memory, and hence to revision, "thinking" may become a defense against further experience. The more unsane appear to see only sameness in events. Failure is built into each new interpersonal situation: "It's the same thing over again," "I know it won't do any good." Such statements lead to further limiting of experience, which in turn leads to further statements of the same kind—in a circular manner. Cases of this kind usually necessitate therapeutic techniques such as hypnosis and free association, which make possible the review of buried experiences. The review of such "lost" information makes possible a new time perspective, and hence changes in thinking and behavior patterns.

A third use of the Structural Differential, to review beliefs, is of key importance, since the inability to change beliefs is conspicuous among the maladjusted and unsane. In a recent article, A. E. Emerson maintains that modifiability of the cell accounts for the adaptability and survival of the species, and suggests that modifiability of our verbal environment or change of beliefs may likewise be essential for human survival. Certainly we see unmodifiability of belief or rigidity of thinking as an underlying symptom of varying degrees of pathology. Brock Chisholm has gone so far as to suggest that the survival of the human class of life may depend on the development of successful methods for the review and revision of beliefs. Our experience in counseling has been that exploration of beliefs is simplified by the use of the Structural Differential, and proves to be a relatively nonthreatening procedure compared with ordinary verbal discourse. The technique is provisionally to accept any beliefs uttered by the counselee and to classify them on the talk$_3$ level. Then descriptive data are sought ("How did you come to these conclusions?") at the talk$_1$ level. As the counselee, in the atmosphere created by the counselor, examines his talk$_3$ as it relates to his talk$_1$, alternative judgments and hypotheses emerge, which then become topics for research and validation.

In deeper degrees of pathology the ability to revise beliefs appears lost. Deeply delusional persons cannot even imagine other ways of looking at or talking about problem situations. And in some cases projection of "blame" onto others seems "logical" to account for beliefs unacceptable to the self. So too in these more serious cases there is *absolute certainty* of belief, even about how *others* feel. Yet the pathological person cannot check or test his beliefs. Here again the role of the counselor-therapist is to allow an atmosphere for gradual validity-testing, by accepting *any* perceptual or verbal information, whatever its content or imagery. With the emergence of historical experiences and reactions, the behavior, the meanings, the verbalized conclusions are reviewed and re-evaluated.

One last example, a relatively common problem, is the physician-referred individual showing variable psychosomatic symptoms suggesting history-determined situational stress, with no medically accountable causes or structural pathology. One such person showed an overdependent relationship to his wife, with tensions seemingly relieved only by occasional temper outbursts followed by remorse and new vows to "control and forget." Effective release of tensions and a new attitude came gradually when lost experiences revealed reactions to the birth of a sibling followed shortly by abandonment by the mother. Overtly expressed resentments of the mother apparently were evaluated as *the* cause of mother's departure, which led to fear of *any* expression of hostility—for fear of new loss—and the now largely automatic pattern of control.

To sum up: by structuring a program for research, by creating a role of sympathetic understanding, by making possible the exchange and free flow of information, and by discussing techniques for proper evaluation, there appears to result a diminishing of compulsive, history-determined behavior, and an apparent increase of choice; in many cases a transformation of attitudes takes place, from the certitudes characteristic of the immature, to incertitude and probability, or what approximates a mature orientation. Increasing adjustability develops as the research program becomes the formulating, structuring, and testing of a series of probability assertions or hypotheses in terms of observable or predictable consequences.

In my experience I have found general semantics indispensable in therapeutic counseling. Knowledge of general semantics increases the counselor's awareness of the specific mechanisms of misevaluation involved in maladjustment and offers him a point of departure in the therapeutic program for which he might otherwise have to grope for a much longer time. For the counselee, instruction in elementary general semantics—for example, learning to differentiate between reports, inferences, judgments, and hypotheses; learning to differentiate levels of abstraction; learning to distinguish between two-valued and multivalued approaches to problems; acquiring the habit of "dating" and "indexing" one's statements; learning about the processes of abstracting and projecting; becoming aware of the common assumptions underlying our ways of perceiving, feeling, and talking about ourselves and others, etc.—gives him a way of *evaluating his own evaluations*, instead of having to submit to (or defend himself against) a counselor's diagnostic judgments.

Hence the emphasis in this paper on the counselor and counselee as a "research team." With the theory provided by the counselor and the information provided by the counselee, the two together examine the counselee's present and past evaluations to see wherein they depart from the "natural (sane) order of evaluation," and to discover in what respects revisions are necessary or possible. It is the impersonality of the approach that does the job, arousing the minimum of defensiveness on the part of the counselee, and stimulating profoundly his interest and intellectual curiosity in the mechanisms of evaluation and misevaluation.

Winter, 1955-56. Dr. Pemberton lives in Mill Valley, California, and is a consultant in psychology and executive methods in Mill Valley and San Francisco. He is a member of the Psychology Examining Committee of the Board of Medical Examiners of the State of California. His paper was presented at the Second Conference on General Semantics, Washington University, St. Louis, June 12, 1954.

The Significance of Being Unique

EARL C. KELLEY

People have a tendency to look askance at those who are different from most other people and especially at those who are so indiscreet as to let their differences show. We give lip service to rugged individualism but bridle when an individual permits himself to be too individualistic. This is noted not only in politics, which is apt to come to mind first, but in clothing, manners, haircuts, tastes, opinions, and attitudes. It is my purpose here to attempt to show that the ways in which an individual is different from all others are not only his most priceless possession, but that these differences are at the very foundation of our society, that they are essential to a democratic society, and that they should be cherished rather than frowned upon.

That no two individuals are alike is too obvious to need elaboration. No two leaves in a forest, no two blades of grass in a pasture can be found to match exactly. Anyone can see that each human being differs from any other not only in physical appearance, but in habits, attitudes, prejudices, and all other attributes which motivate behavior. This holds true in all living things, although the simpler the organism, the less marked the differences appear to be. This principle can doubtless be extended into the inanimate world, but here we are concerned with living things, especially humans.

Nature must cherish uniqueness, because it has gone to great lengths to provide it. I use the word "nature" to identify the creative force in the universe which is known by many names by different people. This should satisfy everyone except those who hold to the mechanistic theory of creation. This creative force, for which I use the word "nature," is continuous; it is now going on, developing an evolving universe. The creative process is not something which was done at one time and finished.

If nature did not cherish uniqueness, not so much would have been done to achieve such infinite variety, for this variety was hard to bring about.

First, nature has provided that no two organisms start life with the same physical equipment. This was accomplished primarily by the development of heterosexual reproduction. By this device, whereby each new individual is made up of parts of two parents, it became almost completely impossible for two individuals to start life with the same structure, with the rare exception of identical twins. The means by which it is assured that no two individuals will have the same cellular structure with which to start life is too complicated to include here, but it was hard come by in the evolution of living things. Considering that uniqueness is essential to the higher development of living forms, the development of heterosexual reproduction stands as perhaps nature's greatest invention since the formation of living protoplasm.

In addition to a unique physical structure, we now have much evidence to show that the cells also provide for unique purpose. In fact, it appears that all living tissue is uniquely purposive. The word "purpose" is used here, somewhat more broadly than is usual, to include all drives, both conscious and unconscious. It indicates the path down which an individual's energies can most easily be spent. The fact that we all have individualized conscious purposes is well known. What ones likes to do, another may not. These can be consciously modified. I can *make* myself eat mashed squash, for example. But most of the individual's purposes are below the level of consciousness and cannot be changed. They are evidently carried in the cell structure, and they operate automatically. Perhaps they are what psychologists have called drives, but there appears to be no need of two words, one for the conscious and another for the unconscious, since the one is merely a continuation of the other.

Having endowed the individual with unique physical structure including its own special set of purposes, nature has further devised ways by which psychological man must be unique in his knowledge and his attitudes. Habits, attitudes, prejudices are as much a part of one's structure as hand, nose, or foot. We can see this when we understand that a structure *is* what it *does*. These psychological factors, not the physical ones, are what control behavior. One can be a demon or a saint with the same physical equipment. In speaking of the psychological self, there is no intention to create another duality. The psychological and the physical are not independent of one another, but the organism operates as a whole—a totality. Because the total organism is all one functioning unit is no reason why we cannot speak of hand, foot, or attitude separately.

The psychological part of the functioning unit which we call a human being is built through the operation of the phenomenon called perception. Perception is what comes into consciousness when stimuli—light, sound, touch, taste, and odors—impinge upon the body from the outside. It is not here intended to deny the existence of extrasensory perception, about which little is known, but to confine this discussion to the "senses" which are obvious to all. With this possible exception, sensory perception is the only means by which one knows anything about what is around him. Organisms can live without perception, but such a life would be like that of a tree, for example, unaware of surroundings and victim of unfavorable environment without being able to modify that environment in any way. So life, as we think of it, depends upon our ability to perceive.

Quite recently we have gained new understandings concerning the nature of perception through the work of the late Adelbert A. Ames, Jr., of Hanover, New Hampshire. Through his laboratory work and his brilliant interpretations of what his visual demonstrations show, we can understand the nature of perception much better than before. It has been thought by most people that perception was very simple; that one merely looked at an object, saw what it was, and that this settled the matter. The object from which the light rays came was the important part of the process, and the person receiving the rays was merely a receptor, took what came to him, and had no control over it. Ames has shown us that we, through our interpretation, make an object what we can, that we never see anything exactly as it is, and that no two people interpret any object exactly the same. Of course, in the case of common, inanimate objects, the difference may be slight, but in uncommon and in animate objects, such as other people, the difference may be very great.

We do not see everything in our surroundings. To do so would bring us such a mass of data, most of them unimportant, that we could not comprehend all of it or deal with it. We, therefore, select what we will see and what we will ignore. The much greater part of our surroundings we ignore.

We see what we select out of our environment, and we select on the basis of two factors. First, we see what we have experience to see. But experience is not enough to account for the selection, because in any scene there are many things with which we have had experience, but which we do not see. The second determining factor is that we see what we purpose to see. This brings into consciousness not only those objects for which we may be looking, but also the ones that are in keeping with our unconscious purposes.

When men are criticized by their wives because they do not notice the curtains in the living room of the hostess and are accused of being unobserving, they can take comfort in the fact that curtains do not fall within the scope of their purposes, and they may even imply that their purposes include only more important matters.

Since no two people can have the same experiences, it follows that each person is unique from all others in this regard. And since each person's purposes appear to be uniquely established when the individual starts life, it can be seen that no two individuals can perceive any object or other person in exactly the same way. What we perceive is added to what we already have as experience and becomes part of the unique experiential background of each individual. It is built into the structure of the psychological self. And so, as we go about uniquely perceiving and adding this to an already unique background, we become more and more different from others as we go along.

This building process makes each person the center of his own universe. He looks out upon the world with "different eyes" from those of any other person. And no one can completely know any other person, because he has to view that person with his own particular equipment of experience and purpose. It also gives each person knowledge no one else has, and the ability to make a contribution to a common problem, if the opportunity comes, which no one else can make. This is a scientific basis for the oft-affirmed belief in the worth and dignity of every human being. The individual is the creator of his own universe, and thus we can see the fallacy of the older belief that the outside object is what is most important in the perceptive process.

The foregoing is intended to show, briefly, how unique each individual is from all others, and how nature has contrived that it be so, first, by furnishing each his own special physical start and then providing that in what he knows, he is continuously built in the direction of greater and greater difference.

Specialization and Democracy

The values which come to the individual from being different from all others are great. Perhaps that is why nature sets such great store by them and has gone to such length to provide them.

The fact that an individual is unique assures him a special place and special worth in his own society. It is precisely because he is different that it is possible for him to make contributions to the welfare of others, and to develop anything that could be called a society. If people were really alike, as we often seem to wish they were; if everyone had the same experiential background, the same knowledge, and the same skills that everybody else had, there would be nothing that individuals could do together. This is true because no one would know anything that all others did not know and hence would not be able to add anything to a common objective. Hence there could be no society but simply a collection of individuals, each going his own way, accomplishing little, because no one can do very much just by himself.

Differences between individuals make specialization possible. All progress depends upon specialization. By progress I do not necessarily mean improvement, but change from the simpler to the more complex. It is specialization which has made it possible for living things to move from the stage of the single cell to the immensely complicated forms of life we now know, culminating in the human body and personality. The amoeba, for example, has probably not progressed for millions of years, and this is doubtless due to the fact that the individuals are so much alike that specialization has not been possible.

No organism can develop much without specialization of its cells so that some cells perform special functions for the whole, and others perform other functions. The human body, most complicated of all living forms, is made up of billions of cells with groups of cells specialized to perform special functions. These billions of cells co-operate in an amazing fashion to bring about the healthy individual. Sometimes, for some reason not well understood, some of these cells cease to co-operate, going off on their own, and this is what is called cancer. This lack of co-operation usually destroys the whole organism.

And so it is in society, which is a co-operating collection of individuals, just as a living organism is a co-operating collection of cells. Individuals perform special tasks for all so that one does not have to make his own watch or his own shoes. All social progress depends upon this specialization which is possible because of individual differences.

Our society, contrary to opinions commonly held, is the most co-operative one that has ever existed. While many cherish the thought that it is highly competitive and enjoy the thought that individuals are primarily bent on the defeat and perhaps the destruction of others, the fact is that most people are working co-operatively in such close relationships that if anyone fails to do his special part, the whole fails. It takes two hundred people, I am told, to produce a pair of nylon hose; thousands have to co-operate to produce one automobile.

It is in part because of this social co-operation that our fear of Communists has been so great. It is said that one Communist, rightly placed, could destroy the electric power of a whole city. It is probably true that he could do so. Loss of electric power would devastate any modern city, so dependent on others have we become. What we fear this one Communist might do is to cease to co-operate.

We can now see, since all progress is made possible by differences, specialization and co-operation, that co-operation is the basic method of progress for all living things. The law of the jungle is not an eye for an eye and a tooth for a tooth, but mutual aid. Below the level of humans, living things rarely prey on their own kind—rarely take more than they need.

The "rugged individualist" who fancies himself a self-made man would be utterly helpless without the co-operation of others made possible by their differences. Even the hermit miser has to have somebody to make that which he hoards. If he tries to make his own, he will be accused of failing to co-operate with the specialists in that field and will be thrown in jail.

The fact that every individual is unique and is uniquely purposive gives scientific support to the democratic ideal. This support from science will strengthen the position of people who believe in the democratic way of life. The democratic ideal, in one form or another, has been a powerful force in the affairs of men, but it is always helpful and strengthening to find that any idea is not just an opinion, but has backing in the very nature of the organism.

Basically, there are only two ways by which a person may be governed. Either he governs himself, within the social scene, or he is governed by someone else. Fascism, Nazism, Communism are all alike in that they are based upon the submerging of the individual and the elevation of another individual or some abstraction, such as the state. The history of the human race has been a continual struggle by which certain individuals have sought to gain domination over others. This domination is a matter of degree, but it is all slavery in a degree. There is very little difference in the attitude toward the common people of Hitler, Mussolini, or Stalin and that of Simon Legree. All of these "masters" held the individual to be a means to an end—their end—and to be devoid of any value in themselves.

When I speak of the individual governing himself within the social scene, I mean that, of course, no individual is ever free to do just as he pleases but has always to consider the rights of others and take care not to invade those rights. If he does not control himself in regard to the rights of others, people will avoid him and deprive him of the benefits of social contact. Then it will not be possible for him to realize his unique potential, and take advantage of his special gifts, because these gifts have value only in relationship to other people. There is, however, a great latitude of freedom without impinging upon the rights of others and within the limits of the obligations of co-operation with others.

The notion of freedom within the bounds of one's responsibility to others does not seem to be comprehended by many people. I have known parents who said that their children were being brought up democratically but who appeared to have confused democracy with anarchy. Freedom without responsibility is anarchy. A family living together co-operatively puts obligations on every member automatically. There are no autocratic bonds half so strong as the feeling of co-operative responsibility. The autocrat cannot watch the individual he dominates all of the time, but no person can escape his own feeling of obligation. When the parent gives the child complete freedom without the responsibility implied in co-operation, the child becomes a tyrant. It is a sad fact of life that, in our present stage of development, someone is always trying to become a tyrant. Whenever anyone succeeds in becoming a tyrant, he automatically makes slaves.

The very fact that the individual is uniquely purposive implies the requirement of freedom. There is no value in being purposive unless one is, in considerable degree, free to pursue his purposes. This freedom is also essential to creativeness which is the growing edge of progress. It is not possible to be creative, to devise and contrive new solutions to problems, if someone else is dominating the thoughts and actions of the contriver. Slavery is not a good climate for creativity.

The fact that all individuals are unique also implies and requires a democratic way of life. It is to the autocrat that differences are anathema. He needs to have individuals who are alike, lest their differences upset his plans for them. The person's unique value cannot be realized unless he is in a position of freedom to make use of it rather than to have it submerged.

The democratic ideal proclaims the worth of every human being, the dignity of the individual, and the right to freedom within the requirements of others. We now can see from biology and psychology that the individual has worth because he has something which nobody else has, and, if he is lost, something will be lost which can never be recaptured. Because of his unique purposes, he can do some things which nobody else can do so well. Freedom, only existent under democracy, is essential to the development of his unique qualities. Every person is entitled to live in dignity not only because it is decent, but because of his unique and irreplaceable values.

The struggle for freedom, which only democracy can furnish, has been going on since the beginning of human history. It has been and is a continuous struggle beginning long before democracy, biology, or psychology were ever heard of, and it will go on as long as there are those who would enslave. The ideal of freedom did not originate with Jefferson or with the barons at Runnymede. We can now come to see, from the very structure of the organism, why this is so. Tyranny has never triumphed in the long run, although the long run has been too long for millions of individuals. Nor can tyranny ever win, because it is opposed by such powerful natural forces. This is true of small tyrannies, such as occur in home and school, as well as the large tyrannies of governments. Tyrannies fail because they do not really attain the objectives which they seek.

Forces against Individualism

Considering the biological basis for uniqueness and the obvious advantages of it to the individual, how can we account for the fact that our culture is so antagonistic to it and does so much to reduce and, if it were possible, to destroy it? How account for the great emphasis on similarity? When man lived in nature, before he became "civilized," everything in his surroundings was unique. This was true because nature never produces two objects or situations which are alike. Nothing was standardized. Every coincidence, every set of circumstances, which man met was new. This called for new responses, new contriving. Old answers did not suffice. And so, man was continuously called upon to invent new responses to new circumstances. This continuous contriving called for the use and exercise of intelligence.

Intelligence is one's ability to contrive new solutions to ever-emerging situations or problems, the capacity to find ways out of dilemmas, to come upon answers which have never been found before, to invent, and to create. Intelligence is developed and expanded through use. It can only grow when the organism is confronted by new situations, where new solutions are called for. Intelligence gains great impetus in the natural world, where all is unique; it gets little chance to develop in a standardized world where answers are already provided and where one answer can be used again and again. When man allows himself to be standardized, he unwittingly robs himself of the opportunity for intellectual development. Through industrialization and its consequent urbanization, man has largely moved from a unique world to a standardized world and thus, in large degree, he has allowed himself to be removed from the need for and the opportunity to develop intelligence.

There are two powerful factors, one very old and one very new, which have worked away from differences in humans and toward an emphasis on similarity. The old one is authoritarianism; the new one is the effect of the machine. There are doubtless many other factors producing these results, but these two seem to be the most important.

Authoritarianism is the situation where one or many individuals is under the domination of another; where the dominator substitutes his own purposes for those of the dominated; where controls and purposes come to the dominated from the outside; where decisions are made and answers provided, not by one's own structure, purpose, and experience, but by those of another.

In spite of our democratic form of government, which works well considering the number of people involved, our culture is almost completely authoritarian, if one considers the day-to-day lives of the people who live in it. Authoritarianism probably started when the first man naïvely sought to gain advantage over his fellows for his own benefit. The notion is naïve because man cannot really profit, except in a narrow and superficial materialistic way, by gaining domination over his peers. By gaining advantage over his peers, he drives them away from him, and thus deprives himself of their unique value. The qualities of being human can be secured only from other humans, and, when one deprives himself of others, he robs himself. Cut off from his human sources, he comes to have less of the attributes of a human being as time goes on.

Not seeing that this deprivation will occur, seeing only the nearby gains, it is perhaps to be expected that authoritarianism would develop. The notion that in the family, for example, somebody has to be the boss was easily come by, since better ways of living together had not been thought out. So father and mother waged a war to see who would "wear the pants," a language symbol implying that it ought to be the father, but that it often is not so. This struggle is joined by the child who, while still in the cradle, may become the autocrat.

Authoritarianism has been powerfully augmented by philosophical ideas and by the operation of institutions. The church has adopted it, seemingly feeling the need of authoritarianism to control its followers who find themselves cast in the role of petitioners for an agreeable immortality which they believe the church has to dispense. Being a petitioner puts one in the position of being unworthy and calls for an admission of guilt. Fear of being denied the boons believed to be held or withheld by the church deepens the sense of guilt and unworthiness until it becomes an all-pervading concept of self which enters into every aspect of the individual's life. Fear of being denied the goods of the world to come, in a person already laden with an ever-present sense of guilt, calls for placating action, and so the supplicant offers repentance and atonement for his sins, further degrading his already low concept of self, causing him to become a person divided against himself.

Another powerful institution which has added greatly to the authoritarian nature of our culture is the school, both public and private. The school is, perhaps, even more influential than the church because it includes everybody, at least for a time. Not all schools, of course, are basically authoritarian in operation. There are principals of schools, just as there are ministers of churches, who take account of individual differences and operate with the development of each special human being as objective. But the basic pattern of schools in general is to ignore the individual and attempt to level out the differences between people.

Learners are ordinarily lined up in rows of seats, and many of them become anonymous, existing on the seating chart only as the one who sits in any particular place. They are required to do the same things and are expected to learn the same lessons. That which is to be learned comes either from the teacher or from a book—nothing from the self or other available selves. Everyone is evaluated by the same examinations, because each has been expected to learn the same things in the same way. In many schools, the examinations are the same not only for the individuals in a class, but between classes, nullifying the individuality of the teacher. The subject is the objective. In some localities, examinations are state-wide and are constructed by people who have never seen either the learners or the teachers. Area-wide examinations are no longer the general practice, but school-wide ones are still common.

There are many devices by which teachers and administrators attempt to reduce individuality among learners. It is frowned upon when a learner, through curiosity, knows something which is ahead of the lesson taught. Parents are often warned not to teach their young children to read, for then they will not be like the others and will not sit still while the others catch up. The standardized "lesson" requires that the learners be alike. School people try to negate or repeal the uniqueness that nature has established by sorting their students so that the teachers will have learners who are more alike than the random group would be. They can do this because the lesson, not the individual, is what matters. When they sort learners in this manner, they have to use some criterion, such as ability to read or IQ, but whatever criteria they use, the learners are all different except in this particular way. But then, if one does not care about social development, this is of no consequence. Indeed, social development is not ignored; it is frowned upon. The most cherished learner is the solitary one who never communicates with the human beings in the adjoining seats.

In some schools, learners are even required to wear uniforms to further reduce their individuality. This would doubtless be more common if parents would buy the uniforms. When school authorities start to tell people what to wear, individuality usually asserts itself, and rebellion is in the air. Other schools even attempt to repeal sex by putting boys and girls in different schools, perhaps to keep the fact of the existence of the other sex a secret.

When we in America established universal education—mass education—the disciples of the "subject" ran into trouble. Many learners were enrolled in school who had not been there before. Many of these newcomers could not or would not learn the lessons set out to be learned. This did not bring about a turn toward teaching for individual differences as might have been expected. Teachers began instead to weaken and "water down" the subject, with the result that a process of leveling out and down took place. This had to be in the direction of mediocrity, so that even those who had previously profited from the "lesson" no longer did so.

All of this striving for uniformity in our schools came from a false, authoritarian concept of the nature of knowledge. In the authoritarian scheme of things, that which lies outside the individual is that which is good. Knowledge was held to be apart from knowing, to lie outside the learner, mostly in books or the teacher's repetition of books. Knowledge could be had by acquisition, by reaching out and taking it. It seems plain now that knowledge and knowing are not separate. Knowledge is what we know after we have learned. It therefore comes after, not before, learning. Since all learning has to be done in the light of individual unique experience and purpose, knowledge is always subjectively held and is never the same as any other person's knowledge.

This authoritarian concept of the nature of knowledge is, indeed, deeply implanted, and it governs almost everything that goes on in our schools, thus adding greatly to the authoritarian nature of our culture. Every bit of learning which really takes place causes people to be more different rather than more alike.

Philosophers, down the ages, have supported and abetted authoritarian concepts for the most part, although, in recent times, there have been notable exceptions, the most important of which is John

Dewey. Most philosophers have not been able to grasp the idea of a changing, evolving universe, with the creative force still in effect, with creation still going on. Therefore, they have sought to find something immutable and stationary on which to hang their arguments. This immutable has to be something outside any individual or any physical thing, because people die, and things rust and crumble. So they have had to invent and cling to abstractions such as the good, the true, and the beautiful. These abstractions were far removed from the individual and were thought to be unassailable. The good lay outside of the individual, reducing his own worth. The precise point, it seems to me, where the philosophers have failed us is that they have not been able to encompass the concept of universal change, have tried to find a static starting point, and have thus given us a static philosophy which is untenable in an evolving universe. Where all is change, a philosopher needs to find his security in change.

Mechanistic and materialistic scientists, so prevalent in the nineteenth and early part of the twentieth centuries, have had their influence in strengthening the authoritarianism of our culture. To them, science was a simple matter, and so, therefore, was life simple. Their immutables were what they called the laws of science, which were nearly all discovered, and soon would be all settled. These laws operated outside individuals and without regard to them. Scientists made up these laws out of what they thought was experimental evidence, but before all of the evidence was seen. Nearly every immutable on which they based their laws has proven to be untrue. But these "scientific" pronouncements have had an enormous effect on the thinking of people. Relativity, the quantum theory, new light on the nature of energy, the destruction of the atom, the interchangeability of matter and energy, have played havoc with the immutable laws of mechanistic science, but they have not greatly altered the mind sets brought about by the teaching of these laws.

In addition to the effect of the authoritarianism on individual differences, we have also the powerful influence of the machine on our lives. I shall not dwell upon the leveling effect of the machine at length, because this has already been done better and more fully than I can do it here. The machine is a standardizer. It makes things all alike without regard for personal taste. We all buy the same things. We listen to the same music, see the same movies, hear the same news. We read the same boiler plate in our newspapers. Like the teacher, the maker of radio and television programs thinks he has to cater to the lowest tastes, and again we are pushed toward standardization and mediocrity, or just a notch below mediocrity. Some even advocate the use of television to replace the teacher so that every child in the land, every period of the day, will look at and listen to the same program every day. So even the little variation introduced by the individuality of the teacher (and many teachers valiantly try to bring about some variation) will be done away with.

Recently we tried to buy a toaster which was not of the "pop-up" variety. We happen to like an individual piece of toast, made by use of a thin piece of bread, personally supervised as to color, buttered, and eaten immediately. Our old toaster had been broken, and no one in any electrical shop would fix it, because parts that were no longer manufactured needed renewing. These parts would have to be made by hand. In every store, the salesman tried to sell us a "pop-up" toaster. If we did not like to have our toast jump at us at dawn, we simply were not in tune with the modern world. Indeed, it has become increasingly difficult to buy a loaf of bread which has not already been sliced, so that the thin piece of bread which we want for toast is hard to come by. "Take a piece of bread which we have established as standard, and parch it in a machine you won't have to watch and can't watch if you want to." But we beat them, perhaps for the last time. We found an amateur who made the parts we needed by hand. He was hard to find, and may be the last one extant.

The authoritarian cannot operate if he has to deal with many differences. He needs standardization and uniformity so that he can reduce the number of factors he has to control. Individual differences are poison to him. Therefore, great effort, is made to render people alike and to ignore what differences remain. In this effort, the authoritarian has been aided by the effect of the machine and its standardizing influence. The effect on individuals has been to cause them to accept what has come to them, not to try to solve problems but to accept ready-made answers. In the degree that people succumb, they have very little use for intelligence, and their intellectual powers become fallow from want of exercise. Not needing to contrive, they are not creative. They constitute a drab society, although many of them have been "educated."

Individuality and the Changing Universe

A person's uniqueness is his most priceless possession. It gives him his reason to be. Powerful forces in our culture seek to reduce or eliminate these differences between people. Now I shall attempt to indicate some ways by which uniqueness may be nourished and developed.

I shall not propose that we return to the good old days when man lived close to nature. Living close to nature was good for the development of uniqueness and for the exercise of man's intelligence, but in many ways such living was not good. For one thing, living in nature was too burdensome; it took too much human energy to produce enough material to support life. Nature was always trying to reclaim the space which had been cleared for raising food. The struggle was continuous and exhausting.

While the machine has had a great standardizing effect on man, its benefits have been enormous. Through its use of energy other than human energy to do work, it has lifted much of the load off the backs of men so that they are able to devote time and attention to better aspects of life. We could not, of course, do away with the machine even if we wanted to. Therefore, we have to learn to live with it, so that the machine is the servant, not the master, of man.

One time during the depths of the depression, I was riding with two others in a car past a place where a steam shovel was excavating a hole for a basement. One said, "Now that's the trouble with us. If that hole was being dug by men with shovels, we wouldn't have all this unemployment and economic stagnation." "Yes," replied the other, "and if all those men had teaspoons instead of shovels, we would all be even richer."

We need to modify our institutions so that they will value human differences. We need to learn how to live with the machine so that it will serve us, rather than control us.

The church could abandon fear as a device in controlling people. It could teach proper relations between people and the universe, including the creative force which many call God, without teaching disrespect of self. It is not necessary to indulge in self-defamation in order to be on good terms with other people, the universe, and the deity in whatever form the individual conceives it. Conformity and expiation are not really essentials for religion. The development of the whole social being is just as feasible through the church as it is in a home and the school. Religion need not rest upon mysticism. It is safer in a changing world when it is based upon the individual's relationship to the universe and all that is in it. This relationship is a continuously changing and emerging one. Self-defamation causes one to lose sight of his own special value.

The best hope of democratizing our culture seems to me to lie with the modification of the school. The home and the church have enormous influence, but they are less accessible. The public school is established, supported and controlled by the people, and any time that the people desire more democratic schools, they can have them. The best way to modify the home is through the school, because most of the students in any school, particularly any high school, will be parents in a few years. The difficulty with parent education as it is now conceived is that it is hard to get access to the parents, especially those needing the education most. The best time to inform a mother concerning parenthood is while she is available in high school, not after she has graduated and already has a baby to take care of. This is not to depreciate the work of those engaged in parent education, but only to point to the opportunities readily available in the school.

The public school, such as we have in America and some other countries, where free education through high school is available to all, is one of the truly great social inventions of all time. It is a readily available agent for social growth which, if we did not have it, would be almost impossible to create. It has many truly dedicated teachers and administrators. It is a giant, with more power for good than any giant ever dreamed of in fairy tales, where anything can happen. But it is a sleeping giant, busying itself in a dream world of the past, not aware of its potentialities. Its attention is on "knowledge" of the past, not seeing the humans of the present, not realizing that there is no knowledge until some one has learned.

If this sleeping giant can be aroused and its attention drawn to its potentialities in the building of adequate human beings equipped to live in a democracy, confident and courageous in the face of the problems which are constantly emerging for each new graduating class (I started to say "each new generation," but new problems emerge much too rapidly for that), then great changes for the better can be brought about in a reasonably short time.

First, the teacher needs to direct his attention to the learner, rather than to the subject. Not that there is anything wrong or evil about subject matter. Subject matter is essential to all learning, since one cannot learn without learning something. But it makes a great deal of difference whether subject matter is an end, or the means to an end. If the end or goal of teaching is the subject, it cannot be the learner. The goal of education should be adequate people, and any subject matter which serves that goal is good.

Teachers need to recognize and nourish individual differences and realize that no item of subject matter is good for everybody or can be assimilated by everybody. There is no very good reason why everyone in a class has to work at the same thing at the same time. Since human beings are unique in interest and ability, it is not really possible for them to do so. The learners we often call gifted can work in areas which challenge them while others find enterprises suited to their special capabilities. Release from the tyranny of the subject can bring an end to the leveling out and watering down process which has been so harmful to learning.

The school is a miniature society with most of the problems of the large society. Through mutual consultation among students, teachers, and administrators, and through honest student participation in school government, individuals can become functioning parts in this society. Such consultation can give each person experience in the operation of a good society and respect for the opinions and peculiarities of others. Experience in good living and in the operation of a good society will serve the individual throughout his life as he brings his influence to bear upon the larger society. The way for youth to learn how to live well in the future is to live well now.

Consultation and involvement in the operation of the school will tend to improve the learner's concept of self. No one can be an effective citizen in a democratic society if he regards himself as inferior. When one does not like what he sees when he looks at himself, he tries to lose himself through identification with the mob, the mass. In a mass, his self can become anonymous. We have many people who identify themselves with "causes," the better to hide themselves. Authoritarian teachers, not so crudely as this, say to their charges in effect, "You don't know anything. I do. So I will tell you. You are to speak when you are called upon. You'd better not stick your neck out." The symbol of the turtle in its shell is an interesting one. A few years of being told one is unworthy is pretty convincing, and so self-haters are built.

To be consulted and to be treated as an individual allows self-respect to develop and grow.

Young people in schools need to have opportunities to do things of their own and on their own. This calls for much doing, rather than so much listening and reading. In this doing, the learner is faced with real contriving and has to use and exercise his intelligence in order to find solutions, in order to get answers. This drives him, not to his desk alone, but to the machine shop, the library, the community. Education is thus broadened and made to deal with the current scene. The contemporary world becomes the prime educator.

Emphasis on problem-solving leads to creativity and to the arts. Creativity is not just a matter of making great pictures or composing great music. It encompasses all that is contrived that is new. Everyone who contrives new answers to problems, new ways to solve dilemmas, creates. Art, in this sense, comes naturally to all who have a chance to contrive. As for that which is now usually called art—painting, ceramics, music, and so on—the creative value of those activities can be greatly enhanced by giving freedom to the creative urge of the learner. There are many art classes in our schools today where creativity is eliminated by the demands of the teacher. The drawing teacher insists that pictures be made to look as she sees the subject, not as the student sees it. Art, then, becomes a matter of copying rather than creating. This applies to all artistic activities which could be so liberating. We have much discipline trouble in our music appreciation classes, because our learners are required to listen, not do, and to appreciate that which they have little opportunity to understand. Appreciation comes after understanding, not before it. Many aspects of creative living will become possible when the sleeping giant awakes.

Living in nature had great benefits for man, but of course we cannot all return to nature. Industrialization has caused many of us to become city dwellers. City living has a standardizing effect on people, because the city environment repeats itself, whereas nature never does. Since urban living is an established fact, we need to do more to bring nature to the city dweller. This calls for more parks, larger parks where nature can be more closely simulated, more opportunities for recreation. Nature itself is recreating in its effect on people. Much has, of course, already been done in this direction, but we need much more, so that the city will no longer be so confining in its effect. Slums are the worst places for people to live from the standpoint of uniqueness. Whenever a slum is cleared, space is provided, everyone gains not only in human terms, but in economic terms as well. The automobile has been a great boon to city dwellers because, through its use, people no longer need to live near the factories and offices where they work. They can live out where there is more space and more opportunity for individuality to be nourished. We are having a hard time, however, learning how to live with the automobile and not die in it.

Learning to live with the machine, gaining its benefits without losing our uniqueness, is one of the great problems of our present society. The use of television, for example, poses such a problem. Television should be a great boon to mankind, but, because we let it use us instead of our using it, it has become a standardizer with grave consequences. Although watching television will probably always lack a good deal from the standpoint of participation, programs could be built which would at least make people think and not call for a stock response with its resulting standardizing effect on people. Great music and great plays, for example, do not call for stock responses but bring forth individual, personal responses. That is one reason why they are great.

Television is a good example of a canned activity, a standardizing triumph of the machine. Living in a machine age, we need to educate our young away from canned activities which do not call for unique responses. Using television as a baby sitter to keep Junior out of Mother's hair educates toward mediocrity and establishes habits of retreat from life. We can own television sets without deliberately training the young to be undiscriminating and without developing habits of retreat. We hear parents complain of their children's passion for comic books, but you can go into almost any living room on Sunday and see Daddy on the floor reading the "funny" paper to his two-year-old. The funny paper is not funny, and it is not written for children—chronological children, that is. But there Daddy is, training his child to become a comic book addict, about which he will later complain.

Avoiding such actions as using television and the comic sheet to "amuse" little children is an illustration of a way by which we can educate away from activities which call for canned responses and a way by which we can learn to live with the machine and its products without allowing it to reduce our individuality.

Perhaps the most all-inclusive thing we can do for individuality is to learn how to live in a changing universe. The fact of change, unless it is indeed a denial of "fact," seems to be one thing we can be sure of. Those who seek an unchanging base on which to stand will always be disappointed and will always be out of tune with the universe. The immutable, if it could be found, or if one thinks he has found it, calls for rigidity and similarity. To some degree, each individual who stands on the immutable blocks the ongoing movement of the creative force which he needs, rather, to facilitate. The person who learns to accept change and looks forward to it has the only security available to humans. He does not know what tomorrow will be like, but he knows it will be different from today. He is glad that this is so, he looks forward to this new tomorrow, and in this, he feels secure. In accepting change, he understands that people are unique and learns to cherish their differences.

Spring, 1957. Dr. Kelley is professor of secondary education at Wayne State University and author of Education for What Is Real *(1947),* The Workshop Way of Learning *(1951), and coauthor of* Education and the Nature of Man *(1952).*

Toward a Theory of Creativity

CARL R. ROGERS

I maintain that there is a desperate social need for the creative behavior of creative individuals. It is this which justifies the setting forth of a tentative theory of creativity—the nature of the creative act, the conditions under which it occurs, and the manner in which it may constructively be fostered. Such a theory may serve as a stimulus and guide to research studies in this field.

The Social Need

Many of the serious criticisms of our culture and its trends may best be formulated in terms of a dearth of creativity. Let us state some of these very briefly:

In education we tend to turn out conformists, stereotypes, individuals whose education is "completed," rather than freely creative and original thinkers.

In our leisure time activities, passive entertainment, and regimented group action are overwhelmingly predominant while creative activities are much less in evidence.

In the sciences, there is an ample supply of technicians, but the number who can creatively formulate fruitful hypotheses and theories is small indeed.

In industry, creation is reserved for the few—the manager, the designer, the head of the research department—while for the many life is devoid of original or creative endeavor.

In individual and family life the same picture holds true. In the clothes we wear, the food we eat, the books we read, and the ideas we hold, there is a strong tendency toward conformity, toward stereotypy. To be original, or different, is felt to be "dangerous."

Why be concerned over this? If, as a people, we enjoy conformity rather than creativity, should we not be permitted this choice? In my estimation such a choice would be entirely reasonable were it not for one great shadow which hangs over all of us. In a time when knowledge, constructive and destructive, is advancing by the most incredible leaps and bounds into a fantastic atomic age, genuinely creative adaptation seems to represent the only possibility that man can keep abreast of the kaleidoscopic change in his world. With scientific discovery and invention proceeding, we are told, at the rate of geometric progression, a generally passive and culture-bound people cannot cope with the multiplying issues and problems. Unless individuals, groups, and nations can imagine, construct, and creatively revise new ways of relating to these complex changes, the lights will go out. Unless man can make new and original adaptations to his environment as rapidly as his science can change the environment, our culture will perish. Not only individual maladjustment and group tensions, but international annihilation will be the price we pay for a lack of creativity.

Consequently it would seem to me that investigations of the process of creativity, the conditions under which this process occurs, and the ways in which it may be facilitated, are of the utmost importance.

It is in the hope of suggesting a conceptual structure under which such investigations might go forward, that the following sections are offered.

The Creative Process

There are various ways of defining creativity. In order to make more clear the meaning of what is to follow, let me present the elements which, for me, are a part of the creative process, and then attempt a definition.

In the first place, for me as scientist, there must be something observable, some product of creation. Though my fantasies may be extremely novel, they cannot usefully be defined as creative unless they eventuate in some observable product—unless they are symbolized in words, or written in a poem, or translated into a work of art, or fashioned into an invention.

These products must be novel constructions. This novelty grows out of the unique qualities of the individual in his interaction with the materials of experience. Creativity always has the stamp of the individual upon its product, but the product is not the individual, nor his materials, but partakes of the relationship between the two.

Creativity is not, in my judgment, restricted to some particular content. I am assuming that there is no fundamental difference in the creative process as it is evidenced in painting a picture, composing a symphony, devising new instruments of killing, developing a scientific theory, discovering new procedures in human relationships, or creating new formings of one's own personality as in psychotherapy. (Indeed it is my experience in this last field, rather than in one of the arts, which has given me special interest in creativity and its facilitation. Intimate knowledge of the way in which the individual remolds himself in the therapeutic relationship, with originality and effective skill, gives one confidence in the creative potential of all individuals.)

My definition, then, of the creative process is that it is the emergence in action of a novel relational product, growing out of the uniqueness of the individual on the one hand, and the materials, events, people, or circumstances of his life on the other.

Let me append some negative footnotes to this definition. It makes no distinction between "good" and "bad" creativity. One man may be discovering a way of relieving pain, while another is devising a new and more subtle form of torture for political prisoners. Both these actions seem to me creative, even though their social value is very different. Though I shall comment on these social valuations later, I have avoided putting them in my definition because they are so fluctuating. Galileo and Copernicus made creative discoveries which in their own day were evaluated as blasphemous and wicked, and in our day as basic and constructive. We do not want to cloud our definition with terms which rest in subjectivity.

Another way of looking at this same issue is to note that to be regarded historically as representing creativity, the product must be acceptable to some group at some point of time. This fact is not helpful to our definition, however, both because of the fluctuating valuations already mentioned, and also because many creative products have undoubtedly never been socially noticed, but have disappeared without ever having been evaluated. So this concept of group acceptance is also omitted from our definition.

In addition, it should be pointed out that of definition makes no distinction regarding the degree of creativity, since this too is a value of judgment extremely variable in nature. The action of the child inventing a new game with his playmates; Einstein formulating a theory of relativity; the housewife devising a new sauce for the meat; a young author writing his first novel; all of these are, in terms of our definition, creative, and there is no attempt to set them in some order of more or less creative.

The Motivation for Creativity

The mainspring of creativity appears to be the same tendency which we discover so deeply as the curative force in psychotherapy—*man's tendency to actualize himself, to become his potentialities*. By this I mean the directional trend which is evident in all organic and human life—the urge to expand, extend, develop, mature—the tendency to express and activate all the capacities of the organism, to the extent that such activation enhances the organism or the self. This tendency may become deeply buried under layer after layer of encrusted psychological defenses; it may be hidden behind elaborate façades which deny its existence; it is my belief however, based on my experience, that it exists in every individual, and awaits only the proper conditions to be released and expressed. It is this tendency which is the primary motivation for creativity as the organism forms new relationships to the environment in its endeavor most fully to be itself.

Let us now attempt to deal directly with this puzzling issue of the social value of a creative act. Presumably few of us are interested in facilitating creativity which is socially destructive. We do not wish, knowingly, to lend our efforts to developing individuals whose creative genius works itself out in new and better ways of robbing, exploiting, torturing, killing, other individuals; or developing forms of political organization or art forms which lead humanity into paths of physical or psychological self-destruction. Yet how is it possible to make the necessary discriminations such that we may encourage a constructive creativity and not a destructive?

The distinction cannot be made by examining the product. The very essence of the creative is its novelty, and hence we have no standard by which to judge it. Indeed history points up the fact that the more original the product, and the more far-reaching its implications, the more likely it is to be judged by comtemporaries as evil. The genuinely significant creation, whether an idea, or a work of art, or a scientific discovery, is most likely to be seen at first as erroneous, bad, or foolish. Later it may be seen as obvious, something self-evident to all. Only still later does it receive its final evaluation as a creative contribution. It seems clear that no contemporary mortal can satisfactorily evaluate a creative product at the time that it is formed, and this statement is increasingly true the greater the novelty of the creation.

Nor is it of any help to examine the purposes of the individual participating in the creative process. Many, perhaps most, of the creations and discoveries which have proved to have great social value, have been motivated by purposes having more to do with personal interest than with social value, while on the other hand history records a somewhat sorry outcome for many of those creations (various Utopias, Prohibition, etc.) which had as their avowed purpose the achievement of the social good. No, we must face the fact that the individual creates primarily because it is satisfying to him, because this behavior is felt to be self-actualizing, and we get nowhere by trying to differentiate "good" and "bad" purposes in the creative process.

Must we then give over any attempt to discriminate between creativity which is potentially constructive, and that which is potentially destructive? I do not believe this pessimistic conclusion is justified. It is here that recent clinical findings from the field of psychotherapy give us hope. It has been found that when the individual is "open" to all of his experience (a phase which will be defined more fully), then his behavior will be creative, and his creativity may be trusted to be essentially constructive.

The differentiation may be put very briefly as follows. To the extent that the individual is denying to awareness (or repressing, if you prefer that term) large areas of his experience, then his creative formings may be pathological, or socially evil, or both. To the degree that the individual is open to all aspects of his experience, and has available to his awareness all the varied sensings and perceivings which are going on within his organism, then the novel products of his interaction with his environment will tend to be constructive both for himself and others. To illustrate, an individual with paranoid tendencies may creatively develop a most novel theory of the relationship between himself and his environment, seeing evidence for his theory in all sorts of minute clues. His theory has little social value, perhaps because there is an enormous range of experience which this individual cannot permit in his awareness. Socrates, on the other hand, while also regarded as "crazy" by his contemporaries, developed novel ideas which have proven to be socially constructive. Very possibly this was because he was notably nondefensive and open to his experience.

The reasoning behind this will perhaps become more clear in the remaining sections of this paper. Primarily however it is based upon the discovery in psychotherapy

... that if we can add to the sensory and visceral experiencing which is characteristic of the whole animal kingdom the gift of a free and undistorted awareness of which only the human animal seems fully capable, we have an organism which is as aware of the demands of the culture as it is of its own physiological demands for food or sex; which is just as aware of its desire for friendly relationships as it is of its desire to aggrandize itself; which is just as aware of its delicate and sensitive tenderness toward others as it is of its hostilities toward others. When man's unique capacity of awareness is thus functioning freely and fully, we find that we have, not an animal whom we must fear, not a beast who must be controlled, but an organism able to achieve, through the remarkable integrative capacity of its central nervous system, a balanced, realistic, self-enhancing, other-enhancing behavior as a resultant of all these elements of awareness. To put it another way, when man is less than fully man—when he denies to awareness various aspects of his experience—then indeed we have all too often reason to fear him and his behavior, as the present world situation testifies. But when he is most fully man, when he is his complete organism, when awareness of experience, that peculiarly human attribute, is most fully operating, then he is to be trusted, then his behavior is constructive. It is not always conventional. It will not always be conforming. It will be individualized. But it will also be socialized.[1]

The Inner Conditions of Constructive Creativity

What are the conditions within the individual which are most closely associated with a potentially constructive creative act? I see these as possibilities:

[1] From "Some of the Directions and End Points of Therapy," by Carl R. Rogers, in *Psychotherapy—Theory and Research Methods*, ed. by O. H. Mowrer (New York: Ronald Press, 1953).

A. OPENNESS TO EXPERIENCE: EXTENSIONALITY. This is the opposite of psychological defensiveness, when to protect the organization of the self, certain experiences are prevented from coming into awareness except in distorted fashion. In a person who is open to experience each stimulus is freely relayed through the nervous system, without being distorted by any process of defensiveness. Whether the stimulus originates in the environment, in the impact of form, color, or sound on the sensory nerves, or whether it originates in the viscera, or as a memory trace in the central nervous system, it is available to awareness. This means that instead of perceiving in predetermined categories ("trees are green," "college education is good," "modern art is silly"), the individual is aware of this existential moment as it *is*, thus being alive to many experiences which fall outside the usual categories (*this* tree is lavender; *this* college education is damaging; *this* modern sculpture has a powerful effect on me).

This last suggests another way of describing openness to experience. It means lack of rigidity and permeability of boundaries in concepts, beliefs, perceptions, and hypotheses. It means a tolerance for ambiguity where ambiguity exists. It means the ability to receive much conflicting information without forcing closure upon the situation. It means what the general semanticist calls the "extensional orientation."

This complete openness of awareness to what exists at this moment is, I believe, an important condition of constructive creativity. In an equally intense but more narrowly limited fashion it is no doubt present in all creativity. The deeply maladjusted artist who cannot recognize or be aware of the sources of unhappiness in himself, may nevertheless be sharply and sensitively aware of form and color in his experience. The tyrant (whether on a petty or grand scale) who cannot face the weaknesses in himself may nevertheless be completely alive to and aware of the chinks in the psychological armor of those with whom he deals. Because there is the openness to one phase of experience, creativity is possible; because the openness is *only* to one phase of experience, the product of this creativity may be potentially destructive of social values. The more the individual has available to himself a sensitive awareness of all phases of his experience, the more sure we can be that his creativity will be personally and socially constructive.

B. An internal locus of evaluation. Perhaps the most fundamental condition of creativity is that the source or locus of evaluative judgment is internal. The value of his product is, for the creative person, established not by the praise or criticism of others, but by himself. Have I created something satisfying to *me*? Does it express a part of me—my feeling or my thought, my pain or my ecstasy? These are the only questions which really matter to the creative person, or to any person when he is being creative.

This does not mean that he is oblivious to, or unwilling to be aware of, the judgments of others. It is simply that the basis of evaluation lies within himself, in his own organismic reaction to and appraisal of his product. If to the person it has the "feel" of being "me in action," of being an actualization of potentialities in himself which heretofore have not existed and are now emerging into existence, then it is satisfying and creative, and no outside evaluation can change that fundamental fact.

C. The ability to toy with elements and concepts. Though this is probably less important than A or B, it seems to be a condition of creativity. Associated with the openness and lack of rigidity described under A is the ability to play spontaneously with ideas, colors, shapes, relationships—to juggle elements into impossible juxtapositions, to shape wild hypotheses, to make the given problematic, to express the ridiculous, to translate from one form to another, to transform into improbable equivalents. It is from this spontaneous toying and exploration that there arises the hunch, the creative seeing of life in a new and significant way. It is as though out of the wasteful spawning of thousands of possibilities there emerge one or two evolutionary forms with the qualities which give them a more permanent value.

The Creative Act and Its Concomitants

When these three conditions obtain, constructive creativity will occur. But we cannot expect an accurate description of the creative act, for by its very nature it is indescribable. This is the unknown which we must recognize as unknowable until it occurs. This is the improbable that becomes probable. Only in a very general way can we say that a creative act is the natural behavior of an organism which has a tendency to arise when that organism is open to all of its inner and outer experiencing, and when it is free to try out in flexible fashion all manner of relationships. Out of this multitude of half-formed possibilities the organism, like a great computing machine, selects this one which most effectively meets an inner need, or that one which forms a more effective relationship with the environment, or this other one which discovers a more simple and satisfying order in which life may be perceived.

There is one quality of the creative act which may, however, be described. In almost all the products of creation we note a selectivity, or emphasis, an evidence of discipline, an attempt to bring out the essence. The artist paints surfaces or textures in simplified form, ignoring the minute variations which exist in reality. The scientist formulates a basic law of relationships, brushing aside all the particular events or circumstances which might conceal its naked beauty. The writer selects those words and phases which give unity to his expression. We may say that this is the influence of the specific person, of the "I." Reality exists in a multiplicity of confusing facts, but "I" bring a structure to my relationship to reality; I have "my" way of perceiving reality, and it is this (unconsciously?) disciplined personal selectivity or abstraction which gives to creative products their aesthetic quality.

Though this is as far as we can go in describing any aspect of the creative act, there are certain of its concomitants in the individual which may be mentioned. The first is what we may call the Eureka feeling—"This is *it*!" "I have discovered!" "This is what I wanted to express!"

Another concomitant is the anxiety of separateness.[2] I do not believe that many significantly creative products are formed without the feeling, "I am alone. No one has ever done just this before. I have ventured into territory where no one has been. Perhaps I am foolish, or wrong, or lost, or abnormal."

Still another experience which usually accompanies creativity is the desire to communicate. It is doubtful whether a human being can create, without wishing to share his creation. It is the only way he can assuage the anxiety of separateness and assure himself that he belongs to the group. He may confide his theories only to his private diary. He may put his discoveries in some cryptic code. He may con-

[2] For this and the idea in the following paragraph I am specifically indebted to my student and colleague, Mr. Robert Lipgar.

ceal his poems in a locked drawer. He may put away his paintings in a closet. Yet he desires to communicate with a group which will understand him, even if he must imagine such a group. He does not create in order to communicate, but once having created he desires to share this new aspect of himself-in-relation-to-his-environment with others.

Conditions Fostering Constructive Creativity

Thus far I have tried to describe the nature of creativity, to indicate that quality of individual experience which increases the likelihood that creativity will be constructive, to set forth the necessary conditions for the creative act and to state some of its concomitants. But if we are to make progress in meeting the social need which was presented initially, we must know whether constructive creativity can be fostered, and if so, how.

From the very nature of the inner conditions of creativity it is clear that they cannot be forced, but must be permitted to emerge. The farmer cannot make the germ develop and sprout from the seed; he can only supply the nurturing conditions which will permit the seed to develop its own potentialities. So it is with creativity. How can we establish the external conditions which will foster and nourish the internal conditions described above? My experience in psychotherapy leads me to believe that by setting up conditions of psychological safety and freedom, we maximize the likelihood of an emergence of constructive creativity. Let me spell out these conditions in some detail, labeling them as X and Y.

X. PSYCHOLOGICAL SAFETY. This may be established by three associated processes.

1. *Accepting the individual as of unconditional worth.* Whenever a teacher, parent, therapist, or other person with a facilitating function feels basically that this individual is of worth in his own right and in his own unfolding, no matter what his present condition or behavior, he is fostering creativity. This attitude can probably be genuine only when the teacher, parent, etc., senses the potentialities of the individual and thus is able to have an unconditional faith in him, no matter what his present state.

The effect on the individual as he apprehends this attitude, is to sense a climate of safety. He gradually learns that he can be whatever he is, without sham or façade, since he seems to be regarded as of worth no matter what he does. Hence he has less need of rigidity, can discover what it means to be himself, can try to actualize himself in new and spontaneous ways. He is, in other words, moving toward creativity.

2. *Providing a climate in which external evaluation is absent.* When we cease to form judgments of the other individual from our own locus of evaluation, we are fostering creativity. For the individual to find himself in an atmosphere where he is not being evaluated, not being measured by some external standard, is enormously freeing. Evaluation is always a threat, always creates a need for defensiveness, always means that some portion of experience must be denied to awareness. If this product is evaluated as good by external standards, then I must not admit my own dislike of it. If what I am doing is bad by external standards, then I must not be aware of the fact that it seems to be me, to be part of myself. But if judgments based on external standards are not being made then I can be more open to my experience, can recognize my own likings and dislikings, the nature of the materials and of my reaction to them, more sharply and more sensitively. I can begin to recognize the locus of evaluation within myself. Hence I am moving toward creativity.

To allay some possible doubts and fears in the reader, it should be pointed out that to cease evaluating another is not to cease having reactions. It may, as a matter of fact, free one to react. "I don't like your idea" (or painting, or invention, or writing) is not an evaluation, but a reaction. It is subtly but sharply different from a judgment which says, "What you are doing is bad (or good), and this quality is assigned to you from some external source." The first statement permits the individual to maintain his own locus of evaluation. It holds the possibility that I am unable to appreciate something which is actually very good. The second statement, whether it praises or condemns, tends to put the person at the mercy of outside forces. He is being told that he cannot simply ask himself whether this product is a valid expression of himself; he must be concerned with what others think. He is being led away from creativity.

3. *Understanding empathically.* It is this which provides the ultimate in psychological safety, when added to the other two. If I say that I "accept" you, but know nothing of you, this is a shallow acceptance indeed, and you realize that it may change if I actually come

to know you. But if I understand you empathically, see you and what you are feeling and doing from your point of view, enter your private world and see it as it appears to you—and still accept you—then this is safety indeed. In this climate you can permit your real self to emerge, and to express itself in varied and novel formings as it relates itself to the world. This is a basic fostering of creativity.

Y. PSYCHOLOGICAL FREEDOM. When a teacher, parent, therapist, or other facilitating person permits the individual a complete freedom of symbolic expression, creativity is fostered. This permissiveness gives the individual complete freedom to think, to feel, to be, whatever is most inward within himself. It fosters the openness, and the playful and spontaneous juggling of percepts, concepts, and meanings, which is a part of creativity.

Note that it is complete freedom of *symbolic* expression which is described. To express in behavior all feelings, impulses, and formings may not in all instances be freeing. Behavior may in some instances be limited by society, and this is as it should be. But symbolic expression need not be limited. Thus to destroy a hated object (whether one's mother or a rococo building) by destroying a symbol of it, is freeing. To attack it in reality may create guilt and narrow the psychological freedom which is experienced. (I feel unsure of this paragraph, but it is the best formulation I can give at the moment which seems to square with my experience.)

The permissiveness which is being described is not softness or indulgence or encouragement. It is permission to be *free*, which also means that one is responsible. The individual is as free to be afraid of a new venture as to be eager for it; free to bear the consequences of his mistakes as well as of his achievements. It is this type of freedom responsibly to be oneself which fosters the development of a secure locus of evaluation within oneself, and hence tends to bring about the inner conditions of constructive creativity.

Putting the Theory to Work

There is but one excuse for attempting to discover conceptual order and stating it in a theory; that is to develop hypotheses from the theory which may be tested. By such testing profitable directions for action may be found, and the theory itself may be corrected, modified, and extended. Thus if this theory which I have tentatively formulated is worth while, it should be possible to develop from it hypotheses which might be objectively tested in classes in the arts; in education outside of the arts; in leadership-training groups whether in industry or the military services; in problem-solving groups of any sort. Let me suggest a few of the general hypotheses which might be given more specific and operational form for any of the above groups. They would apply whether one was concerned with the development of creative artists or creative leaders; with originality of design or creative methods of problem-solving.

HYPOTHESES REGARDING INNER CONDITIONS. 1. Individuals who exhibit a measurably greater degree of conditions A, B, and C (openness, internal locus of evaluation, ability to toy with materials) will, over any given period of time, spontaneously form more products judged to be novel and creative, than a matched group who exhibit a lesser degree of A, B, and C.

2. The products of the first group will not only be more numerous, but will be judged to be more significant in their novelty. (Such a hypothesis could be given operational definition in art classes, problem-solving groups, or leadership-training groups, for example.)

3. Condition A (openness to experience) can be predicted from conditions B or C, which are more easily measurable. (It is not at all certain that this hypothesis would be upheld, but it would be worth careful investigation. If conditions A, B, and C are highly intercorrelated, then they could jointly be predicted from the one which proved most easily measurable. Thus we might gain clues as to how we might less laboriously select graduate students, for example, with a high creative potential.)

HYPOTHESES RE FOSTERING CONSTRUCTIVE CREATIVITY. 4. Given two matched groups, the one in which the leader establishes a measurably greater degree of conditions X_1, X_2, X_3, and Y (psychological safety and freedom) will spontaneously form a greater number of creative products, and these products will be judged to be more significantly novel.

5. Conditions X_1, X_2, X_3, and Y are not of equal importance in fostering creativity. By comparing different groups in which one or another of these conditions is emphasized or minimized it may be possible to determine which of these conditions is most effective in facilitating creativity.

6. A group in which conditions X_1, X_2, X_3, and Y are established should, according to our theory, have more effective and harmonious interpersonal relationships than a matched group in which these conditions are present to a lesser degree. (The reasoning is that if creativity is all of a piece, then a group in which the fostering conditions are established should be more constructively creative in social relationships.)

7. The extent to which different groups in our culture provide the fostering conditions (X and Y) could be measured. In this way one could determine whether creativity is now being fostered to a greater degree by the family group, classes in schools and colleges, bull sessions, social clubs and groups, interest groups, military groups, industrial groups. (One wonders how college classes would show up in such a comparison.)

Conclusion

I have endeavored to present an orderly way of thinking about the creative process, in order that some of these ideas might be put to a rigorous and objective test. My justification for formulating this theory, and my reason for hoping that such research may be carried out, is that the present development of the physical sciences is making an imperative demand upon us as individuals and as a culture for creative behavior in adapting ourselves to our new world if we are to survive.

Summer, 1954. Dr. Rogers is professor of psychology and psychiatry, University of Wisconsin, and author of Counseling and Psychotherapy (1942), Client-Centered Therapy (1951), *and* Psychotherapy and Personality Change (1954). *His paper was presented at the Conference on Creativity, held at Granville, Ohio, December, 1952.*

Toward a Humanistic Psychology

A. H. MASLOW

I begin with a credo, a confession, a personal statement. I've never made it quite this way before because it sounds so presumptuous but I think it's about time for it.

I believe that the world will either be saved by the psychologists or it won't be saved at all. I think psychologists are the most important people living today. I think the fate of the human species and the future of the human species rest more upon their shoulders than upon any group of people now living. I believe that all the important problems of war and peace, exploitation and brotherhood, hatred and love, sickness and health, misunderstanding and understanding, the happiness and unhappiness of mankind will yield only to a better understanding of human nature.

I believe that medicine, physics, law, government, education, economics, engineering, business, industry are only tools—powerful tools, powerful means—but not ends. I think that the ultimate end to which they should all be bent is human fulfillment, human betterment, growth, and happiness. But these tools are all evil in the hands of evil men, and are good and desirable only in the hands of good men. The only way to heal evil men is to create good men. To understand people better, to know what creates them, and to know how to cure the evil and let the good come out, we must know what evil is and what good is, that is, what psychological health is, and what psychological sickness is. And this is the job for the psychologist.

Therefore I feel myself, as a psychologist, to be an important man. I must confess that mostly I feel fortunate at this blessing that has been bestowed upon me. I think being a psychologist is the most fascinating life there is. As a matter of fact I found myself recently (this is a confession too) being kind to people who weren't psychologists, like the rich man who doesn't want to be too ostentatious about his good fortune.

Psychologists must be considered fortunate for several reasons. They can be officially virtuous about being Peeping Toms and asking impertinent personal questions of everybody they run across. They can ask the most embarrassing questions and say, "Well, this is psychological research," and thereby get answers. Not only can psychologists deal with the most fascinating objects in the world—human persons —not only can they by their own studies, their own scientific work, more efficiently work out even their own personal problems as human beings, but most of all they can feel so important. Everything that they discover will be magnified a million times. Learn more about human nature and you thereby automatically learn more about all the works of mankind. The more you know about the human being, the more you know about his products, and the more you can manipulate and better the products as well. Basic to the study of law, of education, of economics, of history, ought to be an improved study of the human being who has made the law and made the history. Paul Valéry has said it well: "When the mind is in question, everything is in question."

It must be quite clear now that I speak out of a special conception of the call of the psychologist, his mission, his vocation. I think that there are rules and responsibilities for him that don't apply to other scientists. I know it sounds a little Messianic, but my reasoning is quite simple. Our most pressing and urgent problems today are problems arising out of human weaknesses—sorrow, greed, exploitation, prejudice, contempt, cowardice, stupidity, jealousy, selfishness. These are all human sicknesses. We already know that we can cure these sicknesses if we can manage them one at a time. Psychoanalysis, for example, is one particular deep therapy, that can manage these problems, given enough time, enough money, enough skill.

If we die in another war or if we continue being tense and neurotic and anxious in an extended cold war, this is due to the fact that we don't understand ourselves and we don't understand each other. Improve human nature and you improve all.

But before you can improve human beings you must understand them. And there it is, just as simple and blunt and unavoidable as I can make it. We just don't know enough about people, and this is the task facing the psychologist. We need psychology, and we need it more than anything else that I can think of, whether more bombs or more religions or more diplomats or more bathtubs. Even more than physical health, more than new drugs, we need an improved human nature.

Furthermore, we need it in a hurry. I have a sense of historical urgency about this. Time's awasting and the dogs of history are barking at our heels. War may break out about our ears any day.

The psychologist has a call, then, in the same sense that a minister should have. He doesn't have the right to play games and to indulge himself. He has special responsibilities to the human race. He ought to feel the weight of duty upon his shoulders as no other scientist needs to. He ought to have a sense of mission, of dedication.

Another point in this credo. By psychologists I mean all sorts of people, not just professors of psychology. I mean to include all the people who are interested in developing a truer, a clearer, a more empirical conception of human nature, and only such people. That excludes many professors of psychology and many psychiatrists. I would include some sociologists, anthropologists, educators, philosophers, artists, publicists, linguists, businessmen—anybody who is pointed in this direction; practically anybody who has taken upon his own shoulders this task that I consider so great and so important.

Since psychology is in its infancy as a science, and so little is known (only the psychologist knows how little this is) by comparison with what we need to know, a good psychologist should be a humble man. Unfortunately, too many psychologists are not humble, but are, instead, arrogant. There is no greater danger than an arrogant psychologist or psychiatrist.

Feeling as I do about psychology—its importance, its unfulfilled tasks, its areas of ignorance, and its tremendous promise—I should like to submit a series of prescriptions as to what psychology needs if it is to realize itself as a science and therefore perform the tasks it must perform for the troubled human race.

1. *Psychology should be more humanistic, more concerned with the problems of humanity, and less with the problems of the guild.*
The sad thing is that students come into psychology almost always with humanistic interests. They want to know about people, what makes them tick, how they can be improved. They want to *understand* about love, hate, hope, fear, ecstasy, happiness, the meaning of living. But what is so often done for these high hopes and yearnings? Most graduate training, even most undergraduate courses, turn away from these subjects (I couldn't even find the word "love" indexed in any of the psychology books on my shelves, not even the ones on marriage). Such topics are called fuzzy, unscientific, tender-minded, mystical. What is offered instead? Dry bones. Techniques. Precision. Huge mountains of itty-bitty facts, having little to do with the interests that brought the student into psychology. Even worse, teachers of psychology try, often successfully, to make the student *ashamed* of his humanistic interests as if they were somehow unscientific. Hence often the spark is lost, and students, becoming graduate psychologists, settle down to being members of the guild, with all its prejudices, its orthodoxies. The creativeness goes, the daring, the unorthodoxy, the sense of high mission, the prophetic sense, the humanistic dedication. Cynicism closes in, and I am horrified to report that most graduate students in psychology speak guardedly of the Ph.D. as the "union card" and expect not to enjoy doing their dissertation research, tending to regard it as an unpleasant job rather than as a privilege, something to get out of the way so they can get a job.

What cultivated man in his right mind would read a doctoral dissertation or an elementary textbook on psychology? How few psychology books there are that I could recommend to the general reader that have the approval of the technical psychologist? The only ones that I can think of which would help people to understand themselves and their friends better are called inexact, unscientific, "clinical." They are said by most technical psychologists to come more from the psychotherapeutic tradition than the scientific. For instance I may recommend Freud and the neo-Freudians, but I doubt that Freud could get a Ph.D. in psychology today, nor would any of his writings be acceptable as a doctoral dissertation. And only a few months ago, in a standard journal of psychology, a presidential address compared Freud with phrenology. And this for the greatest psychologist who has ever lived—at least from the point of view of nonmembers of the guild, who constitute most of the human race.

And what is offered in exchange for Freud, Adler, Jung, Fromm, and Horney? Beautifully executed, precise, elegant experiments which in half the cases or more have nothing to do with enduring human problems, and which are written not primarily for the human species, but for other members of the guild. The guild's disdain for the public's concerns is reminiscent of the keeper at the zoo who was asked whether the hippopotamus was male or female. "Madam," he replied, "it seems to me that that would be of interest only to another hippopotamus."

Psychologists are, or should be, an arm of the human race, a help to it. They have obligations, responsibilities, duties to every person now living, and to everyone who will ever live in the future. They just have no right to play little autoerotic games off in a corner of the laboratory.

2. *Psychology should turn more frequently to the study of philosophy, of science, of aesthetics, but especially of ethics and values.*

I am sorry that psychology has officially cut itself off from philosophy because this means no more than giving up good philosophies for bad ones. Every man living has some kind of philosophy, usually an unconscious, therefore uncriticized, uncorrectable, unimprovable one, that Philipp Frank called a "chance philosophy." If you want to improve it, make it more realistic, more useful, and more fruitful, you have to be conscious of it, and *work* with it, criticize it, improve it. This most people (including most psychologists) don't do.

And I mean more than the philosophy of science. I mean also the study of values, of *why* science is, of what it is for. Where did science come from anyway? Why do we spend so much time on it? What's in it for us? And I mean the philosophy of aesthetics, of creativeness, of the mystic experience, that is, of the highest and deepest experiences the human being is capable of. To concern oneself with these matters is a way of avoiding shallowness and busy work, and of setting a suitably high level of aspiration. If the priests of science themselves are small men, with limited, superficial goals, then the religion of science will be petty and trivial also.

Too many psychologists have looked for their philosophy of science to the mathematicians and physicists of the nineteenth century, and simply imitate them. Their reasoning is apparently that these scientists were successful: let us see how they did it, and imitate them, and then we too will be as successful. But this is foolish. Psychology as a science is in its infancy and has to work out its own philosophy, its own methodology, suitable to its own nature and problems and goals. A little boy doesn't become a man by putting on his father's shoes, smoking his pipe, and trying to speak in a bass voice. He has to *really* grow, not make believe he's already grown.

I don't mean to make heroes out of professors of philosophy either. They're probably no better and no worse than the psychologists (or physicists or chemists). There are as many sterile philosophers as there are sterile psychologists (or chemists or poets). And yet in philosophy there are many growing points, points of penetration and improvement and advancement in human thought. Unless they know the great philosophers, the psychologists are likely to remain arrogant rather than humble, trivial rather than profound, repetitious rather than creative. And they are likely to continue trying to live up to their "little boy" effort to "make like" a Hollywood scientist, to wear a white coat, have a stern, tough look on his face, and not to bleed when cut.

The trouble with many psychologists is that they are content to work with but a portion of the human being, indeed even to make a virtue out of doing so. They forget that ultimately their task is to give us a unified, empirically based conception of the whole human being, of human nature in general, i.e., a philosophy of human nature.

But such a task takes courage and a willingness to step away from the narrow platform of certainty. This certainty is and must be narrow for the simple reason that we just don't know enough about human nature to be sure of anything but small bits of knowledge.

Everyone, even the one-year-old child, has some conception of human nature. It is impossible to live without a theory of how people will behave, of what to expect of them. Every psychologist, however positivist and hard-boiled and antitheoretical he may claim to be, nevertheless has a full-blown philosophy of human nature hidden away in a concealed place in his guts. It is as if he guided himself by a half-known map, which he disavows and denies and which is therefore immune to correction by newly acquired knowledge. This unconscious map or theory guides his reactions and expectations far more than does his laboriously acquired experimental knowledge.

The issue is then not over whether or not to have a philosophy of psychology, but whether to have a conscious or an unconscious one.

Another truth that we have learned from the philosophers is that you must have a map if you are not to waste your time. It may sound sensible to say, "After all, facts are facts and knowledge is knowledge. Let us just accumulate facts of all kinds one by one, only making sure that they are valid and reliable and we will slowly nibble away at the unknown. Slow but sure. Let us have nothing to do with theories —only certain facts."

But we now know that most facts, maybe *all* facts, are expressions of a theory. The anthropologists, particularly the semanticists, have proven that even naming an object, "That is a chair," or "That is a man," is an expression of a world outlook, and that in order really to understand the statement you must know the world outlook.

I am by no means arguing against detailed work, as my own detailed work can testify. Every clash of broad issues eventually works itself down to small crucial experiments, and these experiments ought to be done as well and as carefully as we know how. What use is it doing an experiment if your results tell you nothing for sure? Ultimately, the experimenter, the researcher, is the Supreme Court before which all theories are and must be tested.

Because we know so little for certain about human beings (by comparison with what we should know and would like to know) intuition, common experience, wisdom, intelligence, and insight all become tremendously important. Even a stupid man can understand when there are enough certain facts, but when there are not, only the innately perceptive, wise man can know. Philosophies of human nature have been expounded by theologians, poets, dramatists, artists, statesmen, and industrialists. We should respect these—as theories, as suggestions—almost as much as we should the theories of the psychologist, and use them as frameworks for criticism, for suggested experiments, as tentative road maps to be tested and examined. We can still learn much from Marcus Aurelius, from Goethe, from Spinoza, from Coleridge, although I hope and expect that the day will come when we will know more than any of them, as today any high school boy knows more about biology than Aristotle did. This is the triumph of science, that ultimately it can take the wisdom of the great intuitors, correct it, test it, and come out with a better product, with more certain and reliable knowledge. When the scientists, after years of theorizing, debating, experimenting, checking, and counter-checking arrive at the same conclusion that Rousseau or Shakespeare did, it is not actually the same conclusion. It is now knowledge, whereas formerly it was a theory. And I remind you that we need a principle by which to select from among the various contradictory theories which have been offered. Not only Rousseau's theories must be checked, but also those of Rousseau's opponents. And who is to check them, who is to decide, but the scientist? And on what basis can he decide if not on the basis of empirical research?

We must pay special attention to the synoptic thinkers, the producers of theories of the whole man in his whole world. It is easy enough to develop a sound theory of the learning of nonsense syllables, or of rats running in mazes, or of the conditioning of the dog's salivary reflex. To integrate these miniature theories with the whole of psychology—that is another matter. To relate them to love and hate, to growing and regressing, to happiness and pain, and to courage and anxiety, exposes the weakness of nibbling away at the edges of reality instead of making reconnaissance flights over the whole of it.

3. *American psychology should be bolder, more creative; it should try to discover, instead of try only to be cautious and careful and to avoid mistakes.*

Why is it that there has never been a great American psychologist in the sense of making bold, new discoveries? Our best American psychologists have been excellent scholars, excellent systematizers, excellent experimenters, but *not* great discoverers. All the great breakthroughs, the great innovations have come from European psychologists; all the brands of psychoanalysis, Freud, Adler, Jung, Rank, Fromm, Horney; all the Gestalt psychologists, Wertheimer, Koffka, Kohler, Lewin; the Rorschach test; Goldstein's organismic psychology. Even behaviorism, so specifically American, began with Pavlov.

I have been told that something very similar is true for the other sciences. The most dramatic example of course is atomic physics. Einstein, Bohr, Fermi, Szilard were all European. The United States is way down on the list in the number of Nobel Prize winners when size of population is taken into account, and it would be even further down if wealth and opportunity were also taken into account.

Why is American science so essentially conventional, so hostile to creativeness, to beginnings, to speculation, to unorthodoxy, to really new ideas? Why are American psychologists so characteristically appliers of other people's ideas? Why normally do they despise and attack the innovator for ten or twenty years and *then*, when they've finally got used to the shock of thinking unconventionally, make it conventional, and swarm in with hundreds of working-out experiments on other people's ideas? As Picasso said, "First you invent something and then they make it pretty." Why can't they recognize where they get their ideas from in the first place?

I remember how saddened I was and how irritated by an official report of a major committee of the American Psychological Association on the future of psychological science and its improvement. The recommendations amounted finally to methodological ones mostly; how to be cautious and conservative, how to check, how not to make mistakes, how to pick out other people's mistakes, how to validate, how to be accurate and precise and sure and certain. Hardly a word was there about creativeness, new ideas, sticking your neck out, breaking out of the rut, taking a chance, *encouraging* uncertainty and confusion and exploration. It was so much like the road maps we get at a gas station, telling us how to make our way from known place to known place. Not a word about the no-man's land out ahead, the place where there are no maps and street signs and paved roads, not a word about the pioneering and trail-breaking and sketchy surveying that are necessary *before* the maps can be made.

But once admit creativeness and then you're smack in the middle of a mess of poets, artists, musicians, and other dirty people who don't have a Ph.D. in psychology and are therefore clearly social climbers who don't have any *right* to know anything about human nature. Once you let the door open a crack *anybody* can get in. And then who knows *where* things may lead? As one lady once said, "The horrible danger of murder, rape, and arson is that they may lead you to smoking."

4. *Psychology should be more problem-centered, and less absorbed with means or methods.*

If you are primarily interested in doing what you can about important questions or problems, then techniques, methods, apparatus become secondary. For instance, if your quest is "What is love?" and you propose to do the best you can to find out, then you will stick with the problem even though you have to improvise. And you will have to be content with inexactness and uncertainty in the early stages of exploration. If you insist on using only elegant techniques and demand "scientific" exactness, elegance, validity, and reliability, then you just can't work with this problem and must give it up, because the techniques and methods and machines now available won't help much with it.

Those who *do* insist on precision from the very beginning can therefore never begin. All they can do is to come in on the later stages of development of the problem.

Therefore if you identify science with exactness, with precision, with quantifications, with precisely defined variables, and with good control of all these variables, you have thereby repudiated as "unscientific" all the first stages of work with any problem, when hunches, intuitions, naturalistic observations, speculations, and theories are all you have.

To put it even more bluntly, to define science primarily as method is to make of it a senseless game or ritual. What is it a method *for?* If pertinence, worth, goal, value are understressed, and validity and reliability exclusively sought for, it is very much like boasting, "I don't know or care what I'm doing, but see how accurately I'm doing it."

The situation in American psychology, in which most researchers do what they can do well, rather than what needs doing, is largely due, I think, to this mistaken notion of what science is and should be.

5. *Psychology ought to be more positive and less negative than it is. It should have higher ceilings, and not be afraid of the loftier possibilities of the human being.*

One major shortcoming of research psychology (and of psychiatry as well) is its pessimistic, negative, and limited conception of human beings. It has so far revealed to us much about man's shortcomings, his illnesses, his sins and weaknesses, but rather little about his virtues, his potentialities, or his highest aspirations. This is true for every area of psychology, for all its subdivisions.

I am not calling for optimism. Rather I am asking for realism in the best and fullest sense of the word. To identify realism with darkness, misery, pathology, and breakdown as so many novelists have done in our time is idiotic, but psychologists have committed the same error. Happiness is just as real as unhappiness, gratification is just as real as frustration, love is just as real as hostility.

I want to stress the most important single example of our present mistaken emphasis, namely, the contrast between our knowledge of psychological sickness and our totally inadequate attention to psychological health. Now that I've tried myself to study healthy people, I can understand why this is so. It is a difficult job, ringed about with philosophical reefs of all sorts, particularly in the area of the theory of values. In addition there are cultural problems, methodological ones, and clinical ones. Yet psychological health clearly calls for study. We must know what men are like at their best; not only what they *are*, but also what they can become. The by-products of such knowledge are incalculably important. My own belief is that such a health psychology will inevitably transform our deepest conceptions of human nature. It will wean us away from the almost universal habit of regarding normality as a special case of the abnormal, of being content to regard a healthy human being as simply "not very sick." It will teach us rather that the abnormal is a special case of the normal, and that psychological illness is primarily a struggle toward health.

Another aspect of this same mistake, this preoccupation with the negative, this stress on fear rather than courage, is the great amount of time that has been spent on the defensive processes, on self-protectiveness, on safety and security, and on homeostatic processes. The implication is that life is a process of avoiding pain and of fighting trouble and unhappiness.

But there is another side to the human being and another set of motivations, the positive ones, the tending to grow stronger, wiser, healthier, to actualize one's potentialities, to be curious, to enjoy, to wonder, to philosophize, to be creative. Not only do we adjust, we also rebel.

It is true that we tend to shrink within ourselves when something threatens: we do try to avoid pain. And there is much pain in life for most people. Yet if life were simply an avoidance of pain, why would we not cut our throats, all of us, and thereby avoid pain forever? Clearly life has more to offer than pain. Then why not study this "something more"?

6. *If this is all so, then therapy should be taken out of the office and spread to many other areas of life. Furthermore, it should not only be more broadly used but also more ambitiously defined to include the growth-fostering techniques.*

Some of the more elementary psychotherapeutic techniques can be boiled down to very simple processes that can be taught to teachers, parents, ministers, doctors, and even to all of mankind. Support, reassurance, acceptance, love, respect, the giving of safety, all of these are therapeutic. We know also that many of the good life experiences are therapeutic *through* giving these basic medicines—the good marriage, good education, success at a good job, having good friends, being able to help other people, creative work. All these can be studied more carefully than they have been, so that we can know more about them. And whatever knowledge we do have can be much more widely taught than it has been.

In any case the conception of therapy as getting rid of symptoms and of illnesses is too limited. We must learn to think of it more as a technique for fostering growth and general improvement of the human being, for encouraging self-actualization. This means that many other techniques not now included under the head of psychotherapy will belong there, if only we can expand the meaning of therapy to include all the growth-fostering techniques, the educational ones particularly, and *most* particularly creative education in art, in play, and all other kinds of education that avowedly improve creativeness, spontaneity, expressiveness, courage, and integration.

7. *Psychology should study not only behavior on the surface but much more the depths of human nature, the unconscious as well as the conscious.*

I am aware that this sounds silly, or even fantastic, and yet the truth is that official, academic, experimental psychology does *not* study the depths as it should. It *is* preoccupied with what can be seen, touched, or heard, with what is conscious. The greatest single psychological discovery that has ever been made was the discovery of unconscious motivations, and yet the situation is that the unconscious is still out of bounds for many research psychologists. Its study has been mostly the preoccupation of psychoanalysts, psychotherapists, psychiatrists. Only in the last few years have some experimental psychologists begun to tackle the problem.

The consequence, as judged, let us say, by the standard texts in general psychology, is a kind of half-psychology, in which human nature is presented, so to speak, "from middle C upward." This is like defining an iceberg as only that portion which can be seen above the waterline. Most of the *Journal of Experimental Psychology* is written as if Freud had never lived.

The final product is an "official" psychology which deals with rationality but not with the irrational, with the cognitive far more than with the conative and emotional, with adjustment to external reality and hardly at all to internal reality, with the verbal, mathematical, logical, and physical and hardly at all with the archaic, the preverbal, the symbolic, the illogical, the fluid, the intuitive, the poetic (what the psychoanalysts call "primary process").

Not only do our depths make trouble for us; this is also where our joys come from. If we go about the world not knowing what's going on inside ourselves, not knowing what we're looking for, unconscious of the forces which largely determine our behavior, we are blind to the sources of both our ills and our pleasures. This lack of understanding means certainly a lack of control over our own fate.

8. *Academic psychology is too exclusively Western, and not Eastern enough. It turns too much to the objective, the public, the outer, to behavior. It should learn more about the inner, the subjective, the meditative, the private. Introspection, thrown out as a technique, should be brought back into psychological research.*

American psychology is behavioristic, concentrating on watching the overt actions of others from the outside. This predilection originates in a praiseworthy though naïve effort to be "scientific." Of course it is our hope as scientists to be able to demonstrate, to prove, to repeat the experiment in another laboratory. Yet we must face the hard fact that this is an *ultimate* goal rather than an immediate one. By sticking to the observation of external behavior we must thereby overlook all sorts of human activities which do *not* show themselves externally in a simple form.

Behaviorism originated in a sensible reaction against anthropomorphizing animal psychology, but the reverse error has happened instead, of *rodentomorphizing* human psychology, of studying the person as if he were no more than a complicated white rat. It is truly a mistake to attribute human motives to laboratory animals, but is it a mistake to attribute human motives to humans?

I would like to bring back introspection for another reason that I have recently become impressed with. We are discovering, more and more of us, as we study personality in the depths rather than at the surface, that the deeper we go into ourselves or any other person, the more universal we get. At our deepest levels, we seem to be more alike than different. Therefore if you can manage to get to these depths within yourself (usually the aid of a therapist is needed), you find out not only about yourself, but also about the whole human species. The nonacademic psychologists of the East have always known this; now we in the West must learn about it too.

9. *Psychologists should study more than they have the end experiences as well as the means to ends, the pragmatic, the useful, and the purposive.*

What experiences does man live for? What makes living worth while? What are the payoffs? What experiences in life justify the pains of existence? In other words, which experiences are worth while in themselves? We know that we reach the heights of living in the moments of creation, of insight, of aesthetic experience, of mystic experience, of delight, of love-sex experience. (I have called these the "peak experiences.") Were it not for these, life wouldn't make any sense. We would then be living in order to . . . in order to . . . in order to . . . in order to . . . and so on with no end. We must ask ". . . in order to what?"

Remember too that end experiences need not be *only* the peak experiences of life. We get milder payoffs and rewards in simple zest of living, in enjoying all the activities that are done for themselves and not for the sake of something else. A healthy organism enjoys just *being*. Our overpragmatic psychology, preoccupied with purposive behavior, neglects behavior that is not purposive—that is an end in itself.

10. *Psychology should study the human being not just as passive clay, helplessly acted upon by outside forces, and determined by them alone. It should also study the ways in which he is (or should be) an active, autonomous, self-governing mover, chooser, and center of his own life.*

The so-called stimulus-response psychology has created, without meaning to, what we might call a Stimulus-Response man, passive, responding, shaped, adjusting, learning. With this picture we must contrast the creative, active man, the one who invents, who is responsible, who accepts some stimuli and rejects others, who creates his own stimuli, who makes decisions both about stimuli and about responses.

Perhaps posing this opposition may help clarify why more and more psychologists are getting worried about the concept of "adjustment." Adjustment whether to the culture, to other people, or to nature means being passive, letting yourself be shaped from the outside, living by the will of other people. It is like trying to make other people happy, asking, "What does Daddy want me to be?" instead of asking, "What am *I* like, really? What is my real self?"

Then, too, this is why, increasingly, psychologists criticize the conception of learning as a passive process only.

11. *All intellectuals tend to become absorbed with abstractions, words, and concepts, and to forget raw experience, the fresh and concrete, the original real experiencing which is the beginning of all science. In psychology, this is a particular danger.*

My own remedy for this is to turn to (a) the general semanticists, who devote themselves to this danger in particular, and (b) the artists, whose particular job it is to experience freshly, to see (and help us to see) the world as it is, and not as it looks when screened through a web of concepts, verbalisms, abstractions, categories, and theories.

12. *The lessons of Gestalt psychology and of organismic theory have not been fully enough integrated into psychology. The human being is an irreducible unit, at least so far as psychological research is concerned. Everything in him is related to everything else in him, in greater or lesser degree.*

13. *I believe that psychologists should devote more time to the intensive study of the single unique person, to balance their preoccupation with the generalized man and generalized and abstracted capacities.*

There is one great difference between what psychology studies and what all other sciences study. Only psychology studies uniqueness. One white rat is as good as another, one atom is like another, one chemical like another. Their differences don't really matter. So all other sciences study similarities, which means abstracting. Now psychology has to do this too, but it also has the special task that no other science has (except anthropology) of studying uniqueness.

This has at least one very important consequence that I must mention. In his most essential core, no human being is comparable with any other. Therefore his ideals for himself, the path of growth must also be unique. His goal for himself must arise out of his own unique nature, *not* be picked up by comparison or competition with others. It is dangerous to pick up an ideal for oneself from a father or teacher or some other model or hero. Essentially the individual's task is to become the best *himself* in the world. Joe Doakes must not try to be like Abraham Lincoln or Thomas Jefferson or anybody else. He must become the best Joe Doakes in the world. That he *can* do and only this is possible and even necessary. And here he has no competitors.

14. *Finally, as we get to know more about what the person legitimately wants and needs for his growth and self-fulfillment, i.e., for psychological health, then we should set ourselves the task of creating the health-fostering culture.*

I think that this is, in principle, no more difficult a task than the making of the A-bomb. Of course, we don't know enough to do a really good job right *now*. But part of the ultimate task would be acquiring the necessary knowledge. I see no theoretical reason against this.

Such an enterprise, when it comes, will be the proof that psychology has matured enough to pay off, not only in individual terms, but in social improvement as well.

Autumn, 1956. Dr. Maslow's paper was originally given as a public address at the Cooper Union for the Advancement of Science and Art, March, 1956. He is professor of psychology at Brandeis University; he is coauthor of Principles of Abnormal Psychology *(1941), author of* Motivation and Personality *(1954) and editor of* New Knowledge in Human Values *(1959).*

The Fully Functioning Personality

S. I. HAYAKAWA

Let me start by contrasting two views of security, namely, the static and the dynamic. The static concept of security may be pictured by thinking of the oyster inside its shell, the frightened person behind his neurotic defenses, or prewar France behind the Maginot Line. The main idea in the static concept of security is to build up enough protective walls and to sit still inside them. The "search for security" for many people still is the task of building and mending walls around themselves.

The dynamic concept of security can be pictured by thinking of a skillful and self-confident driver speeding home in the traffic stream along Bayshore Highway. He knows that the highway is dangerous; he knows that he may encounter drunken drivers or cars with faulty brakes, and he knows that a slight error in judgment at sixty miles an hour may result in his not getting home at all. Nevertheless, he is not insecure, he is not frightened; in fact, this daily confrontation of danger doesn't worry him at all, because his security in this dynamic and dangerous situation depends not on walls to protect him from danger, but on internal resources—skill, knowledge, experience, flexibility—with which he knows he can cope with danger.

And in this choice of examples I think I have already indicated that the static concept of security is an illusory one, except perhaps for oysters. Against the background of far more profound psychological experience and knowledge than I can bring to bear on the subject, others can write of how one cultivates through proper teaching and child-rearing methods and self-criticism, the kind of dynamic, inner security which is the goal of education and psychiatry in our times. I myself should like to discuss the question, "Assuming that the search for security has been successful so that you have developed a person who is genuinely free of neurotic anxieties, and therefore free of needless defensive reactions, what would he (or she) look like? What sort of a person would a genuinely sane individual be? What would he be like to have around, to talk with as a friend, to work with as a colleague? That is, how does he distinguish himself from people like us?"

The reason I am interested in this topic is that there is plenty of literature on neurotics and psychotics, telling us how we get to be the messes we are—that is, through being bottle-fed, through being toilet-trained too severely, through living in an overcompetitive culture, through having sexual inhibitions or through having not enough of them, through having had the wrong parents, or through having been subjected to the wrong methods of education, and so on. We have thousands of descriptions of emotional disturbance and its causes, but we have too few descriptions of emotional health. And so, as I say, what does a sane person look like?

One of the bases of my inquiry to this question arises from Alfred Korzybski's claim in *Science and Sanity* that he had given the first clear, definite, functional definition of sanity. The sane individual, he said, does not confuse levels of abstraction; he does not treat the map as if it were the territory; he does not copy animals in their reactions and therefore is not a *dog*matist or a *cat*egorist (the pun is Korzybski's, not mine); he does not treat as identical all things that have the same name; he does not exhibit two-valued orientations in which absolute good is pitted against absolute evil; he does not confuse reports with inferences, inferences with judgmental statements; he is cautious about applying generalizations to particulars.

You will note that this description that Korzybski gives is a negative description, because it says so many things that the sane individual does *not* do. Of course there are positive elements in Korzybski's description of sanity, too. They are to the effect that the same individual is extensionally oriented (that is, he is fact-minded rather than word-minded), he is conscious of his abstracting and of his projecting processes, he is relaxed rather than rigid or defensive, and he is co-operative and mature in his orientations.

Now I don't want to argue with Korzybski's concept of sanity, which I believe is as good as any you can find; nevertheless his account of sanity is at a fairly high level of abstraction. He said, for example, that if our evaluative processes were not crippled by built-in misevaluations, we would all function so well that we could all be regarded as geniuses. Some people have laughed at Korzybski because they thought that he made a vast overstatement when he said this, but I don't think there is anything to laugh at here. We all know people, including people who are very dear to us among our friends and relatives, who we feel would be enormously creative if they only got the bugs out of their systems. Often we feel that way about ourselves. Hence, to cease being crippled by unsound evaluative habits does not seem an unrealizable goal. Maybe we could all be geniuses, or at least a little less removed from the genius class, if we knew how to overcome our misevaluations. But again let me call attention to the fact that the main emphasis of Korzybski's description of sanity is a negative one; that is, that we must stop doing the things we do now that prevent us from functioning better. And so we do not get a picture from Korzybski of the semantically liberated or the same individual.

Professor A. H. Maslow of Brandeis University has done a study of what he calls the "self-actualizing person," in his book *Motivation and Personality*. Dr. Carl Rogers in his book *Client-Centered Therapy* has been trying to isolate the characteristics of what he calls the "fully functioning person" or the "creative person." From these books and others in the same general direction, we get a picture of what modern psychologists—specifically those psychologists whose position is most closely allied to that of general semantics—regard as the psychologically healthy person, that is, the person whose search for security has been successful.

So let's talk about the "genuinely sane person" or, to use Carl Rogers' term, the "fully functioning person." What does he look like? Who is this character? Dr. Rogers' theories are based upon an extrapolation beyond the facts abstracted from successful cases of therapy that he has seen, and the materials for his pictures of the "sane person" are then the experiences and observations of a psychotherapist.

Maslow approaches his idea of the "sane person," whom he calls the "self-actualizing personality," from a different source. He defines the "self-actualizing person" as one who makes "full use and exploitation of his talents, capacities, and potentialities." These people, he says, "seem to be fulfilling themselves and to be doing the best that they are capable of doing. They are people who have developed or are developing to the full stature of which they are capable." In order to isolate the characteristics of the "self-actualizing personality," Maslow started with a rough definition and applied it to those of his friends, acquaintances, and students who seemed to fill the bill. He also studied a number of historical characters or living personalities, about sixty or seventy people altogether, who seemed to meet the requirements. He does not, of course, give the names of all the persons he has studied. Some of them were famous, some obscure. Some whom he thought to be self-actualizing turned out, on closer examination, not to be as healthy as they looked at first. After much careful screening he narrowed down his list to some forty people whom he found to be self-actualizing to a large degree.

And so I shall lump together Carl Rogers' "fully functioning person" with Maslow's "self-actualizing personality" and call this combined abstraction the "genuinely sane individual."

The most impressive fact, as described by both Rogers and Maslow, is that these sane people are not, in the ordinary sense of the term, "well adjusted." The unreflective layman and many schoolteachers and administrators, even some psychiatrists, seem to believe that adjustment to a society, in the sense of complete conformity with the goals, internal and external, of that society, is the goal of mental health. Such a view of adjustment would mean that in Rome you would not only do as the Romans do, but think and feel as the Romans do; that in a money-mad society you too would be money-mad; that in a Nazi society you would be a good Nazi. The "fully functioning personality" is not, in that sense, fully adjusted. His relation to the society around him may be described somewhat as follows: he is *in* and *of* the society of which he is a member, but he is not a prisoner of that society.

On the other hand, the "fully functioning personality" is not an outright rebel against the social norms of a society either, given a halfway tolerable society to live in. Maslow writes as follows of his case studies of "self-actualizing personalities":

Their behavior is marked by simplicity and naturalness, and by lack of artificiality and straining for effort. This does not necessarily mean consistently unconventional behavior. Actually the "self-actualizing personality" is not extremely unconventional. His unconventionality is not superficial but essential and internal. It is his impulse, thought, and consciousness that are unconventional, spontaneous and natural. Apparently recognizing that the world of people in which he lives could not understand or accept this, and since he has no wish to hurt people or to fight them over trivialities, he will go through the ordinary trivial conventions with a good-humored shrug and with the best possible grace. . . . But the fact that this "conventionality" is a cloak which rests very lightly on his shoulders and is easily cast aside can be seen from the fact that the self-actualizing person practically never allows convention to hamper him or inhibit him from doing anything that he considers very important and basic.

Now Carl Rogers states more or less the same thing when he says, "The fully functioning personality is not necessarily 'adjusted' to his culture, he is not a conformist. But at any time and in any culture he would live constructively, in as much harmony with the culture as a balanced satisfaction of his internal needs demanded." In other words, he can take his culture or he can leave it alone as is dictated by his deepest inner needs.

This, too, can be restated in the language of general semantics. One of the most important insights we get from general semantics is that human beings are a "symbolic class of life," from which follow our generalizations about the relationships between symbols and what they stand for. Because we are a symbolic class of life, much of our behavior, many of our needs, are symbolic in addition to being functional.

Let me illustrate this in a humble way. When we are hungry, of course we must eat, but we often eat at more expensive restaurants than we can afford because we hope to symbolize by this choice of restaurant our high social status, and we want to avoid the distasteful low-status symbolism of the modest restaurant where the food is better and the prices are lower. To those whose symbol systems are fixated and who have no self-insight, eating at the most expensive restaurant in town *is* success, while eating anywhere else *is* social disgrace. For symbol-fixated people this kind of identity equation holds for all other social symbols in the way of conspicuous consumption, social rituals, and social behavior. These are the people whose self-respect is *absolutely* dependent on the kind of clothes they wear, the kind of car they drive, the kind of society they are seen with. For these people clothes or cars or country club membership or social ritual are not symbols but ultimate realities.

To know the difference between a symbol and that which is symbolized—the difference between map and territory—is a central idea in general semantics. Of course others before Korzybski had arrived at this conclusion, but Korzybski was alone in making this a central premise of his thinking. Once you have internalized the idea that the symbol is not that which is symbolized, then you come to realize that never to have been invited to join the country club does not mean that your life has been lived in vain, and, *per contra*, it also means that you are able to dine at the country club, when you have to, without acting as if it was going to kill you.

Summed up in general semantics terms, the optimum relation of an individual to his culture can be stated as follows: since the map is not the territory, since the symbol is not that which is symbolized, the semantically well-oriented person is primarily concerned with the territory and not with the map, with the social reality rather than the social façade.

A second fact about the sane person is that, to an unusual degree, his own feelings and emotions, his own resentments and tensions, his attractions and his dislikes are, in Carl Rogers' terms, "accessible to awareness." We all have what Rogers and others have called a "self-concept," that is, some kind of idealized picture of ourselves. Thus, we may think of ourselves as efficient or as inefficient, as hard-boiled or as kindhearted, as lovable or as unlovable, or as artistic or as practical, etc. But also we all have impulses and feelings that do not fit our self-concepts, in that the man who thinks of himself as hard-boiled and tough may feel a twinge of humane sentiment that he would not know what to do with, or the person who thinks of himself as extremely gentle may suddenly find in himself a sadistic impulse. The self-defined highbrow may feel a lowbrow urge to go to a prize fight, while the husband who has been openly scornful of his wife's interest in modern art may unexpectedly find himself warming up to a painting by Miró. What so-called "normal" people do with these wellings of unexpected feeling that arise inside of them, is to suppress them, to deny them to awareness, since to admit them to awareness would require the reorganization of their picture of themselves.

The way in which a genuinely psychologically healthy person differs from so-called "normal" people in this respect is that he is aware of his own feelings, he does not try to suppress them, he often acts upon them, and, even if he does not act upon them, he is able to admit them to awareness. Let me quote Rogers' description of this characteristic. "The person would be open to his own experience. . . . In a person who is open to his experience . . . every stimulus, whether originating in the organism or in his environment, would be freely relayed through the nervous system without being distorted by defensive mechanisms." Carl Rogers talks about one of his patients:

Formerly he could not freely feel pain or illness, because being ill meant for him being unacceptable. Neither could he feel tenderness and love for his child, because such feelings meant being weak, and he had to maintain his façade of being strong. After therapy he can be genuinely open to the experiences of his organism—he can be tired when he is tired, he can feel pain when his organism is in pain, he can freely experience the love he feels for his daughter, and he can also feel and express the annoyance for her when he feels annoyed . . . he can fully live the experiences of his total organism, rather than shutting them out of his awareness. I have used this concept of availability to awareness to try to make clear what I mean by openness to one's own experience. This might be misunderstood. I do not mean that this individual would be self-consciously aware of all that was going on in himself, like the centipede that became aware of all his legs. On the contrary, he would be free to live a feeling subjectively, as well as be aware of it. He might experience love, or pain, or fear. Or he might abstract himself from this subjectivity and realize in awareness, "I am in pain," "I am afraid," "I do love." But the crucial point is that there are no barriers inside himself, no inhibitions which would prevent the full experiencing of his own emotions.

Maslow also is interested in this subject and it is curious how Maslow and Rogers converge from different theoretical sources. Maslow says of the self-actualizing personality, "Their ease of penetration to reality, their closer approach to an animal-like or child-like acceptance and spontaneity imply a superior awareness of their own impulses, their own desires, opinions, and subjective reactions in general."

These characteristics too can be translated into the language of general semantics. The first fundamental postulate of general semantics, as already indicated, is that the map is not the territory and the second postulate is that the map is never *all* of a territory. Now, if we regard the self-concept as the map of the self, we may, if we identify the map with the territory, feel that the self-concept *is* the self, which it is not. In other words, if my self-concept defines me as a gentle, kindhearted person, then *by definition* I don't *ever* have any cruel or sadistic impulses. If therefore sadistic impulses occur, they have to be denied to awareness. In other words, if my self-definition as gentle and kindhearted is rigid enough, I cannot permit myself to be aware of my nonkindhearted impulses, rare as they may be. Therefore, in one respect at least, I shall be like the famous man who shouted, "You know goddam well I never lose my temper!"

Supposing, on the other hand, one were a good general semanticist, aware through internalization of the principle that the map is not all the territory, that the self-concept therefore is not all of the self. In such a case I should, even if I defined myself as "gentle and tenderhearted," realize that this definition does not say all about myself and therefore I should be compelled to state, "So far as I know, and in the situations in which I have found myself, I have been, up to now, on the whole, gentle and tender-hearted. But since I have not been in all possible situations, nor experienced all possible experiences, and since few of us are completely honest with ourselves, there no doubt exist within me feelings I have not recognized in myself, as well as potentialities for emotions that I have not yet had occasion to feel." With such an attitude toward one's own self-definitions we should indeed be, in Rogers' terminology, "open to our own experience."

In short, the serious student of general semantics, as of any other psychological discipline, extending his scientific principles to every concept, including his own concept of himself, would know that every map, including the map of the self, must shade off at the edges into a *terra incognita*. Therefore he expects the unexpected within the area of his own thoughts and feelings, and he is not compelled to deny these feelings to awareness.

Socrates said, "Know thyself." But he also said, "Whatever authority I may have, rests solely upon my knowing how little I know." And what Socrates said about knowledge in general applies with special cogency to self-knowledge. The individual who says, "I know myself," does not know himself. It is the individual who knows how little he knows about himself who stands a reasonable chance of finding out something about himself before he dies.

Another thing about the genuinely sane person which is emphasized, although in different ways, by Rogers and Maslow is that since the map is not the territory, and since therefore knowledge about an event is never the event itself, those who take this fact for granted are not uncomfortable about the fact that they don't know the answers. Maslow says:

Our healthy subjects are uniformly unthreatened and unfrightened by the unknown, being therein quite different from average men. They accept the unknown, they are comfortable with it, and, often are even attracted by it. To use Frenkel-Brunswick's phrase, "they can tolerate the ambiguous." . . . Since, for healthy people, the unknown is not frightening, they do not have to spend any time laying the ghost, whistling past the cemetery, or otherwise protecting themselves against danger. They do not neglect the unknown, or deny it, or run away from it, or try to make believe it really is known, nor do they organize, dichotomize, or rubricize it prematurely. They do not cling to the familiar, nor is their quest for truth a catastrophic need for certainty, for safety, for definiteness, and order. The fully functioning personality can be, when the objective situation calls for it, comfortably disorderly, anarchic, vague, doubtful, uncertain, indefinite, approximate, inexact, or inaccurate.

There is another fundamental principle in general semantics with which many of you are perfectly familiar, that of indexing and dating, as we call it in our terminology. The idea is, of course, that no two individual things or persons or events are ever identical, and that everything in the world is in process, with changes occurring constantly. We have that rule in form A_1 is not A_2; policeman$_1$ is not policeman$_2$; and policeman$_1$ (this week) is not policeman$_1$ (next week), and so on. Most of our errors of evaluation arise, Korzybski said, from identification reactions, in which we ignore the differences between individuals of the same class name, and in which we ignore the changes that occur over time. Another name for the same principle in general semantics literature is extensionality, as opposed to intensionality. The extensional individual responds to similarities *and differences*; whereas the intensional individual tends to ignore differences among things that have the same name. This principle of intensional orientation is illustrated by the saying, "A woman driver is, after all, a woman driver." The extensional individual is highly aware of things, people, and events at subverbal levels, where everything is in process.

It is gratifying to know that Maslow and Rogers describe the fully functioning personality as extensional if we can judge from the following accounts. In Rogers' paper, *Toward a Theory of Creativity*, this concept of openness to experience is further elaborated. Dr. Rogers says:

The creative person, instead of perceiving in predetermined categories ("trees are green," "college education is a good thing," "modern art is silly") is aware of this existential moment as it *is*, and therefore he is alive to many experiences which fall outside the usual categories (in *this* light this tree is lavender; *this* college education is damaging; *this* modern sculpture has a powerful effect on me).

The creative person is in this way open to his own experiences. It means a lack of rigidity and the permeability of boundaries in concepts, beliefs, perceptions and hypotheses. It means a tolerance of ambiguity where ambiguity exists. It means the ability to receive much conflicting information without forcing closure on the situation.

Dr. Maslow has another way of saying this:

Self-actualized people have a wonderful capacity to appreciate again and again, freshly and naïvely the basic goods of life, with awe, pleasure, wonder, and even ecstasy, however stale these experiences may be for other people. Thus, for such people, every sunset is as beautiful as the first one, any flower can be breathtakingly lovely even after he has seen a million flowers. And the thousandth baby he sees is just as miraculous a product as the first one he saw.

And this is simply another way of stating the indexing principle. Thus, $sunset_1$, is not $sunset_2$, $flower_{1,000,000}$ is not $flower_{1,000,001}$, $baby_{1,000}$ is not $baby_{1,001}$. And therefore experience continues to be fresh for the creative person.

Maslow describes this extensionality of self-actualizing people in social relationships in the following terms. "They can be and are friendly with anyone of suitable character regardless of class, education, political belief, race or color. As a matter of fact it seems as if they are not even aware of the differences which often mean so much to other people." In other words, the self-actualizing person *experiences at lower levels of abstraction* than the rest of us. He reacts to the specific $Smith_1$, $Smith_2$, etc. and therefore he concerns himself very little with high order abstractions such as, "He is a Catholic," "He is a Republican," "He is a Negro," etc.

Maslow also says:

> The first and most obvious level of acceptance to be found in the self-actualizing personality is at the so-called animal level. These self-actualizing people tend to be good and lusty animals, hearty in their appetites and enjoying themselves mightily without regret or shame or apology. They seem to have a uniformly good appetite for food, they seem to sleep well, they seem to enjoy their sexual lives without unnecessary inhibition, and so on for all the relatively physiological impulses. They are able to "accept" themselves not only at these lower levels, but at all levels as well, e.g., love, safety, belongingness, honor, self-respect. All these are accepted without question as worth while simply because they are part of human nature, and because these people are inclined to accept the work of nature rather than argue with nature for not having constructed things to a different plan. This interesting point shows itself in self-actualizing people by the lack of disgusts and aversions seen in average people and especially in neurotics, e.g., food annoyance, disgust with body products, body odors, and body functions. . . . One does not complain about water because it is wet, nor about rocks because they are hard. . . . As the child looks out upon the world with wide, uncritical and innocent eyes, simply noting and observing what is the case, without either arguing the matter or demanding that it be otherwise, so does the self-actualizing person look upon human nature both in himself and others.

Another curious fact which I find deeply meaningful and which Maslow points out arises from this childlike quality of perception and feeling in the self-actualized person which makes for a structure of ends and means different from those of other people. For most people, almost everything they do is a means to an end. So far as people who are regarded as normal in the rat race of American life are concerned, ends are often almost impossible to discover: they work in order to eat, they eat in order to work; they play golf in order to keep fit, and they keep fit in order to work better, and they work better in order to be able to afford their golf club fees. Maslow also says elsewhere that people even rationalize fishing by saying, "It is important to be out in the open air," instead of regarding fishing as a pleasure in itself. Here is an example of ends-means relationship with respect to my own children. In Chicago we lived in an apartment with a self-operating elevator. I found that I pushed that button *in order to* get upstairs; but to my children I found that pressing the elevator button and releasing the amazing consequences of that act was a pleasure in itself, to be undertaken leisurely, zestfully, and with sparkling eyes. So it used to take us a very long time to get upstairs. But the point is that self-actualizing people, like children, enjoy as ends in themselves hundreds of little things that to ordinary people are only means. Dr. Rogers says of the same point:

> Such living in the moment means an absence of rigidity, of tight organization, of the imposition of a structure. It means, instead, a maximum of adaptability, a discovery of structure in experience, of a flowing, changing organization of the self and of personality rather than the imposition of structure upon experience.

Another characteristic of the fully functioning personality is that he is a creative individual, sometimes creative in the usual sense of artist, musician, novelist, scientist, or political leader, but just as often creative in smaller, but equally genuine ways, that is, the ability of the carpenter, the office manager, the house-organ editor, the housewife, or the teacher to improvise, for the particular needs of a job at hand, out of the particular materials at hand, a unique and original solution of a problem, a solution that immediately strikes others with a thrill of pleasure so that they say, "How did you ever think of that!" This is what I mean by creativeness.

Maslow writes that there are no exceptions to the rule that self-actualizing people are creative in their own way.

Carl Rogers also has been concerned with this problem of creativity and he says that in a creative person and therefore a fully functioning person, "the locus of evaluation is in the self." It isn't what teachers think, it isn't what the Ph.D. committee thinks, it isn't what the neighbors think, it's what *I* think that matters. Because the fully functioning person's experience, past and present, are accessible to awareness, because he sees freshly and without rigid categorizing or labeling of the situation before him, he ultimately is his own judge of what is the needed solution for any given problem. After all, the solutions of others are merely the solutions of people who weren't in *this* situation, confronted with *this* problem, with *these* materials or with *these* people to work with. Therefore, the fully functioning person, even if he may welcome the praise or admiration of others, is not dependent on others.

Perhaps from this we can give an account in general semantics terms of the creative process. Let me put it something like this: if you see in any given situation only what everybody else can see, you can be said to be so much a representative of your culture that you are a victim of it. In other words, you haven't even got the materials to be original with, since you have before you only "just another" sunset, "just another" tree, "just another" batch of leftovers in the icebox—these are the common abstractions. But if you are extensional about the world around you, open to the uniqueness of every object and event, if you are open, too, about your own feelings, namely, the uniqueness of your tensions and needs at this moment, and of those around you, what is before you is *not* "just another" sunset, or "just another" tree, or "just another" batch of leftovers. And the act of bringing together the uniqueness of yourself at that moment with the uniqueness of your materials at that moment into the solution of the problem is the act of creativity: whether the end product takes the form of a painting, a sonata, a plan for prison reform, or a new kind of casserole dish.

I should like to call in another source of insight on the subject by quoting from the poet and novelist, D. H. Lawrence, when he talks about art.[1] What he says about art seems to me exactly equivalent to what Maslow and Rogers say about the relationship of a genuinely sane person to the world around him:

> The business of art is to reveal the relation between man and his circumambient universe, at this living moment. As mankind is always struggling in the toil of old relationships, art is always ahead of its "times," which themselves are always far in the rear of the living present.
>
> When van Gogh paints sunflowers, he reveals, or achieves, the vivid relationship between himself, as man, and the sunflower, as sunflower, at that quick moment of time. His painting is not the sunflower itself. We shall never know what the sunflower is. The camera will visualize the sunflower far more perfectly than van Gogh ever did.
>
> The vision on the canvas is a third thing, utterly intangible and inexplicable, the offspring of the sunflower itself and van Gogh himself. The vision on the canvas is forever incommensurable with the canvas, or the paint, or van Gogh as a human organism, or the sunflower as a botanical organism. You cannot weigh nor measure nor even describe the vision on the canvas. . . .

[1] "Morality and the Novel," in *Phoenix: Posthumous Papers of D. H. Lawrence* (The Viking Press, 1936).

It is a revelation of a perfected relation, at a certain moment, between man and a sunflower . . . and this perfected relation between man and his circumambient universe is life itself, for mankind. . . . Man and the sunflower both pass away in a moment, in the process of forming a new relationship. The relation between all things changes from day to day, in a subtle stealth of change. Hence art, which reveals or attains to another perfect relationship, will be forever new.

If we think about it, we find that our life consists in this achieving of a pure relationship between ourselves and the living universe about us. This is how I "save my soul" by accomplishing a pure relationship between me and another person, me and other people, me and a nation, me and a race of men, me and animals, me and the trees or flowers, me and the earth, me and the skies and sun and stars, me and the moon: an infinity of pure relations, big and little. . . . This, if we knew it, is our life and our eternity: the subtle, perfected relation between me and the circumambient universe.

Finally, the fully functioning personality is ethical in the deepest sense. Maslow says that his sane people have a sense of right and wrong that is quite clear-cut, but that their evaluations are at deeper levels, rather than at the superficial levels that most people worry about. He says that ordinary "moral" problems fade out of existence for sane people:

It is not so much that the problem is solved as that it becomes clearly seen that it never was an intrinsic problem to start with, but it was only a sick-man-created one, e.g., whether or not one plays cards or dances, or wears short or long dresses, exposing the head in some churches and covering it in others, drinking wine, eating some meats and not others, or eating them on some days and not others.

For the fully functioning personality such problems are deflated. Rogers says on the same point that because the fully functioning personality is nondefensive and because he therefore has access to his own needs and those of others, he can be counted on to be trustworthy and constructive. That is, the unsane individual is moral only with the greatest of effort and often he behaves unmorally and viciously with the best of moral intention. Whereas to the fully functioning personality, as Rogers, Maslow, and Korzybski see him, morality and ethics come naturally, as the result of proper evaluation. A person who is fully open to his own feelings and deeply aware of other people as well, can hardly act blindly or selfishly. He is deeply socialized, as Dr. Rogers says, because "one of his own deepest needs is for affiliation and communication with others. When he is most fully himself—'selfish'—he cannot help but be most deeply identified with others too and therefore his orientation is social in the best sense."

This picture of the sane person may sound like an impossible ideal. I don't want it to sound that way. What is the sane person like to meet? What does he look like? Well, he (or she) may be short or tall, may be thin or fat. He (or she) may wear false teeth or have fallen arches or bifocals. He (or she) may be childlike in some respects and therefore may look childish to his friends and neighbors. Because he is somewhat detached from his culture, he may seem cold and distant to others. But, most importantly, this sane person that I have been describing in the abstract may suffer from anxiety and fear and doubt and foreboding—because such feelings can arise from nonneurotic sources in this troubled world—so that *externally he (or she) may look just as troubled and act just as troubled as a neurotic person*, because there *are* troubles in the world which cause doubt, anxiety, and foreboding. *But his troubles would be real ones and not self-contrived ones.*

I say this last because sometimes we speak of the goals of mental health as if they meant the hope of the emergence of completely happy people in a completely trouble-free world. If such were our goal, it would indeed be an impossible and unattainable one. Actually, it seems to me that the goals of mental health are much more modest. Sanity does not mean the solution of all problems (cultural or psychological or economic or whatever) but merely the abolition or avoidance of those problems which we create for ourselves through lack of self-insight.

Self-insight is necessary and prior to all other kinds of insight. Self-insight is increased, of course, by experience—and by reflection upon experience. Further insights may be derived from literature, poetry, drama, and the arts. All these insights may be ordered and made more meaningful through the study of psychology, cultural anthropology, sociology, general semantics, and other such disciplines. If through such experiences, reflection, and study we are able to increase our self-insight, we shall have made a real start toward seeing more clearly, and therefore beginning to solve, the problems other than psychological that beset this troubled world.

Spring, 1956. Dr. Hayakawa is professor of language arts at San Francisco State College; editor (and founder), ETC.: A Review of General Semantics, *1943 to present. This paper was presented at the Asilomar Conference of the Mental Health Society of Northern California, September 3, 1955; at the annual meeting of the American Occupational Therapy Association in San Francisco, October, 1955; and at the Outdoor Art Club, Mill Valley, California, May, 1956. An earlier version of this paper was presented in the 1954 Lecture Series of the Chicago Chapter of the International Society for General Semantics.*

III. The Arts: Highbrow and Low

As long as the means of [mass] communication are not available for criticism of themselves, as long as we are prevented from thinking about the process by which we are hypnotized into not thinking, we remain at the mercy of our simplest appetites, our immediate and almost childish sensations, and these can be exploited—for the arts most useful to the public are essentially those which can be most effectively turned against the public good.

To know this, to know that we have the right to put them into our service, is the beginning of an intelligent approach to the problems and to the opportunities of the public arts.

GILBERT SELDES, *The Public Arts*

Design as Metaphor

WELLER EMBLER

Before me is a reproduction of a painting by Giorgio di Chirico. What does it mean, this weird picture called "Il Trovatore," and why on earth should anyone have chosen to paint such a picture? The main figure in the painting suggests a man, but its feet are cloven hoofs, its legs and thighs are like the lower appendages of a puppet, joined loosely together, and smoothly shaped out of painted wood. Its torso is a medley of triangles in dark greens, browns, and yellows, a grotesque arrangement of shapes, odds and ends from under the carpentry bench. The figure, like the Venus of Milo, is armless. Its melancholy head is the shape of a football, or an egg, and appears to be stitched down the center and tied round the middle in a bow of black ribbon. The head reminds one of those chickenwire forms used to display millinery in shop windows. The whole mannequin, strange and sad, is supported by wooden braces (for it is not so well balanced as the Venus) and is set off against a background of enigmatic spaces with dusky shadows, against an architectural motive with ominous doors and windows that watch the empty scene intently, and against, in the distance, forbidding bottle-green skies. On the left there falls a mysterious shadow across the piazza floor of the scene, the shadow of a human figure, a stranger, silent, inquiring, reproachful.

It would be difficult to say what this painting "means," though it must stand for something the artist felt or had in mind. The modern artist may seem often not to have premeditated the content or design of his painting, yet his art is not whimsical or casual. He is serious and intends that his art shall be meaningful. What is more, his art invariably has some kind of emotional impact on the observer, though the emotion may not be readily articulated in words or be the same emotion that inspired the painter. What "Il Trovatore" means to me may not be in one-to-one correspondence with what it meant to the painter when he was making his picture. Indeed, the iconography may be, probably was, intensely personal to the painter. But the painting hangs on my wall and "stands for" thoughts and feelings of today. The painting is part of my environment and says something to me which I can translate into words.

The mannequin is clearly a troubadour, for that is the title of the picture. Here lies obvious irony, that this weak, fantastic, patched-up creature should be said to represent the twelfth-century heroic lover, debonair maker and singer of love songs. The figure is no Manrico, nursed and reared by gypsies, duelist, romantic knight. This dreaming puppet is the modern troubadour, ineffectual, with geometry for a heart, but, curiously, like Manrico, a being capable of suffering, and if not a tragic hero, at least a tragic personality.

Why is the di Chirico puppet supported by braces? And what are these braces that keep the figure standing upright? There comes to my mind a sonnet by Matthew Arnold, which is in a way a considerable comment on the painting.

> Who prop, thou ask'st, in these bad days, my mind?
> How much, the old man, who, clearest-soul'd of men,
> Saw The Wide Prospect, and the Asian Fen,
> And Tmolus' hill, and Smyrna's bay, though blind.
> Much he, whose friendship I not long since won,
> That halting slave, who in Nicopolis
> Taught Arrian, when Vespasian's brutal son
> Clear'd Rome of what most sham'd him. But be his
> My special thanks, whose even-balanc'd soul,
> From first youth tested up to extreme old age,
> Business could not make dull, nor Passion wild:
> Who saw life steadily, and saw it whole:
> The mellow glory of the Attic stage;
> Singer of sweet Colonus, and its child.

Ours, if one were to judge only from what has been said about them, are "bad days." And one might well ask whom he can turn to for intellectual and spiritual support in these parlous times. First, says Arnold, Homer, because he was clear-souled. But there is, alas, no Homer in the painting. Nor is there an Epictetus, "halting slave," unless the figure itself is a forlorn stoic, perhaps very much more slave than philosopher. And di Chirico might well have claimed both Homer and Epictetus as countrymen, for he was himself both Greek and Italian. And lastly there is Sophocles, who saw life steadily and saw it whole, as the puppet figure certainly does not. Di Chirico's mannequin sees life hardly at all, except as a riddle, a contemporary sphinx (the shadow in the painting?), who will not be answered and who claims her victims with monstrous indifference. What props our modern figure are the meaningless sticks of modern life, holding the miracle of man (though he sports vestiges of nobility in his blue cloak) by the nape of the neck.

When I look at "Il Trovatore," my attention is called irresistibly to another poem, "The Hollow Men," by T. S. Eliot. Eliot's poem is dated 1925, and di Chirico's picture is dated 1917. One may reasonably suspect that Eliot knew the painting, was even, conceivably, inspired by it, or by any one of the many di Chirico paintings that show strange, puppet-like figures with the egg-shaped heads. These heads, are they filled with straw, fit only to display bonnets?

> The eyes are not here
> There are no eyes here

T. S. Eliot's poem is an illuminating companion to di Chirico's painting. Modern man is frustrated and made impotent by the shadows of fear and anxiety, by the shadows of doubt and self-contempt. For the shadow of doubt falls often

> Between the motion
> And the act
>
> Between the emotion
> And the response.[1]

Di Chirico's straw-filled doll is pinioned to an armature in the city square, alone and desolate in the very sight of a majestic and vigorous past. Di Chirico's painting is a plastic statement of our distance (in emotional perspective) from the wisdom of ancient Greece, from the

[1] From "The Hollow Men," *Collected Poems, 1909-1935*.

castles of Provence, from the glory that was the human figure in the Renaissance, from the glory that was the human spirit in Homer and Sophocles.

Design invariably, from the simplest to the most complex, has meaning. Design is metaphorical, just as language is metaphorical. Patterns, shapes, and outlines express inner thoughts and feelings, give body and form to beliefs and doubts, hopes, ideals, needs. Design is informed thought or emotion, an allegory of that which is within us. Design is communication and is surrogate for the something within which, curiously, is not fully created until it has been given expression formally. Hence design is a making of something, the creation of a pattern which represents the thought or feeling, and at the same time becomes a something in itself, a captured, embodied emotion. In this sense all design is representational. For all design is emblematic of the thought of the designer and says something about him and his society. Design is never really random or accidental or pure. It always has meaning. It is always a thought or a feeling becoming substantial. And the substance is the metaphorical expression of the mind's life. The astonishing thing is that the design should so often say so well what we want it to say, so that sometimes the idea or emotion appears to have been perfectly realized in the design.

Before inquiring further into the philosophy of design, let me illustrate the relationship of design to cultural beliefs and social ideals in a specific culture pattern—the genteel tradition in American life.

The genteel tradition in America had its beginnings in the eighteenth century and was the American democratic equivalent of European aristocratic life. The tradition has persevered into our own times (though it has suffered some changes, to be sure), but it was most vigorous in the early nineteenth century. Though the aim of its social philosophy is happiness, and though as a way of life the tradition seeks to avoid the unpleasant, if necessary by overlooking it, nevertheless, the genteel tradition trusts in the good things of life, believes in being civilized, and is devoted, in a naïve sort of way, to the idea of good will toward men.

Essential to the tradition is a social homogeneity, defined to a great extent, though not exclusively, by wealth and a community of cultivated tastes. In the late eighteenth century and in the early nineteenth century the ideals of taste were derived from European aristocratic society, and the categories of the cultivated life were expressed with insight by Lord Chesterfield as *"les manières, les agréments, et les grâces,"* as manners, the cultivated pleasures, and the graces.

By manners, of course, a great deal more is meant than mere drawing-room poise. By manners is meant that whole social structure implied in the term "good form," form that keeps the world together. Civilization is form, and a civilized society is one which has developed a "style" of behavior, a style made real in ceremony, in social patterns, elegant and complicated, like the figure in the carpet, like a sentence of Henry James.

Form is expressed not only in the ritual of good manners but also in the picturesque, in the composed, or better still, perhaps, in the posed, where space, the space concept, which is basic to the genteel philosophy, is experienced in its deepest sense. Distance lends enchantment to the view, as a genteel poet once said, and the view is of the utmost importance. It is the open window looking out upon the faraway in picturesque composition that is the stamp and seal of this philosophy. And out of space is made the ideal, one might almost say, the beauty of the remote, for it is in the remote that the tradition has most to say, believes in most, and serves as its very foundation— whether it be expressed in the view, or the good things which come from far corners of the earth, a Ming porcelain, an Indian tapestry, or whether it be the liberal and charitable interest which one can show for those at some little remove—can show from a distance to the less fortunate of the earth. It is the vista, given out, perhaps, by aisles of honeysuckle or cedar hedges, the vista of misty blue mountains at the end of the aisle or of a classical summerhouse set in a small court at the end of a pleasant alley, or a vista of the past, of tradition, of history itself, becoming in the hands of the tradition a space idea as much as a time idea, as in scenic wallpaper which pictures clipper ships, and the wide ocean, and, superimposed in the composition, an architectural ruin of ancient Rome.

The feeling is spatial. The ideal is the statuesque, the snapshot, the still life, a kind of frozen space, in which the culture, the vision and image of the good things of life—these parks and parterres and hedges, these views, these ceremonies and rituals of the photograph album, these ancient ruins, abbeys composed in myrtles and ivys, these *objets d'art* from the far corners—are congealed, in which the pleasant, the gracious, the charming, the delightful, the tasteful has been made to abide, to endure, in space, forever.

"The failure of Woolett, Massachusetts," says Maria Gostrey in *The Ambassadors,* "was the failure to enjoy," to enjoy, of course, the agreeable things of life, the cultivated pleasures, as Lord Chesterfield called them, for Woolett was puritan minded, and it was against conscience in Woolett to be "happy." In the social philosophy of the genteel tradition, happiness—serene worldly contentment—is of basic importance, and the authentic Brahmin was educated to the tried pleasures, to appreciation of *tradition* (the mellowed past), to taste in the arts, in literature, in the rare and precious.

But when Lord Chesterfield speaks of *les grâces,* he touches on the vibrant life of the tradition. The Graces, it will be remembered, are the three goddesses of classical mythology who preside over the elegant and refined pleasures of life, enhancing them with brilliance, joy, and the freshness of bloom. Aglaia is brilliance, attending social enjoyments, present wherever there is good breeding and good nature, lending sprightliness, sparkling wit, and polish to discourse. Euphrosyne stands for joy, one who tones down the Dionysian to acceptable proportions, to tasteful entertainment, who inspires gracious living, a general good will, who gives spice to the agreeable things of life. And Thalia represents innocence and new bloom, the naïve, the unsophisticated. She is youth, sweetness, the uncorrupted, the very color and vitality of youth in all its unsmirched blossoming freshness, an adornment, a springtime decoration, a Lady Hamilton as "Nature" by George Romney.

Examples of the genteel tradition in modern painting are to be found in the paintings of Pierre Bonnard, Raoul Dufy, and Henri Matisse. Dufy's "Open Window in Nice" is a polished and felicitous composition. It is a picture of a richly furnished room looking out through open French doors (their long glass windows etched with graceful traceries) upon a Mediterranean scene in profound azure. The room is a tableau, pleasing, sophisticated, reflecting the cultivated sensibilities of those who might really live in such surroundings. But it is the whole painting that delights the eye with subtle harmonies and pleasing patterns suggesting good manners, and, effortlessly, the best of taste. In the paintings of Pierre Bonnard one sees the work of a painter who wished to paint only happy, gracious things, gardens with figures, dinner tables, windows opening out upon quiet landscapes, flowering almond trees. If one analyzes the charm of a Matisse painting, he will find, I think, that it derives from the philosophy of life that emphasizes form—interiors with open windows, decorative figures on ornamental backgrounds (a kind of ceremonial pattern), a cultivated sensibility with experience of the good things (these pineapples and anemones and Japanese objects of art), the pose (the picturesque, the sunlit interior, the still life of flowers and tables and "arrangements," the windows and doors with views, the vista), the remote, that distance that lends enchantment, the exotic—those seraglios and odalisques and arabesques, and Moroccan landscapes, and last but hardly least, the representation of happiness, of the ideal of happiness, that obvious "joy of living" so youthfully expressed, really, in the brilliant colors. The work of art should "not raise problems," said Matisse. "I want people . . . to get a feeling of repose, when looking at my painting." This is the meaning of that exquisite composition, that sorcery of arrangement, that magic of rhythm and color—the genteel philosophy become substance in decorative design.

This, too, is the meaning of handsome magazines like *House and Garden*, the statuesque covers of *Harper's Bazaar* and *Vogue*, the posed covers, and as a fine example of the tradition brought well up to date, of the late *Flair* magazine of the window-vista covers. This is the meaning of the advertising which occurs in these magazines, of the "pose," the "setting," the photographs of far places, the "snapshot" of the family clustered happily around the expensive automobile drawn up before a Georgian entrance in an expanse of wide green lawns.

This is the meaning of scenic suburbia, of the parklike avenues, the "country" lanes, and the picturesque nautical settings where there is so much of everything to contribute to the happy life, where the environment is, as Matisse said of his paintings, "a cerebral sedative, rather like a comfortable armchair." This is the meaning of interior decor, where elegance is employed as representative of the philosophy of the good things, the discerning, the exotic. This is the meaning of that domestic architecture which we recognize as Georgian, the uttermost in refinement, in harmonious proportions, as in the distinguished work of Samuel McIntire, expressing the whole of a tradition. Georgian architecture is the perfect expression of that "reasonable, delightful order" so dear to the heart, so very much the heart of the genteel tradition.

Our inner thoughts and beliefs become substantial in the works of our hands, and if we wish to know what we deeply believe, what we approve of, we have but to look at the things we have made. Consider, for example, Thoreau's house at Walden Pond, which tells us as much about Concord high thinking as the Craigie house does about Cambridge high living in the nineteenth century. I do not know that Thoreau's house could have been called domestic architecture. It was intended only as a "shelter." But it had meaning nevertheless. The little hut was a representation of the whole philosophy of New England transcendentalism. Thoreau chose the kind of dwelling which should in no way be a burden to him, as he had some special business to transact with nature and with himself, and he could not spend his time looking after his property. His house was a protest against the materialistic way of life where "things" count for more than people. But it was more than that. It was a shelter designed to let the owner live by the seasons, even by the parts of the day, morning, afternoon, evening. It was a shelter that left the spirit free to follow its whims. But it tells us even more. It tells us about New England thrift, of the acceptance of the challenge to make do with little, so that the worldly shall not be more than the spiritual. The little hut had above all something most emphatic to say about freedom. It was James Russell Lowell who passed the judgment on Thoreau's *Walden* that has clung to it ever since its publication. "Thoreau's experiment actually presupposed," said Lowell, "all that complicated civilization which it theoretically abjured."

But it was not Thoreau's distaste for civilization that sent him to Walden Pond. Thoreau wished to live for a while on the shores of Walden Pond to see what it had to offer, just as Lowell wished often to travel in Europe to see what it had to offer. Far from abjuring civilization, it was precisely civilization that Thoreau wanted and approved of, the highest kind of civilization, which makes it possible for a man to go to Walden Pond if his business calls him thither, precisely because the mortar does exist, because lumber is available, and lamps, and plows, and books. Civilization makes possible the choice. *To insist through action upon the right to make a choice*—that was the meaning of the house at Walden. Let others do as they wish—make britanniaware lamps at Brook Farm, enjoy the society of the great country houses of England, worship in churches, count money at high desks, or frequent barrooms. Thoreau was a naturalist and a philosopher. So he went to Walden to transact his business. And when Thoreau had had enough of Walden, he left, saying he "had several more lives to live and could not spare any more time for that one." It is no wonder that the house at Walden is no longer standing. It was not important that it should stand after Thoreau left it. It was not a monument. It was a shelter only, from which the spirit could roam at will.

As language is different among the different peoples of the world, so design is diversified according to the various cultures of the world. And the masterpieces of design are outward signs of the subjective life of a people, just as the masterpieces of literature are also confessions of the life within. How diverse and numerous are these masterpieces of design is only too well known today as a result of far-reaching studies in archaeology and cultural anthropology. And without exception, each created article of a culture is a figure of speech, a vehicle made to carry inner thoughts and feelings with more or less power and distinction.

The tree of life has been a symbol from time immemorial, signifying man's undying hope to realize the sources of his existence and to become one with them, in this life and in the life hereafter. In different styles and versions, the flowering tree has appeared over the world, in Coptic textiles of the fourth century, in Persian silks carried to Spain, in Indian tapestries, in Chinese porcelains and embroideries, in illuminated Mexican manuscripts.

The bridge, in its many styles and designs, has stood in all lands and times for coherence, for joining and holding together, from the George Washington Bridge in New York to the covered bridges of New England, from Japanese foot bridges to Maillart's sculptured concrete. How deep a meaning one may attach to the bridge can be seen from the dedicated work of John and Washington Roebling in their Brooklyn Bridge; in the stained-glass, cathedral-like design of Joseph Stella's paintings of Brooklyn Bridge; in Hart Crane's epic *The Bridge*, inspired by the Brooklyn Bridge; in Jo Mielziner's stage setting for Maxwell Anderson's *Winterset*; and in the cluster of emotions attached to Brooklyn Bridge by the people of the boroughs of Brooklyn and Manhattan.

There is profound religious meaning in the design of a Cambodian temple, just as there is in the design of a medieval cathedral and in the Toltec Avenue of the Dead. There is cultural meaning in the construction of a Malayan house on stakes, and in the cliff dwellings of the Pueblo Indians. Consider how freighted with meaning is the Hiwassee Dam of the Tennessee Valley Authority. Its concrete is reinforced with a philosophy of life. (This is no wasteland!) The dam at Hiwassee is a symbol of creativity and co-operation. And the beauty of its engineering derives, in part at least, from what it stands for—unity of purpose among men toward useful and creative and human ends.

Of all design, architecture probably has the most to say metaphorically because it has so much of *history* in it. Architectural design stands for tradition, continuity of human faith, the victory of man over intransigent forces and materials, the past with its wealth of thought and its wealth of feeling. The Greek temple, the Egyptian tomb, the Gothic cathedral—these are the very texture of history, the thought and hope of perpetuation become realized and substantial. The history of Europe is in her ecclesiastical design—Romanesque, containing reminiscences of the Crusades and of Byzantium and the East; Gothic with its great vaults and stained glass expressive of medieval religious fervor, its slender piers and flying buttresses metaphors in stone of medieval logic; Renaissance in its rich worldly beauty emblematic of Renaissance humanism; Baroque a sign of the vastness and grandeur that was the mind of the seventeenth century.

The early history of America is clearly presented in New England church architecture, an architectural design embodying all the puritan virtues. In the simple, harmoniously proportioned, many-windowed, steeple-topped, white wooden buildings built to the Glory of God and the Holy Commonwealth is represented divine orderliness and austerity and candor. There is nothing inexplicable here, no flesh, no appetite, no vanity, nor worldly longings. Here is purity and that clear defiant individualism which believes in the unencumbered exploration of the self toward personal salvation, that single-minded pursuit of perfection, that insistence upon personal identity, and that polar solitude which is, to the puritan, of all things most godlike. This church is a part of our history, and even to those who do not take part in its devotions or believe in its philosophy, its architecture is meaningful as history, is full of the ideals of a great tradition. Architecture is not frozen music, but through its symbolic form, it is frozen history.

What, if one stops to think of them, is one to make of his surroundings, the things he looks at, the materials he uses, the objects, breaking up space, in and around which the routine of his daily life takes place? Our environment is inevitably a projection in design of what we believe about life. If we were to choose the modern design which seems to say most about the twentieth century, which appears to be most widespread and meaningful, we should probably select that which is based on the cube or rectangle, or, reducing the design to its simplest and most telling element, the horizontal straight line. It is tempting to look for a meaning in the free forms of contemporary design, in the organic line rather than the straight line, in the biomorphic rather than the geometrical pattern. And indeed there is much that is significan socially and psychologically in contemporary abstract painting (in the work of Jackson Pollock and Willem de Kooning, for example), in ceramics, and particularly in sculpture, where the organic form expresses primordial emotions and strange psychological insights with vivid intensity. In fact, the free sensitive organic line has meaning in it as yet incapable of being articulated in social and psychological language. Nevertheless, the most common shapes in modern design are for the most part those based on the straight line, and this is most obvious, of course, in modern architecture.

A great deal has already been written about the early history of cubism as a strong and authoritative art movement originating largely with Dutch and Parisian painters in the early part of the century. The social and philosophical meaning of cubism is of chief interest to us here. In many ways the history of the twentieth century has been expressed in modern cubist design. For example, one must observe that it is closely related to theoretical science in its emphasis on a space-time dimension and on the principle of simultaneity; in its research into space, as with Parisian cubism, and into time, as with Italian futurism. One must also be impressed with the cubist's philosophical questioning of reality itself and with the social protest implied in the breaking up (the deformation) of the "old" reality and its rehabilitation into a new, more harmonious composition, which shall be a little nearer the eye's desire if not the heart's.

Yet cubism has even deeper meaning psychologically. The cube, the rectangle, the square, and the line are signs of pronounced inner feelings. One would be rash, perhaps, to say "precisely" what these feelings are, for they are clearly not the same to everyone. Yet we may be reasonably certain of this, that linear design is very nearly always symbolic of the intellectual, not as distinguished from the emotional, but as different from the organic or "natural." The straight line stands for basic simplicity, for directional movement (e.g., in the rectangle), for horizontal drive, for a balance of tensions in the right angle, and for crisis, as in the intersection. Specifically, the long straight line of the rectangle stands for energetic horizontal movement. Modern architecture is linear in design, the rectangle being its basic shape. The dynamic character of this horizontal movement, imaginatively pioneered by Frank Lloyd Wright, is an expression of our new inner orientation to the space-time continuum which, when expressed in terms of everyday happenings, is simply a sensitiveness to new energies and to their expression in terms of *speed and change*. A feature of modern design is its minimum of detail and ornament, its simplicity and directness, its compelling immediacy, powerful movement in something like Picasso's "Guernica" mural, sudden drama of blacks and whites in interior decoration, instantaneity of appeal in popular advertising. The machine, modern architecture, cubistic abstract painting, bridges, industrial engineering, and advertising design are all emblematic of the new personality which believes in speed and change. Nikolaus Pevsner has described very well what it is we respond to in modern linear design, when, in writing of the work of Walter Gropius, he says,

Glass walls are now clear and without mystery, the steel frame is hard, and its expression discourages all other-worldly speculation. It is the creative energy of this world in which we live and work and want to master, a world of science and technique, of speed and danger, of hard struggles and no personal security, that is glorified in Gropius' architecture. (*Pioneers of Modern Design*)

The straight line is our tree of life. The source of our life and the nourishment of our being appear to derive from the hidden energies of which the horizontal drive is sign and symbol as well as effect—the articulation of speed in the train on the track, the automobile on the parkway, the airplane in its path, the propulsion of the world's commerce from destination to destination across the earth, inflexible and with fierce determination.

But there lingers in one's mind a doubt that modern design can remain purely abstract and intellectual and compulsive in its movement. The feeling for something a little more "human" and less "driven" is being expressed in recent developments in linear design. What may have started as an articulation of speed and change only and for their own sake has been considerably sweetened by the milk of broader social philosophies.

Though we do not respond to the lotus flower or the spreading tree of life, we find spiritual sustenance in certain patterns of cubes and squares and rectangles that are symbolic ritual performances of *freedom*. The line is authority, *but space is freedom*. The tension between space and boundary is fully suspended in the square, whose right angles are, in effect, movable in any direction, making the possibility of more room everywhere. In modern design space is not cramped but flexible. Instead of being cabined and confined, we are emancipated emotionally in the feeling of being able, like the cube, to expand limitlessly in all directions simultaneously. The sense of free movement is embodied ideoplastically in the United Nations Buildings in New York. In outer appearance, the Secretariat may resemble a colossal filing cabinet, indifferent to flesh and blood of humans. But when the Secretariat and the Assembly building are seen together (from any position) the design becomes symbolic of free, plastic movement, space expanding with the undulations of the human spirit, flexible and hospitable to human ideas and feelings. It is not without meaning that the United Nations Buildings should be on the bank of a great river, tributary leading to all the corners of the earth, nor in a great city opening out with concourses in every direction. Nor are the spacious foyers, flowing into each other and looking out on so many sides on broad plazas and terraces merely decorative in purpose. The easy gracious movement of ramps and corridors, of outgoing glass walls, of waves of space and open areas bespeak the ideal of the unimpeded flow of people, expanding emotionally to embrace more than ever was embraced before in the history of the world. In this design, symbol of inner hopes and aspirations, we can be reassured that people are striving still for freedom. So too in much contemporary domestic architecture we find this understanding of ideal human wants. In the work of Marcel Breuer, Mies van der Rohe, Philip C. Johnson, Charles Eames, Richard Neutra, Eric Mendelsohn, Gregory Ain, and many others, we see imaginative expressions of inner ideals of freedom. These architects have been inspired by more than a playing with space, more than with the creation of works of art. As I have said in another place, "Their buildings are materialized philosophy— the old but still the very best philosophy, the philosophy of freedom. Their creations say that we ought to live in and be surrounded by an environment that makes in every way for the free, uninhibited spiritual growth of each human being, by an environment that encourages each personality to grow and mature. The new philosophy of design, with its intermingling of inner and outer spaces, with its invitation to communicate, with its purity of motive and its spiritual values, is a philosophy of good will outgoing to all men." Modern design is a metaphor of our longing for freedom and in many ways an attempt to accomplish this longing in reality.

Design is inspired from within. When we look at nature—sand dunes or mountain lakes, woods, the sea, desert or prairie or upland pasture—we see only those details and make only that arrangement of the parts which will form a hieroglyph of our inner life. Oscar Wilde's paradox that nature imitates art (that a London fog is a copy of a Monet painting) is more than a half-truth. It is we who make the design in what we see, and the design is a statement of what we believe. One can make a picture out of the boles of several trees arranged in concert for the eye, as Cézanne painted them, or as one might see them in a public park or through one's picture window. Or we can draw a shell or a leaf as we see it, or want to see it, so that our drawing shall be a pictorial representation of our thoughts about the leaf, adding tone and color and *chiaroscuro* to add depth and subtleties to the meaning we are imparting. And when we choose our surroundings (if we have a choice), we choose intentionally and according to our prejudice the cottage by the waterfall or the city apartment, and we decorate these dwelling places with our cherished beliefs as well as with our dearest possessions.

No taste, say interior decorators, is inexcusable. It is worse than bad taste. For no taste implies no beliefs about life. Tastes vary, however, for we are not inclined to agree about the details or the ultimate nature of the good life. Just as men speak their ideals with many tongues, so men speak their ideals in many patterns of design. Health and pleasure arise from the infinite variety that is called forth in the articulation of the ideal; and we turn to the myriad expressions of this various world for refreshment, for beauty, and, really, for a better understanding of the ideal thoughts of the mind of man.

Winter, 1954. Professor Embler is chairman of the department of humanities at the Cooper Union for the Advancement of Science and Art, New York City. His other writings on metaphor include "Metaphor and Social Belief," in S. I. Hayakawa (ed.), Language, Meaning and Maturity; "The Novel as Metaphor," in ETC., Autumn, 1952; "Metaphor in Everyday Life," in ETC., Winter, 1958-59.

Sexual Fantasy and the 1957 Car

S. I. HAYAKAWA

American males, according to a point of view widely held among Freudian critics of our culture, are afraid of sex. If a woman indicates to a man that she loves him and desires him, the chances are that she will scare him away. Her open manifestation of desire is likely to arouse, not his enthusiastic response, but his underlying anxieties. For endemic among American males, so the argument goes, is, if not impotence, the fear of impotence. Behind the masculine front lies the anxious question, "Am I really male?"

Such critics of the culture point to the American form of stag party, which has superficially the comforting implication of men being he-men together, as but one of a number of disguises which sexual anxiety can take. The implication of stag parties that the stags don't think about is that it is an institutionalized way of running away from women—running away from the real tests of being a lover, husband, father, and a man. But sex is not too far away from any stag party—a sniggering, surreptitious sex interest such as is shown in a news story like the following:

HOLLYWOOD, FEB. 9 (UP)—Police today released several husbands who were arrested while allegedly watching a lewd movie at a lodge hall while their wives played bridge in a room next door. Officers said 62 men were arrested last night after a policeman climbed a telephone pole and watched the movie through a window. Detectives said the hall had been rented by a Knights of Pythias group for a "business meeting."

The real giveaway as to the psychology of the men in this situation is contained in the last paragraph of the story:

On the way to jail, one suspect said, "Boy, a life sentence isn't going to be nearly long enough." Another asked, "Where do you join the Foreign Legion?"

And well they might join the Foreign Legion. For they insult their wives doubly, first by declining or fearing to respond fully and joyfully to their wives' sexuality, and secondly by gratifying themselves instead with the mental masturbation of obscene movies. For all too many American men a wife is not a wife but a mother substitute, alternatively loving and punitive, someone to run away from when one wants to be naughty, and then returns to, to be spanked and forgiven.

Such assertions as the foregoing about American men are familiar enough in the writings of Karl Menninger, Franz Alexander, Karen Horney, and others with a psychoanalytic orientation. They are also familiar through the writings of nonpsychiatrists like Philip Wylie, with his diatribe against momism. I myself have been tempted to dismiss these charges as unfair generalizations, based too much on experiences with patients, and not enough on observations of the majority. All American men aren't like that—I have argued—not even most of them.

But in 1957 I am being contradicted. I am being contradicted by perhaps the most powerful voice in America—the voice of that industry upon whose prosperity rests, we are told, the prosperity of the nation, namely, the automobile industry, which appears to have decided that the supplying of means of transportation is but a secondary reason for its existence, and that its primary function is the allaying of men's sexual anxieties. As if to back up with a fifty-million-dollar bang what psychoanalytic critics have been saying about the American male, the automobile industry is saying in 1957: "The fundamental fact about American male psychology is the fear of impotence. Let's give the men, therefore, the One Big Symbol that will make them feel that they are *not* impotent. Let's give them great big cars, glittering all over and pointed at the ends, with 275 h.p. under the hood, so that they can feel like men!" For, as the consumer motivational research people must have told the powers-that-be in the industry, this is what will make men trade in their present cars and put themselves into hock for 1957 models. The motivational research people do not survey merely the patients of psychoanalysts; they survey the entire buying public. And what most of the public wants, it appears, is a potency symbol.

Granted that a car is transportation. Granted that restless annual style changes and the quest for novelty are necessitated by business competition. Granted that a car is a prestige symbol, a personal symbol, or what you will. Granted even that many cars have always been for many men unconscious symbols of potency. The 1957 cars are nevertheless unique in sacrificing *all* else—common sense, efficiency,

economy, safety, dignity, and especially beauty—to psychosexual wish fulfillment.

Few people actually need more than 40 h.p.—the Volkswagen has only 36 h.p. and is still capable of violating the top speed limit in practically any state of the union. But since the U.S. is a lavish economy, let us say that the average buyer of an American automobile is entitled to at least 85 h.p., and for a luxury car with power-driven accessories, he is entitled to 160 h.p.—the rating of the 1951 Cadillac.

What about the horsepower above 160? I believe it can be safely said that every single horsepower above that figure is purely symbolic, and has *nothing* to do with transportation except to make it more hazardous. The 160 h.p. car can provide more than enough size, speed, and power to serve not only all conceivable practical purposes to which a passenger car can be put, but also to gratify the normal amount of will to aggression.

The argument that horsepower above that figure can contribute to safety because it enables you to pull ahead in passing is convincing only to those whose personal inadequacies leave them wanting to be convinced. No sensible driver ever finds himself in this most easily avoided of avoidable dangers. (If you find yourself in a tight situation where you need this extra "pull ahead" power, it's time you pulled over to the side of the road to sober up before proceeding.) Hence I repeat, every horsepower above 160 is purely for the gratification of one's fantasy life—in the psychiatric sense.

The bolt-out-of-the-blue performance that enables most V-8's these days to accelerate from a standing start to 60 m.p.h. in eleven seconds or less is again purely symbolic. If you are not a bank robber (and most of us are not), what's this unused and unusable acceleration for, if not for psychological satisfactions? And the ability of most cars nowadays (even including what used to be called the "economy" Big Three) to attain speeds of 125 m.p.h. and over again has no function other than to say to the buyer, who even on the open road rarely gets a chance to do 80, "Don't feel badly because you are a dubiously satisfactory bedmate. You're a *mighty* potent fellow. You are Captain Midnight! You are Buck Rogers!"

Even more revealing than horsepower or acceleration is design. First of all there is, of course, the rocket ship motif. As Freudian students of space-ship and rocket-travel literature have pointed out—I think especially of such students of the subject as the late Dr. Robert Lindner of "The Jet-Propelled Couch," Dr. Rudolph Ekstein of the Menninger Foundation, and Dr. Robert Plank of Cleveland Heights —space ship fantasies are deeply related to difficulties in interpersonal relations. As the individual retreats into himself because he feels powerless to deal effectively with the living men and women around him, he often lives increasingly in a fantasy world of power and heroic action in distant, interplanetary spaces. The seven-year-old cuts box tops from cereal packages and gets himself a space helmet to act out his fantasies. The thirty-five-year-old buys a Plymouth Fury. Both reveal themselves to be in their sexual latency period, which is all right, of course—for the seven-year-old.

And to continue on the subject of design, there are the protuberances, the knifelike projections, the gashes, the humps—all dazzlingly colored and outlined in strips of chrome. The symbolism of these is enough to make Dr. Freida Fromm-Reichmann blush—and she doesn't blush easily.

Once, a score or more years ago in Kobe, Japan, I saw in the

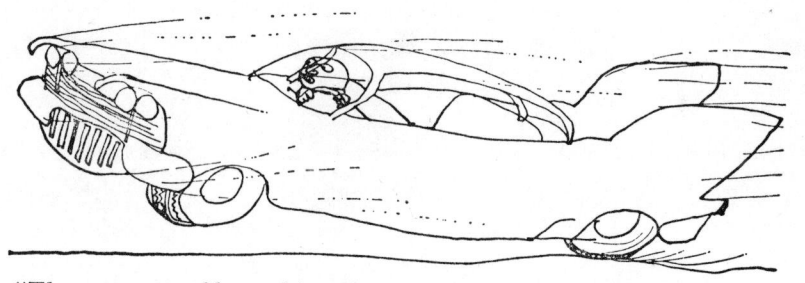

"The seven-year-old gets himself a space-helmet to act out his fantasies. The thirty-five-year-old buys a Plymouth Fury."

foreign section a "sex store"—a place where sexual curiosities could be bought—erotic art, indecent appliances of various kinds, all apparently calculated to awaken sexual interest in those whom age or dissipation had enfeebled, or to serve as collectors' items for those whose sexual life was mostly at the imaginative or symbolic level. Among the items on display was a collection of rubber contraceptives fantastically designed. Some were surrounded with knifelike or sawlike rubber fins, others were covered with big rubber spikes, some were fringed with tassels, some were ornamented like the noses of fighter planes with fierce bird and animal heads.

These pathetic potency symbols for the impotent and near-impotent come to mind as I contemplate such monstrosities as the 290 h.p. Mercury Turnpike Cruiser, the 345 h.p. De Soto Adventurer, and the 375 h.p. Chrysler 300-C.

The cars of 1957 have two disadvantages when compared with the obscene little objects in that store in Kobe. First, they are a menace to public safety—and quadruply so when their possessors are under the influence of liquor. Secondly, how can they serve as fetishes to be collected when you can't even get them into your garage?

Spring, 1957. S. I. Hayakawa is professor of language arts at San Francisco State College; editor (and founder), ETC., 1943 to present.

Illustrations for this article were prepared by Frank Lobdell of the California School of Fine Arts, San Francisco, California.

Why the Edsel Laid an Egg:
Motivational Research vs. the
Reality Principle

S. I. HAYAKAWA

The following are later reflections on the American automobile, aroused by the many letters which I received in response to my article, "Sexual Fantasy and the 1957 Car." Among the questions raised by my correspondents is why automobiles are discussed at all in a journal of general semantics. This question is easily answered. As *ETC*'s cover says, it is "concerned with the role of language and other symbols in human behavior and human affairs."

The automobile is certainly one of the most important nonlinguistic symbols in American culture. As the advertisements keep telling us, it is one of our ways of telling others who we are, from Cadillac as a "symbol of achievement," to Ford as a symbol of "young-mindedness," to Plymouth, which says, according to a recent ad, "We're not the richest people in town, but we're the proudest. We're the kind of family that gets a big bang out of living." Even those who simply want transportation, with no fads or frills or nonsense, can buy a Jeep and "say" so. The auto makers are therefore the grammarians of this nonverbal "language," and shortcomings in the "language" are necessarily shortcomings in the range of expression available to the consumer.

Different people have different needs, with respect both to transportation and self-expression. Hence there should be, in a rich economy like that of the United States, variety in automobiles no less than in other facets of life. Hence I believe that manufacturers should build *some* cars of very high horsepower for those who need such cars, whether for practical or psychological reasons. I do not object to *some* cars being styled to allay unconscious sexual anxieties or to provoke space ship fantasies, if people want such cars. *Some* cars should be little and unpretentious, because there are many modest, unassuming people in the U. S., hard as this may be to believe on the basis of car ads. And since, as one obscene cigarette ad puts it, some people "like their pleasure BIG,"[1] *some* cars, whether for practical or psychological reasons, should be big. Some people love ostentation; hence it is inevitable and necessary in a free economy that

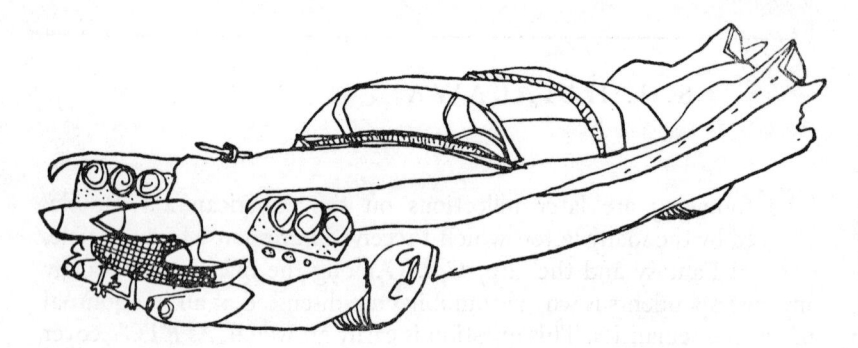

manufacturers produce for their benefit *some* huge and suitably dazzling ostentation wagons.

My quarrel with the American automobile industry in 1957 was not that it produces overpriced, overpowered, oversized, and overelaborate cars, but that it produces them almost to the exclusion of all other kinds. Except for some interesting experiments at the fringes of the market by American Motors and Studebaker, the dominating forces in the industry—General Motors, Ford, and Chrysler—are still carrying on in 1958 their assault on consumer intelligence. The "Big Three" are producing no cars that are not expensive, hideous, and (except for a few sixes) costly to operate and powered far beyond the needs of the ordinary motorist.

[1] See Vance Packard, *The Hidden Persuaders* (New York, David McKay, 1957), pp. 127-129; also Chapter VIII, "The Built-in Sexual Overtone."

The Chevrolet, already too long, low, and broad in 1957 for the practical, day-to-day chores to which Chevrolets have been put ever since I can recall, is 9" longer, 2½" lower, and 4" broader in 1958. Mercury ("The big M"—for masculinity?) offers engines from 312 to 400 h.p. in its "Marauder" line.[2] Again we are being told that what we need is power ("Try the B-12,000 engine. It puts 12,000 pounds of thrust behind every engine stroke!"), Gull-Wing fenders, Swept-Wing styling, with Turbo-Flash performance, in Firesweep Corsair Star Chief hardtops with that Bold New Look. Again the explicit statement of the sex theme, "Hot, Handsome, a Honey to Handle."

For what? For Father to commute seventeen miles to work—a distance which, with favorable traffic conditions (and they are not always favorable), he will cover at an average rate of 30 m.p.h. For Mother to drop Chrissie off at dancing school, stopping at the supermarket and the public library on the way back. For Doug, the candy salesman, to make his calls on neighborhood stores. For Florence, the social caseworker, to visit her clients. For Pete, the insurance adjuster; for Stanley, the instructor at the university extension center; for Andy, the television repair man—all of whom need their cars for their work and their occasional holiday week-ends.

It does not come altogether as a surprise, therefore, that in the spring of 1958 the volume of new automobiles sales was crushingly disappointing to the trade. The Edsel laid a colossal egg. *Time* (March 31, 1958) reported that the sale of "medium-priced" cars fell disastrously. The manufacturers blamed the recession.

One wonders, however, whether the recession itself is not partly to be blamed on the carmakers who, in defiance of all rational consumer interests—economy, convenience, safety, maneuverability, and beauty—have been trying to foist upon the *majority* of the public fabulously overpriced jukeboxes such as only people of deprived origins or the neurotic would want to buy and only the prosperous can afford to maintain. What I objected to in the cars of 1957, and what I still object to in 1958 is the assumption apparently held by carmakers—an assumption revealed in the 200-plus h.p. engines and the

---

[2] "After psychiatric probing a Midwestern ad agency concluded that a major appeal of buying a shiny new and more powerful car every couple of years is that 'it gives him (the buyer) a renewed sense of power and reassures him of his masculinity.' " Packard p. 79.

tailfins and the spaceship platforms with which they equipped the lowest-priced and most popular cars, the Ford, Plymouth, and Chevrolet—that *the majority of the population is mentally ill.*

The trouble with car manufacturers (who, like other isolated people in underdeveloped areas, are devout believers in voodoo) is that they have been listening too long to the motivation research people. Motivation researchers are those harlot social scientists who, in impressive psychoanalytic and/or sociological jargon, tell their clients what their clients want to hear, namely, that *appeals to human irrationality are likely to be far more profitable than appeals to rationality.* This doctrine appeals to moguls and would-be moguls of all times and places, because it implies that if you hold the key to people's irrationality, you can exploit and diddle them to your heart's content and be loved for it.

The Great Gimmick of the motivation researchers, therefore, is the investigation of irrationality, of which we all have, goodness knows, an abundance. Many people (perhaps most) have sexual anxieties and fears of impotence, as the motivation researchers say. Many upward-strivers (most, I am sure) like to impress their neighbors with the display of costly status symbols. Many people (surely not most!) allay their feelings of inadequacy with spaceship fantasies.

But what the motivation researchers, many of whom call themselves Freudians, do not bother to investigate, since it is too obvious, is rationality—or what Freud called the reality principle.[3] Father may indeed see a bright-red convertible as a surrogate mistress and the hardtop as a combination wife-and-mistress, but he settles for a lesser car than either because Chrissie is going to an orthodontist. Doug, in his secret fantasies, screams along the track of the Mille Miglia at 200 m.p.h., but in actuality, especially when his wife and children are with him, he never drives above fifty-five. Andy's dreams are crowded with jet-propulsion themes which clearly mark him as haunted by feelings of sexual inadequacy, but on his eighty-five dol-

[3] "But what about those consumer-motivation studies . . . ? The trouble here seems to have been the elemental mistake on which research can founder—failure to ask questions which elicit meaningful replies. For example, the Ford Motor Company asked no questions at all about: car prices, cost of upkeep, cost of operation, rising insurance rates, growing difficulty in parking, irritation at cars too long for garages, etc. In fact, the consumer research program . . . completely ignored automobiles as functioning machines of transportation." *Consumer Reports,* April, 1958, p. 218.

lar-a-week salary he cannot be snow-jobbed into a conviction that his self-respect requires him to maintain a car that swallows six dollars' worth of gasoline every two hundred miles and costs a hundred dollars to repair every time his fender is dented.

What the motivation researchers failed to tell their clients (perhaps because they hadn't thought of it themselves) is that *only* the psychotic and the gravely neurotic *act out* their irrationalities and their compensatory fantasies—and it is because they act them out that we classify them as mentally ill. The rest of us—the mildly neurotic and the mature, who together constitute the majority (among whom I make bold to include myself)—are reasonably well oriented to reality. We do not indulge our fantasies unless it is socially and psychologically safe to do so (as in taking fencing lessons or marching in regalia in a Shriners' parade) and within our financial means (as in reading paperback murder mysteries).

Motivation researchers seem not to know the difference between the sane and the unsane. Having learned through their "depth" techniques that we all have our irrationalities (no great discovery at this date), they fatuously conclude that we are equally governed by those irrationalities at *all* levels of consumer expenditure—although it doesn't take a social science genius to point out that the more expensive an object is, the more its purchase compels the recognition of reality. The fact that irrationalities may drive people from Pall Mall cigarettes to Marlboro or vice versa proves little about what the average person is likely to do in selecting the most expensive object (other than a house) that he ever buys.

The trouble with selling symbolic gratification via such expensive items as the Phallic Ford, the Edsel Hermaphrodite, and the Plymouth with the Rear-End Invitation is the competition offered by much cheaper forms of symbolic gratification, such as *Playboy* (fifty cents a copy), *Astounding Science Fiction* (thirty-five cents a copy), and television (free). When, on the advice of their voodoo men, automakers abandon their basic social function of providing better, safer, and more efficient means of transportation in favor of entering the business of selling dreams (in which the literary and entertainment industries have far more experience and resources), they cannot but encounter competition which they are not equipped to meet.

The consumer rush to the little foreign cars does not appear to me a passing fad, although Detroit is trying to reassure itself by saying that the foreign-car trend has reached its peak. The Morris Minor, the English Fords, the Hillman, the Simca, the Volkswagon, the Volvo, the Fiat, and all the other lovely little bugs that we see today in increasing numbers are cheap to operate. As for what they "communicate," they give out simple, unassuming messages devoid of delusions of grandeur. Their popularity indicates a widespread reassertion of an orientation toward reality, which says that $1,600 is less than $2,800, that 30 miles per gallon is cheaper transportation than 8 to 13 miles per gallon, that a 155" Renault is easier to park than a 214" Dodge. The very people who are writing the ads for Plymouth, Ford, Chevrolet are driving DKW's, MG's, and Triumphs, while their bosses, the agency heads, ride around in Jaguars and Bentleys. It will take the American auto industry five years, if not a decade or two, to regain the respect and confidence of its friend, the American consumer.

Now that American automakers, with hundreds of thousands of unsold cars on their hands, are in such deep trouble, you would think that they would turn away in disgust from the voodoo men who gave them such a bum steer. But they are slow to learn. *Consumer Reports* (April, 1958) quoted as follows from *The Wall Street Journal:* "Ford Motor has called on the Institute for Motivational Research to find out why Americans buy foreign economy cars."

Although the answer is right there in the question, I am sure that the Institute for Motivational Research is not so stupid as to point out this fact to the Ford Motor Company. I foresee, therefore, years of prosperity ahead for the Institute for Motivational Research, for Social Research, Inc., and all the other Shamans of the Hard Sell. But will Ford be able to survive another round of good advice such as they got on the Edsel?

Spring, 1958. Dr. Hayakawa is professor of language arts at San Francisco State College; editor (and founder), ETC., 1943 to present.

Illustration by Frank Lobdell of the California School of Fine Arts, San Francisco, California.

The Language of Pictures

PAUL R. WENDT

Man has been communicating by pictures longer than he has been using words. With the development of photography in this century we are using pictures as a means of communication to such an extent that in some areas they overshadow verbal language. The science of semantics has studied the conveyance of meaning by language in considerable detail. Yet very little is known as to how pictures convey meaning and what their place is in the life of man.

Perhaps this neglect may be due to the poor repute pictures have in our society as a means of communication. For example, in the field of education, pictures, as a part of the group of audio-visual materials available to teachers, are still considered supplementary rather than complementary to other teaching materials such as textbooks or other purely verbal materials. The term audio-visual "aids" persists, although a number of educators have tried for a decade to persuade their colleagues to discontinue its use on the basis of its connotation of (1) something used by poor teachers who cannot teach without gadgets, (2) a luxury to be trimmed off the budget in hard times, and (3) a mental crutch for backward pupils.

Pictures are of course surrogates for experience. As such they may be said to be closer to extensional meaning than to intensional meaning. At least their position lies in between these two. They are not always close to the actual experience even though the school of "you press the button and we do the rest" implies that merely pointing the camera at Aunt Minnie results in a good likeness to cherish when she is not around. Neither are pictures symbols as words are symbols, since even Aunt Minnie's nephew, age four, can recognize her snapshot though he cannot read.

Pictures are a language in themselves. They are not merely limited representations of reality operating within narrow limits of expression. On the contrary photography is a very flexible medium with a wide range whose limits have not yet been sighted. The range extends from absorbing realism to a fairly high level of abstraction. Let us consider the realistic end of the scale.

The tendency today is to say that the heydey of the movies is over. Television is gnawing at the vitals of Hollywood. But the powerfully realistic effect of the film remains. The other day the writer showed to one of his classes a film, *The Cinematographer*, which purports to show the work of the director of photography in a large studio. Excerpts from several dramatic films were shown to illustrate the different types of scenes a cinematographer encounters. None of these excerpts was longer than one minute. After the film ended some members of the class complained that the excerpts were so realistic and exciting that they "lost" themselves in the content of the episodes and completely forgot that the purpose of the film showing was to study cinematography. Each episode in turn caught these students up in a rich representation of reality. The excerpts were very dissimilar in content so that it was a wrench to change from one scene to another. Nevertheless the students were deeply involved in each excerpt in turn, and only when the lights came on in the classroom did they remember where they were.

Motion pictures are a powerful medium of persuasion. Hitler's films of the bombing of Warsaw were such terribly realistic records that they could be used as a tool of conquest. At times a motion picture may seem even more realistic than the real experience.

At the other end of the scale from realism to abstraction, pictures have many qualities of language. Like words every picture has a content of meaning partly intensional, partly extensional. Whether this meaning is more or less extensionally clear or abstractly difficult to understand depends of course on many factors inherent in the viewer, such as his past experience. But it also is dependent on factors in the picture itself which we might call the grammar of photography.

Composition is all important. In chirographic, or hand-made, pictures composition is achieved sometimes by selection of the point of view but more often by manipulation of space relationships of objects perceived or imagined. The still photographer, unless he is using techniques which are essentially chirographic, such as retouching, montage, or collage, is bound by the objects of reality as the eye of his camera sees them. He achieves composition by painstaking selection of the camera angle, by using a variety of lenses, by choice of filters and emulsions, and by controlling lighting on the subject or scene. Choosing a camera angle may take a professional photographer days of continuous effort, even though television camera operators may be forced to do it in seconds. The angle and the lens used for the shot determine the basic composition. The lighting, however, gives the photographer an enormous range of control over the representation of reality. High key photography in which all the values are crowded toward the whites and light grays, gives the impressions of light, of lightness, or happiness, or innocent pleasures. Low key photography with many shadows and low values is appropriate for mystery, danger, depression. Every textbook in photography contains the series of portraits of a model taken with different lighting effects, showing how one face can be made to look like many strange people. Pictures have affective connotations.

These constitute the grammar of photographs. The analogy holds even down to details such as synizesis. Two crucial objects in a picture, like two syllables, can be blended and not discriminated from each other, thereby changing the meaning entirely. Even though the photographer uses lighting and other techniques to separate the two objects, the viewer may still misread the picture because of lack of experience or poor viewing conditions. Always it is important to remember that pictures, like words, are merely surrogates for reality, not reality itself.

In motion pictures we find the syntax of photography. Motion pictures present a flowing discourse in picture surrogates. Like a paragraph, a motion picture sequence is a highly structured time-space analysis and synthesis of reality. Using individual "shots" like words, the sequence inflects the static frame of film by motion. One scene with motion by actors or by the camera resembles a sentence.

Short dynamic scenes have the same effect as blunt statements. Longer scenes with complicated changes in composition created by camera movement have somewhat the effect of compound sentences.

Pictures, like words, must make a logical continuity, according to accepted rules. For example, a motion picture showing two people conversing must first show them more or less side-to, to establish their relative positions. Then as each speaks he is shown over the other's shoulder. This is the familiar "reverse-angle" shot. That this is a culturally based convention of film syntax is shown by the experience of representatives of the U. S. Office of Information who have found that natives of foreign countries who have not seen motion pictures cannot "understand" the reverse-angle shot. They cannot adjust to our stereotyped representations of reality. They don't understand our language of pictures. Similarly, most of the action in a motion picture must be "matched." That is, if an actor is shown walking up to a door in a distant shot, the following close-up should show him approximately in the same position as he was in the last frame of the long shot. "Matching the action" is a convention in cinematography, part of the film language. It is not always used. When the tempo of the film is fast it is common practice for the editor to elide some of the action, as an author does when he wants the same effect. And of course films *can* compress time dramatically.

Paragraphing is accomplished by the traditional fade-out and fade-in, or by the dissolve or optical effect as soft or hard "wipes." The pace of the narrative is determined more by the film editor than by the script. The editor of words clarifies the presentation of content by eliminating words, sentences, paragraphs, and even chapters. The film editor clips out frames, scenes, sequences, and even large parts of a film (resulting sometimes in "the face on the cutting room floor"). The book editor may achieve lucidity by rearranging the author's text, moving paragraphs and chapters. The film editor boldly changes the order of film sequences. Both the book editor and the film editor can have a decisive influence on the style of the finished work. Both can call for rewriting or new photography. Both can affect the pace of the manuscript or the "rough cut." Both are experts in grammar, syntax, and style.

More important than the mechanical analogy to words are the semantic dimensions of pictures. Every photograph is an abstraction of an object or an event. Even the amateur, ignorant of the plasticity of the medium, makes an abstraction of Aunt Minnie when he presses the button. Only a few of Aunt Minnie's characteristics are recorded on the film.

The professional photographer in control of his medium knows he is abstracting. If he is competent he abstracts to a purpose. Knowing he cannot possibly record the whole event, he sees to it that the abstracting preserves those features he wants to present to the picture-reader. By manipulation of the variables at his command, he lets us "see" the event as he thinks it should be "seen." If he is a news photographer he probably wants to present a "realistic" event, full of details, although often he is working under such handicaps of haste that the picture as we see it in the newspaper has become simplified and perhaps indistinct. Then it lacks background or environment, it lacks the richness and crispness which a realistic picture must have. Some news pictures are so simplified that they look like symbolizations. They fit the definition of a symbol as "that which suggests something else by convention."

The fashion photographer, however, preparing for an advertisement in *The New Yorker*, controls the photographic medium to produce a simple, stylized figure, often against a blank background. This picture is realistic only to a limited extent and approaches the characteristics of a symbol. Carried even further a photograph can be almost purely symbolic, devoid of the very characteristics that are usually associated with photography. Take as an example the famous combat photo of the planting of the American flag by Marines on the summit of Mount Suribachi. There is nothing in the frame but the men struggling to raise the flag and a few rocks of the mountain top. This picture has been accepted as a symbol. It has even been reproduced in bronze in Washington, D. C., as a memorial to the Marines. We accept a statue as a symbol. But here is a case where the statue was copied directly *with little change* from a press shot.

At this point we may consider a paradox. *Life* magazine a few years ago ran a series of photographs called "What's in a Picture." One showed a tired interne in a hospital having a quick cup of coffee while still in his surgical gown. Another showed a boy and his dog walking the railroad track. In a third Cardinal Mindszenty was on trial in Hungary. A fourth showed the exhaustion in the face of a combat Marine. There is no doubt that these pictures rate among the most graphic that have ever been taken. In fact, this is why *Life* ran them as a separate series, to show that some of the best pictures need no explanation. This, however, is a characteristic of symbols, and these pictures achieve their greatness because they present symbols—the American doctor, a typical boy, the horror of brain-washing behind the Iron Curtain, and the life of a front-line soldier. It is a paradox that these most graphic pictures are symbolic. They are *at the same time* very real and very symbolic.

A picture is a map, since there is not a one-to-one correspondence between elements of the picture and elements of the event. We might say, as J. J. Gibson says about the retinal image, that a picture is a good correlate *but not a copy* of the scene photographed. A picture definitely has structure. It is a configuration of symbols which make

The Map Is Not the Territory

it possible for us to interpret the picture, provided that we have enough experience with these symbols to read the picture.

Pictures can be manipulated like words so as to seem to change their referents. The motion picture editor can lengthen and shorten individual scenes and place them in such a juxtaposition in a carefully planned tempo as to create an impression foreign to the events photographed. It would be possible to assemble a number of pictures of active American businessmen and cut them together to give the impression of frantic competition for money when this did not exist in the actual situations.

Once we have established the fact that photographs of events are *not* the events, that they show by intent or accident only a few characteristics of events, we have the perspective to question some reactions of people to pictures. In spite of decades of visual education there still are teachers who will not use teaching films when they are easily available. This refusal has been dismissed as conservatism, laziness, and poor teaching. Could it be that some of these teachers, projecting films in undarkened rooms on a wall (for want of a proper screen) and with a screen image not large enough to give a realistic effect, have unconsciously concluded that motion pictures are not enough different from words to bother with? Obviously the great asset of films is realism, which gives the pupils a chance to identify with characters on the screen and "lose" themselves in the picture. When this realism is wiped out by poor reproduction or poor projection, the faint images on the wall lose details, become more outlined and stylized, and have little advantage, if any, over words. Like words they are so vague that they can be interpreted individually by each viewer. Pictures, unlike words, depend very much indeed on the quality of their reproduction for the kind and amount of meaning the picture-reader gets from them.

Because of the plasticity of the photographic medium it is well that there are few pictures that do not have captions. In a sense these are indices like Interne$_1$, Interne$_2$. We feel the need of captions on pictures as we do not feel the need for indices on words. Yet we usually feel that pictures are much more likely to be completely self-explanatory than words.

General semanticists know it is hard to make the average person realize that he brings meaning to the word, that the word does *not* contain any meaning. A word is just a series of hentracks which we are told authoritatively stands for a certain concept.

It is still harder to convince anyone that we also bring meaning to a picture. If the picture is well within our previous experience it means something. What it means depends on the kind of our experience. The picture of any political figure is interpreted in radically different manner by opposing parties. City children react differently to a picture of a cow than do farm children. Thus pictures can reinforce stereotypes because the characteristics of people or events which the photographer presents through the medium are not strong enough to overcome the "embedded canalizations" in the reader.

When the picture is not within the range of our experience we react to it almost as little as to an unknown word. Scenes of mass calisthenics performed by ten thousand Russians mean to us little more than "mass conformity," whereas they may originally have been meant to express "ideals." Strange animals are to us just configurations of light and shade on paper. If they move on the screen we can apply more of our experience to understanding what we see. Professional photographers, like teachers, have their readers carefully estimated. Like teachers, they see to it that their pictures contain plenty of the familiar (to their particular reader) and some of the unusual. We are able to reach out a short distance into the unknown from the solid base of our own experience. The difference here between words and pictures is that the distinction between the known and the unknown is sharpened by pictures. If we read that an emu is like an ostrich, only larger, we have a vague idea about it. If we see a picture of an emu we remember more clearly the features similar to an ostrich and perhaps notice how the emu is different and new.

Pictures are multiordinal. They are interpreted on different levels of abstraction. We have seen this happen in the *Life* series mentioned above. Our Aunt Minnie is just another aunt to strangers; they think she looks like the Genus Aunt. The fact that pictures are interpreted on different levels is the basis for some items in some common intelligence scales. The lowest level is that in which the child merely enumerates objects and people: "I see a woman and a girl and a stove," etc. This is analogous to the descriptive level of words. A higher level of reaction would be description and interpretation such as, "The woman is probably the girl's mother and she is cooking her supper."

A picture causing a semantic disturbance is familiar to everyone. "Oh, that doesn't look like me at all. What a terrible picture!" Or the vacationers who have rented a lake cottage on the basis of glamorous pictures in an advertising folder get a shock when they find that the lake is much smaller than they thought, that the trees are scrubby, and that the cottage is in disrepair. Visitors to California complain that the "blue Pacific" is not always blue, as the postcards invariably show it. Or they say, "Is *that* Velma Blank, the great movie star?" It is in situations like these that we can best realize that pictures, although somewhat better than words, are only maps of the territory they represent.

Pictures can be self-reflexive. A photograph of a photograph is a standard method of reproduction, for example, in the making of filmstrips. It is by such reproduction that it is possible to present to congressional committees photographs which seem to show members of the cabinet or senators in conversation with persons with whom they never exchanged more than a word.

Pictures, then, have many of the characteristics of language, not in the figurative sense of "the language of flowers" but in the very real characteristics of structure (syntax, grammar, style) and of semantics. The most crucial characteristic is that pictures are abstractions of reality. A picture can present only a few of the aspects of the event. It may, under the strict control of the photographer, become as abstract as a symbol.

It is most urgent that there should be more awareness of the abstracting power of photography, that pictures *do lie*. Instead we find great naïveté. People believe what they see in pictures. "One picture is worth a thousand words" not only because it is more graphic but because it is believed to be the gospel truth, an incontrovertible fact. A teacher may present her pupils in a big city with a side view of a cow. They should then know what a cow is! Little do they dream that to a farm boy a cow is a complex of associations which even four hours of movies could not present. We find pictures used as "illustrations." They are inserted in textbooks as a last resort to relieve the copy. One picture of Iowa in the geography text must suffice for Iowa. The author says, "This is Iowa." The general semanticists would recognize this as the error of "allness," ascribing to a word all the characteristics of the thing abstracted from. The danger of "allness" is so much more lively in the case of pictures than in the case of words because everyone assumes pictures *are* reality.

Of course pictures provide us with more cues from reality itself (cues for eliciting the meaning we bring to the picture) than the arbitrary hen tracks we call "words." But the basic error is to fail to realize that the meanings of pictures are not in the pictures, but rather in what we bring to them.

Summer, 1956. Dr. Wendt is associate professor of education at Southern Illinois University, Carbondale, Illinois.

A Grammar of Assassination

MARTIN MALONEY

The typical book titles of our age are not THE AGE OF REASON, *but* THE AGE OF LONGING, THE AGE OF ANXIETY, THE POLITICS OF MURDER, THE STRATEGY OF TERROR, THE AGE OF TERROR.
—PETER VIERECK

Let me lend you THE HISTORY OF CONTEMPORARY SOCIETY. *It's in hundreds of volumes, but most of them are sold in cheap editions:* DEATH IN PICCADILLY, THE AMBASSADOR'S DIAMONDS, THE THEFT OF THE NAVAL PAPERS, DIPLOMACY, SEVEN DAY'S LEAVE, THE FOUR JUST MEN.
—GRAHAM GREENE, *The Ministry of Fear*

It is an oddity of an odd age that critics of contemporary American society should concern themselves so often with the symbols, rather than the facts, of violence. At a time when his study windows might almost have rattled to the remote explosions on Yucca Flat, or to the coughing of Korean sniper fire, Canon Bernard Iddings Bell was busy citing the current *literature* of violence as another symptom of the Common Man's decline:

The most popular novelist in America today ... is ... almost ludicrously savage in his substance and his style. He writes tales of a violence that is near to madness plus a degenerate sexuality. His best-selling production reaches its climax when a woman, physically beautiful and fascinatingly wicked, undresses herself, with an almost incredible particularity of lascivious description, in the presence of a libidinous and savage hero. When she is quite bare, the hero shoots her twice in the belly. As she dies, she cries, "How could you?" He replies, "It was easy." End of book. Over one million, two hundred thousand copies of this masterpiece have been purchased. The sale of all his books, essentially the same in plot with minor differences of decoration, has passed the ten million mark in four years. This pander is indeed an exceptionally low creature, but he is at the moment the Common Man's delight.[1]

This is, I suppose, a relatively sophisticated kind of criticism, with which we can agree in principle, at least. Popular literature is certainly, in its own manner, intensional and stereotyped; its enormously wide diffusion suggests that it relates to the structure of social character, or of society. For this reason it is worth study, though perhaps a different sort of study from that which Canon Bell accords it.

A second example: In 1953 Mr. Jack Mabley of the Chicago *Daily News* conducted a spectacular if short lived campaign against the literature of crime available to children on television. Mr. Mabley apparently monitored a good deal of the dramatic programing on Chicago television stations; with loving care he listed and tabulated the symbolic acts of violence, ranging from simple assault through mayhem to homicide, which he found represented on the flickering screens. He was thus able to include in his reports some fairly impressive totals of human destruction, including some detailed and gruesome descriptions of specific examples, which lost very little in the retelling. This information was headlined in the *Daily News* over quite a long period, seemingly as a demonstration of the depravity of television broadcasters, or of American children, or of parents, or of society in general, with the obvious exceptions of Mr. Mabley and the *Daily News*.

A third and final exhibit is provided by Mr. Edmund Wilson, a literary critic of reasonable distinction and an exceedingly serious-minded man where the literary arts are concerned. A dozen or more

[1] Bernard Iddings Bell. *Crowd Culture: an Examination of the American Way of Life* (New York: Harper & Brothers, 1952), pp. 31-32.

years ago, Mr. Wilson read some detective stories—the first literature of this sort, he remarks, that he had sampled since 1907. As a result of this experience, Mr. Wilson wrote:

> My final conclusion is that the reading of detective stories is simply a kind of vice that, for silliness and minor harmfulness, ranks somewhere between smoking and cross-word puzzles. Detective story readers feel guilty, they are habitually on the defensive, and all their talk about "well-written" mysteries is simply an excuse for their vice, like the reasons that the alcoholic can always produce for a drink. One of the letters I have had shows the addict in his frankest and most shameless phase. This lady begins by pretending, like the others, to guide me in my choice (of detective novels), but she breaks down and tells the whole dreadful truth. Though she has read, she says, hundreds of detective stories, "it is surprising," she finally confesses, "how few I would recommend to another. However, a poor detective story is better than none at all. Try again. With a little better luck, you'll find one you admire and enjoy. Then you, too, may be
> A MYSTERY FIEND."
> This letter has made my blood run cold; so the opium smoker tells the novice not to mind if the first pipe makes him sick; and I fall back for reassurance on the valiant little band of my readers who sympathize with my views on the subject.[2]

There are two questions which seem to be raised by these quotations. 1. Is crime fiction actually worth all this comment? 2. If so, is the critical apparatus suggested in these quotations adequate to deal with the subject matter? Let us, for a moment, assume that we have made positive answers to the first question, and go on to the second.

I do *not* think that the critical apparatus of Bell, or Mabley, or even Wilson, is adequate to discuss present-day crime fiction, because it seems to me that each of our three critics fails to recognize this form of popular literature as something separate from "serious" writing.

Whoever discusses the present-day, melodramatic tale of crime and violence is talking about a special form of popular art. Popular art, I conceive, may be defined as a kind of communication which uses many of the techniques of the fine arts, and which sometimes has the general appearance of fine art, but which is, in various important aspects, a profoundly different sort of thing. The fine arts normally

[2] Edmund Wilson, "Who Cares Who Killed Roger Ackroyd?" in *Classics and Commercials* (New York: Farrar, Straus, 1950), pp. 263-264.

express the insights of an artist into the nature of his experience, his subject matter, and his medium; for such insights, popular art usually substitutes formula—the formula plot, the formula design, the formula melody. A work of fine art is intended to communicate to others, but it requires that the others contribute importantly in the way of understanding and appreciation. A work of popular art makes no such demand, or at any rate, as modest a demand of this sort as possible. It is usually directed at the largest possible audience of

Dawn of Literacy

viewers, listeners, or readers, whether or not they are able to contribute anything to the process of communication. A work of popular art, in practice, is judged by the number of people who consume it.

The popular arts, thus roughly defined, are a new phenomenon in the world. They depend absolutely for their existence upon a highly developed technology; the works of Mickey Spillane, which Canon Bell has read with such horror, would be inconceivable in a society which did not command the technical ability to reproduce them inexpensively some thirteen million times over. Mr. Mabley, for his part, might be struggling with the analysis of sports or politics, were it not for the efforts of Zworykin and Marconi and Fessenden and Conrad. It is thus, I think, a mistake for anyone to talk about the popular arts of the twentieth century as if they were the same as the fine arts of the sixteenth century. And it seems to me that this mistake is precisely the one which our critics usually commit. Mr. Wilson condemns the present-day detective story because it is not as good literature as Dickens or Poe or Thackeray; Canon Bell finds it vulgar because it seems not to be as sophisticated as the literature which the better people of the eighteenth century enjoyed.

The observations of these critics are accurate enough; they are also unimportant. We shall never understand or control or deal with the popular arts by simple condemnation. A quotation from a recent article by Weller Embler suggests—if we may now proceed to our original question—the vital importance of sound criticism in this area, together with an apparatus for achieving it:

Though our world of today is one of extreme violence, it is not true that people living the everyday routine lives of our society are either given to or are the subjects of violent acts. Though it would be insane to deny the abundance of rape, murder, mayhem, manslaughter, suicide, torture, assault, arson, enslavement everyday everywhere, still, considering the density of modern society, there is not as much actual overt violence as one would suppose from the evidence of motion pictures, comic books, radio, and cheap fiction. On the other hand there is universal inner violence, fear, and treachery. It is the great inner conflicts and tensions that modern story-telling describes; and it is the translation of fiction's outward beatings, stranglings, stabbings, and shootings into our own inner struggles that we make when we read or listen.

Since the tempest within will not submit to description in words of exact reference, the tempest without must serve as metaphor to tell about the soul's life. Modern fiction has chosen the device of *hyperbole* with which to show forth the inner life—all the shocks the spirit's heir to in our time—the insults, the humiliation, the sacrifice, the moral corrosion. For the most part, the modern story-teller chooses to deal with the extraordinary incident. Being more dramatic, it is more immediately understandable, reflects more directly the conflicts of everyday life. The violence and the fear of violence that is in us and so much a part of our psychological life are amplified many times in the metaphor of melodrama. The terror of the cinema screen and the ferocity of, for example, *Sanctuary* are mirrors held up to the terror and rage of our inner lives. Thus, the age of anxiety gives away its inner tensions in the works of popular writers like Graham Greene, James M. Cain, Dashiell Hammett, Mickey Spillane; in the cartoons of Charles Addams; in the plays of Tennessee Williams and Arthur Miller; in the operas of Carlo Menotti; in the films of Alfred Hitchcock, Billy Wilder, Raoul Walsh, Carol Reed, and Roberto Rossellini. Not that violent death does not occur in daily life, still it occurs but seldom to the 13,000,000 people who read the fiction of Mickey Spillane. Modern novels and motion pictures express our fears, our desires, our anxieties, our hate, all that troubles inwardly—frustration, fear of poverty, of spinsterhood, of losing status, of loneliness, discrimination, humiliation, shame, heartache, of being sacrificed, of slavery, and of tyranny.[3]

I do not think it matters greatly whether we take the tales of violence as a *History of Contemporary Society* in an unlimited series of volumes, or as a metaphor of the soul's plight in the atomic age. The fact remains, in either case, that here again the symbols of fiction and drama perform their immemorial function: they permit human beings to say the unspeakable, and they make possible the verbal solution of problems which are, in the flesh, insoluble.

The literature of crime and violence, however crude the connoisseur of letters may judge it, however shocking the moralist may think it, is thus no trivial thing. Like most of our entertainments—and especially those which strive to be most entertaining and least meaningful—it conceals some grave and terrible problems. An anatomy of this literature—what I have called here "a grammar of assassination" —remains to be constructed. The chief purpose of these notes is to sketch the bare outlines of such a grammar. To do this, we must examine briefly the history of this special branch of literature.

As everyone knows, the modern crime story begins with a segment of the work of Edgar Allan Poe. Poe wrote only three detective stories—*The Murders in the Rue Morgue, The Mystery of Marie Roget,* and *The Purloined Letter.* As Edmund Wilson correctly points out, Poe was probably interested chiefly in writing a story which should turn about the solution to a puzzle, which should exploit his own keen interest in the processes of reasoning. In so doing, he created the first true hero of detective fiction—a *private* detective, incidentally, and the first watson.[4]

[3] Weller Embler, "The Novel as Metaphor," *ETC.,* X (1952), 3-11.

[4] Dr. John (or James) Watson's last name has become, to detective story writers, a common noun. A watson is the admiring and naïve associate of the detective (usually of the brilliant amateur class).

Throughout the last century, the detective story prospered modestly. There was Wilkie Collins, with his rather dull and complex novels, *The Moonstone* and *The Woman in White*; there was Gaboriau with his Inspector LeCoq, whom Sherlock Holmes once called "a miserable bungler." Dickens attempted the detective story, especially in his unfinished novel, *The Mystery of Edwin Drood*. It was not, however, until Dr. Arthur Conan Doyle's tale, "A Study in Scarlet," appeared in the *Strand Magazine* in London in the 1880's that the detective story began to show signs of that enormous popularity which it later achieved.

It is possible to name stories of crime and detection which long antedate Poe. Voltaire's *Zadig*, on one occasion, becomes almost indistinguishable from Holmes or Dupin. So does D'Artagnan, in one episode of *Le Vicomte de Bragellonne*. There is even a rather typical tale of deduction in the Old Testament, which tells how Daniel exposed the chicanery of the priests of Baal. But a more important observation is this: all stories of crime appear to embody one of those myths so meaningful and so essential to human understanding of life that they appear in an endless variety of forms back to the remotest antiquity. This is the dual myth of flight and pursuit, the ancient theme of guilt and punishment.

To some extent all stories are embodiments of this theme. No living man fails to pursue, more or less effectively, the goals he is able to construct; nor does any living creature fail to flee destruction, or at least, whatever it can recognize as destruction. And the processes of flight and pursuit seem, in most cases, to be rationalized by the concept of personal guilt and personal responsibility for one's acts. A great number of stories and plays, based largely or wholly on this theme, examine with special care the motives and behavior of pursued and pursuer, and attempt to demonstrate the tragic or comic or melodramatic possibilities of the theme of pursuit. Thus, the story of Telemachus' search for his father in the *Odyssey*, the relentless pursuit of Jean Valjean by the terrible Javert in *Les Miserables*, and the chase sequences in some early American film comedies, all make some use of this theme. So does Francis Thompson in *The Hound of Heaven*; so does Dante in *The Divine Comedy*. So, in a direct and obvious way, does the crime story.

With this general theme of pursuit and flight as a starting point, we may isolate some of the common terms in the detective stories of

Conan Doyle. We should first observe that the grammar of the Holmes stories—and of many other, but not all, detective stories—is peculiar. The statement of each story implies a previous statement, which is initially concealed from the reader, but without which the story could not exist. Sometimes these implied statements are exceedingly complex: Enoch J. Drebber must first, in the deserts of Utah, commit a dreadful wrong against Jefferson Hope; Hope in turn must wreak his long-delayed vengeance upon Drebber one foggy London morning at 3, Lauriston Gardens—all this before Mr. Sherlock Holmes can conduct his investigation which Watson so fancifully entitled "A Study in Scarlet." This feature of the grammar of the Holmes stories is crucial; its function is to establish guilt and responsibility for the acts described, and without it the entire character of the pursuit would alter significantly.

As for the stories proper, they involve but a single verb: to pursue. The pursuit is, as a rule, symbolic rather than physical. As Holmes remarks on one occasion, "We have not yet grasped the results which the reason alone can attain to. Problems may be solved in the study which have baffled all those who have sought a solution by the aid of their senses." But on occasion the chase can be active enough; see for instance the pursuit of Jonathan Small down the Thames in "The Sign of Four."

The actions antecedent to pursuit vary a good deal; but they have one characteristic which recurs frequently. A surprising number of the stories hinge on the commission of such minor crimes as theft, embezzlement, arson, fraud, and blackmail. One of the early stories, "A Case of Identity," involves no legal offense at all. In these cases, the stake for the pursued might be exposure, imprisonment, disgrace, or simply the contempt of all right-thinking men. The symbols of death and violence were by no means essential to this world.

As for Holmes himself, the actor in these tales, we may readily see that Doyle invented many adjectives to describe him; he is shown as a musicologist (his monograph on the polyphonic motets of Lassus was the last word on that abstruse subject), as a cocaine user, research chemist, and amateur boxer. Many of these characteristics were dropped or contradicted in later tales; nearly all are individually unimportant. The essential adjectives which describe Holmes are three in number: he is superhuman; he is a private detective, not a public official; and he is a defender of "the right" as "the right" is understood by all right-thinking men. He is not necessarily concerned with the law. James Windibank, in "A Case of Identity," has broken no law; yet Holmes demonstrates the coldest anger and contempt for his somewhat unethical behavior, and even threatens to horsewhip him. On the other hand, Holmes almost jovially permits a certain Captain Jack Crocker, who has—out of the purest motives—crushed the skull of Sir Eustace Brackenstall with a poker, to go free. ("The Adventure of the Abbey Grange," in *The Return of Sherlock Holmes*.) As for the actual officials of the law—the incredibly bumptious and obtuse Inspector Lestrade, for example—they are obviously beneath anyone's contempt.

We might summarize the world of the Sherlock Holmes stories (which is typical of detective stories of the period, for these tales were widely imitated) in this fashion. It was a world in which law was operative, but in a limited way; it was a world in which a gentleman's code of right and wrong transcended the law when it did not supplement it. It was a world in which the business of upholding the right fell upon the shoulders of private men rather than public officials. And finally, it was a world in which there were few gradations in the moral code; black was black and white was white; a theft discovered might be as fatal to a man's future as a murder discovered.

Let me be quite clear; this world, and the attitudes which informed it, were the peculiarly personal products of Doyle himself, as anyone familiar with his life can attest. But that it was an intelligible and acceptable world to large numbers of persons in Britain and America may be inferred from the immediately enthusiastic reception which the stories received, and by their long-continued popularity. Then too we must remember that these stories have added, perhaps permanently, to the language and to our stock of stereotypes, and so to our "knowledge" of human motives and behavior.

Two changes in the grammar of the crime story occurred after the first successes of Sherlock Holmes, but long before Doyle wrote the last of the stories in the *Casebook* (around 1922), both changes being more or less to the same purpose, but quite different in detail.

One of these changes was to slip the story proper from the pursuit back to the action which antedated and motivated the pursuit. This meant, of course, that the chief actor was now the pursued, the offender, the criminal, and that the action concerned chiefly his crime and subsequent flight. Perhaps the best British examples of this changed pattern may be found in the works of E. W. Hornung (*The Amateur Cracksman*, 1899; *The Black Mask*, 1901; *A Thief in the Night*, 1905; *Mr. Justice Raffles*, 1909). Holmes, representing as he does an extralegal code of ethics, can and does sometimes stand outside the law; his behavior, since it is always directed toward a "good" end, can be rationalized. Raffles' behavior, on the other hand, since it violates not only the law, but to some extent the "gentleman's code," cannot be so lightly treated. Holmes, it is notorious, not only "lived happily ever after" despite his occasional illegal behavior, but seems to be immortal; Raffles, on the other hand, necessarily died young; he atoned for his many misdeeds during the Boer War. As George Orwell points out:

> Raffles is presented to us . . . not as an honest man who has gone astray, but as a public school man who has gone astray. His remorse, when he feels any, is almost purely social; he has disgraced "the old school"; he has lost his right to enter "decent society"; he has forfeited his amateur status and become a cad. Neither Raffles nor Bunny (his friend and accomplice) appears to feel at all strongly that stealing is wrong in itself. . . . They think of themselves not as sinners but as renegades, or simply as outcasts. And the moral code of most of us is still so close to Raffles' own that we do feel his situation to be an especially ironical one. A West End club man who is really a burglar! That is almost a story in itself, is it not?[5]

The British preference in wrongdoing, if we may judge by the Raffles stories and others of similar pattern, is for highly skilled and somewhat genteel thievery. Americans, with a long tradition of horse-trading behind them, seem to have preferred fraud to outright burglary, as exemplified in the "Get-Rich-Quick" Wallingford stories of George Chester, or O. Henry's sketches of the chicaneries of Jeff Peters and other con men.

The other grammatical alteration in the crime story pattern is perhaps less interesting. Writers of the conventional (usually British) detective story discovered that no crime save murder was really worth dramatization; here the chase, in itself, had a real point to it. The stake at both ends was death; the killer must be killed lest he kill some more.

But even this use of the most extreme symbols of violence did not save the detective story of the early 1900's, in most cases, from dull-

[5] George Orwell, "Raffles and Miss Blandish," in *Dickens, Dali and Others* (New York: Reynal and Hitchcock, 1948), pp. 203-204.

ness. Most of the stories and plays of this period were highly conventionalized puzzle pieces; see for example the collected works of Agatha Christie, Anna Katherine Green, or Mary Roberts Rinehart. The victim did not bleed genuine blood; and if the hero was sometimes "in danger," it was as if a chess piece had been endangered in a game. I do not bewail simply the absence of blood; the story and the characters were usually missing too. In these stories we usually find a collection of almost excessively respectable authors and genteel readers (the late President Wilson, for one) perpetuating and popularizing a literature of violence, a kind of phenomenon which neither Mary Roberts Rinehart nor most of her devoted circle of readers ever had the temerity to examine at very close range. The point of the crime story or play was said to be the puzzle it propounded: whodunit? Readers were urged to rationalize their excursions into symbolic murder on the grounds that the experience sharpened their wits.

The next step in the development of the crime story was a natural one. Convinced—and correctly so—that the consumers of crime stories were more interested in vivid, realistically appointed writing than in puzzles, certain American writers began to produce highly realistic and brutal tales of murder; of these, one of the first and the best was Dashiell Hammett. The sawdust-filled baronet with an Oriental dagger planted in the center of his shirt disappeared; in his place appeared the shabby and furtive racketeer shot bloodily to death in a dingy city street. Raymond Chandler says of Dashiell Hammett's early writings that he

gave murder back to the kind of people that commit it for reasons, not just to provide a corpse; and with the means at hand, not with handwrought dueling pistols, curare and tropical fish. He put these people down on paper as they are, and he made them talk and think in the language they customarily used for these purposes.[6]

This new concept of the crime story, which has of course been reflected in film, radio, and television productions of the cops-and-robbers sort, has made some essential changes in our grammar of assassination. The act of pursuit becomes almost exclusively physical, and often extremely violent; it is a long step from Holmes pondering the significance of a flake of cigar ash in his study to Hammett's Con-

[6] Raymond Chandler, "The Simple Art of Murder," in *The Pocket Atlantic* (New York: Pocket Books, 1946), p. 210.

tinental Op who, on one occasion, stuffs a length of copper wire into his pocket because it's just the right length to go around somebody's neck. The verb "to pursue" now becomes almost synonymous with "to destroy." In addition, the old adjectives of the crime story are lost or discarded, and new ones are found to describe both the antecedent statement (the crime) and the story statement (the pursuit). The black-and-white universe of Holmes vanishes. In the new world, the burden of guilt for crime tends to spread so that no one is free of it; law and conscience alike are shaken—neither the police nor the courts nor his next-door neighbors are necessarily on the side of the good man, who thus becomes a desperately solitary figure. Chandler describes this change admirably:

> The realist in murder writes of a world in which gangsters can rule nations and almost rule cities, in which hotels and apartment houses and celebrated restaurants are owned by men who made their money out of brothels, in which a screen star can be the fingerman for a mob, and the nice man down the hall is the boss of the numbers racket; a world where a judge with a cellar of bootleg liquor can send a man to jail for having a pint in his pocket, where the mayor of your town may have condoned murder as an instrument of money-making, where no man can walk down a dark street in safety because law and order are things we talk about but refrain from practising; a world where you may witness a holdup in broad daylight and see who did it, but you will fade quickly back into the crowd rather than tell anyone, because the holdup men may have friends with long guns, or the police may not like your testimony, and in any case the shyster for the defense will be allowed to abuse and vilify you in open court, before a jury of selected morons, without any but the most perfunctory interference from a political judge (p. 212).

This is indeed a world of anarchy, in which the act of violence becomes the core. But a completely anarchical universe is difficult to imagine, and still more difficult to write about. What holds the Hammett-Chandler world together? Into this world, Chandler says

> down these mean streets a man must go who is not himself mean, who is neither tarnished nor afraid. The detective in this kind of story must be such a man. He is the hero, he is everything. He must be a complete man and a common man and yet an unusual man. He must be, to use a rather weathered phrase, a man of honor (p. 214).

So we return, by somewhat devious ways, to the essentials of the world of Sherlock Holmes. But where the morality of Holmes was a morality shared with all right-thinking men, the morality of Sam Spade and Philip Marlow is private, unshared, and unspeakable. Nevertheless, the morality of Sam Spade exists—or at least, we are so led to believe.

Since Hammett, no completely defined new patterns have emerged in the crime story. The perpetually interesting question is: what next? What new patterns can the vocables of violence assume?

It appears to me that two patterns have begun, rather tentatively, to emerge. I have been speculating for several years whether the time is not ripe for a new Raffles to appear, his story to be the legend of the "nice chap" who unfortunately goes about killing people. Several attempts have been made in this direction, in published fiction, in broadcasting, and in films. A recent motion picture, *The Sniper,* presented the story of a charming, handsome, all-American boy who went about shooting strange women because they reminded him of his mother. And of course, there was Chaplin's film *Monsieur Verdoux,* the fable of a kindly and dapper little businessman who— unable to find more suitable work—goes into the business of marrying elderly spinsters, and murdering them. Chaplin, a man of rash courage in more ways than one, justifies Verdoux in the film: why should societies either capable or presently guilty of genocide look askance at this little man who, for the best of reasons, has destroyed only twenty or so aged and not very interesting women? In general, of course, this pattern seems rather difficult to popularize; I suspect that our future experience of it will be confined to a few, occasional, and perhaps brilliant examples.

The alternative pattern is, of course, already rather widespread. We remarked a moment ago that the personal and secret integrity of Chandler's and Hammett's heroes is all that holds their universe of violence together. But suppose that that integrity (whatever it may amount to) fails? What then? The answer is that we then get the paranoiac universe of Mickey Spillane, in which the world is a dark, terrifying, and hostile place, where elaborate and deadly plots are commonplace, where no man is free of guilt, and where the only response to any situation is violence, violence first and last. For Philip Marlow's sense of honor, Mickey Spillane's Mike Hammer substitutes a lively gift for hallucination, complete with phantom bells ringing inside his cranium in moments of crisis.

I assume, however, that scholarly readers with a laudable interest in social phenomena will already be familiar with Spillane's works, and with the critical comment about him; so I should like to pass on to another, less familiar work of the same general school. This is a novel by Sterling Noel, entitled *I Killed Stalin* (New York: Farrar, Straus and Young, 1951). The hero of this remarkable book is Alexis Ivanovitch Bodine, born in Brooklyn to White Russian parents, a former OSS man with a record of service in Yugoslavia during World War II. He is abruptly recruited by an American espionage organization referred to as Bureau X, which is so secret that nobody appears to know what its purpose is. As an employee of this organization, Bodine is planted in the American Communist party, where he rapidly qualifies himself as a saboteur. The Communist groups with which he is affiliated are, of course, quite as secret as Bureau X. Eventually he is shipped off to the Soviet Union, where he becomes almost instantly a colonel in the Red Army and commanding officer of another organization called Arbat 568, which is even more secret than anything he has belonged to so far, but the purpose of which is all too clear. Arbat 568 is the organization which murders and cremates enemies of the regime. Bodine finds this work rather depressing at times, but not beyond his capacities. The sole motivation for this entire rigmarole, from Bureau X through an assortment of assassinations, plots, and counterplots to Arbat 568, is the killing of Joseph Stalin. As presented in Noel's book, this political murder is quite purposeless: the United States and the Soviet Union are not at war when it is projected, and it is not expected that the death of the dictator will accomplish anything very startling. In a rather strained effort to provide some motivation for the killing, Noel shows the Soviet Union attacking the West a day or so before Bodine finally gets Stalin in front of the sights of a rifle.

The interesting thing about *I Killed Stalin* is that in this *reductio ad absurdum* of the crime story, it is no longer possible to tell the pursuer from the pursued, or the good from the evil. Anyone can be anything; characters change their faces with the fluidity of nightmare. Suspicion is the normal evaluation of character, and automatic violence is the signal response to suspicion. The grammar of assassination, at this point, disintegrates almost wholly: what remains is a verb, an endlessly active verb, whose significance is compounded of sterile sexual pursuit, destruction, and torture.

Now why—if at this point I may venture the question—why is the detective story, or any other branch of popular literature, worth all this critical pother? My answer would be along these lines. To a large extent our semantic environment conditions all of us, shapes our goals, our attitudes toward others, toward ourselves, toward society. To a large extent, within the past fifty years or so, our semantic environment has become mechanized: our lives are swamped in the endless flood of symbols poured over us daily by our complex communications network, much of which is beyond our control. No one can wholly avoid contact with the mass media: even those who, by prodigious effort, fail to attend the movies, or to watch television, are brought in contact with the content of these media at second hand, through their children, friends, and neighbors.

The reverse of these observations also appears to be true. If we may correctly remark that our semantic environment (which is now crowded with the symbols of violence) is inescapable, and that it conditions us all to some extent, we may also note that the semantic environment, in a kind of unholy antiphony, supplies the responses to the questions raised by our fears, our anxieties, our unachievable desires. "The tempest without," says Weller Embler, "must serve as metaphor to tell about the soul's life." More than this, we might add: the "tempest without" may be regarded as part of, a complement to, "the soul's life."

Mickey Spillane's work is still being avidly consumed, via film, radio, and books. Sterling Noel has published a second novel, much like his first. A book warning the public of forthcoming invasions of Earth by flying Venusian saucers has just reached the best-seller lists. Is it too much to suggest that millions of people immerse themselves in this sort of witch's broth because it provides a "normal" intellectual climate for them? that literature which becomes popular does so because it dramatizes and complements most effectively the inner tumult which its readers experience?

We cannot of course transfer literally the symbols of the literature of violence to the life of the soul. And no doubt there are many who would find this literary world incredible and horrifying if they were forced to regard it as in any sense "real." For in this world, the world which we have been examining, a man lives dreadfully alone, clutching the secret of his own goodness to himself. And outside is a world of unfathomable evil, half concealed by grinning masks which only parody goodness. One's next-door neighbors, the cop on the corner, the judge in his chambers, the minister in his pulpit, the huge, mock-heroic, mock-beautiful faces of celebrities, senators, generals, even presidents—one by one they slip their masks to reveal the demon beneath. And yet, one is reassured. In this universe a champion will arise, evil will be bloodily suppressed, and all one's anxieties will be melted in the heat of violence.

Is this world an echo, a reflection, of the inner world in which millions of us live? If it is, then I do not think that censorship or protests directed at broadcasting networks, the Johnston office, book publishers, or the press will avail us much. We are not dealing with the stupidity or malpractice of a small group of communicators, but with a whole society badly in need of therapy. This therapy must be self-administered, and we must rely on the agencies available for the task: schools, churches, such civic, business, and professional organizations as have any direct influence on public attitudes, the media of public communication, and above all, any individuals with a modest preference for sanity and some notion of how to achieve it.

I suppose it to be true that unsanity is catching; it spreads with equal facility from an obscure person with few contacts outside his family, from a great man standing before the television cameras, from the pages of a cheap book or a not-so-cheap magazine, from a classroom lecture or a Sunday morning sermon. But I like to think that—contrary to the normal laws of medicine—sanity can be contagious too. If it is, it will be contracted from individuals, whose range of influence may be great or small. And if that is so, we can scarcely have too many carrying its virus.

Winter, 1954. This paper is based on a lecture given before the Chicago Chapter of the International Society for General Semantics, March, 1953. Dr. Maloney is associate professor of radio and television in the School of Speech, Northwestern University.

Communication in Science Fiction

ROBERT PLANK

Growing like a mushroom, science fiction has in a few years achieved the status of a major literary genre in its own right. It has hardly yet, however, been subjected to systematic investigation. One of the first problems to be faced would be that its rapid sprouting must, obviously, be a symptom of whatever it is that is peculiar about the present state of our civilization. But what is that? One expects science fiction to be particularly concerned with science, in the usual sense of the word. It is surprising to find that this is not so. These systems of fantasy are, rather, preoccupied with communication.

It may be that this preoccupation is the key to the question of how science fiction reflects broader trends of our times. For it is the same focus of interest which characterizes semantics; and the same preoccupation has played a growing role in our social and political life, coming to the fore in the importance of such concepts as the "iron curtain."

The science fiction literature of the last few years offers an abundance of material to illustrate the various forms that the preoccupation with communication may take. The classical guise is perhaps that displayed in "Discontinuity" by Raymond F. Jones (*Astounding Science Fiction*, October, 1950).

The central character of the story is Dr. Mantell, a scientist who has "provided the medical world with its most brilliant technique in thirty centuries of its history. . . . With one sweep he eliminated the centuries old butchery of lobotomy and topectomy which had maimed hundreds of thousands in its long fad" (p. 83). This he achieved by the "Mantell Synthesis": "He could tear apart the brain of a man, cell by cell, and reconstruct it in the image of a living human being" (p. 79). The operation proceeds by building "blank molecules" which are then "punched" with data from "giant pattern molecules." A "semantic selector" is built in.

However, Mantell's experiments had led to "intensifying the very conditions they were designed to heal. In a hundred cases of extensive brain damage, his process had restored life, but only in varying degrees of hopeless aphasia. At first the public hailed the magnitude of his stride, then, revolted by the horror of his failures, they had turned against him with a mighty clamor" (p. 83).

At the beginning of the story, after fifteen years of married life, Alice Mantell, with the help of her lover, has attempted to murder her husband, but has succeeded merely in bashing his head in. Mantell's coworkers, finding him after his wife's assault more dead than alive, decide to put him together again by subjecting him to the "Mantell Synthesis." The result is that he is restored to complete health—in fact, he feels better than ever before—but he finds himself totally unable to communicate with other people, either by speaking or writing.

It is noteworthy that no other symptom is mentioned, yet the reaction to his condition is drastic. Dr. Vixen, Mantell's chief assistant, "was staring, his face reflecting sickness of heart" (p. 85). Dr. Mantell himself "knew what his fate would be. Visual, auditory, ataxic aphasia—schizophrenia—they would put a label on him and lock him in a jail. They'd lock him up for the rest of his life because somehow he had become imprisoned behind an incredible wall of communication failure" (p. 86).

So he escapes from the Synthesis Laboratory to a suburban insane asylum. There he finds several of his former patients who are in custody, and he is overjoyed to discover that he can talk to them. The cause of the *supposed* failures of the Mantell Synthesis is found: having "semantic selector banks" built into them, the brains of the synthesized have been freed of so much ballast that they, far from being schizophrenic, aphasic, etc., are really "the most completely sane people the world has ever known" (p. 97). Their communication system is so nearly perfect that they can have no truck with the poor linguistic systems of communication of us nonsynthesized folk—an astonishing situation which is explained as follows: "All are beyond our comprehension because, as Shannon demonstrated so long ago, a channel cannot pass a message of greater entropy than the channel capacity without equivocation. Since we demand zero entropy and ordinary communication employs so much higher values, we understand nothing" (p. 99).

The rest is easy. Putting the Mantell Synthesis into reverse gear as it were, some "entropy" is reintroduced into the brain of one of the synthesized. Then two people—one of them Alice Mantell—are kidnaped and synthesized. These cases—both striking successes since they are made over into perfect beings—convince Dr. Vixen. " 'If those two could be changed,' he whispered half to himself, 'the whole world can be made over. I am next. You'll let me be next?' he demanded urgently. 'And after me, the whole world' " (p. 109).

All this sounds quite puerile. Surely one would not find a story of this sort in a purportedly scientific book. But, as Hayakawa points out,[1] one does. To anyone who has read some of those "case histories" on which L. Ron Hubbard built his doctrine of "Dianetics" (the "Modern Science of Mental Health"), the motifs and the atmosphere of "Discontinuity" have a familiar ring. And one might doubt whether Jones would have displayed so much crusading zeal at the end of his story, were it not for the impression that his fantasy is backed by a new method which can solve the problem of communication once and for all.

What is noteworthy about both Jones's science fiction and Hubbard's fictitious science is that they give expression to the feeling that present methods of communication are unsatisfactory; according to both, not only technical means must be improved but also underlying mental processes. Communication is by definition interpersonal, but both Jones and Hubbard identify it with an inner mental process. The demand for better communication changes in this way into a demand for clearing the mind.

This is to be achieved by a posttraumatic reconstruction comparable to birth—Mantell, awakened from Synthesis, "endured the pains of primal birth" (p. 84). A similar rebirth theme appears in Dianetics.

[1] "From Science-fiction to Fiction-science," *ETC.*, VIII (1951), 280-293.

Any person who is not thus reconstructed, or who does not possess that perfect communication system which is actually beyond human reach, is flatly labeled insane. Fear of insanity is an obviously dominant motif, though it is largely disguised as fear of the treatment meted out to the insane—which is distorted beyond recognition. We may note the obsession with the "butchery" of lobotomy, which is referred to as though it were an extremely common psychiatric practice.

The world of such stories—many modern science fiction tales as well as Hubbard's "case histories"—is peopled with individuals who are able to exert a powerful influence on human minds, and especially on the mind of the hero. Depending on the place of those

Flight from Reality

persons in the pattern of interpersonal relationships, this influence may be beneficent or sinister. It is, of course, always an essentially magical influence. It is a strongly directive communication, and usually perpetrated by methods which are outside of normal human experience, if not outside of experience altogether.

It would thus seem that there is a compulsive need which forces the author of science fiction to deal with the problem of communication. It must not be overlooked that there is also a technical requirement of his craft which exerts a powerful pressure in the same direction.

While the foregoing is true of much of science fiction, it is even more universally true of a literary genre which is not identical with science fiction but has ties with it—utopian fiction. All utopias and a large proportion of science fiction stories are concerned with depicting a society and way of life which is different from that in which the author actually moves. He must therefore transpose his hero into an alien world by letting him sink into a magic sleep to wake up in another century, by letting him travel to a faraway and hidden place, or by some more abstruse method. The preferred vehicle nowadays is, of course, the space ship.

All those travels to distant stars, into the future, or more modestly, just to uncharted islands of the Pacific, raise tremendous problems of interpersonal communications. Older authors generally ignored them. Their globetrotters, space travelers, and shipwrecked sailors land on a foreign shore and begin blithely to talk and to listen to the natives as though the language gulf did not exist—an unrealistic procedure which could only be justified as long as the problem of communications just did not evoke any interest.

This situation changed with Kipling, who included in his collection *A Diversity of Creatures* (1912) a very odd short story, "Easy as A.B.C.," in which he equipped an expeditionary force with all the paraphernalia a signal corps could dream of. This interest in communication has of late become more marked. Communication now plays a paramount role in the works of practically all science fiction writers and utopists.

In one group of them, communication is sinister, technical, and a one-way process. The "telescreen" in the late George Orwell's influential novel *1984* and the "mending apparatus" in "The Machine Stops" (an anti-Wellsian short story by the famous British writer E. M. Forster) are almost diabolical devices by which the powers that rule the world crush the individual. Such contraptions were not known to earlier authors.

In another group, represented by Olaf Stapledon's *Odd John* (a fantasy on the idea of development, by mutation, of a supernormal type of man) and by a host of lesser works, communication means telepathy. This is not a new idea. The motif of telepathy is found in old works like Cyrano de Bergerac's *Voyage dans le Soleil* and in such intermediate works as Wells's *Men Like Gods*; but it is now used much more freely. Telepathic powers, especially as part of the endowment of a new species or of robots, have become quite commonplace in science fiction.

The common denominator of all these devices is that they provide rapid and penetrating communication by short-cutting the more conventional medium of language. It cannot be a matter of mere chance that the shift to this concept coincided with the catastrophe of 1914 which has been conceived of as the great breakdown of understanding, and that it has paralleled the emergence of disciplines specifically dealing with communications, such as significs, semantics, and cybernetics.

Nor is it to be overlooked that these fictitious methods of communication obviate the necessity of confession. In 1984, the special twist that confessions are exacted even though the authorities, thanks to their privileged means of communications, have known everything all along, becomes to the author the crowning abomination. In some science fiction stories, telepathy—in the hands of the forces of law—is a powerful weapon against evil schemes. What telepathic forces would mean in a patient-psychotherapist relationship can easily be inferred. It should also be noted that the idea of telepathy is markedly close to the patient's delusion that his mind is being read and influenced, which is so common in paranoid schizophrenia. Herein lies the real connection between the communications problem and psychosis which was dimly seen in Jones's "Discontinuity."

All the elements which have been gradually evolved in science fiction tie in with various phenomena of our culture outside of science fiction. All centering around the problem of communication, they form a complex pattern; we can recognize two strands in it.

One is a well-known phenomenon, though clothed in a new and unusual garb: the desire to be removed from the earth; to be reconstructed; to be able to make confessions without having to put them into words; to escape the consequences of being declared insane—all this is known to the psychotherapist as resistance.

This, however, is but one side of the picture: that same desire to escape from this world; to be reborn; to obtain a clearer mind; to be endowed miraculously with a better system of communication; that paradoxical doubt about the place of sanity (are the psychotic on the outside of reality, looking in, or are we?)—all these are manifestations of the anxiety and discomfort which have characterized the most recent stage of our civilization.

These are the tendencies which flavor the peculiar atmosphere of science fiction. They are, to a surprising degree, identical with undercurrents that characterize much of the actual world in which we all live. The same parallelism which prevails with regard to communications could also be demonstrated as far as some related complexes of ideas are concerned, such as the by now rather trite motif of space travel. Inside science fiction as well as outside it, all these imaginative attempts to escape emotional discomfort may gain even greater importance if present trends continue.

The emergence of a deviant emotional climate in a civilization, as the rise of the Nazis taught us to our sorrow, is not a matter ever to be taken lightly. There is an adage that when a man lies prostrate, if no angel lifts him up, the devil will.

Autumn, 1953. Robert Plank (LL.D., M.S.W.) is a clinical social worker, Veterans Administration Mental Hygiene Clinic, Cleveland, Ohio.

Popular Songs vs. the Facts of Life

S. I. HAYAKAWA

Because I have long been interested in jazz—its history, its implications, its present developments—I also listen to some extent to popular songs, which are, of course, far from being the same thing. Up to now my interests in general semantics and in jazz have been kept fairly clear of each other. But since both interests are manifestations of the same nervous system, I suppose it was inevitable that someday I should talk about both jazz and semantics at the same time. My present subject is, therefore, an attempt to examine, from a semantic point of view, the *words* of popular songs and jazz songs in order to discover their underlying assumptions, orientations, and implied attitudes.

First, let me clarify the distinction between popular songs and jazz. In "true" jazz, as the jazz connoisseur understands the term, the basic interest on the part of both musician and listener is in the music as music. Originality and inventiveness in improvisation are highly prized, as are the qualities of instrumentation and of rhythm. Popular music, on the other hand, stands in about the same relationship to jazz as the so-called "semiclassics" stand in relation to Bach, Beethoven, and Brahms. Just as the musical ideas of the classics are diluted, often to a point of inanity, in the "semiclassics," so are the ideas of jazz (and of semiclassics) diluted in popular music—diluted, sweetened, sentimentalized, and trivialized.

Now the contrast between the musical sincerity of jazz and the musical slop of much of popular music is interestingly paralleled in the contrast between the literary sincerity of the words of blues songs (and the blues are the basic source of jazz inspiration) and the literary slop in the majority of popular songs. The words of true jazz songs, especially the Negro blues, tend to be unsentimental and realistic in their statements about life. (In saying "Negro blues," I should add that *most* of these are written by Negroes, but some have been written by whites under Negro inspiration.) The words of popular songs, on the other hand, largely (but not altogether) the product of white song writers for predominantly white audiences, tend toward wishful thinking, dreamy and ineffectual nostalgia, unrealistic fantasy, self-pity, and sentimental clichés masquerading as emotion.

We have been taught—and rightly—to be more than cautious about making racial distinctions. Hence let me hasten to explain that the differences between (predominantly Negro) blues and (predominantly white) popular songs can, in my opinion, be satisfactorily accounted for without "racial" explanations. The blues arise from the experiences of a largely agricultural and working class Negro minority with a social and cultural history different from that of the white majority. Furthermore, the blues—a folk music which underwent urbanization (in New Orleans, Chicago, New York, Memphis, Kansas City, and elsewhere)—developed in an economic or market situation different from that in which popular songs, aimed at mass markets through mass entertainment media, developed.[1] With these cultural and economic conditions in mind, let me restate the thesis of this paper, using this time the terminology of general semantics: *The blues tend to be extensionally oriented, while popular songs tend to exhibit grave, even pathological, intensional orientations.*

Perhaps I can make my thesis come to life by discussing a specific area of emotion about which songs are written, namely, love, in the light of what Wendell Johnson calls the IFD disease—the triple-threat semantic disorder of Idealization (the making of impossible

---

[1] I might add that I do not know enough about folk music among the whites (hillbilly music, cowboy songs, etc.) to be able to include these in my discussion. Hence in comparing *folk* blues with *commercial* popular songs, I am comparing two genres which are not strictly comparable.

and ideal demands upon life), which leads to Frustration (as the result of the demands not being met), which in turn leads to Demoralization (or Disorganization, or Despair). What Johnson says in *People in Quandaries* (Harper) is repeatedly illustrated in the attitudes toward love expressed in popular songs.

First, in looking forward to love, there is an enormous amount of unrealistic idealization—the creation in one's mind, as the object of love's search, of a dream girl (or dream boy) the fleshly counterpart of which never existed on earth:

> Will I ever find the girl in my mind,
> The girl who is my ideal?[2]

> Every night I dream a little dream,
> And of course Prince Charming is the theme,
> The he for me. . . .[3]

Next, of course, one meets a not-altogether-unattractive person of the other sex, and the psychological process called projection begins, in which one attributes to a real individual the sum total of the imaginary perfections one has dreamed about:

> I took one look at you,
> That's all I meant to do,
> And then my heart stood still . . .[4]

> You were meant for me, I was meant for you. . . .
> I confess, the angels must have sent you,
> And they meant you just for me.[5]

Wendell Johnson has commented frequently on what he calls a prevalent belief in magic. Some of his clients in his speech clinic at the University of Iowa, he says, will do no drills, perform no exercises, read no books, carry out no recommendations; they simply seem to

---

[2] "My Ideal," by Leo Robin, Richard Whiting, and Newell Chase. Copyright, 1930, by Famous Music Co.
[3] "The Man I Love," by George and Ira Gershwin. Copyright, 1924, by Harms, Inc.
[4] "My Heart Stood Still," by Lorenz Hart and Richard Rodgers. Copyright, 1927, by Harms, Inc.
[5] "You Were Meant for Me," with lyrics by Arthur Freed, melody by Nacio Herb Brown. Copyright, 1929, by Robbins Music Corp.

expect that now that they have come to THE right speech clinic their stuttering will somehow magically go away. The essence of magic is the belief that you don't have to do anything—the right magic makes all effort unnecessary.

Love is depicted in most popular songs as just this kind of magic. There is rarely an indication in the accounts of love euphoria commonly to be found in these songs that, having found the dream girl

or dream man, one's problems are just beginning. Rather it is explicitly stated that, having found one's ideal, *all* problems are solved:

> We'll have a blue room, a new room, for two room,
> Where every day's a holiday, because you're married to me....[6]

The "Blue Room" song hints at what other songs often state, namely, that not only are emotional problems (and apparently economic problems) automatically solved by finding "the sweetheart of all my dreams"; the housing problem is also solved:

[6] "Blue Room," by Lorenz Hart and Richard Rodgers. Copyright, 1926, by Harms, Inc.

You'll find a smiling face, a fireplace, a cozy room,
A little nest that's nestled where the roses bloom. . . .[7]

In a bungalow all covered with roses,
I will settle down I vow,
I'm looking at the world thru rose-colored glasses,
And everything is rosy now.[8]

That, then, is the idealization. And students of general semantics know from reading Wendell Johnson what *that* leads to. The unrealistic expectations—for love is never expected to last for any shorter a period than "forever"—result inevitably in disappointment, disenchantment, frustration, and, most importantly, self-pity. Hence:

I'm all alone every evening,
All alone, feeling blue,
Wondering where you are, and how you are,
And if you are all alone too.[9]

What if it turns out that he wasn't all alone at all, but two-timing her? She complains bitterly:

You were only fooling,
While I was falling in love.[10]

Little you care for the vows that you made,
Little you care how much I have paid. . . .[11]

But in spite of the disappointments he has caused, she still loves him:

Yesterday's kisses are bringing me pain,
Yesterday's sunshine has turned into rain,
I'm alone because I love you,
Love you with all my heart.[12]

[7] "My Blue Heaven," by George Whiting and Walter Donaldson. Copyright, 1927, by Leo Feist, Inc.
[8] "Looking at the World Thru Rose Colored Glasses," by Tommy Malie and Jimmy Steiger. Copyright, 1926, by Pickwick Music Corp.
[9] "All Alone," by Irving Berlin. Copyright, 1924, by Irving Berlin.
[10] "You Were Only Fooling," with words by Billy Faber and Fred Meadows, music by Larry Fotine. Copyright, 1948, by Shapiro, Bernstein & Co.
[11] "Somebody Else Is Taking My Place," by Dick Howard, Bob Ellsworth, and Russ Morgan. Copyright, 1937, by the Back Bay Music Co.—assigned to Shapiro, Bernstein & Co. Copyright, 1941, by Shapiro, Bernstein & Co.
[12] "I'm Alone Because I Love You," words and music by Joe Young. Copyright, 1950, by M. Witmark & Sons.

> Am I blue, am I blue,
> Ain't these tears in these eyes telling you.[13]

> How can I go on living, now that we're apart?[14]

She admits vociferously, "I'm a fool to care," but she wallows nevertheless in self-commiseration:

> No day or night goes by,
> That I don't have my cry. . . .[15]

The next stage in the progress from disenchantment to demoralization and despair is, of course, another popular song theme, "I'm through with love, I'll never love again"—a theme which has such variants as these:

> I'll never love again,
> I'm so in love with you.
> I'll never thrill again
> To somebody new. . . .[16]

> And if I never fall in love again, that's soon enough for me,
> I'm gonna lock my heart and throw away the key.[17]

And what is the final stage? Students of general semantics are familiar enough with psychiatric concepts to know that when the world of reality proves unmanageable, a common practice is to retreat into a symbolic world, since symbols are more manageable and predictable than the extensional realities for which they stand. The psychiatric profession classifies this retreat as schizophrenia, but that does not prevent it from being the theme of a popular song:

> I'm going to buy a paper doll that I can call my own,
> A doll that other fellows cannot steal. . . .
> I'd rather have a paper doll to call my own
> Than a fickle-minded real live girl.[18]

---

[13] "Am I Blue," by Grant Clarke and Harry Akst. Copyright, 1929, by M. Witmark & Sons.

[14] "Have You Ever Been Lonely?" with words by George Brown (Billy Hill) and music by Peter de Rose. Copyright, 1933, by Shapiro, Bernstein & Co., Inc.

[15] "I Need You Now," by Jimmy Crane and Al Jacobs. Copyright, 1953, by Miller Music Corp.

[16] "I'll Never Smile Again," with words and music by Ruth Lowe. Copyright, 1939, by Pickwick Music Corp.

[17] "I'm Gonna Lock My Heart," by Jimmy Eaton and Terry Shand. Copyright, 1938, by Shapiro, Bernstein & Co., Inc.

[18] "Paper Doll," by Johnny Black. Copyright, 1915, by E. B. Marks.

This, then, is the picture of love's unhappy progress, as presented by the song writers of the commercial song-publishing world. The unrealistic emotions and the bathos of popular songs have, of course, long been notorious. It may well be asked if songs can be otherwise and yet be popular.

In answer to this question, let me next present the problems of love as seen by the writers of blues songs, such as are the basis of jazz. The first thing to be noticed is that the object of love is not idealized, but is looked at fairly realistically. It is one thing to call a pretty girl an angel, but quite another to look at angels as they are seen in "Harlem Blues":

> Now you can have your Broadway, give me Lenox Avenue,
> Angels from the skies stroll Seventh, and for that thanks are due
> To Madam Walker's Beauty Shops and the Poro System too....[19]

Shortcomings of character or appearance in the object of one's love are candidly acknowledged:

> The man I love's got lowdown ways for true,
> Well, I am hinkty and I'm lowdown too.[20]

> You're so mean and evil, you do things you ought not to do,
> But you've got my brand of honey, so I guess I'll have to
>   put up with you.[21]

In other words, there is no to-do made about looking and looking for an ideal girl or man—one adjusts oneself to the kind of women and men that actually exist. Refraining from "always chasing rainbows," the people depicted in the blues appear to save themselves a vast amount of emotional energy.

The loved one's imperfections, however, do not appear to stand in the way either of the intensity or durability of one's affections, as is indicated in this lament over a woman's death:

> I tried to keep from cryin',
> My heart felt just like lead.

---

[19] "Harlem Blues," by W. C. Handy. Copyright, 1922, by W. C. Handy; copyright renewed. Included in A *Treasury of the Blues*, ed. W. C. Handy (New York: Simon and Schuster, 1949).

[20] "The Basement Blues," by W. C. Handy. Copyright, 1924, by Handy Bros. Music Co., Inc.

[21] "Goin' to Chicago Blues," by Jimmy Rushing and Count Basie. Copyright, 1941, by Bregman, Vocco and Conn, Inc.

> She was all I had to live for,
> I wish that it was me instead....[22]

Furthermore, there is no magical attitude toward love indicated in the blues. Love means a mutual human relationship, and therefore there are duties and responsibilities, no less than there are rewards. In its crudest and most elementary statement, the duty is financial:

> You want to be my man you got to give me $40 down,
> If you don't be my man, your baby's gonna shake this town.[23]

> You sittin' down wonderin' what it's all about,
> If you ain't got no money, they will put you out,
> Why don't you do right, like some other men do?
> Get out of here, and get me some money too.[24]

In general the duties described are those of living up to one's obligations as a mate, of providing that minimum of dependability that makes, as they say, a house a home:

> Kind treatment make me love you, be mean and you'll drive me away,
> You're gonna long for me, baby, one of these old rainy days.
> Yes, I love you, baby, but you don't treat me right,
> Walk the streets all day, baby, and never come home at night.[25]

---

[22] "St. James Infirmary," by Joe Primrose. Copyright, 1930, by Gotham Music Co.

[23] "The Memphis Blues," by W. C. Handy. Copyright, 1912, by W. C. Handy. (Included in *A Treasury of the Blues*.) When the lecture on which this paper was based was delivered in San Francisco, it was extensively reported in the San Francisco *News*. In the correspondence columns of the *News* a few days later, there appeared a protest from a reader who remarked regarding my quotation of these lines, "It is good to know that our future teachers [at San Francisco State College] are acquiring moral and spiritual values by getting the good honest feel of the brothel." Mr. Ralph Gleason, writing in the musicians' magazine, *Down Beat*, and taking his interpretation of my lecture from the letter writer in the *News*, worked himself up into quite a moralistic lather against what he imagined to be my recommendation of love on a cash-down basis over white middle-class morality. I trust it is not necessary to explain that what I am doing here is attempting to draw a humorous contrast between love regarded *as magic* and love (including facsimiles thereof) regarded as *involving mutual obligations*. The statement that love involves obligations is not entirely absent, of course, from popular songs. A recent example is "Little Things Mean a Lot," by Edith Lindeman and Carl Stutz (New York: Leo Feist, 1954), which, as sung by Kitty Kallen, a few years ago enjoyed vast popularity.

[24] "Why Don't You Do Right?" by Joe McCoy, Copyright, 1942, by Mayfair Music Corp.

[25] "Blues in the Dark," by Jimmy Rushing and Count Basie. Copyright, 1943, by Bregman, Vocco and Conn, Inc.

And the famous blues singer, Bessie Smith, gives the following advice to girls—advice which is full of the sense of one's own responsibility in a love situation:

> So if your man is nice, take my advice,
> Hug him in the morning, kiss him every night,
> Give him plenty loving, treat him right,
> For a good man nowadays is hard to find.[26]

The physical basis of love is more candidly acknowledged in the blues than in most popular songs. I am indebted to Dr. Russell Meyers of the University of Iowa Hospitals for the following observation about Jelly Roll Morton's "Winin' Boy Blues," in which there occurs the line, "Pick it up and shake it, life's sweet stavin' chain."[27] Dr. Meyers equates this line to Herrick's "Gather ye rosebuds while ye may," translating thus: "A 'stavin' chain' is the heavy chain used by loggers to bind together logs to be floated down river, so that it is metaphorically that which binds together, i.e., sexuality; the idea is, as in Herrick, that you shake it now, while you are still able."

Popular songs, to be sure, also refer to the physical basis of love, but usually in extremely abstract periphrasis, as in "All of me, why not take all of me?" In the blues, however, as in the Elizabethan lyric, the subject is treated metaphorically. The following is from a song made famous by Bessie Smith:

> You better get yourself to a blacksmith shop to get yourself overhauled,
> There ain't nothing about you to make a good woman bawl.
> Nobody wants a baby when a real man can be found,
> You been a good ol' wagon, daddy, but you done broke down.[28]

So there are disappointments in love in the blues, no less than in popular songs. But the quality of disappointment is different. The

---

[26] "A Good Man Is Hard to Find," by Eddie Green. Copyright, 1917, by Mayfair Music Corp. This song is not of Negro composition and is not, strictly speaking, a blues. However, ever since its famous rendition by Bessie Smith (Columbia 14250-D), it has been part of the blues repertory.

[27] See General 4004-A, in the album *New Orleans Memories*, by Jelly Roll Morton.

[28] "You've Been a Good Ole Wagon" (Smith-Balcom), sung by Bessie Smith (Columbia 14079-D; re-issue, Columbia 35672). Copyright by Leeds Music Corporation, 322 W. 48th St., New York, N.Y.

inevitability of change in a changing world appears to be accepted. Conditions change, people change, and in spite of all one can do to preserve a valued relationship, failure may result:

> Folks I love my man, I kiss him morning, noon and night,
> I wash his clothes and keep him dry and try to treat him right.
> Now he's gone and left me. . . .[29]

> I've got a hard-working man,
> The way he treats me I can't understand,
> He works hard every day,
> And on Sat'day he throws away his pay.
> Now I don't want that man,
> Because he's done gone cold in hand.
>
> Now I've tried hard to treat him kind,
> But it seems to me his love has gone blind.
> The man I've got must have lost his mind,
> The way he treats me I can't understand.
> I'm gonna get myself another man,
> Because the one I've got done gone cold in hand.[30]

The most vivid statement of a sudden change of situation, involving desertion and heartbreak, is made in "Young Woman's Blues," by Bessie Smith:

> Woke up this mornin' when the chickens were crowin' for day,
> Felt on the right side of my pilla, my man has gone away.

Her reaction to this blow, however, is not, as in popular songs, any giving away to self-pity. The song continues:

> I'm a young woman, and I ain't done running round.[31]

---

[29] For this and several other quotations from blues songs in this paper, I am indebted to Professor John Ball of the Department of English, Miami University, Oxford, Ohio, who, as a student of jazz, has transcribed from his record collection the words of many blues songs, including many which have never appeared in print.

[30] "Cold in Hand Blues" (Gee-Longshaw), sung by Bessie Smith (Columbia 14064-D; re-issue, Columbia 35672). Copyright by C-R Publishing Co., 2908 Americas Bldg., Rockefeller Center, New York.

[31] "Young Woman's Blues" (Bessie Smith), copyright, 1927, by Bessie Smith; copyright renewed, 1954, by Empress Music, Inc., 119 W. 57th St., New York 19, N.Y.

In other words, she may be hurt, but she is far from demoralized. This refusal to be demoralized under conditions which in popular songs call for the utmost in wailing and self-commiseration is repeatedly to be found in the blues. Instead of the self-abasement that we find in the "kick-me-in-the-face-again-because-I-love-you" school of thought, the heartbroken men and women of the blues songs regroup their emotional forces and carry on without breakdown of morale. The end of a love relationship is by no means the end of life. As Pearl Bailey has sung:

> Gonna truck downtown and spend my moo,
> Get some short-vamp shoes and a new guy too . . .
> Cause I'm tired, mighty tired, of you.[32]

There is, then, considerable tough-mindedness in the blues—a willingness, often absent in popular songs, to acknowledge the facts of life. Consequently, one finds in the blues comments on many problems other than those of love, for example, the problem of urban congestion, as in "I'm going to move to the outskirts of town," or of alcoholism, as in the song, "Ignorant Oil." There is also much folk wisdom in the blues, as in "Nobody knows you when you're down and out," or in such observations as:

> Now if a woman gets the blues, Lawd, she hangs her head and cries,
> But if a man gets the blues, Lawd, he grabs a train and rides.[33]

I am often reminded by the words of blues songs of Kenneth Burke's famous description of poetry as "equipment for living." In the form in which they developed in Negro communities, the blues are equipment for living humble, laborious, and precarious lives of low social status or no status at all—nevertheless, they are valid equipment, in the sense that they are the opposite of escape literature. "Rock Pile Blues" states explicitly what the blues are for:

> My hammer's heavy, feels just like a ton of lead,
> If they keeps me slaving someone's gonna find me dead.
> Don't mind the rock pile, but the days are oh so long,
> Ain't no end of misery, that is why I sing this song.[34]

[32] "Tired" (Roberts and Fisher), sung by Pearl Bailey (Columbia 36837).
[33] See note 29. Memo to Professor Ball: Where on earth did you find this, John?
[34] "Rock Pile Blues," by Spencer Williams. Copyright, 1925, by Lincoln Music Co. (Included in *A Treasury of the Blues*.)

As a student of general semantics, I am concerned here with two functions which literary and poetic symbols perform with respect to our emotional life. First, by means of literary symbols we may be introduced vicariously to the emotions and situations which we have not yet had occasion to experience; in this sense, literature is preparation. Secondly, symbols enable us to organize the experiences we have had, make us aware of them, and therefore help us to come to terms with them; in this sense, literature is learning.

If our symbolic representations give a false or misleading impression of what life is likely to be, we are *worse* prepared for life than we would have been had we not been exposed to them at all. The frustration and demoralization of which Wendell Johnson writes are of necessity preceded by the expectations created by unrealistic idealizations. This is not to say, of course, that idealizations are in themselves unhealthy; they are a necessary and inescapable product of the human processes of abstraction and symbolization, and without idealizations we should be swine indeed. But there is a world of difference in the semantogenic effects of *possible* and *impossible* ideals. The ideals of love, as depicted in popular songs, are usually impossible ideals.

Hence the question arises: do popular songs, listened to, often memorized and sung in the course of adolescent and youthful courtship, make the attainment of emotional maturity more difficult than it need be? It is almost impossible to resist having an opinion on this question, although it would be hard to substantiate one's opinion except on the basis of considerable experience in contact with the emotional problems of young people. Mr. Roy E. Dickerson, executive secretary of the Cincinnati Social Hygiene Society, who has had this experience, has offered the following comment on the thesis of this paper:

> In my judgment there is no doubt about the unfortunate influence of IFD upon the younger generation today. I detected it, I think, in even such a highly selected group as the delegates to the Seventh National Hi-Y-Tri-Hi-Y Congress held under the auspices of the National Council of YMCA's at Miami University recently. I had the pleasure of handling the group of the section of the Congress which gave attention to courtship and marriage. It was still necessary to debunk some super-romantic concepts.
>
> I am up to my eyes in marriage counseling. I feel that I am consulted again and again about ill-considered marriages based upon very super-

ficial and inadequate ideas regarding the nature of love and how it is recognized.

The existence of the blues, like the existence of occasional popular songs with love themes which do not exhibit the IFD pattern, demonstrates that it is at least possible for songs to be *both* reasonably healthy in psychological content *and* widely sung and enjoyed. But the blues cannot, of course, take over the entire domain of popular song because, as widely known as some of them have been, their chief appeal, for cultural reasons, has been to Negro audiences—and even these audiences have been diminishing with the progressive advancement of Negroes and their assimilation of values and tastes in common with the white, middle-class majority. Furthermore, while there is lyricism to be found in blues *tunes* and their musical treatment, the *words* of blues songs are notoriously lacking in either lyricism or delicacy of sentiment—and it would seem that popular songs must, to some degree, supply the need for lyrical expression, especially about matters of love.

With all their limitations, however, the blues demonstrate that a popular art can function as "equipment for living." Cannot our poets and our song writers try to do at least as much for our young people as Bessie Smith did for her audiences, namely, provide them with symbolic experiences which will help them understand, organize, and better cope with their problems? Or, if that is too much to ask (and perhaps it is, since Bessie Smith was, in her own way, an authentic genius), can they not at least cease and desist from further spreading the all-too-prevalent IFD disease?

Winter, 1955. Dr. Hayakawa is professor of language arts at San Francisco State College, editor (and founder) of ETC., 1943 to present. This paper was originally presented at the Second Conference on General Semantics, held under the auspices of Washington University and the St. Louis Chapter of the International Society for General Semantics, at St. Louis, Missouri, June 12, 1954.

It was also presented before the Associated Students of San Francisco State College at Nourse Auditorium, San Francisco, July 8, 1954. On this occasion the lecture was illustrated by music performed by the Bob Scobey Frisco Jazz Band and Claire Austin. The writer wishes to thank again, for their excellent and spirited contribution to the program, the performers of that evening: Bob Scobey (trumpet), Fred Higuera (drums), Dick Lammi (bass), Bill Napier (clarinet), Wally Rose (piano), Jack Buck (trombone), and Clancy Hayes (banjo and voice). Whatever was left unclear in the speech was made more than clear by the skillful interpretive singing of Mr. Hayes and the deeply felt blues-singing of Mrs. Austin.

The materials of this paper were again presented at the Folk and Jazz Festival at Music Inn, Lenox, Massachusetts, September 5, 1954. Music on this occasion was supplied by the Sammy Price Trio, with blues-singing by Jimmy Rushing and Myra Johnson. They were also presented, with the assistance of the Bob Scobey Frisco Band and Lizzie Miles, blues singer, before audiences at Beloit College, Northwestern University, University of Chicago, and Purdue University, January and February, 1956. The writer is deeply indebted to all these gifted performers for their sympathetic understanding of the argument of this paper.

IV. Language and Thought

For one who knows no language but his own the correspondence of words and things is an assumption almost inevitable. For him then the words are not merely conventional symbols for things but real properties of the things; and a grasp of the relations of words is a grasp of the things themselves. It is then a disillusionment to discover, upon learning a foreign language, that what can be expressed in a word in one tongue requires a pair of words or a whole phrase in another, and that between no two languages is there more than a rather loose correspondence of word to word. This wrenches the word loose from the thing; it also introduces what is for me the most characteristic product of philosophical reflection: namely, a consciousness of the variety of human points of view. And the fact that this consciousness is slight in ancient philosophy, acute in all of the modern period, may be traced, I think, to the fact that the modern philosopher lives and works in a world of many tongues where the Greek philosophers knew only one. And I will go a step further and suggest that this experience of language which the ancients lacked is the most important item in any education for reflective thought.

WARNER FITE, "Experience with Languages"

The Blind Men and the Elephant: Three Ends to One Tale

RAYMOND J. CORSINI

Many centuries have passed after the fact, but is it possible to discover the end of the tale of the Blind Men and the Elephant? Ali thought the Elephant to be like a spear, Bul like a fan, Con like a wall, Dor like a tree stump, and Eri like a rope. What happened thereafter has not been told. It is possible that man's fate depends on the end of the tale. Three endings are given below: the reader may take his choice.

END ONE

Ali, the eldest, spake: "I am the eldest, and consequently the wisest. I am also the first to have felt the Elephant and now the first to speak about him. Moreover, I felt him carefully, to the very end. He ends in a sharp point. He is hard, long, and smooth, and is like a spear which curves gently. My description of the Elephant may be regarded as definitive."

Bul spoke next: "It is true, Ali, that you are aged. Hence your faculties are dim. Also, if you are right, then I must be wrong. This is impossible, since phenomenologically reality is as I see it. Far from being like a spear, the Elephant is soft, wide, flat, and pulpy—very much like a fan."

"Reality is reality," stated Con. "I kicked the Elephant. He is massive, like a wall. He is limitless, infinite. I could find no end. Oh, the poverty of philosophy, the smallness of men who reduce infinity to the proportions of their own mean perceptions!"

Dor began to whirl his staff about his head, screaming: "No, no, no. Wrong, wrong, wrong! I started with fundamentals, from the ground up. The Elephant is like the trunk of a tree. By Allah and Moreno, you are all wrong."

At this point, his mouth frothing, Eri began to lay about him. "Liars, Adlerians, Catholics, Negroes. . . ."

Then the others began to labor each other with *their* heavy, iron-shafted staffs, yelling meanwhile, "Infidels, Rogerians, Trotskyites, Mormons, Semanticists, Jews, McCarthyites, Collectivists, Syndicalists, Behaviorists, Episcopalians, Dianeticists, Transactionists, Freudolators. . . ."

After a while, all was quiet. And when people came by, they found that all but one of the Blind Men were dead. One of the passers-by knelt beside the sole survivor, and seeing the dying man's lips moving, bent close.

"The others, are they dead?"

"Yes."

"Ah, then . . . then . . . I am right. The Elephant is like. . . ." But he then expired, and to this day no one knows what the Elephant is like.

End Two

Seminar-wise, the Blind Men gathered at a conference table, and Ali, the eldest, spake: "We have long been curious to know exactly what an Elephant is like, and we have already gathered enough preliminary data to indicate that each of us has had different perceptions. Since the whole is at least the sum of its parts, let us try to reconstruct the beast by correlating the data we have gathered. From my experiential frame of reference, this is how the Elephant appears to me. . . ."

And so the Blind Men discussed the Elephant at length, and finally they arrived at an integration and summation of their perceptions. Thus they created what might be called the Eclectic Elephant, which was approved by all concerned, and became The Elephant. The Elephant was concluded to be a creature which had for a head a single spear-shaped protrusion; probably for decoration, but perhaps for protection from the sun, it had a kind of shade or parasol or fan; protrusion and fan were mounted on an enormous, wall-like body, upheld by a single stump-like leg; the creature ended with a rope-like tail.

A joint monograph on the Elephant was written by the Blind Men and was published in the *Hindustani Journal of Experimental and Comparative Zoology*. It remains the basic reference on the subject.

End Three

Ali, the eldest, spake: "It is evident that since we are blind we cannot really know what the Elephant is like." Bul nodded, "We can each get a part of the beast, but the whole escapes us. Our limitations are only too evident. And even a combination of our perceptions . . ."

". . . is inadequate," added Con, "because the whole is more than . . ."

"There is probably more to the Elephant than what we have felt," stated Dor. "Perhaps if we called in still another blind man to feel the Elephant, he would see it as a volley ball, a lawn sprinkler, or an Austin car. We can never hope to understand. We are too mean and limited to obtain a just conception of this vast and noble beast. How may we ever realize this?"

"There is only one way," suggested Eri. "It is evident that what we must do to understand the Elephant is to ask someone who can *see*."

"A higher authority!" the other Blind Men shouted. "That's what we need."

So they went to consult a child of high reputation—the same child who had seen the Emperor as he was. "What is the Elephant like?" they asked.

"He is purple, has three heads, sixteen legs, crawls on his belly, and eats with his nose."

"And the spear?"

"It grows from his three eyes and is twelve ells long."

"And the fan?"

"He has hundreds. They flap in the wind."

"And the wall?"

"It extends for miles."

"And the stump?"

"A wartlike decoration."
"And the rope?"
"He hooks it on trees and climbs it."
And so the Blind Men were content.

Summer, 1955. Dr. Corsini, who has had wide psychological experience in schools and correctional institutions, has contributed papers to many psychological journals. He is associate director of Daniel D. Howard Associates, an industrial consulting firm in Chicago.

The illustration for this article is by George A. Taylor, of Chicago, Illinois.

A Chinese Philosopher's Theory of Knowledge

CHANG TUNG-SUN

Generally speaking, there are two kinds of knowledge, the perceptual and the conceptual. Take a table or a chair for instance. It can be touched and perceived directly. This is perceptual knowledge. The uniformity of nature and the idea of a Supreme Being, on the other hand, cannot be verified by the senses, and causality, teleology, and the like are also conceptual in nature. It may be noted that perceptual knowledge cannot be outside the conceptual, nor can conceptual knowledge be separated from the perceptual. As a matter of fact, any conceptual knowledge contains perceptual elements and vice versa. The differentiation between the two is always for the mere convenience of discussion. They do not exist separately.

The kind of knowledge treated in this essay, it will be seen, is not perceptual but conceptual knowledge. Insofar as the conceptual guides the perceptual, the importance of the former surpasses that of the latter. This point is often neglected by the empiricists, but from the standpoint of cultural history it is desirable to have it emphasized.

Conceptual knowledge is also interpretative in nature. By interpretation we understand the manipulation of concepts and the employment of categories. For instance the apprehension of a flower is a perception, but it is an interpretation to say that flowers are derived from leaves, or that the formation of the flower is for the purpose of reproduction. In an interpretation of this kind at least the following concepts are being used: any event must have its antecedent; each change must have its cause; and, the final result in a concept of evolution is so much the more derived from interpretation. Therefore, interpretative knowledge, because it contains concepts and results in concepts, is conceptual knowledge. The manipulation of concepts is for the purpose of interpreting perceived facts. Thus, it is evident that conceptual knowledge is interpretative knowledge, and interpretative knowledge is theoretical knowledge.

At this point we may mention the thesis of Pareto,[1] the Italian sociologist, for purposes of comparison. According to him, theoretical knowledge has very mixed elements: descriptive elements, axiomatic elements, concrete elements, and imaginary elements, in addition to those appealing to sentiments and beliefs. He also classifies theoretical knowledge into two kinds: the experimental and the nonexperimental. And, with these two as *matter* he has as *nexus* the logical and the nonlogical. Thus there are four classes, the logico-experimental, the nonlogico-experimental, the logico-nonexperimental, and the nonlogico-nonexperimental. In this connection we are not interested in developing his theory, but merely in pointing out that his experimental knowledge is outside the theoretical knowledge discussed herewith.

His distinction between the logical and the nonlogical indicates that the nonlogical is not very important, but the term "the logical" itself seems very ambiguous. The thought of man may not necessarily be in agreement with formal logic, but it cannot be otherwise than in agreement with *a* logic. We are treating, therefore, not formal logic but real logic. The type of logic used by Chinese philosophers is different from that of the West, while the Hindus may have a logic different from both the Chinese and the Western. Logic follows the trend of culture. Western scholars often mistake their logic for the universal logic of mankind, as we have seen in the case of Kant. We will have more to say on this point later. It suffices here to say that the distinction between the logical and the nonlogical is of no particular importance, because there is no theoretical knowledge which does not imply real logic. It sounds like nonsense to speak of

[1] Vilfredo Pareto, *The Mind and Society,* tr. Andrew Bongiorno and Arthur Livingston.

nonlogical theoretical knowledge. Pareto has made a real point in saying that approval and disapproval of nonexperimental knowledge depends upon sentiment, and thereby speaks of the "logic of sentiment." But from the logic of sentiment we must exclude experimental knowledge before we can go any further. What we are interested in here is a kind of knowledge which is both interpretative and conceptual and outside the experimental.

The newly arisen Vienna school has noted this point. Rudolf Carnap, for example, has made a distinction between the problems of facts and the problems of logic in his book *The Logical Syntax of Language*. The former are those arising from facts while the latter are problems of words symbolizing things, and of the judgments which are made about things. This distinction may be of use by bringing before us the fact that much of our knowledge is not directly related to things, but merely to views about things. This kind of knowledge has a great place in human life. In our discussion we are dealing with this kind of knowledge which in concrete cases is comprised of political thought, social thought, philosophical thought, and moral points of view, as well as the theoretical part of religious beliefs. Scientific knowledge, apart from its experimental elements, belongs here also in the form of interpretative theory.

It is worth while to note that experimental knowledge is guided by conceptual knowledge. Alfred North Whitehead is very clear on this point in *Adventures in Ideas*. According to him, science is a synthesis of two kinds of knowledge, one direct observation, the other interpretation. Thus he speaks of "observational order" and "conceptual order." The former is explained as well as supplemented by the latter. Points of view among scholars may differ as to the priority of the two, but since the emergence of higher animal forms, both of them have coexisted. New observations may modify original concepts while new concepts may lead to new points of observation. We may take the evolution of physics as an example. Newtonian physics starts with matter in the form of concrete things. Hence the conceptions of absolute motion, and absolute space and time. But modern physics takes cognizance of concrete matter only as a point in the framework of time and space. Hence, what Whitehead calls "simple location" is discarded. From this it may be seen that the development of physics follows the conceptual scheme which is employed in it. In addition to Whitehead, V. F. Lenzen, the American physicist, in his *The*

Nature of Physical Theory has illustrated the changes and developments of physical concepts in relation to physics. In the field of biology, Woodger in his recent book, *The Axiomatic Method in Biology*, has also demonstrated very clearly that categories have guided observation. All these examples show that experimental knowledge is perceptually derived knowledge which is guided and influenced by underlying nonexperimental knowledge or conceptual knowledge. It is easy to see that experimental knowledge can modify conceptual knowledge, while it is not so obvious to many people that conceptual knowledge may be underlying and guiding the perceptual knowledge.

Another point to be made concerns the social nature of conceptual knowledge. All experimental knowledge is derived from the senses, and thus is individual and private, in other words, nonsocial. Consequently, perceptual knowledge can hardly be social knowledge. Yet no knowledge can do away with its social content, the emergence and existence of which occur only in the field of interpretative knowledge. Samuel Alexander has pointed out in *Space, Time and Deity* that the problem of valuation has a social nature, and that without presupposing society we cannot speak of value. It is needless to say that valuation is possible only in the field of interpretative knowledge. So far as perceptual knowledge is concerned, by the nature of the fact that it is private and individual, there is no problem of objective valuation. The importance of perceptual knowledge is self-evident, while nonexperimental knowledge is apparently unimportant because its importance is not so evident, though nevertheless real.

The reason for the social nature of theoretical knowledge is not far to seek; it is that it is thinking expressed in terms of language, which in scientific terminology is called "linguistic thinking." It is needless to say that language is a social product. Although the child's language has a stage of monologue, it is self-evident that language implies or presupposes an audience. Primitive man, we are told, often takes language as a concrete entity. The lower the culture, the greater the power of words. In primitive society language has magical power, therefore there is a direct connection between language and thought. If a primitive man is accused of being a thief, he most certainly becomes angry. But in modern society a sophisticated person can turn aside this accusation by a smile, provided he is innocent. We may take the degree of the power of words as a gauge to measure the development of an ethnic intellectual development. This point has been sufficiently demonstrated by modern students of child psychology and "primitive mentality," so we do not need to dwell upon it any further.

The arguments thus far seem to reveal the discrepancy between language and things, and thus to advocate the emancipation of thought from language. Almost all the philosophers, from remote times to our own, have been aware of the limitations imposed by language, with the implication that real thinking cannot be clothed in language. The ordinary view is something like this: thought is primary, and with new terms thought has a better chance for expression. But this argument does not necessarily reveal the nature of the development of human thought. As a matter of fact, it is better to say that language has been a contributing factor rather than an obstacle to the development of thought. Viewing human history as a whole, any new creation in language, e.g., new terminology, represents a development of thought along a new line. Language and thought are fundamentally indivisible. Any thought can only be articulated through language or symbol. That which cannot be thus articulated most likely will not be counted as thought. Although language and thought cannot be absolutely identified with each other, they cannot be separated. It is not that language limits thought or hinders it, but rather that language creates thought and develops it. Should we consider the two points together, namely, that thought develops with language and that language is a form of social behavior, it will be clear that apart from the experimental elements all knowledge is social.

With the cognizance of the determination of thought by social conditions, there develops the sociology of knowledge. But the sociology of knowledge has shown only that human thought is determined by socially visible or invisible forces without realizing that apart from all these immediate concrete forces there are underlying social forces of a remote nature. We may identify these remote forces with cultural relations. All thought, in addition to being influenced by our immediate social environment, is also molded by our remote cultural heritage. The immediate forces determine the trend of our thought, while the remote cultural heritage determines the forms in which thought is made possible. All these forces help to determine interpretative knowledge. With different interpretations come different cultures. And, being born into different cultures people learn to interpret differently. Thus we may use culture to explain categories, and categories to explain mental differences, e. g., those between the West and the East.

With regard to types of language, a distinction may be observed between "emotive language" and "referential language." The first is used to arouse, with necessary gestures and appropriate sounds, the corresponding gestures or mental attitudes in the person to whom they are addressed. The latter is used to refer to things and ideas about things, largely in terms of organized symbols or articulate language. According to Darwin, the animal expressions in the form of singing and roaring may be taken as the precursors of human language. Thus emotive language is nearer to elemental expressions and more concerned with mental attitudes while referential language, being nearer to abstract thinking, is more concerned with grammatical constructions than mere changes in sounds.

With grammar and sentence structure comes logic, and in this connection we have to deal for a moment with the nature of logic. Western logicians take it for granted that the object of logic is rules of human reasoning. This assumption, however, is not quite justified. Take Aristotelian logic, for example, which is evidently based on Greek grammar. The differences between Latin, French, English, and German grammatical forms do not result in any difference between Aristotelian logic and their respective rules of reasoning, because they belong to the same Indo-European linguistic family. Should this logic be applied to Chinese thought, it will prove inappropriate. This fact shows that Aristotelian logic is based on the structure of the Western system of language. Therefore, we should not follow Western logicians in taking for granted that their logic is the universal rule of human reasoning.[2]

In so far as the object of logic lies in the rules of reasoning implied in language, the expression of reasoning must be implicitly influenced by language structure, and different languages will have more or less different forms of logic. Hence the difference between Chinese logic and Aristotelian logic. The traditional type of subject-predicate proposition is absent in Chinese logic. According to the usage of Western logic, in such a sentence as "A relates to B" the form is not a subject-predicate proposition but a relational proposition. Another sentence

[2] [See S. I. Hayakawa, "What Is Meant by Aristotelian Structure of Language?" in *Language, Meaning and Maturity* (New York: Harper, 1954).]

like "A is related to B" is in the form in question, because there is the distinction between the subject and predicate. For both forms, however, there is in literary Chinese only one, that is, *chia lien yi*. Although we may say colloquially *chia shih lien yi*, the function of the *shih* is that of the so-called "empty words," which are used only for emphasis or intonation, without any grammatical function. Both of these Chinese propositions mean the same thing, without grammatical distinction except that the latter is more emphatic. Neither is a subject-predicate proposition. *Lien* relates the two terms *chia* and *yi* but it is not a copula.

Regarding the "empty words" such as *che, yeh, hu, tsai, yi, wei,* and so forth, they were not primarily so, their original meaning having been lost. Their function is based on their sounds. As such sounds do not have proper characters, they are represented by characters of similar sounds, which are called "borrowed" words. Such a "borrowed" use denotes only the sound without any implications as to meaning. The original characters had their own meaning. For example, the *wei* mentioned a moment ago originally meant *hou* or "apes." It is the sound, not the meaning of the original, which is borrowed. In the formula "... *che* ... *yeh*," *che* serves the function of a comma and *yeh* that of a full stop. According to the types of language mentioned above, the referential and the emotive, the Chinese "empty words" are emotive words. These empty-emotive words are closely related to the ideographic nature of Chinese characters, on which we will have more to say later. Now it suffices to say that Aristotelian logic is based on the sentence structure characterized by the subject-predicate form. Should we alter the sentence structure, the validity of the traditional Aristotelian logic may be questioned. With these preliminary remarks we may proceed to a discussion of the differences between the Western linguistic family and the Chinese language, and their respective influences on logic.

Western thought is in the last analysis confined to Aristotelian logic although later developments in logic have gone beyond the Aristotelian type. Modern mathematical logic, for example, is only an extension of formal logic. In no way can it unify all the forms of logic. The reason why Bertrand Russell is opposed to the idea of substance lies entirely in the fact that he has discovered a new logic not based upon the form of subject-predicate proposition. As a matter of fact, however, this new system of logic applies, apart from mathematics, only to the physical sciences. It is not applicable to the social sciences. Therefore, traditional logic is still the "living logic" in the mind of Western thinkers. Now it can be shown that the "ten categories" and the later modified "five predicables" in Aristotelian logic are based on Greek grammar. And so long as definition and division are derived from the "ten categories" and the "five predicables" they in their turn are limited by Greek grammar. The "fallacies" pointed out by Aristotle are essentially those found in the Greek language.

Apart from the obvious examples mentioned above, the basis of Aristotelian logic may be seen definitely to lie in the subject-predicate form of language structure. It is seen in the English sentence "it is," which means "it exists." The verb "to be" has the meaning of existence, and Western logic is closely related to the verb "to be" in Western languages. It must have occurred to the readers of Plato that the verb "to be" is quite rich in meaning. Many philosophical problems come from it. Because the verb "to be" has the meaning of existence, the "law of identity" is inherent in Western logic; without it there can be no logical inference. Western logic, therefore, may be called "identity logic."

The law of identity does not merely control logical operations such as deductions and inferences but also influences concepts of thought. As we know, Aristotle's philosophy was made possible entirely by the use of "identity logic." For him the substance is merely derived from the subject and the verb "to be." From the latter, because its implication of existence leads naturally to the idea of "being," and from the former because in a subject-predicate proposition the subject cannot be eliminated. From the indispensability of the subject in a sentence, only a short step leads to the necessity for a "substratum" in thought. For example, when we say, "This is yellow and hard," yellowness and hardness are the so-called "attributes" which are attributed to something, the something in this case being "this." The "something" in general is the substratum. With a substratum emerges the idea of "substance." The idea of substance is indeed a foundation or fountainhead for all other philosophical developments. If there is any description, it becomes an attribute. An attribute must be attributed to a substance, thus the idea of substance is absolutely necessary in thought in the same way as the subject is absolutely necessary in language. This is the reason why in the history of Western philosophy, no matter how different the arguments may be, pro or con, about the idea of substance, it is the idea of substance which itself constitutes the central problem.[3]

The English word "it" also has its own peculiarities. It is a non-definitive. It denotes *something,* but not what. Once the *what* is stated there develop the subject and predicate, or in other words, the substance is characterized by its attributes and the attributes are attributed to the substance. Thus, the separation between existence and whatness was the fundamental condition under which the concept of the substance was born. And this condition is expressed only in Western language structure. It may be agreed then, after considering the peculiarities of the verb "to be" and the word "it," that many philosophical problems are merely problems of language.[4]

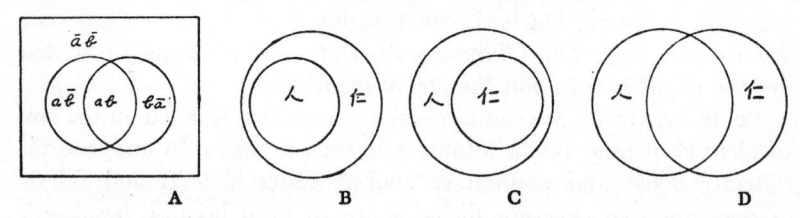

The Chinese language has its own peculiarities. First, it is not essential for a Chinese sentence to have a subject. It is often understood. In a sentence like *hsueh erh shih hsi chih pu yi yueh hu* ("When we study and constantly review it, is it not pleasant?", or *kou chih yu jen yi wu o yeh* ("If there is devotion to benevolence, there is no evil"), the subject is eliminated. Examples of this kind are too numerous to mention. The above two are random examples from the *Analects.* Secondly, in Chinese there is no verb "to be" comparable to the English form. The colloquial *shih* does not convey the idea of existence. The literary *wei* on the other hand conveys an idea of *ch'eng* which means "to become." But in English "becoming" is exactly opposite to "being." Such a formula as "... *che* ... *yeh*" does not mean anything identical, and consequently does not constitute

[3] [On subject-predicate structure, see A. Korzybski, *Science and Sanity: An Introduction to Non-Aristotelian Systems and General Semantics,* (Lakeville, Conn., 1950), pp. 62, 85, 92, 131, 189, 190, 224, 306, 371. On "substance," see A. J. Ayer, *Language, Truth and Logic* (New York, 1936), pp. 28, 32-3, 50, 195.]
[4] This view differs from that of the Vienna school in that, according to that school, once language is clearly defined, some problems will cease to exist. But it seems to me that there are problems arising from language which indicate emotive drives which cannot be eliminated.

a logical proposition in the Western sense. If we say *"jen che jen yeh"* ("To be a man is to be human"), we cannot say the first *jen* is the subject and the second *jen* (written with a different ideograph) the predicate. In such a sentence the idea cannot be expressed diagrammatically, as is often used in Figure A in the case of Western logic.

The other figures B, C, D cannot convey the exact idea of the sentence. It may be either of the three, or it may be in between the three. This is the best proof of the absence of the word "to be" in Chinese.

We have seen above that Western logic is essentially based upon the law of identity.[5] Division, definition, syllogism, and even conversion and opposition are based upon it. All these are correlated and constitute a system. The basic structure of Chinese thought is different from this system. *The Chinese system of logic, if we may call it a system, is not based upon the law of identity.*

Let us begin with Western logical division. As it is based on the law of identity, it must be dichotomous in such forms as "A and not-A," "literary books and nonliterary books." Cases like "A and B" or "Good and Evil" are not dichotomous in form because besides A and B there may be C and besides Good and Evil there may be Not-Good and Not-Evil. Thus, there is the need in classification for the rule of exclusiveness. But Chinese thought puts no emphasis on exclusiveness, rather it emphasizes the relational quality between above and below, good and evil, something and nothing. All these relatives are supposed to be interdependent. In a sentence like *yu wu hsiang sheng, nan i hsiang ch'eng, ch'ng tuan hsiang chiao, ch'ien hou hsiang sui* ("Something and nothing are mutually generative; the difficult and the easy are mutually complementary; the long and short are mutually relative; the front and the rear are mutually accompanying"), we have a logic of a quite different nature.

Next we come to the discussion of definition. In Western logical definition it is necessary to make the sign of equation between the *"definiendum"* and the *"definiens."* For example, "A triangle is a portion of a plane bounded by three straight lines." But in Chinese thought the problem of equation between the two is never thought of. For example, "wife" is denoted as "a woman who has a husband."

This cannot constitute a definition in Western logic, in which it

---

[5] The rules of "contradiction" and "excluded middle" are simply corollaries of the law of identity.

must be condemned as a fallacy, or as begging the question, but it is characteristic of Chinese logic. *Chuan chu* or the "inverted use of a word" in classical commentaries belongs to the same category. So also the "metaphoric" use or *chia chieh*. The most important concept in ancient China might be said to be concerned with "heaven" (*t'ien*), but according to the definition in the *Shuo Wen*, *t'ien* means the "human head" or that which is above the head. It is evident that that which is above the head may not necessarily be "heaven." There may be many other things such as clouds, wind, the moon, birds, and what not. This "indicative" method of definition is quite different from the Western type. Examples of this sort of definition, such as *jen che jen yeh, yui che yui yeh* ("To be a man is to be human; to be correct is to be accommodating") are too numerous in the Chinese classics to need mention here. It suffices here to point out that in addition to its difference from the Western type of definition, a Chinese term may also be explained or indicated by another term similar in sound and associated in meaning. To explain a term by means of others of similar sound is inconceivable in Western logic, for Western logic always aspires to be detached from language, and the explanation by means of sound is merely linguistic, it contains no logical implications. In short, it may even be safe to say that ancient Chinese literature contains no such method of definition as that found in the West.

It may be well at this juncture to discuss the Chinese characters *fei* and *pu*. In an English sentence like "A is not-B" or "A is not B" the affirmative or negative nature is easily determined. But if in Chinese we say *chia fei yi*, it may mean either the first or the second. The difficulty is not so apparent in this simple proposition, but it is clear that conversion is unnecessary and opposition impossible. In the nature of the case it is, therefore, evident that Chinese thought cannot be placed in the Western logical framework. We must give it an independent name.

It may be proposed to call this type of logic "correlation logic" or "the logic of correlative duality." This type of logic emphasizes the relational significance between something and nothing, between above and below, and so on. It is expressed sufficiently in the *Book of Changes*. Although modern archaeologists may not accept the *Book of Changes* as one of the earliest records, we cannot say that it does not contain the traditional thought of China. The most dominant note here is the so-called *i yin i yang chih wei tao* ("The positive and negative principles constitute what is called tao or nature"). With *yang* or the positive principle we presuppose the *yin* or the negative principle, and with the *yin* we presuppose the *yang*. Each is dependent upon the other for its completion. Other examples like *kang* and *jou*, *chin* and *t'ui*, and *chi* and *hsiung* are exactly similar.[6] Should we wish to adopt a terminology much in vogue, we might call this way of thinking an illustration of "dialectical logic." But this term is very ambiguous, and its historical allusions do not allow it to be adopted in this connection. We will have to be content with noticing that Chinese ways of thinking are different from those characterized by the use of the law of identity. Without defining the different terms used, it is impossible to speak intelligibly in the West. But the Chinese language, which is characterized by the use of correlation logic, has nothing to do with identification. Rather it uses antonyms to make an idea complete.

Opposition as a means of expression is not only used in propositions like "death without passing away," "a great sound but scarcely audible," "the greatest omen without being visible," "nonresistance means strength," or "the most fluent speech seems to stutter," but it is also used to denote a single term. In the *Shuo Wen*, for example, "outgoing" means "incoming" and "disorder" means "order." In this case, it is better not to consider the words as having contradictory meanings, because it is the meaning, not the word, which awaits its opposite for a complete illustration of the connotation. For example, *ch'u* ("outgoing") must wait for *chin* ("incoming"). Without *chin* there cannot be *ch'u*. Other examples such as *luan* ("disorder") and *chih* ("order"), and *kung* ("tribute") and *tz'u* ("grants") are similar in nature. The explanation of the word "to sell" is also given by means of its opposite "to buy." "To sell" and "to buy" in contrast to each other become clearer, because buying and selling constitute the same transaction when viewed from the different standpoints of the buyer and seller. From this it is seen that Chinese thought is not based upon the law of identity, but takes as its starting point relative orientation or rather the relation of opposites. This type of thought evidently constitutes a different system. This system is probably related to the nature of Chinese characters. Being ideographic, Chinese characters put emphasis on the signs or symbols of objects. The Chinese are

[6] Emotive and phlegmatic, assertive and resigned, lucky and unlucky.

merely interested in the interrelations between the different signs, without being bothered by the substance underlying them. Hence the relational or correlational consideration.

The ideographic nature of Chinese characters influences not only the structure of the Chinese language but also the thought or philosophy of the people as well. The *Book of Changes* may be taken as the best example. Most probably words were originally coined as tokensymbols. Thus, it is said "the sage arranged diagrams (*kua*) in order to see the significance of any sign (*hsiang*)." Although we are not

Metalinguistics: Words Fashioning Thought and Vice Versa

quite justified in saying that the diagrams are the original Chinese characters, it may at least be granted that they are similar in nature to Chinese characters. The creation of the diagrams served the purpose of divination, but there must have been previously arranged limits of possible combinations for the purpose of divination. Each combination is a possible sign. "Heaven indicates good and bad fortune by signs which are signified by the sages." The "sages" must have been such heroes of cultural history as Pao Hsi Shih, to whom the discovery of the diagrams was attributed. It may be said that the signs do not merely symbolize something external but also indicate possible changes. For example, it was from the *yi* diagram that farming implements were invented, and from the *li* diagram that fishing nets were invented. Dr. Hu Shih has well said, "Confucius was of the opinion that with the genesis of the signs there come things. The signs are the primeval archetypes after which things are modeled."

According to ancient Chinese thought, first came the signs, then the development of things. This assertion is quite different from that of the West. Although platonic ideas have a superficial resemblance, it must be remembered that Plato's "ideas" are self-existent, which is not true in the case of the eight diagrams. As we have seen, Western thought is consistently based on the idea of substance. Consequently there is the need for a substratum, and the final result of this trend of thought gives rise to the idea of "pure matter." It is characteristic of Western philosophy to penetrate into the background of a thing, while the characteristic of Chinese thought lies in exclusive attention to the correlational implications between different signs, such as *yin* and *yang*, *ho* ("involution") and *p'i* ("evolution"). It is also because of this fact that there is no trace of the idea of substance in Chinese thought. It should be noted that the presence of an idea gives rise to word forms with which to express it. In China there is no such word as substance. Such words as *t'i* ("body") and *yung* ("function"), *neng* ("knowing"), and *so* ("known") in their function of expressing subject and object came from the translation of the Buddhistic scriptures. It makes no difference to the Chinese mind, whether or not there is any ultimate substratum underlying all things. Because the Chinese characters are ideographic, Chinese thought takes cognizance only of the signs and the relations between them.

It must be evident thus far that there is not only a close relation between logic and language, but that a logical system must presuppose a philosophy, that is, cosmology and the philosophy of life. Chinese cosmology may be called "significism" or "omenism." The Chinese character *hsiang* which we have translated as "sign" has all the meanings of the English words phenomenon, symbol, and omen, but it must be noted that behind the *hsiang* no concrete things are implied. Its signification is only concerned with human affairs. Thus a sign is for the purpose of giving lessons to the people, and consequently, all the heavenly phenomena such as stars and comets were taken as evil omens. The Chinese cosmogony characterized by omenism is essentially a practical guide to human life. In this point it also differs from the West. It may be true that in Western philosophy, cosmology is a preliminary step to the philosophy of life, but the two cannot be confused. Chinese thought, on the contrary, does not make any distinction between the cosmos and all the problems of human life.

According to Western tradition philosophy may be classified into ontology, cosmology, and the philosophy of life. In China there are only cosmogony and the philosophy of life, without any ontology or cosmology proper, and even cosmogony is absorbed into the philosophy of life. The reason for this lies in the neglect of the law of identity on the part of Chinese thinkers. Even such expressions in the *Lao Tzu* as "*t'ien ti ken*" and "*tao chi*" are only concerned with the origin of the universe. In spite of the fact that the later development in the *Chuang Tzu*, in such a sentence as "Whether an object is made or unmade it remains the same thing," is often alleged to be similar to Western substance, the aim of *Chuang Tzu* is only "the proper degree of adjustment." Consequently, his identification of the cosmos with the self is only a sort of mystic experience. In other words, he is concerned with "participation" or "transduction"[7] rather than with the problem of existence. The book *Chuang Tzu* has a mixed origin. It is doubtful whether there may not have been insertions and alterations on the part of the Wei and Chin scholars, but it is evident that the author's ideas are more or less similar to those of the Hindus.

The later cognizance of the problem of substance on the part of the Chinese is due to the influence of India. The ethical systems of the Sung and Ming dynasties are merely reactions against Buddhism. It is often said that Western philosophy began with the idea of substance and later got rid of it, and that China originally did not have it—but later acquired it. She acquired it through cultural contact, a fact which raises problems which cannot be discussed here. Our problem is whether or not there are original forces which still underlie Chinese thought, whether, for example, the Chinese mind is still characterized by neglect of the idea of substance. The weight of evidence, in spite of abundant Western influences, is that it is.

Because the idea of substance is related to the idea of causality most of the sciences are still determined by the concept of causality. At this point it may be said that Kant was the first to reveal the mystery of Western thought. He is not surpassed by anyone, even today. He puts the idea of reciprocity between the ideas of substance and causal-

[7] These terms are borrowed from Jean Piaget, *The Child's Conception of the World* (New York and London, 1929).

ity in order to make the three interdependent. Consequently, wherever there is causality there must be reciprocity, and wherever there is reciprocity there must be substance. No one of the three is dispensable. From this we may learn that the idea of causality is derived from that of substance. That causality is later combined with substance gives rise to the idea of the atom. On this ground is based our thesis that in Western thought religion, science, and materialism are interdependent, a position which is not taken by recent Chinese scholars.

Roughly speaking, there are two forms of religion in the West, the early Greek type and the Christian type. The first is neither monopolized by the Greeks nor is it exclusively Western. It is similar to that of the early Chinese life. It should be remembered in this connection that in Greek mythology there are potentialities of materialism. And the early religion of China, as of all early societies, was close to Nature. But when theology developed it had to be based upon the idea of substance. The idea of the Supreme Being or a Creator is closely correlated with the idea of Substance. Furthermore, it is also closely connected with the idea of identity. Metaphysics, which is based on substance, is religion. An Ultimate Reality is in essence God. Thus it may be maintained that metaphysical or ontological philosophy is a type of religious thought. The logic characterized by the law of identity underlies this type of religious thinking. Finally, it may be said that ontology in philosophy, the idea of God in religion, and the law of identity in logic are in essence one and the same thing.

Oswald Spengler has shown in *The Decline of the West* that "there is no natural Science without a precedent Religion." Whitehead also maintains that the development of modern science was closely related to the religious beliefs of the medieval ages. So long as science is related to religion it is to be understood that in Western culture the two are but different streams from the same fountainhead. They are not so much opposed as ordinarily assumed. But this should not be understood in causal terms; the one does not determine the other, they are both parallel developments from a common origin. Thus although science and religion are opposed to each other on the surface, they are not opposed in their innermost nature.

Furthermore, Spengler has informed us that Catholic cosmology and materialism are not different things, but the same thing expressed in different terminology. Leaving aside Catholicism, we may say that materialistic thought is based on the idea of atoms, and the idea of atoms is related to the ideas of substance and causality. We may maintain that there are three fundamental categories in Western thought, substance, causality, and atoms. Religion has a foundation in substance. With causality science is developed, and from atoms materialism is derived. Behind these three categories there is another to string them together, namely, that of identity. The French philosopher Emile Meyerson has done a service in pointing out in *Identity and Reality* that all scientific theories and quests are concerned with identity. It may be easily seen that with identity there must be substance; with substance there must be causality; and the atom is between the two. Thus Western thought is essentially based on these four categories. Without understanding the importance and priority of these categories, we cannot thoroughly understand Western culture and thought.

Chinese culture, on the other hand, has no relation whatsoever to the above-mentioned categories. Let us begin with early religious life in China. The Chinese religious life is not very unlike that of the Greeks. Yet religious ideas in China were not associated with the rituals of worship and the institution of official temples. It is not certain whether there were any other deities before the concept of Heaven arose. But so far as Heaven and God are concerned, the Chinese have never been concerned with them primarily. When we speak of Heaven we have in mind only Providence, which is merely a manifestation of Heaven. In other words the Chinese are concerned with the will of Heaven without being too particular about Heaven itself, because according to the Chinese point of view the will of Heaven is Heaven itself, and to inquire into Heaven without paying attention to its will is logically inconceivable in China. Heaven and the will of Heaven are the same thing. There is not first Heaven and later the manifestation of its will. Because Heaven and its will are identical, the Chinese have never considered Heaven as an entity, and so long as it is not an entity it is not a substance. Thus the Chinese Heaven has no relation whatsoever to the Western substance. . . . Through divination the gap between man and Heaven is bridged. The Chinese are only interested in knowing the will of Heaven in order to seek good fortune and to avoid misfortune. As to the nature of Heaven as such they are indifferent. This fact shows that the Chinese have not applied the category of substance to the idea of Heaven and have not taken Heaven as the ultimate stuff of the universe.

Another point of interest is the fact that most of the statements concerning the will of Heaven in the *Shang Shu* indicate only the transfer of political power among different dynasties or from one dynasty to another. Political power was alienated in China in two ways, the hereditary and the revolutionary. When hereditary rule was abused it gave rise to revolution. No trouble arose in the case of the hereditary transfer, but there had to be a justification for a revolution, and the justification was found in the will of Heaven. Such a revolutionary transfer has great political and social consequences. That this is attributed to the will of Heaven is evidence that all great changes are beyond the control of the human will, and that the will of Heaven is only manifested in politics and social life. This is just the reverse of the case in the West in which the concept of substance was taken as the basis for its emphasis on religious thought.

In this connection something might be said about the changes and influences of religious life in China and the West. In the West the Greek type of religious life ended by the time of the unification of the Roman Empire, but the new form of religion survived the decay of feudalism. Consequently, Western religion and politics are dual currents. Chinese religious life, which bore many resemblances to that of Greece, was a powerful support of Chinese feudalism, which was similar to the European. In the time of the *Ch'un-Ch'iu* feudalism was shaken and the thought of the people was no doubt affected. Hence such statements as "The Heavenly path is far and the human path near," and "What has Heaven said? Yet the four seasons are functioning regularly." Confucianism, without having done away with the doctrine of Heaven, pushed it beyond human affairs. This type of thought had a tendency to make religious belief less influential in China, and later there was only politics and no religion. The same trend is manifested in thought, and we may recapitulate by saying that the law of identity in logic, the subject-predicate proposition in sentence structure, and the category of substance in philosophy all have religious thought as a background. This is characteristic of Western culture. Correlation logic, nonexclusive classification, analogical definition, all have political thought as a background. This is characteristic of Chinese culture.

These two types of thought differ not only in their categories and their basic rules of logic but also in their attitudes. In putting a question about anything, it is characteristic of Western mentality to ask

"What is it?" and then later "How should one react to it?" The Chinese mentality does not emphasize the "what" but rather the "how." Western thought is characterized by the "what-priority attitude," Chinese by the "how-priority attitude." In other words, Western people use the "what" to embody and absorb the "how." The "how" is to be determined by the "what." The Chinese on the other hand use the "how" to imply the "what." The "what" type of thought may develop through religion to science. This is one of the characteristics of scientific thought. The type of thought characterized by emphasis on the "how" can develop only in the sociopolitical sphere, especially in connection with the problem of ethics. Neglect of the "what" accounts for the neglect or absence of epistemology in China.

That Chinese thought always centers on human affairs while neglecting Nature may thus be accounted for. It is often alleged that in Chinese philosophy there are disputes between nominalism and realism and the problem of the relation between Man and Nature, thus implying that Chinese philosophy is similar to Western philosophy. In fact, it is not so. The Chinese interest in the problem of nominalism and realism, as well as in the problem of the relation between Man and Nature, is concerned with sociopolitical thought and the philosophy of life.

Chinese and Western thought differ also on the question of inference. The syllogism, which is based on the law of identity, is the form of inference in Western logic, while the Chinese use analogy instead of inference. The formula mentioned above, *jen che jen yeh*, is a type of analogical thinking. Other examples from Mencius are more to the point, for example, "The goodness of human nature is like the downward tendency of water" and "Does not life mean nature just as white means white? Does not the whiteness of a white feather mean the whiteness of white snow, and the whiteness of snow mean the whiteness of white jade? . . . if so, then is the nature of the dog similar to that of man?" Such examples in Mencius are too numerous to need further quotation. I. A. Richards in his *Mencius on the Mind* contrasted this type of argument with the Western type. The former may be called the "logic of analogy." This logic, as a matter of fact, though it cannot be appropriately applied to scientific thought is what is largely used in sociopolitical arguments. Analogical argument indeed is one of the characteristics of political thought. Marxism may be taken as one of the best examples. The formula, Thesis-Antithesis-

Synthesis, which is to be applied to any historical process, is analogical in nature. In the same way we may consider the transformation of seeds into trees, as the antithesis of the seeds. So also the theory of the class struggle is argument by analogy. Without criticizing the fallacy implied in Marxism it may be profitably observed that the Marxian philosophy is political in nature.

The type of thought primarily interested in politics may also have some connections with language. Thus, Confucius was for the "rectification of names" or *cheng ming*. The rectification of names was not advocated by Confucius for the sake of logic but rather as the means by which the order of society was to be maintained. Hence the saying, "If names be not correct, language is not in accordance with the truth of things. If language be not in accordance with the truth of things, affairs cannot be carried on to success. When affairs cannot be carried on to success, proprieties and music will not flourish." The function of the rectification of names lies in the discernment between what is above and what is below, the determination of the superior and the inferior and the distinction between good and evil. Its aim lies in human affairs rather than in logic. For example, to kill a king is called murder or *shih*, implying that this involves a violation of the superior by the inferior. The killing of an inferior by a superior is called execution or *chan*, implying that the executed is justifiably punished according to law. For the emperor to travel is called *hsing* or "to favor." To "come directly" is called *lai* and "to come to settle" *lai kuei*. To go from the local districts to the central government is "to go up" or *shang* as in the expression "to go up west" and "to go up north." And to go from the central government to the local regions is to "go down" or *hsia*, such as to "go down south," to "go down east." There are similar distinctions in English as seen already in these translations, but their emphasis is not so obvious and systematic. Dr. Hu Shih considers all these distinctions merely those of parts of speech with grammatical functions. He further remarks, "Confucius by rectifying the names is the first logician in China." But such, as we have seen, is not the case.

Further proof may be found in a comparison with Western grammatical changes. Take the English word "sense" for instance. Its changes may take the following forms: senses, sensation, sensational, sensible, sensibility, sensum (sensa), sensationalism, senseless, sensitive, sensitivity, sensibly, sensory, sensorium, etc. All these forms are derived from the same root. Because of the use of inflections, cases, or other grammatical forms the "form" is an essential element in Western thought. In spite of the fact that the Aristotelian idea about "form" may be different from that of Bacon and the Baconian "form" from that of Kant, it may be observed that among all of them there is something basic and uniform, namely, the emphasis on the idea or "form." The Chinese characters are ideographic; though they have radicals or *p'ien p'ang* they do not have roots. The radicals are used merely for the purposes of classification, for example, certain words belong to the realm of water and others to the realm of plants. Whenever there is a new idea a new word must be invented, a new word not derived simply from a root. Chinese ideographs are not subject to grammatical changes; there is no inflection, declension, or conjugation.

As the creation of new words must be based upon the needs of society, it is interesting to note that the most numerous terms in China come from two realms; the one, kinship, illustrated by *po* or father's elder brother, *shu* or father's younger brother, *t'ang* or paternal cousin, *piao* and *yi* or other forms of cousins; the other from the realm of ethics, illustrated by *chung* or loyalty, *hsiao* or filial piety, *lien* or frugality in taking and *chien* or frugality in spending. All the fine shadings in Chinese terminology in these two fields may be lumped together in such English terms as brothers, uncles, cousins, frugality. Such a lumping together is justifiable in the West, but in China all the differences must be preserved owing to their social significance, and we may attribute such fine shadings in Chinese terminology to the rectification of names.

It should be explained also why the type of thought which is interested in politics values more highly the logic of correlation. The reason lies in the fact that in social phenomena anything may be considered in terms of correlations, such as male and female, husband and wife, father and son, the ruling and the ruled, the civil and military, and so forth. It is but a short step from this realm to that of cosmology. For example, we say, "With Heaven being superior and the Earth inferior the universe is fixed." Furthermore political affairs may have cosmological implications; for example, from the positive and negative principles in the cosmos we may derive the principle of evolution and involution underlying the universe and human affairs, finally to be developed into such concepts as proper rule or disorder in political affairs. It should be remembered that this type of thinking is characteristic of political and social thinking.

Even in this, however, there is a difference between China and the West. It is true that Marxism has done away with the law of identity, and has advocated the law of opposition in thinking, being essentially a philosophy concerned with political and social affairs. But its difference from Chinese thought lies in the fact that while Marxism puts emphasis on opposition and thus class struggle, Chinese thought puts emphasis on the result or adjustment of such an opposition. When Mencius said, "Mental laborers rule while manual laborers are ruled," the emphasis is on the division of labor, and mutual aid as conceived by him is thus made possible. In contradistinction to the Chinese logic of correlation, the Marxian type of logic may be called the "logic of opposition."

Now we are in a position to discuss the relation between logical categories on the one hand and human nature on the other. With a given event, we may have different interpretations. For example, sunset is an observed phenomenon concerning which there may be different interpretations, such as, the sun goes beneath the earth westward, or, the earth turns eastward. It is therefore that identity, substance, and causality are all interpretations, or concepts employed in the act of interpretation, and these concepts themselves are interpretative in nature.

But it may be asked, from what do these interpretations arise and how do they become valid? We may borrow the terms from Pareto without following him in their further implications. According to him there are "residues" and "derivations." The first are the emotional drives, and the latter, outward manifestations or rationalizations. A distinction may be made between two kinds of residues, namely, the "residue of persistence" and the "residue of dominance." From the "residue of persistence" develops religious thought; and the category of substance, the subject-predicate proposition, the logic characterized by the law of identity, and the concept of causality developed thereby are its derivations. From the "residue of dominance" comes all social thought, political theories, and the concrete institutions developed thereby. All the derivations are derived from residues which are rooted in emotional drives. In order to express these emotional drives there are all the religious and political developments or derivations.

Students of culture cannot afford to forget that these residues, persistence and dominance, are universal traits of man. And it must be granted that it is not only in the social and political fields but also in the linguistic and mental fields we can see the universal traits of man. The reason why there are cultural differences between China and the West seems to lie simply in the development and underdevelopment of the derivations along certain lines. It is not that the Chinese do not have the "residue of persistence," but in their original culture or derivations it is not developed. But once in contact with India, the Chinese gave a warm reception to its religion, because Buddhism aroused the "residue of persistence" dormant in the Chinese nature. Chinese culture being underdeveloped in this respect, Buddhism found in China a second home.

Neither is it that the Western people do not have the residue of dominance. Western philosophy is certainly a transformation of religion. Kant, as we have known, in his study of knowledge has given a theoretical justification for the existence of substance. But his *Critique of Pure Reason* has left room for his *Critique of Practical Reason*. If in knowledge the substance is not revealed, it is certainly in conduct that it is realized. In these respects Kant, although trying to analyze Western thought, is limited by it. His attitude, it must be remembered, is the traditional Western attitude, namely, that of using religion as an indirect means for approaching society and politics. From this it may be observed that all Western metaphysics is essentially sociopolitical in nature. But the relation between the two is not so obvious. It is to the credit of Marxism that this point is clearly grasped. It is a pity however that it has too narrow a conception, in taking classes for society. Metaphysics was taken as merely a rationalization of social and political thought. The pure theoretical aspect of Western philosophy is nothing but a disguised form of sociopolitical thought. This observation may seem to be exaggerated, but as a matter of fact, philosophy is part of culture and culture always constitutes a total configuration. Politics, society, and human life cannot be divorced from philosophy. It is often alleged that philosophy is primarily concerned with the unraveling of the secrets of the universe, but this view seems very superficial. Two attitudes are usually taken toward the social and political problems of the present. The one attitude seeks to conserve, the other to change conditions. Marxism may have gone too far in identifying idealism with conservatism and materialism with revolutionism, but the fact remains that idealism and materialism are related to society and politics.

It is on this ground that the views of the Vienna school, for example those of Carnap, should be reconsidered. Carnap considers all philosophical propositions as "nonsense" because they are not verifiable. He needs hardly be reminded that there is much in human knowledge that cannot be verified; and we cannot say that anything that is not verifiable is not true. Rousseau's famous sentence "Man is born free" cannot be verified. Yet it helped in contributing toward American independence and the French Revolution. Social thought is not concerned with verification. It is *unverifiable* but *realizable*. This is the basis for the Determination of Man to combat Nature, as we say in China. Western metaphysical thought is nothing but sociopolitical theory in another form. And consequently, philosophy has this unverifiable but realizable nature.

Before concluding this essay, my own theory of knowledge may be briefly formulated. It seems to me that human knowledge may be considered in four groups, each penetrating into and dependent upon the others. The first is the external "structure," which accounts for immediate sensation. The external world being merely "structure," we can only know its "mathematical properties," to borrow a term from Russell. As to its qualitative nature, we know nothing. But it must be pointed out that these mathematical properties are not static and rigid, but flexible and changeable. The second group is the "sensa," to use the terminology of neo-realism. Our sensation is a curious thing. Although externally aroused, it is different from the external world in nature. There may be said to be correspondence and not identity between the two. Sensation by its nature is something independent. The third group consists of "constructions." The ordinarily perceived tables, chairs, houses, friends, and what not, are "constructions." These constructions are often taken naïvely as independent self-existent things. But as a matter of fact, these things are constructed through the perceptions of the observer. The fourth group is what we have already discussed as "interpretation." These four groups are interdependent.[8] Comparatively speaking, the first two are more closely related to the external world and, therefore, more objective, while the last two are more closely related to the inner

[8] [Compare Korzybski, *op. cit.*, Chapter XIV, "On Abstracting."]

world and, therefore, more subjective. The process from the last two to the first two may be called the process of "attachment," while the reverse may be called that of "detachment." Theoretical knowledge is a process of detachment. After detachment theoretical knowledge still invisibly underlies positivistic knowledge. The problem of validity occurs only after the process of detachment. Because of the fact that there may be different interpretations, the problem arises as to which is right and which is wrong, or which is reasonable and which is not. (As a matter of fact, from the cultural point of view there is only difference, and no correctness or incorrectness.) And this is characteristic of theoretical knowledge to which philosophy, social thought, political theories, and religious beliefs all belong.

In conclusion, we may say we have discussed the following points in order to show that human culture[9] constitutes a whole. First, what is Western philosophy? Second, what is the relation between language and thought? Third, what is the relation between logic and philosophy? Fourth, what is the relation between philosophy, society, politics, and religion? Sixth, what is the relation between theoretical knowledge and perceptual knowledge? Seventh, what is the relation between human nature and culture (between "residues" and "derivations")? Eighth, what is the difference between Chinese and Western thinking processes? All these points have been discussed from the point of view of philosophy; if they have any bearing on sociology, evaluation and criticism must be left to the sociologists.

Should the reader have had the patience to follow through all the discussion, it may have seemed to him that the writer has been guilty of eclecticism. But there is eclecticism and eclecticism. Should eclecticism prove useful in offering a more synthetic view of all the related problems, it does not need too much apology.

Spring, 1952. This article appeared originally in the Yenching Journal of Social Studies, *Vol I, No. 2, 1939 (Peking). It is a translation, by Mr. Li An-che, of Chang Tung-sun's original paper in Chinese which appeared in the* Sociological World, *Vol. X, June, 1938, under the title, "Thought, Language and Culture."*

[9] Culture in our discussion is confined to the mental aspect. Its material aspect being outside the scope of the essay, this is not discussed. This should not however be taken as implying that culture has no material aspects.

The editor is indebted to Mr. T. H. Tsien, Librarian of the Far Eastern Library of the University of Chicago, who, in 1952, provided the following information about Professor Chang Tung-sun:

"Born in 1884; studied in Japan; chief editor of the Shanghai Times and many periodicals; acting president of China College, Shanghai; a student of Western philosophy, especially of Bergson; author of many Chinese works on Western philosophy, and translator of Plato and Bergson; professor of philosophy in Yenching University; a leader of the Chinese Democratic League and a member of the Central Committee of the Chinese People's Government since 1949."

What Phonetic Writing Did to Meaning

RICHARD DETTERING

I. THE SEARCH FOR A CRITERION OF MEANING

One of the categories by which a great deal of classical and western philosophy can be interpreted is the choice of a criterion for determining the meaning of words. Much history is compressed therein; suffice it to say that the choices have ranged from subsistent Platonic forms to particular organizations of sense experience. The early "logical positivists," following Hume and Mach, especially stressed the latter; and it was from this stress that Korzybski and the first "general semanticists" got many of their assumptions. But more recent events have brought a surprising change. Some of the more prominent heirs of "logical positivism," for example the "analytic school" now flourishing in England—and with the support of such original positivists as Wittgenstein and Ayer—have come to abandon reference to the empirical world as the requirement for meaning. As J. L. Evans, one of the leading "analytic" spokesmen, recently put it:

> We can now see that to say that either names or descriptions are meaningful is merely to talk about the rules governing their use, and in neither case does talking about the rules involve a relation of correspondence or any other relation between the term and an entity or person in the world.

What Richard von Mises called "connectibility" with the stock of linguistic rules has, at least in these circles, come to replace empirical "verifiability" as the main criterion of meaning. Meaning is to be determined syntactically, *intra*linguistically, without reference to *extra*linguistic facts.

While forceful arguments have been raised by such logicians as Willard V. O. Quine and Max Black against the adequacy of the new *intensional* tests of meaning, faith in the old empirical criterion has not been restored. Instead we have from within the empiricist family an admission of failure in the long attempt to pin down linguistic expressions to mean particular, concrete sense data. At least the one important conclusion being reached here is that names and descriptions do not copy or correspond to what they name and describe, but that they derive their meaning from the cognitively significant *whole sentences* in which they occur. How these sentences relate to the events they report is another and more difficult matter to be touched on later. What interests us immediately is why Western empiricism has been unable to establish meaning by matching words with things. We shall try to find the answer in linguistics rather than philosophy, by exposing the implications of a well-known but extremely slighted characteristic of our Indo-European language family—the phonetic nature of its writing.

It will be our contention that the usual effort to invest individual words with meaning has rested on the false assumption that words are self-sufficient elements of language. This assumption arose in part from our grammar in which subjects behave as *constant bodies* clothed in *varying* predicates, and thus gain a seeming independence from the rest of language. But, to anticipate some of the conclusions of our forthcoming analysis, there has been another, less noticed factor behind our attribution of meaning to separate words. This arises from the confusion of two distinct functions of our *written* word. On the one hand we have its *phonetic* function, by which it comes to *stand for* another symbol, namely, its corresponding speech word. In performing this task our written word often acquires the capacity to abbreviate or substitute for other words indefinitely according to grammatical and logical rules. On the other hand, we have its *designative* function by which the word is said to *name* some "object." Our written word in any natural language must always fulfill the first function; it must stand for a speech word—that is *why* it is written. But only in *some* cases does it *name* an "object," that is, only when its corresponding speech word names an "object." In our highly literate culture we tend to forget to apply this basic test of a written word's *naming* power. If the written word is merely pronounceable it plays its primary role and, especially if it is a noun, we are prone to concede it the additional role of being a name as well. From this habit serious errors have arisen. In dealing with our so-called "higher abstract terms" we do not recognize that their "abstractness" often consists solely of an extension of their original phonetic function, in their acquired *exchangeability* for a plurality of other words. Hence we are apt to regard such words as the *names of abstract things*. By our historical argument we will attempt to clarify the basic linguistic conditions for these functions of *naming* and *standing for*. This will lead us to judge meaning through a pragmatic analysis of language rather than in the traditional terms of "ideas," "perceptions," or "objects." Many fine philosophic points will remain unresolved and certainly no adequate or final concept of meaning will be found, but we may be able to make some progress in attaining a more scientific and operational approach to the problem of meaning in our Western languages.

What our culture today is in part confronted by is the collapse of a "picture theory" of language. While this theory best thrived during the great mathematico-deductive achievements of Western thought, it was strongly supported by the image theory of mind developed in British empiricism. Now although "correspondence theories" of truth are not completely *passé* and are still being developed in increasingly subtle form, there is no longer an implicit assumption that all objects or events described in language are in some sense picturable. This leads to an important distinction.

The most completely picturable things are particular objects, like Mont Blanc, President Eisenhower, the Empire State Building. To a lesser degree it is also possible to picture such objects *as* members of a class: we can picture mountains, men, and buildings. The picturability of objects *as class members* depends on the amount of similarity between the members of the class. What is actually pictured in such cases is a low-order abstraction—but abstraction nonetheless. We can call such abstractions "perceptual abstractions" because they rest on the sensory similarities between particular "objects"—things which, like our three examples, are constantly peaked, two-legged, windowful. But these "perceptual abstractions" do not determine many of the other "groupings" we make from our experience: of wealth, equipment, honesty, intelligence, etc. Leaving aside for the moment the precise nature of these latter groupings, we can agree to call them "conceptual" and the terms that designate them "conceptual abstractions."[1] What the members of these groups have in common is, in any case, not something that can be regarded as a "sensory similarity."

Now a "picture theory" of language is most plausible when linguistic abstractions are "perceptual." As we go up the abstraction ladder, however, the picture metaphor becomes less and less tenable. We can literally *photograph* any particular sensible object, like Hayakawa's "Bessie the cow"; we can *paint* a reasonably communicable picture of cows generally; we can very roughly *sketch* quadrupeds, perhaps needing the aid of some conventional sign; but going beyond in any higher abstract direction—to mammals, organisms, farm assets—we are clearly stymied. No word, idea, or image having any important physical or sensory resemblance to these latter classes is possible. Perhaps this is why the medieval "nominalists," the precursors of modern empiricism, agreed that such universals or classes were only "names" for collections of particulars. On the other hand, the scholastic "realists," who believed in the existence of classes or universals, had recognized the importance of these high-order abstractions in human thought, scientific as well as theological, and refused to dismiss them as mere "names," but instead, following Plato, reified them as conceptual entities. It is interesting to remember, however, that *both* of these Christian philosophies, in their polar opposition, nevertheless assumed that the function of language was somehow to reproduce, or *re-present*, that which it describes.

If we take the word "picture" too literally, of course, we can make all kinds of respectable philosophies look absurd. However, we are here primarily concerned with the criterion of meaning; and when we consider the historical development of language we shall see that the caricature we have drawn is not so farfetched after all.

II. The Relation of Writing to Speech

In order to discuss meaning it is advisable first to consider separately its existence in speech and writing. A chronological historical treatment is feasible, here, because most linguists agree on the main developmental stages of human discourse. Speech, by all accounts,

---

[1] The distinction between "perceptual" and "conceptual abstractions" is similar to the traditional metaphysical distinction between "concrete" and "abstract universals."

came first; as Leonard Bloomfield says: "Men spoke as far back as we know anything about them. . . . Writing appears, by contrast, as a modern invention." Speech can thus be treated historically, as well as theoretically, in isolation from other major forms of communication.

1. *The Nature of Meaning in Speech*

Communicative speech seems to have its origin at the point where vocal noise-making begins to have definite and uniform effects on the behavior of other human beings. The animal world, of course, exhibits this phenomenon too, but both the animal utterance and response are not only instinctual but their correlation is relatively inflexible. The human infant has at first no language but a cry, which soon develops into a variety of sounds. William Entwistle writes:

> Prattle becomes meaningful when a second person . . . attaches a meaning by showing a reaction which baby can then reproduce at will. . . . The parents are anxious to attach meaning to any distinctly articulated syllables and they show profitable reactions. Baby notices that sounds, at first casually uttered, produce invariably certain reactions. He begins to use them on purpose.

We can now distinguish three aspects of oral communication: (a) the *manipulative* (or propagandistic, or hortatory) in which the main function of speech is to secure a desired response from another organism; (b) the *expressive* (or poetic) in which speech conveys some information about the condition of the speaker, for example the presence of hunger or pain; and (c) the *assertive* (or scientific) in which the speech directs attention to or conveys information about some part of the environment. It is clear that no fully enculturated speech can be wholly free of any of these three functions. The differences can be only in emphasis. But it also seems clear that the manipulative function is not only first genetically, but in a strict sense underlies all speech activity and determines the specific operations of the other two functions.[2] If other organisms ceased all response to our speech we

[2] There is a legitimate argument here that the expressive or aesthetic function of speech appears first, as testified by the child's enjoyment of his own voice. But this seems to confuse the quality of the sounds *per se* with the sounds as expressing a need or condition of the speaker. It is the second which is "expressive" in our sense, and which develops in the way it does *only* because it has somehow rendered the significant adult (the mother) manipulable. In a sense the difference is like that between (nondesignative) music and (designative) poetry.

would stop talking. And our expressive and assertive speech tend to acquire whatever rules in the long run best serve the manipulative function. Quoting Clark Hull:

> Perhaps the most typical form of social behavior is found in speech and other types of communicational pure stimulus acts; i.e. acts whose function is purely to stimulate other organisms. Our primary interest in language here is in a kind of feedback from the social to the individual economy, most readily seen in the reaction to the inanimate environment. This is the immensely important role that verbal symbols (acquired originally in social situations) later play in the solution of problems presented by a purely inanimate environment. Perhaps originally through the aftereffects of the reinforcement resulting from the reduction of needs mediated by following verbal directions of symbolically more sophisticated persons, a child begins tentatively to secure analogous stimulation by himself speaking relevant words. By trial and error certain combinations or sequences of self-uttered words are found to mediate problem solution and are therefore reinforced; other combinations do not mediate the reduction of needs and are therefore extinguished.

Speech is thus fundamentally a social and intersubjective occurrence. Meaning in the scientific or assertive sense, along with the emergence of formal "rules of logic," occurs as a relatively late development. To be studied, an "objective statement" must in some sense be artificially isolated from the whole human context in which speech ensues. Nevertheless the appearance of assertive language is the most revolutionary characteristic of human symbolism, and, as Hull says, "the most highly adaptive, the most efficient and flexible means for mediating survival ever evolved." There are now two important features of this *assertive* function of speech which must be understood.

First, such assertion initially takes place as a response to some external stimulus, a response which is in turn directed as a stimulus to some second person. The utterance in effect "conveys the information" that some particular stimulus has been received by the speaker. The value or utility of the utterance thus requires the acknowledgment on the part of the hearer of some socially established causal sequence. For example, the sound: "There is a fire," is interpreted as an *effect* of a stimulus of fire upon the speaker. This sequence must previously be ratified by society in order for the auditor to react as expected. The essential point here is that the spoken utterance thus acquires its assertive meaning by convention—and not by any intrinsic relationship or similarity to the stimulus. There is generally no literal reproduction or re-presentation of the stimulus by the speech sound. Save for the infrequent cases of onomatopoetic speech, which are not considered particularly significant in speech development, there is very little possibility of such literal representation. Experiences which are visual, tactile, olfactory, or gustatory cannot be easily imitated in sounds. Speech sounds are signs, not pictures.

The second feature of spoken assertion, when isolated from writing, is the particularity and concreteness of its references. The stimuli which are capable of being described by speech (in isolation from writing) seem on the whole confined to individual objects or events and easily identifiable species, like mountains, men, and buildings. There is overwhelming anthropological testimony for Entwistle's statement:

> The incomplete significance of primitive languages arises from their excessive concern with the concrete. Circumstances to be analyzed require abstraction, and of the smallest degree of abstraction such communities seem to be incapable.

Of course "perceptual abstraction" of the kind we discussed is involved here; otherwise there would have to be a different sound to denote every new tree or every new bear. But beyond this level, based on *sensory* similarity, preliterate cultures are generally unable to go. There are few generic nouns or verbs or abstract relational expressions. There is scant evidence of what modern psychologists call "transfer of learning." The first speakers were extreme nominalists.

Preliterate speech, then, clearly established a socially accepted sign relationship between symbols and objects, rather than a pictorial relationship. This nevertheless allowed symbolism in the human sense to arise; voluntary sounds became surrogates for objects. But the range of objects symbolized was unusually restricted, and empirical reference or meaning was confined to the level of "perceptual abstraction."

2. *The Nature of Meaning in Picture-Writing*

Speech and writing are so intertwined today that we even use the term "language" (much to Bloomfield's objection) to subsume both. But the origin of writing was quite independent of speech. As A. C. Moorhouse says in *The Triumph of the Alphabet:*

We can examine and appreciate the pictorial and ideographic signs of any people who have ever existed, without troubling to know what words they spoke. Yet for all the things for which there were signs, there were also words. Between the words and the signs, however, there was originally no link at all.

Writing began with drawing. Primitive drawing seems to have been motivated by magic and religion. One of the chief aims in drawing the picture of an object on the wall of a cave seems to have been to get control of the object. "Today," as J. Vendryes says, "there are savages who still completely identify the object with the image." At this point, it is important to remember, drawing had not yet become symbolic. The picture was not yet—in the minds of such people—a substitute for the object; it *was* the object. The separation of the two was the first important step. As Vendryes has put it, "Immense progress was achieved when men learned to draw and make the picture the emblem of the object." Here for the first time symbolism became representational. "Out of this ideographic writing," says Vendryes, "was born the earliest writing which we know, and from it may be traced every system of writing used by man."

At this point the link between speech and writing had not yet been forged. We should stop here to ask what is the status of meaning with such ideographic script. It is much the same as with a photograph or a representational painting. As with preliterate speech, its reference is empirical and concrete; it does not go beyond the "perceptual abstraction" level of individual objects or events or common species. But *unlike speech,* in pictographic writing we have a literal re-presentation or imitation of the object. The common *visual* medium allows a photographic reproduction. Here, then, is the only kind of formal symbolism in which a "picture theory" of language is not at least highly metaphorical, in which such a theory is strictly appropriate and justified. And here, *again unlike speech,* the factors of empirical identification, denotation and assertion become primary in meaning, while intersubjective communication is secondary and derivative. The original motive is to recreate, capture, or control the object pictured; then to represent it and depict something about it; and only finally—and usually *after* speech has intervened—to send a message to another person, to *use* the picture to make an assertion. Here in "picture-writing" extralinguistic reference, which can (as we have already shown) be only artificially isolated within speech, comes forth in its purest state. The "purity" of this state does not tend to remain, however, because the connection of drawing with speech soon gets established.

3. The Subsumption of Writing to Speech

At the beginning there was no necessary association between speech and writing. The picture of a bear, for instance, has no resemblance or intrinsic relation to the speech sound "bâr." The two eventually got connected because they both referred to the same kind of object or species. The connection was achieved, however, because speech began to *use* writing—and not vice versa. This fact is so important that Bloomfield, for example, calls *only* speech by the name of "language," and calls writing, along with gestures, mimicry, expression, and handling activities, a "language substitute." This taking over of writing by speech passes through several stages. As Bloomfield says:

> Apparently, *words* are the linguistic units that are first symbolized in writing. Systems of writing which use a symbol for each word of the spoken utterance, are known by the misleading term of *ideographic* writing. The important thing about writing is precisely this, that the characters represent not features of the practical world ("ideas"), but features of the writers' language; a better name, accordingly, would be *word-writing* or *logographic* writing.

The transition to logography is a moment of great historic significance. At this point the picture of a bear no longer finds its main function in representing an actual bear or the class of bears, but in being a substitute for the speech sound "bâr." Here, for the first time, the empirical reference of writing begins to diminish. The written symbol instead comes to stand for the spoken symbol. There is obvious utility in this ambassadorship. Written symbols are more tangible, they can be preserved, they can be transported long distances in space. They do duty for a spoken symbol more reliably than the spoken symbol can do duty for itself. Yet they do not *re-present* or reproduce the spoken symbol; one cannot draw a sound. What is most crucial, however, is that up to this time most words, *both* spoken and written, have played their full role in *naming* some *extralinguistic* thing. Now, for the *first* time, a symbol acquires the additional role of *standing for* another *symbol*. It can readily be seen what possibilities are thereby opened. The relation of synonymy appears; abbreviation, definition, and logic are made possible. The extent to which this possibility is *realized*, however, *depends on the development of two further states of writing—the syllabic and the phonetic*.

Writing at this point still has the pictorial form, although the pictorial meaning has begun to be threatened. As Bloomfield says, however:

> The main difficulty about logographic writing is the providing of symbols for words whose meaning does not lend itself to pictorial representation. Thus, the Egyptians used a character that represented a tadpole to symbolize a word that meant "one hundred thousand," presumably because tadpoles were very numerous in the swamps. The Chinese symbol for the word "good" is a combination of the symbols for "woman" and "child."

Such devices become very inconvenient, however, as a culture grows more complex. The most common way out, therefore, was to make puns, "to use the symbol of some phonetically similar word whose meaning is picturable." This we know today as "rebus-making." Historically, it led to the emergence of phonetics. As Vendryes puts it:

> The symbolic value of the sound soon came to coincide with the symbolic value of the image, and could replace it at need. The image and the sound could be substituted for one another. Once the equivalence of the two had been arrived at, the image could be treated, first as the emblem, then as the graphic transcription of the sound. . . . Phonetic writing had been created.

As most words in preliterate speech are monosyllabic, the chief effect of these script-sound substitutions and especially of the device of "punning," was for written signs to come to stand, not for speech words, but for syllables. "The symbols in this way," writes Bloomfield, "may take on a more and more constant *phonographic* value: they become *phonograms*—that is, symbols not for linguistic forms, but for phonetic forms." The commonest result was "a set of *syllabic* symbols," which are still found in many languages.

But complete phoneticization had not yet occurred because syllables are compound sounds. Most scripts never went beyond syllabilism. But there was one remarkable exception. According to Bloomfield:

It seems that only once in the history of writing there has been any advance beyond the syllabic principle. . . . At an early date—certainly before 1500 B.C.—Semitic-speaking people became acquainted with Egyptian writing, and hit upon the idea of setting down words in their language by means of the twenty-four simplest Egyptian symbols.

If this was a cultural accident, it was one of the most momentous in the history of man. By no longer standing for syllables, script could no longer, in its component figures, stand for words; it began to stand for atomic sounds, for phonemes. And in standing for phonemes, writing dropped the last vestige of any *possible* empirical representation. Thus our phonetic alphabet began. It is absolutely imperative to remember here that *only* the Indo-European language family ever passed into this last phonetic stage. The rest of the world's languages (with the possible exception of modern Japanese) never fully experienced this transition. They have thus tended to retain in part an ideographic picture script. Their writing still tends to have meaning in a direct reference to the empirical world. As a result, according to Lancelot Hogben in *From Cave Painting to Comic Strip*, "two fundamentally different kinds of writing exist in the world today." The one is "sign-writing," represented by Chinese, the other is "sound-writing," represented by our own Roman alphabet. It is the implications of this division we must next explore, especially in respect to the problem of meaning.

III. The Symbolic Implications of Ideographic Script

Languages whose script was never fully phoneticized have tended to retain many of the meaning relationships of hieroglyphical or picture writing. In modern Chinese, for example, the sign for "man" is still a biped-like figure. Although Chinese script has lost most of its overtly pictorial characteristics, it still retains meaning apart from its relation to speech. Every meaning, therefore, has its own unique script symbol; and these script symbols still stand for empirical phenomena directly. They are associated with the speech words only by happening to relate to the same objects. As a consequence we have what is to us a strange linguistic situation. In Hogben's words:

People in different parts of China speak languages which are of the same parentage as are most of the languages of Europe which is smaller than China; but the speech of people in Canton is as unintelligible to the people of Peiping as is Portuguese to nearly all Norwegians. In spite of this they can all understand the same statements in writing, if they read at all; and if they read fluently, they can all read the same classics.

In Chinese culture as a national unit it is thus the writing which carries the major burden of communication. The script has retained empirical meaning in its own right. It has never become fully subordinate to speech or wholly a substitute for speech. Therefore meaning in the Chinese language retains many of the characteristics of the primitive and quasi-literate cultures. Though no longer pictures, Chinese script words still tend to refer to the kind of phenomena which are *picturable*. They have direct extralinguistic reference—and usually to individual objects or species on the levels of "perceptual abstraction." For "conceptual abstractions," Chinese still uses indirect devices—combining "pictures" on the perceptual level, as in the instance of "good" being a combination of "woman" and "child."

It is difficult not to believe that this Chinese linguistic situation is closely related to, if not principally responsible for what we Westerners regard as the baffling, mystical, and untheoretical quality of much Oriental thought. As F. C. S. Northrop has expressed it in *Meeting of East and West:*

> The meaning of Oriental civilization—that characteristic which sets it off from the West—may be stated very briefly. The Oriental portion of the world has concentrated its attention upon the nature of all things in their emotional and aesthetic, purely empirical and positivistic immediacy.

In such a language in which symbols tend to refer solely to nonsymbolic things, theoretical abstractions and logistic formulations face tremendous obstacles. Indeed, philosophy, theology, and science, as we have known them in the West, would hardly seem likely to arise. And such seems to have been the case. Consider those highest-level abstractions like "being" and "essence" on which the West has built such vast and dazzling cosmologies. Peter A. Boodberg writes that "one of the cardinal peculiarities of the Chinese language is the absence in it of any term or set of terms even remotely congruent with the enormous linguistic and philosophical area covered by the etymon and the derivatives of *esse* and of 'being' in Indo-European languages." Western semanticists who envy this happy escape of Eastern thought should remember, however, that this impotence to abstract has also prevented the East from developing a science based on concepts like "force," "energy," and "matter."[3] In fact, the whole medieval period, with its fantastic edifice of scholastic metaphysics, may in one way be regarded as a kind of preparatory calisthenics, a proving ground for essential linguistic exercises, to make the "abstractions" of Galilean and Newtonian science possible.

We should not make the mistake, however, of calling the Chinese language "deficient" and our own language family "normal." It is Indo-European language which, strictly speaking, is abnormal and has slipped into the advanced phonetic stage where "abstraction" can be wrought for all its worth. It is the consequences of this accident which now interest us, keeping in mind the contrast with Chinese.

IV. THE SYMBOLIC IMPLICATIONS OF PHONETIC SCRIPT

The characters of our own alphabet were originally pictures of things (in their geometrical aspects), but, as in the course of centuries they have come to stand for phonemes, their ideographic quality has completely disappeared. Whereas Chinese characters stand directly for empirical objects, our characters (and their combinations) now have to go through the speech sounds to which they are assigned, and are therefore able to indicate empirical phenomena only in the most roundabout way. Our reading and writing activities thus necessitate our thinking in terms of some previously formulated set of rules establishing equivalence between symbols. In order to apprehend the meaning of most of our written words, we must know which vocal symbols are to be substituted for them. Once the habit of thinking this way has developed—and it developed many centuries ago—there remain few bounds to "abstract" intellectual expansion. Once spoken and written symbols are taken to be interchangeable, it is only a variation on the same theme for written symbols to stand for other written symbols, single symbols for groups of symbols, etc. The process is limited only by our discretion.

In the West, then, it is only our speech which, rigorously speaking, has direct empirical reference. And it is only *some* of our speech which has that, especially those sentences containing the preliterate nouns and verbs having ancient roots in our indigenous language. Much of our contemporary speech, on the contrary, has been developed by its

[3] It has been suggested by Northrup, Hayakawa, and others, that the superior advance of Japanese over Chinese science may be due to the fact that the Chinese ideographs, when borrowed by the Japanese, lost their original "empirical" meaning and were learned as abstractions.

association with writing—the slave has taken over the master. In a phonetic script any written word is a prescription, a recipe, for how to speak it. Now it has been common in the past when a preliterate culture begins to get literate, for it to borrow the script and literature of an older literate culture and more or less arbitrarily assign the imported alphabet to the speech sounds of its own dialect. This is what happened, for example, when English appropriated the Latin script which the Roman extension had made available. Under such conditions, especially when a literate clergy is in charge, writing is bound to exert considerable sway over the native tongue. Not only does it tend to affect the way many old words are pronounced and used, but it brings new words into the spoken vocabulary.

It is interesting in the case of English that most of the remaining Anglo-Saxon terms are those which name the simple and familiar things: parts of the body, like "hair," "nose," and "leg"; objects of nature like "stream," "tree," "rock," and "star." Most of our "conceptual abstractions," on the other hand, most of our higher generic terms, are drawn from the classical languages. A curious example is the introduction of the word "animal" by John Trevisa in 1395. The conscious intent here was to bring in a higher abstraction to cover *all* mobile living creatures; the words *"deór"* (from which "deer" is derived) and *"bestias,"* an earlier Latin immigrant, had long been used to denote the quadrupeds. Yet the public response was to use the new word "animal" merely to *replace "bestias"*; and more than two centuries later scribes were complaining about this narrow adaptation based on "ignorance of the Latin tongue." The scribes, as we know, lost the battle, save in academic circles, and most people still use "animal" as synonymous with "beast" today. The dualism of the prevailing religion was doubtless so great that no particular convenience was seen in a word which lumped men and beasts together. Yet the intellectuals have continued to find "animal" convenient for precisely this reason. We can easily contend that this verbal lumping has served to name the *common quality*, the perceptual similarity, of men and beasts, i. e. their breathing, pulsating behavior. But this common quality could already be *described* without bringing in a new word. The reason the *word* "animal" was introduced was to eliminate the need for such description and to abbreviate the compound substantive "men and beasts"—in short, for reasons of logical economy. When we consider more extreme conceptual terms like "wealth," "equipment," and "property," the reason becomes even more apparent. It is difficult, if not impossible, to isolate any perceptual similarity for which such words "stand." It seems more plausible to say that the introduction of these terms *as terms* was dictated by syntactical convenience. So considered, such abstract words are simply abbreviations.

This brings us to the crux of our original distinction between "perceptual" and "conceptual abstractions." It has been the traditional view that this distinction is only one of degree, or abstraction "height"; that in both cases the mind is simply *abs-tracting*, drawing some *common quality* away from objects; and that on the higher levels, where this "common quality" cannot be perceived by the senses, it is "perceived" by the intellect—a theory arising with Plato's forms and developed in Aristotle's notion of "essence." Now the argument presented here is the antithesis of this classical concept—so much so, in fact, that we must regard the very word "abstraction" as disastrously ambiguous when applied to these two kinds of intellectual process. *All* organisms—the amoeba as well as the human being—abstract in the "perceptual" sense; they have to in order to survive. This is a matter of heredity or of primitive conditioning, of learning similar responses to similar stimuli. Having acquired language and having been subject in our training to make subtle discriminations of similarity among stimuli, it is understandable that humans should *name* these similarities and generically classify them as "common qualities." But this is still a form of perceptual discrimination. It is our view that when we get beyond this level, that with "conceptual abstracting," a radically different kind of operation takes place—one of which only humans are capable and which only humans with phonetic writing have found easy. Such "abstraction" does *not* require any recognition of stimulus similarity or of "common qualities"; it only presupposes some kind of purpose or usefulness in *symbolically* uniting two or more things, or, better yet, in uniting two or more symbols under one. It is more like what we do when we pick eleven men at random and designate them as "Group A," another eleven as "Group B," etc. No "common quality" is relevant to such grouping, yet by it we may be able to solve some complex problem of subsistence or transportation. In such procedures we get involved in the systematic interchanging and combining of symbols—symbols which may or may not have a direct empirical function. This is clearly a business, not of perception, but of logic. Yet it leads to a highly pragmatist and operationalist theory of knowledge. And it indicates why the kind of laboratory activity on which Western science is based finds mathematical and logical calculation as essential as empirical reports. Our Indo-European language habits have made such accomplishments supremely possible.

V. Additional Considerations

Recent speculations on two sophisticated subjects are closely related to the foregoing treatment. First is the study of the linguistic effects of human laziness. The desire to conserve intellectual labor has been commonly noted in Western history: by Occam with his "laws of parsimony" (Occam's razor), by Mach with his "principle of economy," more lately by George Zipf in his controversial elaboration of "the principle of least effort," and by contemporary cybernetics and information theorists. Let us consider a preliminary contention of Zipf, that it is to the interest of the speaker to say as much as he can with as few words as possible; if he could say all he wanted to by *one* word, he would surely do so. The auditor, however, has opposite interests and wants messages "spelled out"; he checks the speaker's tendency to consolidate his meanings. Once the speaker's language is sufficiently learned, however, the auditor, who may by now be using the language himself, comes to accept and even appreciate the speaker's standard abbreviations; then he would rather hear "EDC" than "European Defense Community." So if the speaker keeps control the trend toward abbreviation eventually gets the upper hand. Granting this powerful underlying drive in the evolution of discourse, it would seem to follow that those languages whose words are most free of empirical reference would show the strongest valence toward economical compressions, permutations, and substitutions. To the degree that a word is tied by specificity of empirical meaning, it will resist such internal linguistic manipulation. The inability of the non-Indo-European cultures to detach words from their extensional referents and give them an independence and sovereignty in their own realm, has stopped (or at least delayed) these cultures from capitalizing on the enormous potential of language as a logical system. To the degree, on the other hand, that a word is cut off from empirical meaning, it can be shifted to different "jobs" within the language and serve the end of more efficient and frugal communication. This fact is what causes people to claim that logic "can say nothing about the world"; but it also describes an important difference between the "abstract" languages of the West and the "concrete" language of China. Phonetic symbols have allowed us to economize.

Secondly, our attention is called to the current explorations in British "analytic philosophy" as to the difference between the meaning of words and the meaning of sentences. If words and descriptions find their meaning in their rules of usage, it is very difficult, according to such philosophers as Gilbert Ryle, to apply this criterion to sentences which do not normally have rules for their employment in the way that individual words do. Without delving into this argument or in any way trying to settle a question with which some of the busiest philosophers in the world are now engaged, we can at least indicate a few of the conditions for the inquiry which follow from the historico-linguistic analysis we have given.

At the outset it is essential to distinguish the "parts of speech" from the "parts of writing," and to remember the phylogenetic priority of speech. In the functions of speech which we outlined it would seem to be the spoken *sentence* which serves as the basic linguistic *stimulus-unit*, i.e., *only* the spoken sentence can normally become the complete and adequate symbolic substitute for a nonlinguistic stimulus. The individual sound words belonging to the sentence at best provide what Hull has called "fractional anticipatory reactions"; they give a clue or hint as to what the finished sentence will be like. In listening to oral discourse we all do to some extent what the Germans do when they breathlessly suspend their response while awaiting that final verb! The words, along with the syllables and phonemes of speech, thus acquire their significance retroactively from the subsequently completed sentence.

With phonetic writing the situation is entirely different. The alphabetic characters and the words of writing fulfill at least their primary duty the moment they are comprehendingly read: they have indicated what phonemes (or phonemic compounds) are to be vocally or subvocally substituted. The written sentence is thus an artifact, a pure construction from a set of such phonemic and syllabic instructions. Its main distinction is that from long practice and association it can be more or less read as a unit, permitting the substitution of the appropriate "natural" spoken sentence to occur forthwith. Whereas in speech the word shares in the sentence-gestalt and participates in whatever external relationship the sentence bears, the phonetic written word in its fundamental work cannot stand for anything save its oral counterpart—the spoken word.

This deprived stimulus-substitution value of our written words has perhaps caused us to invent objects for which these words supposedly stand. The exact locus of these invented objects, at any rate, seems to have determined some of the principal differences between our historic metaphysical systems. "Ideas," "concepts," "images," "substances," "physical objects," and "sense data" have all been veterans in this fictional role. To oblige our more "abstract" words we have created "forms," "essences," "universals," and "classes." The subject-predicate structure of our language, whereby nouns could reject their verbs and pose freely as representatives of nonlinguistic things, has of course immensely aided this reification. Yet much of this fantasy might have been avoided had thinkers understood the phonetic nature of our Western writing. Our *spoken* words have been so dependent on their respective sentences that they could have never commanded such mischief.

It is our demure little *written* word sitting there on paper *as if* it named, represented, or pictured *something*, which has sent philosophers scurrying for its external mate. In the non-Indo-European picture scripts a word *was* a picture—it was meant to be. It was easy therefore to point out what kind of thing it pictured. This was the function of the word. And while the picture word performed this function well, it was thereby prevented from engaging in complicated economizing and substitution relationships and developing "higher" theoretical disciplines. But our Western script words were devised to assist and supplement our speech. They were never constructed to usurp the function of the spoken sentence or to be vicars for events. In fact they have, as an extraordinary by-product of their original service, done something far more important. They have organized among themselves. They have acquired the function of *levers* for logically moving great masses of other words and so have done tasks they could never do separately as empirical delegates. In thus producing the miracle of Western "abstract thinking," they have become our efficient servants either to remake or destroy our civilization.

Winter, 1955. Dr. Dettering is associate professor of language arts, San Francisco State College. He has been assistant editor of ETC. *since 1956.*

Technological Models of the Nervous System

ANATOL RAPOPORT

It is not often that a book written in another age suddenly acquires an astonishing up-to-date-ness. This does happen when some prophecy suddenly passes from the realm of the fantastic to the realm of the imminent. Such a prophecy was contained in the book *Erewhon* by Samuel Butler, written in 1872. The prophecy has to do with the evolution of machines, particularly machines endowed with a property which has seldom been attributed to machines—intelligence. As stated by Butler in rather poetic terms, the prophecy envisages a world in which the machine becomes the dominant system of organization (in the way living things are systems of organization). Like living things, the machines of the future metabolize, reproduce, maintain themselves, and in general seem to have an aim in life. The one frightening thing about the *genus machina* is its parasitic dependence on the *genus homo*. The mechanism of natural selection is supposed to function in such a way on that form of "life" as to select those variations which are especially capable of catering to the compulsions of human beings—namely, their compulsions of caring for machines. Gradually, what had started as a symbiosis between man and machine passes into parasitism, so that finally man becomes domesticated by the machine.

Almost the same prophecy is stated in more realistic terms by N. Wiener in his *Cybernetics* (New York, 1948). Wiener envisages the Second Industrial Revolution ushered in by machines able to perform tasks requiring an average intelligence with the resulting dislocations and crises similar to those which followed the First Industrial Revolution, when the "stupid" machines first appeared on the scene of history.

Our purpose here is not to discuss the merits or the limitations of these prophecies, but rather to point out that the sudden dramatic revival of the "intelligent machine" idea (be it a metaphor or a myth or a profound insight) is indicative of a really significant historical event—a major intellectual revolution.

Like the Second Industrial Revolution of which Wiener writes, this intellectual revolution is also the second in recent times. The first one occurred in the seventeenth century with the creation of mathematical physics. Perhaps I should make clear what I mean by an intellectual revolution. I think of such revolutions metaphorically as crystallizations of thinking around new, powerful concepts. In the seventeenth century these central concepts were those of mechanics—force, momentum, particularly energy. They become the central concepts of classical physics and of technology which came into being during the First Industrial Revolution.

The second intellectual revolution, now occurring, brought forward another powerful new concept, that of "quantity of organization," a concept of high degree of sophistication and bearing within it the seeds of extremely far-reaching consequences. It is this concept, also called negative entropy and "amount of information," which makes the anthropomorphic conception of the machine especially intriguing, particularly because through it the common features of "intelligent" or "purposeful" behavior of the higher animals and "automatic" behavior of "higher machines" are made apparent.

Now the personification of machines and "mechanization" of organisms are not new. The former has mythological roots in the medieval legends of the Golem and the Homunculus. The latter appears, for example, in the writings of Descartes.

The question "Are living beings machines?" has long been treated as a metaphysical question, presumably answerable on metaphysical grounds. Since metaphysics is more or less a lost art, we must learn to look at that question somewhat more critically, that is, with semantic awareness. We must translate it into other questions, such as, "To what shall the name 'living thing' be applied?" and "To what shall the name 'machine' be applied?" "Is there an overlap among the referents of the two terms?"

Putting the question this way, we see that the answers to the first are relatively clear while the answers to the second are not nearly so clear. Barring certain borderline cases (viruses, etc.) we have no difficulty recognizing the class of objects to which the name "living thing" can be unambiguously applied. Not so with machines. This is so because living things are "given." They have remained about the same for as long as we can remember. But machines have evolved rapidly within the span of human history. We realize keenly that there are machines today which our grandfathers could not have dreamed of, and, by extrapolation, we feel that we can't really say what the limits of the world of machines may be. If we think about the matter a little more, we realize that machines in their evolution undergo "mutations" of tremendous magnitudes. Where it takes eons for a new biological species to develop, a new technological "phylum" has on occasion come into being within a generation.

By a technological phylum I mean something similar to a biological phylum. If the latter is defined by a very general plan of organization in a wide class of living things, the latter is defined in terms of a *principle of operation*. We can, if we wish, distinguish four technological "phyla," which came into being successively.

The first phylum we could call *Tools*. Tools appear functionally as extensions of our limbs and they serve primarily for transmitting forces which originate in our own muscles. In the transmission of force, sometimes a mechanical advantage is gained, as in the crowbar, a screw, or a pulley. However, the work done by a machine of this sort is actually work done by our own muscles. Therefore a machine of this kind, a tool, does not give the impression of "independent" action, and so it did not occur to anyone to compare tools to living things.[1]

With the second phylum it is a somewhat different story. This second phylum of machines we could call *Clockworks*. In a clockwork a new principle of operation is at work, namely, the *storing* of mechanical energy. A typical clockwork is wound up, that is, poten-

[1] However, personification of weapons does occur. Note also the legend of the Sorcerer's Apprentice.

tial mechanical energy is stored in it, which may be released at an arbitrary later time and/or over a prolonged period of time. A clockwork does give the impression of autonomous activity, and doubtless this crude resemblance of a clockwork to a living thing (residing in its quasi-autonomous activity) gave the craftsmen of the late Middle Ages and of the Renaissance ideas of constructing mechanical dolls and animals. Perhaps the first ideas of automata sprang from the same sources. Characteristically, Descartes speculated on the possibility that animals were elaborate clockworks and, equally characteristically of his age, excluded humans from this class, as possessors of "souls."

We may observe in passing that the bow and the catapult are also clockworks by our definition, since mechanical energy is stored in these machines to be released later (in the case of the crossbow, it may be released much later). However, the "autonomous" action of these machines is so brief that they do not give even the appearance of being "alive."

The first comparison of living things to machines, therefore, was made with regard to clockworks. It is not surprising that this metaphor was not particularly fruitful for the understanding of the living process. We know now, of course, that *energy* is stored in living things, but this energy is not stored in the form in which it is stored in clockworks (mechanical stress) and so was not recognized as such. Living things are not wound up to keep going, and this absence of the most essential characteristic of a clockwork in living things made the early mechanical interpretation of life a sterile one.

This comparison got a new lease on life with the appearance of the third phylum of machines. This phylum includes primarily the *Heat Engines*. Again an entirely new principle enters into their operation. As with tools and clockworks, the output of the heat engine is an output of energy which has been put into it. But whereas the energy put into the earlier classes of machines was in the form of mechanical stress, which is obviously associated with our own muscular effort, the energy put into a heat engine is contained in a *fuel*.

Consider the vital difference between the two situations. It is obvious even to a child that the tool is not autonomous, because the tool is geared at all times to muscular effort. A child or a very primitive person may believe that a clockwork is autonomous, but it is still easy to convince him that it is not, because the winding up is still a result of someone else's muscular effort. No such effort is apparent in the fuel. Fuel is "fed" to the heat engine. The analogy to living things (which also need to be fed in order to operate) becomes ever stronger.

The comparison between heat engines and organisms passed beyond the metaphorical stage and bore real scientific fruits. It became apparent that fuel is in a very real sense the food of the engine and equally apparent that food eaten by organisms likewise functions as "fuel." The principle of energy conservation was shown to hold in living things—a serious blow to the contentions of the vitalists, which sent them on their long and tortuous retreat. Biochemistry was born. More and more processes characteristic of life were shown to be instances of processes reproducible in a chemical laboratory. An analogous revolution was occurring in technology. In fact, it would be not inaccurate to say that the First Industrial Revolution occurred when it became apparent that machines could be constructed which did not need to be "pushed" but only "fed" in order to do the work.

Driven out of physiology, the vitalists took refuge in psychology. Here, in the realm of thought and purpose, of emotion and insight, they felt they would remain safe from the onslaught of the mechanists, materialists, determinists, and reductionists. The label "nothing-but-ism" was derisively pinned on the philosophical outlook of those who believed that even the most complex manifestations of the living process, including the intricacies of men's psyche, could somehow be described in terms of analyzable behavioral components which, in turn, could be related to observable events in space and time.

And so the focus of the battle between the vitalists and the physicalists shifted to psychology, where it remains at this time. The line between the two camps is, of course, not sharply drawn. Like the political spectrum ranging from extreme left to extreme right, the range of convictions concerning the nature of mental processes stretches from extreme behaviorism to vitalism or mysticism. The gestaltists can, perhaps, be assigned intermediate positions.

I am sure the main outlines of the controversy are known. The opening offensive was undertaken by the behaviorists, the champions of what in some circles bears the unattractive name of S—R psychology. The method has a strong physiological bias. Technological analogies are frequently invoked. The earliest of these was the "telephone switchboard" model of the central nervous system. The environment was supposed to act on the organism by a series of stimulus configurations, which activated combinations of receptors, which initiated impulses, which traveled along nerve fibers, passed through the central nervous system to other nerve fibers and into the effectors, whose activity accounted for the overt behavior of the organism, which was proclaimed to be a sole legitimate object of study in psychology. Behavior was viewed as a grand collection of units called reflexes.

The model was seen to be inadequate from the start. If to every configuration of stimuli there corresponded a definite set of responses, how was learning (the acquisition of new responses to the same stimuli) possible? However, the seemingly embarrassing question proved a blessing in disguise, for the discovery of the conditioned stimulus by physiological means strengthened the reflex theory of behavior. It was shown that the paths of the impulses could be *systematically* changed. The switchboard model was shown to be still useful. Learning was accounted for by the "switchings" of the connections.

Hot on the heels of the behaviorists' successes, however, came a more serious critique, called *gestaltism*. Gestaltism deserves serious attention, because its ideas were the direct precursors of a new approach to the theory of the nervous system, which is the subject of the present discussion. The gestaltist critique was not simply a reiteration of the vitalist faith and did not confine itself to derisive labels like "nothing-but-ism" directed against behaviorism. It was much more specific and constructive and was based on at least two clearly identifiable characteristics of behavior, which did not seem to fit into the behaviorist scheme, namely, the recognition of "universals" and the equifinality of response.

The recognition of universals means the following. Suppose an organism learns to respond to the sight of a particular square in a certain way and to a particular circle in a different way (say, open a box marked with a square but not with a circle). The phenomenon is clearly an instance of conditioning. A strict behaviorist (telephone switchboard) explanation would have to rest on the assumption that the stimuli originating from the receptors activated by the sight of the square are "switched" by the conditioning process to paths leading to the proper effectors for opening the box. However, it is known that the conditioned stimulus can be varied considerably *after* the conditioning has been established and still elicit the response. For example, if the original conditioning was to a white square on a black background, it can be subsequently changed to a black square on a white background, which, at least in the retina, excites the *complementary* receptors, i.e., precisely those which were *not* involved in the conditioning process. Roughly speaking, the organism responds to the square as a "square," regardless of the receptors involved. Hence the emphasis on the term *gestalt* (the configuration perceived as a whole, rather than a complex of elementary stimuli). The gestaltists maintained that the behaviorists' emphasis on the stimulus response pathways detracted from the importance of "universals" or abstractions in the act of perception.

(If a counterargument is offered to the effect that in the perception of a geometric figure only the receptors affected by the edges of the figure are involved, it can be countered by other interesting evidence, such as the well-known phenomenon where familiar maps are not recognized if the continents appear in blue and oceans in yellow, or the still more baffling phenomenon that the shapes of objects can be recognized regardless of position, size, or orientation.)

The equifinality of response argument is even more powerful. It has been observed that once an animal has learned to perform a task (say, to run a maze to a reward) it will perform that task with whatever means are available to it. If its legs are amputated, it will *roll* through the maze. Clearly, such behavior cannot be explained in terms of a series of reflexes, each setting off the next, since the performance may involve totally different effectors each time.

This equifinality of response naturally leads one to talk of *purposeful* behavior, in which only the *goal* is relevant and not the particular configuration of neural events which come into play. This seeming inevitability of invoking teleological notions opens the door to more vitalist arguments. The notion of "purpose" seems to resurrect the ancient classification of causes into "efficient" and "final" and to give new life to the ailing idea that the behavior of living and nonliving things cannot possibly be governed by the same set of laws.

It is at this point that the concepts associated with the fourth phylum of machines become exceedingly important. We recall that the first phylum (tools) operated primarily as force transmitters; the second phylum (clockworks) as storages of energy resulting from mechanical stress; the third phylum (heat engines) as transformers of different forms of energy into mechanical energy. Now the fourth phylum of machines operates on the principle of storing and transmitting something called *information*.

Already the telephone switchboard model of the nervous system employs a technological analogy with a communication device rather than a conventional engine. The primary concern of psychology is not so much with "What makes the organism active?" as "How does it know what to do?" Not the source, the transformation, or the utilization of energy by the organism is of prime significance but its *organized* disposition. What the psychologist actually studies is not how much activity has been performed but the sequence of specifically directed acts, which when organized one way may give one set of results and organized in another way (or randomly performed) may give an entirely different set, even though the amount of energy expended remains the same. To give a homely example, consider the difference between closing the door and then turning the key and turning the key and then closing the door. The machines of our fourth phylum are primarily concerned with *systematizing* operations in which utilization of energy is involved. The amount of energy used is not important. The "power" of these machines is not "muscular" power but "mental." The giants among them are capable of receiving, transmitting, and storing complex sets of directions, i.e., large amounts of "information." This is why technological analogies with these machines are of particular interest in psychology. These machines simulate not muscular effort (as their ancestors did) but human intelligence.

Just as the concept of energy and its transformations was able to explain the "activeness" of organisms, which could not be explained on the basis of externally applied stress (as tools are activated) or by internally applied stress (as clockworks are activated), so the concept of "information" promises to do the same for a much larger area of the living process, namely, the "intelligent" and "purposeful" aspects of living behavior.

What is this thing called information? There is now a wealth of literature on the subject and it is not within the scope of this presentation to develop the ideas of this literature, I think, however, that a reasonably good idea of the nature of "information" can be given by a few examples. I will not attempt to make these ideas precise. I will try to appeal to intuitive understanding, even at the risk of being vague.

Information bears a similar relation to energy as organization to effort. One can best see this in an example where the inadequacy of a theory based on energetic considerations alone is obvious. Consider the automobile traffic in a large city. Suppose the proverbial man from Mars decided to study this traffic. He might measure the rate of flow of cars along the city's arteries. He would correctly relate that flow to the speed with which the cars traveled and, being a good physicist, he would relate the speed to the power of the engines. And so he would be satisfied, perhaps, in explaining the rate of flow by energetic considerations.

Next suppose that all the traffic lights failed. Certainly the speed of the cars and thus the rate of flow of traffic would be reduced. Suppose our Martian stuck to his conceptualization in terms of energetics. He would then have to ascribe the reduced flow (or speed) to some failure of the automobile engines, and he would be wrong. The failure is not of the engines but of the traffic lights. True, it takes energy to activate the traffic lights, but it is negligible compared with the energy it takes to move the cars. Energy has therefore little to do with the traffic problem under consideration. The key concept is not that energy but of *directions for the utilization of energy* (commands "stop" and "go" properly patterned), i.e., a matter of *information*. If the traffic lights are not functioning, the driver of a car does not know what to expect at each intersection and, playing safe, he slows down. The accumulated slow-downs of all cars at all intersections turn out to have a greater effect on the over-all slowing of traffic than the occasional full stops at the red lights. In the case of regulated traffic lights, set for certain speeds, the flow of traffic is most efficient. The cars are, in effect, "organized" or bunched up along the roads in such a way that the bunches on one system mesh with the empty spaces on the system perpendicular to it, and the flow is continuous without stops.

Examples can be multiplied at will. Children well trained in fire drills leave a burning building in a surprisingly short time, while a disorganized mob may never leave it. The success of a military action depends both on fire power and on proper co-ordination of the units. Fire power is measurable in terms of energy units, but co-ordination is measurable in terms of something else: the rate of flow of information and the precision of timing in carrying out the sequence of necessary steps. Productivity of an industry depends on the amount of power available (energetics) but to no less extent on the skill of the workers (co-ordination of activity within the individual) and the skill of management (co-ordination of activity of the several workers). While it was traditionally assumed that these co-ordinating functions must be performed by "reasoning beings," i.e., men, it became gradually apparent that a great many of them could be performed automatically (by traffic lights instead of policemen, IBM machines instead of filing clerks, automatic steering mechanisms instead of helmsmen, electronic computers instead of human calculators). There arose then the intriguing idea that there may be a general "psychology" applicable both to the behavior of these devices and at least to certain aspects of human behavior.

Historically the technological analogies purporting to explain the behavior of living things have been geared to prevailing technological concepts. As technology became more involved, the analogies could be extended to more facets of behavior. We are now entering a new technological era—the era of "intelligent machines," called automata and servo-mechanisms. The understanding of the principles on which these machines are constructed and operate promises to extend our understanding of the living process still further.

We must, however, if we are to say something significant, indicate more specifically where that promise lies. We have two pieces of evidence in support of our rather optimistic view. The first is the tremendous stride forward in the understanding of the living process, which resulted from the previous discovery of just one far-reaching principle—that of transformation of energy. The second is the progress being currently made in the analysis of the vague teleological and vitalistic notions of "purpose" and "intelligence."

Let us recall, at the risk of becoming repetitious, why the understanding of the living process presents difficulties. Living things seem to differ from nonliving in three fundamental respects (immediately apparent to the naïve observer).

1. They seem to be "autonomously" active (i.e., the motive power seems to come from the inside rather than be impressed from the outside as in the case of moving inanimate objects).

2. They seem to be guided by purpose and intelligence.

3. They maintain their integrity, grow, and reproduce.

The first technological analogy (with the clockwork) attempted to explain only the first of these characteristics and it did so very poorly. A clockwork is, to be sure, activated from the "inside" for a while, but there is no question about what the source of this activation is. The clockwork simply gives a *delayed* response to a stress (a push) impressed on it.

It is different with a heat engine. There is no obvious push there. The engine is *fed* in a very real sense and is activated by the food it "eats." The analogy to a living organism is in the case of a heat engine far from superficial. But the "muscular effort" of the engine is still externally directed. The locomotive is guided by the rails; the boat by the rudder. A simple engine is "told what to do" at every step of the process. Here the analogy with the living organism fails.

Now it is clear why the development of automata and servos naturally extends the analogy. The mechanisms of *control* are now built into the machine. We now want machines to behave "purposefully" and intelligently and since we have to design the machines, we have to analyze the notions of purposefulness and intelligence into component parts.

Really no sharp distinction can be drawn between intelligence and purposefulness. Any definition of one is sure to involve the other. Let me therefore describe very roughly the present status of "intelligence" and/or "purposefulness" in our machines which will then naturally lead me to the concluding remarks on the modern ideas of the nervous system. I view "intelligent" machines as consisting of two kinds, automata and servo-mechanisms. The only distinction I make between them is that the automaton is guided by a program of discrete steps or directions fed into it, while the servo-mechanism is guided by observing the effects of its action on the outside world. Thus a jukebox which plays a number of selections in the order selected by the customer (in response to the buttons pushed) is an automaton, and so is an electronic computer. A target-seeking torpedo, on the other hand, or a gyroscope, I would call a servo-mechanism. Both exhibit "purposefulness" and "intelligence," although if we adhere to the intuitive popular meanings of these terms, the servo-mechanism seems to specialize in purposefulness and the automaton in intelligence. This seems so, because the automaton seems to be able to follow *explicit* directions, "When so and so, then so, unless so or so, in which case so . . ." (the program), while the servo seems to be guided by a goal. This difference is only apparent. To an outsider, the automaton may well seem to be guided by a "goal" ("Find the solution of this equation") while someone intimately familiar with the operation of a servo can describe its operation in terms of a program.

This equivalence of "program" and "goal" is the principal idea of the modern theories of the nervous system. One point must be kept in mind, however. Program and goal may be logically equivalent, but it does not by any means mean that a description of an operation of an organism or a machine is equally convenient in terms of one or the other.

Let us take a trivial example. We wish a ball in a cup to "seek" to come to rest at a particular point. Here the desired behavior of the ball is described in terms of a "goal," and nothing is simpler than to design a device which will exhibit just such behavior. Take a cup of any convex shape and place it so that the desired point is the lowest. To describe the same kind of behavior in terms of a "program" would necessitate an infinite number of statements, each of which tells which way the ball is supposed to move if it finds itself in a particular position. Such a description in terms of discrete statements (an explicit program) is, of course, out of the question. A description of "intermediate complexity," however, can be given, namely, as a set of differential equations of motion which imply a stable equilibrium at the desired point.

Of the three descriptions clearly the first "stating the goal" of the ball is the simplest. What enables us to realize this "goal" by a mechanical device is our ability to see the problem as a whole. Similar considerations apply, I believe, to the theory of the nervous system.

The first attempt to account for gestalt phenomena in strictly behaviorist terms was made by McCulloch and Pitts in 1943. They showed that any pattern of behavior which could be described by *a program* was realizable in an automaton of a specified construction and (herein lies the importance of their idea) they gave an "algorithm" for the construction of the automaton based on the program. Automata, of course, operate on the same principle. The limitations of this approach, however, are immediately evident. The *whole difficulty* is to describe the action of the nervous system in terms of a program of discrete elementary steps.

The task looks more hopeful if "goal-seeking" steps are allowed in the description of the program. If, for example, the construction of a mechanism for keeping a certain muscle tone constant is known, one of the directions in the program may read, "Plug in that mechanism." Thus with one stroke an immense number of elementary steps is "described."

The value of information theory in this approach to the nervous system is now apparent. The McCulloch-Pitts picture represents behavior in terms of firing patterns of individual neurons. With 10^{10} neurons in the human body, there are $2^{10^{10}}$ such possible patterns at each instant of quantized time. This number is utterly unthinkable. Nothing whatsoever can be said of a system with that many distinguishable states where nothing is known about how the states are to be classified.

To put it in another way, the amount of information per unit time needed to describe such a system is 10^{10} bits (the amount of information coming over an ordinary telegraph wire is considerably less than 5 bits per unit time). It is quite another matter, however, when subsystems are "organized" to work in prescribed ways, when touched off by proper signals. The *amount of organization* of such subassemblies *reduces* the amount of information necessary to transmit over the channels.

This consideration leads to two complementary conclusions. Rigidity of behavior in organisms requires smaller capacities of channels over which information flows. Contrariwise, greater channel capacities allow for greater flexibility of behavior.

We are thus led to ideas of the nervous system which involve not minute blueprint structures (a hopeless approach because of the tremendous complexity of the nervous system) but which involve over-all statistical concepts such as channel capacity, storage capacity, and other parameters familiar to the modern communication engineer, such as redundancy, signal-to-noise ratios, etc.

They are concepts analogous to the over-all concepts in terms of which the operation of the "muscle engines" is understood: power, efficiency, compression ratios, etc.

It is the development of the corresponding *over-all* concepts of communication and complexity which made intelligent machines possible and which gives us promise of future understanding of living behavior, particularly of the functions of the nervous system.

I need not, I hope, emphasize that none of these considerations is relevant to the question of whether thinking machines "really think." I admit I do not understand the question. The really pertinent question is whether similar *abstractions* can be utilized in both the theory of intelligent machines and in the theory of living behavior, particularly that governed by the nervous system.

We know that both organisms and machines receive, transmit, store, and utilize information. The question of how information is "utilized" is particularly interesting. We now know what food is used for: three things, namely, as a source of heat, a source of locomotive and chemical energy, and a source of materials for growth and restoring worn-out tissues. All these elements are being constantly dissipated by the organism: heat by conduction and radiation, energy by motion, materials through breakdown and excretion.

Can it be that besides energy in the form of food and sunlight, organisms also feed on something called "information," which serves to *restore the order*, which is constantly being dissipated in accordance with the Second Law of Thermodynamics?

The formal mathematical equivalence between entropy (the measure of disorder in a physical system) and information (as defined mathematically) was commented on by Shannon, Wiener, MacKay, and others. Can it be that this is no mere formal mathematical equivalence, such as obtains between an oscillating mechanical system and the analogous electrical one, but a more fundamental equivalence such as that between heat and energy or between energy and matter? Can it be that 1.98 calories per degree mole (the difference in entropy between two moles of two separated perfect gases and two moles of their mixture in equilibrium) is *actually* equivalent to 6.06×10^{23} bits of information—the amount it would take to separate the mixture into the constituent parts in terms of yes-no decisions?

If there is such a conversion factor, how do the information-receiving, information-transmitting, and information-storing organs operate to convert information into negative entropy or its concomitant "free energy" and, perhaps, vice versa?

The intriguing nature of these questions has stimulated some of us to undertake the study of communication nets from the information-theoretical point of view. This approach necessitates the description of such nets not in terms of detailed structure but rather in terms of gross statistical parameters. The flexibility and far-reaching adaptability of the behavior of higher organisms almost demands this sort of approach. Perhaps the most fundamental characteristic of living behavior as distinguished from that of man-designed machines is in the *sacrifice of precision* for safety. It is not important that a response be precise but rather that an equivalent response be given under a great variety of conditions or handicaps. It is more important to be "roughly" correct in practically every case than be "precisely" correct in every case but one and altogether wrong in that one. It is necessary to relate totally new situations *approximately* to situations already experienced, and it is necessary to leave certain portions of the nervous system "uncommitted," so that new behavior patterns to meet new situations can be organized. When machines are built possessing these characteristics, we may expect an even closer analogy to the workings of actual nervous systems. That the day is not far off can be inferred from the fact that mathematicians like von Neumann already do not shirk from theoretical investigations aimed at throwing light on the most typical of life processes—reproduction. I am referring to his recent calculations on the number of elements required in an automation which can not only perform specific tasks assigned to it but also is able to reproduce itself, given a mixed-up aggregate of its elementary constituents. An actual materialization of such a machine would, of course, give startling reality to the prophecy in Butler's *Erewhon.*

Such is the state of our present studies, which are extensions of the technological analogies of the living process, particularly of the integrating functions of the nervous system. It is hoped that these studies are now approaching a level sufficiently sophisticated to yield enlightening and lasting results.

Summer, 1954. This paper was presented at the regional research conference of the American Psychiatric Association held at the National University of Mexico, Mexico City, March, 1954. Formerly of the Committee on Mathematical Biology at the University of Chicago, Dr. Rapoport is now associate professor at the Mental Health Research Institute, University of Michigan. He is the author of Science and the Goals of Man *(1950),* Operational Philosophy *(1953), and of many scientific articles and monographs. He has been associate editor of* ETC. *since 1945.*

The Psychology of Heresy

HANS H. TOCH

The psychology of social movements must comprise principles which are independent of the characteristics of individual movements. They should be valid, whether applied to the Mau Mau, the Peasants' Revolt, the Ku Klux Klan, or the Children's Crusade. One must be able to derive inferences from studies of the medieval Church which can clarify aspects of modern political movements. It is the purpose of the following to illustrate this possibility.

As an arbitrary problem we shall consider that of disagreement between members and leaders of movements on matters of doctrine. Such disagreement represents deviation, which is a recognized problem area in social psychology. Jahoda, Deutsch, and Cook have noted that "the study of deviants (for example, unprejudiced individuals in a prejudiced group) may serve to highlight the social norms and practices from which they are deviating. It may indicate the types of pressures to conform and the socio-psychological consequences of non-conformity; perhaps it may even help to reveal the methods by which social changes may be produced."

Another reason why deviations are important lies in the fact that the deviant is a member of the group from which he deviates. Except for his deviations, he shares the majority's goals and premises. A deviation therefore is not a mere conflict, but a symptom of stress in the group.

Heresy

The term "heretic" was coined by leaders of a movement (the Church) to refer to members of the movement who differed from them on questions of doctrine. The label carried derogatory connotations. One of these connotations was that "heresy means . . . the warping of a system by exception," by "picking out one part of the structure," implying that the heretic destroys a self-contained, inherently indivisible whole.[1]

Another such connotation was that of self-appointed authority, of an upstart assuming jurisdiction over a province reserved (by tradition, established hierarchy, or the natural order of things) for experts. "Something self-chosen is maintained here, in contradistinction to the acceptance of something objectively inherited; precisely therein lies the defection."[2]

Still another implication was that of subversion. Thus Webster defines heresy as "an opinion held in opposition to the commonly received doctrine and *tending to promote division or dissension.*" Cardinal Newman described heretics as "assuming the office of the tempter," and endangering the souls of thousands.

The verdict of the Council of Geneva which condemned Servetus to be burned at the stake, reads in part: "You have tried to make a schism and trouble the Church of God by which many souls may have been ruined and lost, a thing horrible, shocking, scandalous and infectious. . . . For these and other reasons, desiring to purge the Church of God of such infection and cut off the rotten member . . . we now in writing give final sentence and condemn you."

Russian Communists have frequently been accused of similarly "troubling" the existence of their movement. Deviation at times be-

[1] Hilaire Belloc, *The Great Heresies* (London: Sheed and Ward, 1938), p. 5.

[2] Harnack, in J. Brosch, *Das Wesen der Heresie* (Bonn, 1936), p. 113.

Such suggestions have appeared even in the literature of general semantics. For example, in the "Author's Note" which prefaces *Selections from Science and Sanity* (Lakeville, Conn., 1948), A. Korzybski warns against "confusion": "In Vol. III, No. 4 of *ETC.*, there appears a five-page glossary of terms used in General Semantics, all of them fully explained in *Science and Sanity*. Practically every 'definition' misses the main point and trend of my work. For instance, what is said in the glossary about the use of the term 'semantic' in my 'General Semantics,' i.e., in a new theory of values, is entirely misleading. Such initial errors lead automatically to further more aggravated misinterpretations."

comes synonymous with treason, as in the Russian Treason Trials of the thirties and forties. The official history of the Bolshevik party states, in language somewhat reminiscent of the Servetus verdict: "It may seem to some that the Bolsheviks devoted far too much time to this struggle against the opportunist elements within the Party, and that they overrated their importance. But that is altogether wrong. Opportunism in our midst is *like an ulcer in a healthy organism,* and must not be tolerated." (Italics supplied.)

In a similar vein, Lenin has said, "If we judge people by what they actually advocate, it will be clear that 'freedom of criticism' means freedom for an opportunist trend in Social-Democracy, the freedom to convert Social-Democracy into a democratic party of reform, the freedom to introduce bourgeois ideas and bourgeois elements into socialism."

A distinct parallel is evident between the medieval conception of heresy and that of contemporary definitions of similar phenomena.

The Obverse of the Coin

In the above quotations, the process of heresy is viewed as a negative one, something destructive, offensively aggressive, and antithetical to the established order.

Individuals who are characterized as heretics, however, generally regard themselves as in possession of a positive interpretation, a constructive and objective set of beliefs. As Chesterton put it, "The heretic was proud of not being a heretic. It was the kingdoms of the world and the police and the judges who were heretics. He was orthodox. He had no pride in having rebelled against them; they had rebelled against him.... If he stood alone in a howling wilderness he was more than a man; he was a church." In other words, it is the leader who is seen as having deserted the cause, departed from the true path, or destroyed the movement.

Trotsky writes: "From the time that I entered into opposition to the bureaucracy, its courtier theoreticians began to call *the revolutionary essence of Marxism*—Trotskyism.' At the same time, the *official conception of Leninism changed from day to day becoming more and more adapted to the needs of the ruling class.*" (Italics supplied.)

With even more emphasis, Avvakum declares, after being expelled from the Russian Orthodox Church for deviations: "[The excommunication] *came from heretics,* and in Christ's name, I trample it underfoot . . . they are God's enemies, and, living in Christ, I do not fear them . . . all we need do is to spit on their doings and their ritual, and on their new-fangled books, then all will be well."

It appears that both the heretic and the leader are exponents of views they regard as legitimate interpretations of official dogma. Each sees the situation in his own fashion, which represents reality to him. Each perceives the other as holding a dangerously erroneous interpretation. This being the case, the problem may be regarded as one of conflicting perceptions.

Heresy has been defined as ideological deviation. This definition is implicit in the ecclesiastical use of the word as referring to improvisations in matters of dogma, as well as in what Communist

The Seeing-Eye Dogma

theoreticians refer to as the "Intra-Party Struggle," the suppression of deviation on "matters of principle."

A leading Chinese Communist defines "questions of principle" as "questions of the methods of observing and treating problems according to general rules of development." He continues: "We cannot afford to be muddled on questions of principle. If errors arise in principle, not only specific errors arise, but also systematic, consistent errors, errors in related practical problems."[3] Conversely, "in ordinary political questions and in questions of purely practical nature, it is possible and, moreover, obligatory to compromise with those in the party who hold differing opinions."[4] Only questions of principle, and "such practical questions which do involve principle" are matters on which correction is imperative.[5]

[3] Lin Shao Ch'i, in C. Compton (ed.), *Mao's China: Party Reform Documents 1942-1944* (Seattle: University of Washington Press, 1952), p. 220.
[4] Stalin, in C. Compton, *op. cit.*, p. 198.
[5] C. Compton, *op. cit.*, p. 222.

The specific statements or practices which are seen as involving principle may appear insignificant, even picayune, when viewed by an outsider. The bloody religious wars in the Russian Orthodox Church centered around whether one should cross oneself with two (as against three) fingers, and a few similar details. However, as has been pointed out, "the excommunicated Raskolniks felt that important issues were at stake. They believed . . . that rites reflect different interpretations of the cardinal Christian dogmas dealing with the blessed Trinity, the nature of our Lord, and the doctrine of the Church. The Raskolniks therefore accused the Orthodox of adopting such heresies as Arianism, Macedonianism, Nestorianism, and papism."[6]

The area of potential ideological conflict is thus that sphere of thinking and opinion in which specific statements are seen as carrying general implications. Deviations from officially sanctioned opinions come to denote *divergencies in outlook and viewpoint transcending their content*. Heresy is synonymous for the diagnosis of such denotations, for the isolation of basic differences in the way leader and member perceive things.

Current Illustrations

A few examples may serve to illustrate the dynamics of heresy in a variety of settings. One such setting is the British Sunbathing Association, in which several members recently fomented division by proposing that "naturist" be used as a substitute term for "nudist."

"Attempts are being made to form a rival organization," gravely announced general-secretary Arthur Hodgson. . . . One of the leading figures of the proposed break-away organization is a man who says that the term nudist denotes someone who wants to throw off his clothes at every opportunity. He favors the term naturist—someone who sheds his clothes only because he appreciates the benefits of it. (New York *Post*, September 29, 1953)

It is clear from this statement that we are not faced with a mere controversy about terminology, but rather with a fundamental difference in the way the movement is perceived. Some sunbathers seem to place greater emphasis than others on therapeutic and hygienic aspects of sunbathing. Further examination might possibly reveal

[6] S. Bolshakoff, *Russian Nonconformity* (Philadelphia: Westminster Press, 1950), p. 55.

that loss of prestige from membership in the nudist colony had led to the adoption, by some nudists, of an outsider's outlook about nudism. It has, after all, been shown that members of unpopular minority groups tend to adopt hostile attitudes toward their own groups in the face of social pressure.

One of the areas in which a Jew's perception of Jews can become manifest is that of the Zionist issue. Among the American Jewish community the majority of spokesmen and opinion leaders are vocal pro-Zionists. An exception is the American Council for Judaism, one of whose officials, Rabbi Berger, recently declared: "We have rejected not only the theory but the practice of medievalism which regards Jews as some kind of an exclusive fraternity. . . . Judaism is not what goes on in Israel or in the omnibus fund-raising campaign. Judaism transcends language. Judaism is justice and righteousness—even for the Arabs. For Judaism is of the heart—and the mind. . . . Judaism is a series of moral postulates. . . ." (*New York Times*, May 10, 1953)

In a reply by a Zionist official, the A.C.J. was accused of "(giving) aid and comfort to the enemy" and spreading "a type of propaganda not normally encountered outside the lunatic fringe of anti-semitism."

The perceptual differences underlying attitudes toward the Zionist problem are only too evident from the above. While in the one instance Judaism is conceived of as a set of ethical principles, it is regarded in the other as a group whose cohesiveness is essential because of pressures from a hostile environment.

It is often questionable whether sufficient communality of premises for common group membership exists for individuals seeing things in such diverse fashion. This argument is applicable to many compromise government coalitions. An illustration is provided by the resignation, from President Eisenhower's first cabinet, of former Labor Secretary Durkin. According to a *New York Times* article, "there were . . . evidences that Mr. Durkin did not fit on the team. He was reported to have told a friend that when he walked into a room 'everybody stopped talking.' At one of his infrequent news conferences it was noted that he referred to the Administration and Administration groups as 'they' rather than as 'we' " (September 11, 1953).

It is this " 'they'-feeling" toward one's formal membership group, indicative of other allegiances, which often constitutes the basis for dissent. The fear of this type of process occurring prompted the recent "worker-priest" controversy in the Catholic Church. A warning to priests working in Italian factories and the subsequent prohibition of the French working-priest plan, seem to have been based on experiences with transfers of allegiance by worker priests from the Church to the labor movements, i.e., of their excessive identification with purely working class interests. "Some of the priests," according to the *New York Times*, "have become so immersed in their work that they have come very close to supporting the Communist Party line" (August 17, 1953).

Many cases of dissent are related to disapproval of official actions based on different perception of what constitutes a reasonable rate of progress, or different opinions as to what measures are called for under given historical conditions. The history of the Soviet Communist party is replete with instances of individuals for whom Lenin was moving either too fast or too slow. There are many occasions in which the dissenter is an advocate of the *status quo* rather than a proponent of new measures.

Ideological dissent not only ranges over the entire scale of conservatism-radicalism but can also cover, in terms of content, every aspect of a movement's ideology. This is illustrated by the listing of heresies culled from the East German press by the U.S. High Commission in Germany:

Trotskyism, Zionism, cosmopolitanism, objectivism, particularism, bureaucratism, unionism, diversionism, schematism, imperialism, Titoism, pacifism, conciliationism, individualism, factionalism, practicism, neutralism, relativism, critical realism, militarism, chauvinism, Social Democratism, opportunism, careerism, equalitarianism, theoreticism, formalism, naturalism, collaborationism, kulak attitude, lack of vigilance, lack of class consciousness and uncritical attitude. (*New York Times*, January 25, 1953)[7]

Any area where differences in perception can arise is a potential region of dissent; any point officially defined in a particular way, unless it be a truism, provides the possibility of a difference in perception, and is therefore a possible trouble spot.

[7] An even longer listing of "isms" has been culled by Rapoport from Lenin's *Materialism and Empirio-criticism*. Some of these are "isms" which met with Lenin's favor, but most fall into the same category as those in the U.S. High Commissioner's list. Several items, in fact, seem to have withstood the test of time. See A. Rapoport, "Dialectical Materialism and General Semantics," *ETC.*, V, 81-104 (Winter, 1948).

Heresy and Dogma

A perceptual difference need not lead to overt conflict, however, or to the expulsion or defection of the dissenter. What does in fact occur is to a large extent determined by the ideology within which the difference has manifested itself. Some systems contain few formal definitions or dogmatic premises, and hence allow latitude in interpretation. L. S. O'Malley has written of the Hindu religion, for example, that "owing to the absence from Hinduism of definite dogmas and the non-existence of a central controlling authority, nonconformity can scarcely be said to exist, and new sects are constantly being formed by men who think they have discovered a new road to eternal truth." Edmond Taylor observes that, as far as the Hindu is concerned,

> An individual . . . may feel that his path is the best for himself—or even for all men—but . . . he is not disturbed when others take different paths, because *what is important to him is not the path but the ultimate goal.* . . . Carried over into politics this attitude makes for mutual tolerance among followers of different political creeds having roughly similar goals, and even a measure of understanding among those who pursue antithetical goals—doubtless the Hindu has a vague feeling that, just as all religious paths lead to God, so do all political paths lead to human betterment.

Another religious group whose beliefs are so broadly defined that they can comprise those of other sects is the Bahai movement. Members of this movement consider all other denominations as manifestations of Bahai, which is "the sublime idea in which all other creeds converge." Such religious liberalism can result in eclecticism, as in Annam, a country in which no practical distinction is drawn between religions. The same individual "is often Buddhist, Taoist, Confucianist all in one" and attends various pagodas and temples at random, according to Gabrielle Vassal.

The importance of the extent to which an ideology is dogmatic rests in the fact that to this degree it invalidates, as "incorrect," alternative interpretations. The deputy governor in Arthur Miller's *The Crucible* declares that "the shining sun is up, and they that fear not light will merely praise it." The more "lights" are defined, the more shadows are implicitly created.

It is for this reason that the closed system provides the most fertile ground for ideological conflict. Given the fact that a closed system is "a universal method of thought which claims to explain all phenomena under the sun," according to Arthur Koestler, minimum latitude is left for differences in interpretation. G. C. Coulton has noted this, in discussing the Inquisition: "When once a church has claimed for its exclusive province the whole of human life, both on this earth and in eternity, then no other creature can move without in some sense attacking this position. It is one of the advantages of the Roman Church ... that she occupies a position from which she can complain of every innovator as a trespasser, an interloper, a disturber of the settled peace."

Koestler observes with regard to Communism that "disagreements which in the normal world are settled by argument, become in the all-or-nothing atmosphere of the closed system acts of treason, heresy, and schism." Heresy is the concomitant of dogma, and the relationship is a direct one.

Sacred Cows

In addition to dogma, a related condition which turns differences into conflict is the importance assigned to the area in which the conflict arises.

Heresy trials and witch hunts took place in New England in the late eighteenth century because the colonists saw the world in exclusively religious terms. In this context, "Antinomians, Quakers and Baptists were viewed much as we view the carriers of the small-pox or typhoid fever germ. With no knowledge of the laws of nature or the findings of modern science, shut in on all sides by mysterious forces of evil, threatened constantly by devils and witches, placing the emphasis mainly upon the life in another world and accepting implicitly the theological dogma that all values rest ultimately upon religion, it is not surprising that the presence of the heretic caused consternation, persecution was thought necessary to social health, and toleration meant the spread of deadly poison gas."[8] When we regard an area as important, we become acutely aware of attempts to question our premises in this area, and intolerant of those who dare to tamper with them. Orthodox views become sacrosanct, and divergences of opinion intolerable.

Once a dogma or sacred cow is seen as threatened, a conflict is gener-

[8] J. M. Mecklin, *The Story of American Dissent* (New York: Harcourt Brace & Co., 1934), pp. 125-126.

ated. The type of argument usually employed is familiar to semanticists. It consists in this case of dividing humanity ideologically into two halves. One of these is "us"—white, good, right, true-blue, and all-American; the remainder becomes "they"—dark, evil, hostile, alien, and dangerous. The dichotomy is all-inclusive. "He that is not with me is against me," Christ is quoted as declaring, "and he that gathereth not with me scattereth abroad." "But you must understand, sir," patiently explains Miller's deputy governor, "that a person is either with this court or he must be counted against it; there is no road in between. This is a sharp time, now, a precise time—we live no longer in the dusky afternoon when evil mixed itself with good and befuddled the world."

Once the dichotomy has been set up, it almost follows that the slightest deviation from the positively valued category could be placed into the negatively valued one. The process has been eloquently described by Rapoport in his discussion of Lenin's polemical methods. In the case of an adherent who expresses one or two deviant ideas, for example, one dismisses his remaining, orthodox views as secondary, points to his inconsistencies, and shows that he unconsciously belongs in the enemy camp or that his thinking inevitably leads there. Lenin's two categories were socialist (good) and bourgeois (bad). It followed that "to belittle the socialist ideology *in any way*, to turn from it *in the slightest degree*, means to strengthen bourgeois ideology." (Italics supplied.) The persecution of heretics is plausible, once this premise is accepted.

Two Working Principles

It has been suggested above that the problem of heresy can be regarded as a perceptual one. Although the study of perception traditionally concerns itself with the way relatively simple stimulus configurations are translated into psychological data, the relevance of a perceptual approach to social psychology has been repeatedly proposed. Hadley Cantril argues that "a clear understanding of perception ... has just as much relevance for someone concerned with the nature and significance of attitudes and opinions as it does for someone whose chief interest may be the time error or size constancy. For principles of psychology, once we discover them, must—if they are principles—be applicable to all of man's experience." [9]

[9] Hadley Cantril, "The Nature of Social Perception," *Transactions of the New York Academy of Science*, X (1948).

One of the principles discussed by Cantril is that "perception seems clearly to result from the weighing and integrating of a whole host of factors . . . the factors introduced into this weighing process are those which have been learned largely unconsciously from past experience."

Could not such a notion be entertained with respect to heresy? Koestler describes his conversion as a "computation [which] was carried out by an erratic, partly unconscious, piecemeal kind of reasoning, until the conclusion was finally present in my mind—like the result which appears on the dial of electronic calculators." Douglas Hyde, who left the Communist party to become a Catholic, states that during a long period of time, "even though I was losing my health because of the accumulating secret doubts and misgivings, I still could not think of myself as anything but a Communist." Gabriel Almond, in his monumental study of Communists who became defectors, points out that the process of defection is mostly cumulative, in that it cannot be traced to a starting point. It is conceivable that most—if not all—members of social movements have latent reservations which, given sufficient reinforcement, can result in dissent.

Another perceptual principle cited by Cantril is that "the weighing process, resulting in a perception, goes on for a purpose." In other words, "perception is part and parcel of purposive activity and cannot really be understood except in that context." Almond has shown that every Communist sees the party he joins in line with his own purposes. He may leave when these purposes are neglected or frustrated, and his image of the party changes.

Heresy has frequently arisen in movements whose systems of beliefs did not meet the psychological requirements of their membership. Niebuhr has noted that Christianity has been torn by dissent whenever it grew "philosophical, abstract, formal and ethically harmless in the process." Maurice Simon makes a similar observation with regard to the Chassidic heresy among the Jews of Southern Poland. He points out that this group "felt that their spiritual needs were being neglected by the Talmudic Scholars, whose arid discussions on fine points of law they were incapable of following. They were lost sheep . . . who were waiting for a shepherd to lead them back to the fold." Movements tend to disintegrate when they frustrate needs on a wholesale basis.

If purposes are not satisfied by current beliefs, a new ideology may be built up which stands in conflict with these beliefs. The discrepancy is sooner or later perceived and overt dissent results. However, this may occur under conditions other than dissatisfaction. The following are some of the conditions that may be differentiated:

1. The needs and purposes originally operating no longer exist. Any change in purposes tends to bring with it new ways of perceiving things.

2. More specifically, the objectives satisfied by membership may have been temporary, holding within limited conditions only. Once these objectives are satisfied, the movement can be less selectively perceived, and "unfavorable" aspects are noted.

3. In the course of working and living in the movement and acting with regard to concrete aspects of it, the individual will find assumptions about the movement invalidated, if actions based on them consistently turn out unsuccessful and predictions always prove unreliable. Even people whose need to fool themselves about social reality is very great have at their disposal only limited perceptual mechanisms with which to accomplish this self-deception. The very magnitude of the task often defeats it from the outset. Thus, to see a circle as a square, even if one desperately needs a square, is a much more difficult feat to sustain than to perceive, say, a trapezoid as a square. Predictions regarding the "square" would lead to failure, just as a fly believing a window to be empty space will land against it until it changes its mind. Learning is often the result of failure through the following up of mistaken hypotheses. A Communist who regards the party as an expression of love and charity *learns* and becomes disillusioned in the face of perceived manifestations of hatred and violence in situations where he expects understanding and forgiveness.

4. In the course of acting within his movement, an individual also comes to encounter aspects of it not included in his picture of the movement. This often leads to the conclusion that the movement has changed, and that these aspects have actually not been there before their "discovery." The member may then declare that the movement has "betrayed its principles" or is being led astray from its righteous path.

5. Similarly, a member's perception of his movement may be so static and rigid in content that it is not possible for him to absorb new policies, modifications, or unorthodox tactics when they do arise. Almond has noted that every "zig" and "zag" in Communist party

functioning brings its waves of defections. This is true of most other movements too.

Critical events or periods of crises tend to make for ideological revaluation, and to create situations favoring ideological conflicts within groups. Not only do crises crystallize latent perceptual discrepancies, but they also tend to undermine the motivational basis for perceptions. Crises also occasion ideological consolidation. Crisis situations are thus a multifaceted breeding ground for heresy.

The above statements about ideological conflict and dissent point up the kinds of working principles one can use in considering social movements. In each case they serve to place different pieces of social behavior under common headings and to include social behavior under categories applicable to human behavior in general.

Summary

Deviations are important manifestations of social change. Specific deviations tend to represent fundamental differences in outlook between members and leaders of a movement. These in turn tend to have a motivational basis.

Dogmatic propositions promote deviations because they circumscribe "correct" interpretations. The same holds for premises which are strongly endorsed. Polarized thinking develops in such instances.

Ideological differences have been hypothesized to result from cumulative unconscious elaboration of latent doubts and reservations. Frustrated needs were shown to be instrumental in bringing such processes to a head. A number of ways in which this occurs have been differentiated. Several such conditions occur in crisis situations.

This paper has represented an effort to apply working principles from the study of human perception to a problem in social movements. Illustrations have been selected from many different types of movements to point up the general applicability of these principles.

Autumn, 1957. Hans Toch is assistant professor of psychology, Michigan State University. The author is indebted to Dr. Hadley Cantril for initiating the research on which this paper is based. He is also indebted to E. K. Hall, Jr., of the Inwood Institute, who assisted the project financially.

Language and Truth

WELLER EMBLER

Learning to call things by the names that general agreement has bestowed upon them is an elementary exercise of the mind, one which we associate with the education of small children. The first step in teaching a child to talk usually consists of a fond parent's pointing to an object and repeating a word, such as "cow," or "horse," or "dog." The purpose of this exercise is, of course, to teach the child to connect the word with the thing. And when finally the little one himself points with his finger and says "cow," the happy parents applaud with pardonable pride. It is thus that the learning process proceeds—with the picture books that make cows so very cowlike, with trains, automobiles, and other readily available vehicles, with edible substances, with heat and cold, with the names of aunts and uncles, and so on. As we know from this experience with children, the mere accumulation of name words is but a beginning, a first faltering, unsure step toward knowledge.

There are some people who, intellectually at least, never seem to rise above or go beyond the mere naming of things, which for them constitutes knowledge, even truth. We all remember how when we were small boys and girls we had a playmate whose irritating business it was to learn by heart the names of certain objects, such as those which make up the equipment and parts of sailboats, the substance and manufacture of marbles, or the terminology used in dress-making, or the names for tools in a carpenter's shop, and who turned the conversation whenever possible (which was most of the time) upon the subjects he knew so well, tense in argument over whether this was a this or that a that, and hilarious when he caught you in error, maddening because he was so often dead right.

Unhappily, this pride in so low an order of mental activity may be found in adults in varying degrees of intensity. That man is not hard to find who has studied up in advance of an occasion the names for things which are bound to become a considerable part of the conversation. Inevitably he will bring the talk around to what he has studied to remember—statistics, perhaps, the population of a certain city, some odd detail which *you* would have to ransack your memory for (providing you had time, which of course you never do); or he will engage you in conversation about the names of plants or animals or machines and their parts, or certain facts to be discovered from looking at maps, like distances between villages, or perchance dates (where he can be exasperatingly correct), like 1066 A.D., or even, indeed, the names of musical compositions or the titles of paintings, usually those of the old masters (Rembrandt particularly has been chosen for this sort of idle entertainment), and so on *ad nauseam*.

Now to be sure, a knowledge of names is indispensable in the struggle of the human race for survival. We all like to feel secure that when we ask the druggist for aspirin, we shall get aspirin and not bichloride of mercury tablets. We depend with a childlike faith on names, that they will go with that which we have been taught to expect them to go with. And in the higher reaches of thought, in the physical and biological sciences, a classification is a meaningful arrangement, and names become tools without which civilization, to say nothing of human thought itself, would be very nearly impossible. Yet even here one can be misled into thinking he knows something when he doesn't. Unless one has some kind of plan or purpose for the use of his knowledge, some imagination, in short, the memorization of names can be a waste of time.

When I was an undergraduate, I used to help my roommate, who was a forestry student, with his study of *Gray's Manual of Botany*. We had our taxonomic hours once a week when I would hear him recite from memory the divisions, the orders, the families, the genera, and the species of the flowering plants and ferns treated in the seventh edition of *Gray's Manual*. To this day I remember the names of some of the families, the rose family, for instance, which is called *Rosaceae*; the pulse family, *Leguminosae*; the beech family, *Fagaceae* (which I enjoyed hearing about more than many of the others as it had to do with trees I particularly admired—the beech, the chestnut, and the oak). But since at the time I speak of, these fearfully learned names (established by international congresses of botanists) meant nothing to me, and as I had no use to put them to, I knew the names only as prodigious to spell and for the most part ludicrous to hear. To a plant scientist, the name *Lentibulariaceae* (bladderwort family) is something he keeps to himself, seldom venturing it upon a lay company. With men of true learning—in the sciences, in the humanities, in the professions—the using of names with precision is a mark of skill and the result of long training.

If the using of names with precision within the context of an occupation is of a higher order of mind than mere information as to the names for things, the making up of names, the giving of names to things requires real creative ability. Naming a continent (Africa, Asia, America) would be a grave responsibility and would, I should think, call for a poet, or someone, at any rate, with an active, rich, and philosophic imagination. Consider the pain (though not perhaps depth of imagination) that often accompanies the naming of children and how in older times a contemplative working of the mind must have been required to suggest those Mercys and Charitys and Hepzibahs. Indeed, the giving of names summons up now a fine technique, now philosophic insight, now the folk wisdom of a people. It takes learning and understanding to give names to trees—for instance, the Judas tree, blushing as it does a pale pink in the spring, the Woman's Tongue tree of tropical climes with its clusters of dry pods that chatter in the slightest breeze. How were the names Hibiscus and Oleander arrived at as names for the shrubs they signify? Who decided upon Magnolia and Holly, and how did the Algonquins come to fancy Tamarack for the American Larch? The names of flowers, plants, and herbs are often richly suggestive and in time, after long association with what they stand for, become haunting and lovely: the Damask Rose (which Katherine Anne Porter says was the first recorded name of a rose), the Musk Rose, the yellow Eglantine, the Cup of Hebe—

Tansy, Feverfew, Nightshade, Hyssop, Lavender, Monkshood, Foxglove, Rue. Think at what a loss one would be to have to fancy names of places like Saranac, Capri, Madagascar, Paris, Soho, Damascus, or even Londonderry and Vermont. Tools have astonishing names, and one cannot but wonder who it was who told first how they should be called: awl, scythe, capstan, jackknife, colander. And what a brave world is it that hath in it such names as cashmere, velvet, cambric, canvas, silk, and chiffon. Naming the stars was no child's play, and now that we have them fixed who would venture to say whether they could be better named: Orion, Aldebaran, the Pleiades, the Hyades. And one would have to climb Parnassus more than halfway to fashion names for the gods—Tammuz, Osiris, Dionysus, Apollo. What a noble work of man, this making of names to stand for all the things of this various world, the things that can be seen and touched, and worked with, and names, too, for all the insubstantial pageants of the mind.

If the learning of names is an elementary exercise of the mind, the learning of facts is scarcely more, though as with naming, the learning of facts is another step in the direction of truth and can be made up of richly satisfying lessons. Most human beings have an instinct for facts, for those facts, at any rate, which it is profitable for them to have an instinct for. We often surprise an aura of truth shining through facts; and it is perhaps our own discovery of facts that means most to us educationally.

But one has to be wary. What are facts? Facts are not, it seems, always facts. Things are not always what they are *said* to be. Let us suppose that we are walking in a museum and that we stop before a painting which suddenly demands our attention. On the frame at the bottom is printed in black letters the name of a famous painter, Botticelli for instance. Let us suppose further that we are students of art appreciation and are so pleased with our discovery that we tell it to our teacher. Our teacher, being a knowledgeable person, replies that he is acquainted with the painting, that it is such and such a style, but that it is really "contemporary Botticelli." In other words, the painting was not done by Botticelli himself but by someone "of the school of Botticelli," one of the master's students perhaps. Our teacher informs us that many paintings whose artists are unknown but which are typical of a master are said to belong to a school and often carry the name of the painter whose style, etc., they so closely resemble. If one of us has the temerity to observe that since it is not a fact that Botticelli painted the picture, his name should not be attached to it, our teacher may well reply that if we like the picture and it says something to us, what difference does it make (except to professional art historians) who painted the picture.

In our hypothetical case, it has now become necessary to dismiss from our minds the name of the painter of the picture as irrelevant. Instead, our interest lies in certain critical refinements and niceties of explanation as make a statement of fact not a statement of fact. Often, it seems, we are less interested in "facts" and more interested in what we say about them, and consequently, it is the talking about them that becomes important. We refine upon the so-called facts, modify and color them, put them on condition, and make them provisional.

Yet certain facts are so persistent that they will not knuckle under —the facts one works with, for instance. A poem by Robert Frost entitled "Mowing" comes spontaneously to my mind, especially the last six lines:

> Anything more than the truth would have seemed too weak
> To the earnest love that laid the swale in rows,
> Not without feeble-pointed spikes of flowers
> (Pale orchises), and scared a bright green snake.
> The fact is the sweetest dream that labor knows.
> My long scythe whispered and left the hay to make.[1]

It is a commonplace, of course, that Americans are a practical people (not caring enough, perhaps, for the imaginative and speculative), with a long heritage of faith in facts. That the early Puritans were a practical band of pilgrims is well known. Though they toiled in the wilderness to build a Holy Commonwealth, still they had a considerable regard for the practical affairs of everyday life. The church had its awe-inspiring words, but the woodpile was a fact of life. Not a few of our steeple-crowned forebears would have agreed quite readily with the Connecticut Yankee in Rose Terry Cooke's novel *Steadfast*, who says: "At heart every human being has the infidelity of the Apostle Thomas hidden in some shadowy recess, where it whispers to itself, 'I will not believe what I do not see and touch.'"

[1] Excerpt from "Mowing" in *Complete Poems of Robert Frost*. Copyright, 1930, 1949, by Henry Holt and Company, Inc. By permission of the publishers.

Even Emerson the idealist paid his respects to the hard facts on many an occasion:

> Bulkeley, Hunt, Willard, Hosmer, Meriam, Flint,
> Possessed the land which rendered to their toil
> Hay, corn, roots, hemp, flax, apples, wool and wood.

Though it is in the realm of the moral and spiritual that we expect to find the abiding *abstract* truths, there where the masonry of accumulated facts has been transformed into the ideal design, nevertheless it is to the concrete everyday facts, objects of use and beauty and wonder—the inorganic earth substances, and air and fire and water, all the growing things of the earth and all the living creatures, all the people of the earth, and the works of their hands and minds, and the records of all their lives—it is to these that we turn for reassurance of the reality of the world and for support of our endeavors in it. One does well to hold fast to "facts" as firm friends to go by his side in the pursuit of the higher truths.

In the Ford Times Special Edition (Number 2) *New England Journeys*, there is a short piece by William Faulkner called "A Guest's Impression of New England." In this little appreciation Mr. Faulkner tells a revealing story.

One afternoon (it was October, the matchless Indian summer of New England) Malcolm Cowley and I were driving through back roads in western Connecticut and Massachusetts. We got lost. . . . The road was not getting worse yet: just hillier and lonelier and apparently going nowhere save upward, toward a range of hills. At last, just as we were about to turn back, we found a house, a mailbox, two men, farmers or in the costume of farmers . . . standing beside the mailbox, and watching us quietly and with perfect courtesy as we drove up and stopped.

"Good afternoon," Cowley said.

"Good afternoon," one of the men said.

"Does this road cross the mountain?" Crowley said.

"Yes," the man said, still with that perfect courtesy.

"Thank you," Cowley said and drove on, the two men still watching us quietly—for perhaps fifty yards, when Cowley braked suddenly and said, "Wait," and backed the car down to the mailbox again where the two men still watched us. "Can I get over it in this car?" Cowley said.

"No," the same man said. "I don't think you can." So we turned around and went back the way we came.

Most of us spend most of our time getting and giving information. Certain pieces of information are basic to survival, the "where it is and how to get it" kind, and for the most part this simple information is readily available if we care to make use of it. Indeed, it is the purpose of the social order to make information available, and fortunately certain pieces (such as vital statistics) are required by law to be published. But in the socially less well-regulated affairs (or socially not regulated at all), information is by no means easy to come by or necessarily known or understood though it might stare one in the face. The location of an unknown oil deposit takes time and skill to find; if one really loses a twenty-dollar bill, information as to its whereabouts is impossible to get; if criminals wanted by the police are successful in hiding out against the law, information about them may be available, but it is not forthcoming; if one wants to know what the future movement of certain stocks is going to be, he has to have information which is apparently very difficult for the average man to find and, if achieved, is not always reliable anyway. Though actuarial tables will predict the probable length of your life, absolute information about your longevity is nowhere to be had. Information as to whether one has achieved salvation is, mostly, I believe, a jealously guarded secret; information about whether one is really loved is often singularly difficult to draw out; information about one's future prospects, though it *may* lie in the palm of one's hand, is by no means infallible even if offered; information about the plans of one's enemies can be got, but it is not always trustworthy and often requires such delicate interpretation that most of us lack the key required for decoding the messages. Then again, what passes for information today may turn out to be but opinion tomorrow—to emend Henry Thoreau. Dependable information about the nature of the physical world, about the universe and universes at large, is mighty hard to come by, though of course physicists and astronomers lay claim now and then to the receipt of valuable disclosures.

When we try to find out information about ourselves, we are altogether too often at a loss which way to turn. The doctor cannot always tell us what is wrong with us, nor can the psychiatrist. Information about oneself is very nearly the hardest information to get and may require the sufferings of Oedipus and a lifetime to achieve. Our "selves" lie buried deep, like hidden treasures, and the maps we have drawn up about ourselves are not so easy to follow as those we have made of the public highways.

Because we know so little about ourselves, or because the information we have got is so garbled, we have to ask ourselves over and over again what our conduct should be in this or that predicament. Where can we learn how to behave? There are books in abundance, there is the law, there are other people who will suggest the rules for our conduct. For want of dependable information, we often resort to what the Existentialists call "role-playing." We learn the kind of conduct expected of a person who engages in our kind of activity, and we try to behave according to the stereotype established for that activity. Information about how to play a role is helpful in a com-

How Do I Know What They Are Unless I Label Them?

plicated society, but following it to the letter is, after all, denying one's own uniqueness and cutting one's self to the common pattern.

Except for downright dangerous indifference to accurate information (say the information on labels in a druggist's shop), we tend to believe what we want to believe. So deeply embedded in us is the will to believe what it suits us at the moment to believe that we stand in need of constant correction, of being corrected by others around us who do not cherish the same illusions as we do. Curiously, it is easy to believe what one wants to believe. Facts are not so stubborn and brutal as we have been led to think, and one can get information which will support his wishful thinking without much trouble. Misinterpreting information is a common enough practice, but willful perversion or misconstruction of information is a daily strategy. Deep inner desires will cause outward facts to suffer rare changes; wanting things desperately enough will change the face of reality altogether, so that what seems and what is become two different realities. Sophistical or false interpretation of factual information colors ethics, judgment, taste. As our desires become more intense, we tend willfully to alter, in our minds, the nature of the world around us.

When Prospero in *The Tempest* tells Miranda how his brother, the false Antonio, usurped his dukedom, it was because, Prospero says, he had given Antonio too much trust, and too much power, so that being thus lorded

> Not only with what my revenue yielded,
> But what my power might else exact, like one
> Who having into truth, by telling of it,
> Made such a sinner of his memory,
> To credit his own lie, he did believe
> He was indeed the duke.

Because information about anything beyond the time of day or one's neighbor's telephone number often requires such toil to secure, is often unreliable, and often, also, so set with thorns, true information is one of the most precious of man's acquisitions and the purpose of all his searching. Is it any wonder that information is power? We make a great effort to share certain kinds of information, the discoveries and findings of medicine, for example; unshared information, military secrets for instance, can be used as a weapon, giving the owner unimaginable power and profit. There are times when we have some but not all the necessary information; there are times when we are not willing to give up the information we have; now and then we are unwilling to receive information, if it is of a kind painful to us; and there are many instances where we do not know how to go about getting information. This explains why education today is devoted almost exclusively to the principles for procuring information, is devoted to skills and training in the use of instruments designed to extract information from intractable and obstinate sources.

The most accurate and dependable information we have for practical daily use is achieved through the techniques and principles of research developed by modern science in all its branches. And modern science has built up an enormous body of information which it is constantly measuring, sifting, and interpreting, so that it may be made applicable in human affairs. Since the seventeenth century, the people of the Western world have looked to science for information about the world; and science, as a method of investigation, has proved miraculously successful and effective.

If knowledge of naming and of facts, if the accumulation of information and the testing and weighing of it are the materials of learning, creative use of the materials, as in the making of judgments and the finding of truths is the final goal of learning—that is, of an education. It is of judgment and truth that I should like to speak in the remainder of this essay.

The formation of value judgments takes time—more time, usually, than we feel we can give, in this workaday world. As a matter of fact, centuries may be required to sift the best from all the many contenders in all the fields of human experience—in social institutions, in political thought, in literature and the arts, as well as French cooking. Time, we say, is the judge, but time has always needed allies, generations of human beings whose wish is to be civilized. Perhaps the most important part of all higher education is the learning to discriminate, to distinguish among all things to find that which is best and most worthy to be preserved. The monuments of a civilization survive because, after long acquaintance with them, a people have valued them worthiest of survival, have found them lasting in value and worthy of preservation. There is a difference betwen a crab apple and an orchard apple (as I believe John Burroughs, the naturalist, once pointed out), between a just government and a tyrannical one, between the *Iliad* and hundreds of forgotten war novels since the time of Homer. And the difference between these examples is not quite a matter of personal taste, despite the theory of cultural relativity. It is very real, as most people know.

As with the gathering of information, the making of judgments is often conditioned by prejudice toward those judgments which it will benefit us personally to make. Objectivity is a rare talent and always has been. Wishful thinking often dictates what we shall like and hold good. If our interests are at stake (and in matters of taste our *feelings* are certainly involved), we *can* prefer the monstrous to the beautiful and good. All the subtle demands of vanity and self-interest, of the ego studying to be heard in the world tend to make our judgments deeply subjective. But who can say absolutely what is good and what is beautiful?

How shall we learn to judge? How shall we judge, for instance, the value of a work of art? What standards shall we employ? At this point I shall certainly disappoint some of my readers. I cannot give the answer ready-made; for if I could, there would have been little purpose in the thoughts I have thus far labored to bring forth. Fashions change, fads come and go, but somehow through that drop-by-drop process known as education, the superior things remain and serve as touchstones for the future. To emend the Spanish philosopher José Ortega y Gasset, it is the daily plebiscite of civilized people carrying the vote for the best that makes the best survive. The formation of taste is not alone a matter of learning the rules. It is rather more a matter of immersing oneself in that which has been tried and found good, in the accumulated body of judgments of the people of a culture. It is the purpose of higher education, and the purpose of the humane studies especially, to help all students to learn to distinguish between that which is good and that which is not so good, so that they may participate in the universal judging of the best. It is the price of civilization that people must evaluate and re-evaluate, else a culture will fall into a state of maximum mediocrity. And if we tremble and grow faint before the task of making the great judgment, of judging, that is, between good and evil, it is no wonder, since this task has plagued mankind from the beginning of time. But we know only too well that we cannot surrender, nor even despair.

"You are too fond of your liberty," said Mrs. Touchett to her niece, Isabel, in Henry James's *Portrait of a Lady*. "Yes, I think I am very fond of it," Isabel replied. "But I always want to know the things one shouldn't do." "So as to do them?" asked her aunt. "So as to choose," said Isabel.

So as to choose—not only between right and wrong among the strictly moral issues, but among all the multitudes of ideas of our time. And that is where, in our time especially, the agitation lies—in determining what to choose, surrounded as we are by such abundance, such unimaginable plenty, not only in material goods and things, but in ideas, theories, possible beliefs. We enjoy a feast of notions, that is, more probably than we need. Our world of ideas is like an enormous department store where we move idly from counter to counter, trying to decide what we should like to have and whether we can afford the intellectual purchases we might make—for there are entanglements in the big purchases. For one thing we may have to keep up the payments; and in any event we have to protect our prizes from thieves and destroyers. Moths creep into ideas, too. Shall we put all our intellectual and emotional savings into something that will rust when exposed to a little damp air? Sometimes we toy with gewgaws or with the trinkets laid out in an inviting display. We wander through the bargain basement among the cheaper thoughts, those that may serve for a time. Some notions take our fancy, the work of far romantic places and peoples, ideals which have grown up in other cultures than our own. Toward some ideas we are curious, are not sure, and we entertain mingled feelings about them. Toward some we are detached and critical. For some notions we have no use at all, and we hardly see them. Toward some we are attentive; some, in the light, spacious higher galleries, we behold with rapture.

And what shall we wish to save and to keep permanently after we have brought our purchases home and viewed them in a more sober moment; for we shall have to decide sooner or later what to keep and what to throw away. I venture to say that if ever we bring ourselves to make the final choices, we shall discover that they are very simple ones—the image of a landscape that speaks of all the possibilities of freedom; the possession of a love that is all-consuming; the ripening knowledge of what a great poem is saying; the daily revelations of a work of art; the full possession of a disciplined mind; the words of a philosopher that never diminish in their power to help us; the music that does not diminish in its power to move us; the infinite satisfactions of a great religious belief; a noble friendship; a wholly unselfish way of life. But it must be remembered that all these are choices which when we have made them have ruled out the many other possibilities; and it is therefore incumbent upon us to select with the greatest care, lest through ignorance we let the prizes slip through our fingers, remembering also (as Mr. E. M. Forster says in his essay "What I Believe") that "there lies at the back of every creed something terrible and hard for which the worshipper may one day be required to suffer."

Anyone who has the temerity to speak of "truth" usually finds that he is performing verbal dances around the *word* truth, rather than letting truth perform for itself. The truth is as hard to talk about as it is to tell, though it is not, I think, so hard to find as people say, nor so ready with a dusty answer. If there is one thing certain, the truth will not be caught *once and for all* in a net of words alone, nor does it like to be imprisoned in a theory; it is much too fond of its liberty. At the outset of any inquiry into the nature of truth, one has, in my opinion, to begin with "facts," that is, with things themselves.

The gross material facts of the world are ready at hand for use in giving mode to the truths drawn from the well of being; and literature and art and history and philosophy and science are the crafts that shape the disembodied truth and make it concrete. Observe how music gives measure to *time,* how painting and architecture and sculpture inform *space,* how history gives a scheme to *past* and *present,* how science makes arrangement of *cause* and *effect,* how philosophy builds the structure of *thought* and literature makes epiphanies of vague *justice, beauty,* and *love.* And do not mistake that the toil exacted to tell the truth is more prodigious than the labors of Hercules, more passing strange, more abundant of enemies and frustration, more unlikely of adjournment. But it is to literature and particularly to the art of poetry that in closing I would turn now, well aware that the same justice might be done the sciences and all the humane studies.

Sun, gold, light, queens, flame, dawn, heart, moon, tears, fields, time, mountains, darkness, wind, the sea, gardens, lions, trees, home, dreams, night, roses, the grave, stars, nightingales—these veritables have been the substance of poetry for a very long time, sense experiences used to express by proxy the thoughts and feelings that are imaginative life. Every now and then someone cries out against them as overworked and worn out. It is not so much that they are overworked, for they are indefatigable; it is rather that they backslide and refuse to work for some masters. Though the rose, for instance, may have become commonplace in our gardens (as well as in poetry), it is still a flower whose charms are inexhaustible. The rose by no means appeals to all poets in the same way. Each poet will request it to carry *his* message. But like the dawn, and fire, and darkness, and the sea, the rose is always accommodating, if the poet is well-intentioned toward it.

> Oh, my luve is like a red, red rose,
> That's newly sprung in June . . .

sang Robert Burns. Roses are lovely and so are young Highland girls. The poet was moved by the analogy that spoke unhesitatingly to him as appropriate and true. With A. E. Housman, roses mostly fade—in fields where "rose-lipt girls are sleeping." With T. S. Eliot the rose is self-conscious, at least the roses of "Burnt Norton" have "the look of flowers that are looked at." And Gertrude Stein, bored, perhaps, with antique similitudes, or indignant with the age-long using of the rose as servant to help any poet on with his singing robes, will have it that "the rose is a rose," only itself with its own life.

The common object is known in its immanence, but not until it is touched by the hand of poetic metaphor is it informed and made vivid with the rich garments of thought and feeling. The metaphor of poetry redeems the thing itself, saves it from being the clod and lump mere use and wont have made of it. Finally, however, it is in the design which the chosen objects make that the truth is realized and becomes a firm and permanent truth of the world, a truth not made but rather "discovered" by the poet, a truth perpetually verified by the experience of mankind.

> *Fame* is the spur that the clear spirit doth raise
> (That last infirmity of Noble mind)
> To scorn delights, and live laborious days;
> But the fair Guerdon when we hope to find,
> And think to burst out into sudden blaze,
> Comes the blind *Fury* with th' abhorred shears,
> And slits the thin spun life. But not the praise,
> *Phoebus* repli'd, and touch'd my trembling ears;
> *Fame* is no plant that grows on mortal soil,
> Nor in the glistering foil
> Set off to th' world, nor in broad rumour lies,
> But lives and spreads aloft by those pure eyes,
> And perfect witness of all-judging *Jove*;
> As he pronounces lastly on each deed,
> Of so much fame in Heav'n expect thy meed.

An abstract *Fame* has here in the hands of Milton become a poetic fact and a massive truth.

But eventually even the poet has to confess that

> Words strain,
> Crack and sometimes break, under the burden,
> Under the tension, slip, slide, perish,
> Decay with imprecision will not stay in place,
> Will not stay still.
> (T. S. Eliot, "Burnt Norton," *Collected Poems, 1909-1935*)

From the last and highest promontory of time, we may see that the truth is not made up of words at all, only that we have had to use words to lure it from its hiding places. And after all is said, it may be (if we can *know* what this means) that the truth is not more than being itself, innocent, eternal being.

But here and now we are obliged to use language and human thought with which to draw up our agreement with reality. Truth is the name we give to the highest and deepest insights, the fruit of long experience, to those ideas and phenomena which have stood the test of our straining at them, which we have judged most likely to endure, which are universally human, and about which disagreement is only inconsequential quibbling.

Unfortunately, the wish for power is sometimes greater than the wish for truth. People sometimes invent the "truth" where it suits them to do so. And sometimes the "truth" seems to be whatever strong and powerful men say it is, and we are stampeded into thinking something is true that deep within us we know is not. The work of our time which deals most commandingly with the willful perversion of truth is George Orwell's 1984. "You believe that reality is something objective," says the novel's Party leader, O'Brien, something "external, existing in its own right." O'Brien is talking to Winston Smith, the unregenerate believer in the ultimate victory of truth and humanity over power and the Party. O'Brien refers to Winston Smith sarcastically as "the last man." He says to him:

When you delude yourself into thinking that you see something, you assume that everyone else sees the same thing as you. But I tell you, Winston, that reality is not external. Reality exists in the human mind, nowhere else. Not in the individual mind, which can make mistakes, and in any case soon perishes; only in the mind of the Party, which is collective and immortal. Whatever the Party holds to be truth *is* truth. It is impossible to see reality except by looking through the eyes of the Party. That is the fact that you have got to relearn, Winston. It needs an act of self-destruction, an effort of the will.

Winston Smith withstands as long as he can the torture and the degradation. He insists heroically that reality is not a matter of power and propaganda. Men are not "infinitely malleable." "There is something in the universe . . . some spirit, some principle . . . that the power-mad will never overcome."

That spirit, that principle, is the indifferent, innocent truth, indifferent, that is, to parties and politics, by nature incapable of self-corruption. It is that which we are a part of and is a part of us, that which is ours as well as everyone else's; it is individualistic as well as communal, the possession of all people, like life and hunger and time, self-evident like fire and air and one's personality, inhabiting space, yet individually experienced as wholly and legitimately one's own, which cannot be gainsaid, short of bitter divorce between the nature of the world and human thought. For human thought searches out the closest possible correspondence between things in the outside world and our inner understanding of them, it seeks (with a hopefulness which if it were naïve would be intolerable mockery) the near-perfect adaptation of a sane intellect to a sane world. And that is why the human perversion of even the smallest truths strikes us as so perilous, and why the perversion of the massive truths becomes so unforgivable. One may well shake one's head with George Eliot's puzzled Mr. Tulliver over the thought that a perfectly sane intellect is hardly at home in an insane world—is hardly at home, that is, in a world made insane by those who, power hungry, prefer darkness to light.

Winter, 1955-56. Professor Embler is chairman of the department of humanities at the Cooper Union for the Advancement of Science and Art, New York City.

Index

Abbreviations, in language, 340
Abrahamson, Julia, 51
"Abstract" languages of the West, 341, 342
"Abstraction," word, 339
Abstractions, in counseling, 151; levels of, 112, 203, 328; in philosophy, 164; in phonetic writing, 327; photographs as, 250-251; of science, 336-337
Academic psychology, and Eastern thought, 198, 199
Action, alternative courses of, 142
Adaptation to environment, 173
Addams, Charles, 261
"Adjustment," concept of, 199-200
Adler, Alfred, 190, 193
"Adventure of the Abbey Grange, The," 264
Adventures in Ideas, 301
Aesthetic function of speech, 329n
Aesthetics, philosophy of, 190
Aglaia, 226
Ahmadi Muslims, 71-72
Ahrarists, Pakistan, 72, 73
Ain, Gregory, 233
Akst, Harry, 284n
Alcoholism, 289
Alexander, Franz, 236
Alexander, Samuel, 302
Alien Registration Act (1938), 78
"All Alone" (song), 283n

Almond, Gabriel, 368, 369
Alphabet, beginnings of phonetic, 335
"Am I Blue" (song), 284n
Amateur Cracksman, The, 265
Ambassadors, The, 226
America, genteel tradition in, 224-226
American Council for Judaism, 363
American males and sex, 235-240
American Motors, 242
American Occupational Therapy Association, 217
American Psychiatric Association regional research conference (1954), 357
American Psychological Association, 194
American psychology, 193-195
American Revolution, 14
American science, 193-194
Ames, Adelbert, Jr., 75-76, 154
"Amount of information," 344
"Amount of organization" in information theory, 355
Analects, 307
Analogical argument, 317-318
"Analytic school" of philosophy, 325, 341
Anderson, Maxwell, 229
Anglo-Saxon terms, 338
Angry Boy (film), 139
"Animal," word, 338

INDEX

Animal level, acceptance at, 212
Annam, religions in, 365
Antinomians, 366
Antonyms in Chinese thought, 310
Anxiety of separateness in creativity, 180
Architecture as communication, 228, 229-233
Arens, Richard, 78, 87
Aristotle, concepts of, 17, 192, 304, 305, 306, 319, 339
Arnold, Matthew, 222, 223
Art, classes, 169, 184; as communication, 221-234; criticism, vocabulary of, 104-105; and fully functioning personality, 214-215; popular vs. fine art, 258-259, 260
Artists, maladjusted, 178
"As if" attitudes, 128-129
Asbury, Luther, 242
Asilomar Conference of the Mental Health Society of Northern California, 217
Assassination. See Crime stories
Assertive aspect of oral communication, 329, 330-331
Associated Press, 78, 80, 84
Assumptions, 151
Astounding Science Fiction, 245, 272
Atomic physics, 193
Attitudes, emotional, 39
"Attributes," of substances, 306-307
Audio-visual "aids," 247
Austin, Claire, 291-292
Authoritarian teachers, 168
Authoritarianism, 160-165
Automata, 343-357
Automobiles, learning to live with, 170; motivational research vs. reality principle, 241-246; and sexual fantasy, 235-240
Autonomous activity in machines, 343-357
Avvakum, 360-361
"Awaring," 132
Axiomatic Method in Biology, The, 302
Ayer, A. J., 307, 325

Bach, Johann Sebastian, 279
Bacon, Francis, 319
Bahai movement, 365
Bailey, Pearl, 289

Ball, John, 288n, 289n
Baptists, 366
"Basement Blues, The" (song), 285n
Basie, Count, 285n, 286n
Bateson, Gregory, 125
Beethoven, Ludwig van, 279
Begum Liaquat Ali Khan, 69
Behavior and information theory, 343-357
Behaviorism, 193, 198, 347
"Being" and "essence," 336
Bell, Bernard Iddings, 256-257, 258, 259, 260
Belloc, Hilaire, 359
Beloit College, 292
Bentley, Arthur, 75
Bentley automobile, 246
Berger, Rabbi, 363
Bergson, Henri, 324
Berlin, Irving, 283n
Biochemistry, 347
Black, Johnny, 284n
Black, Max, 326
Black Mask, The, 265
Block organizations, civic, 40-50
Bloomfield, Leonard, 329, 331, 333, 334
"Blue Room" (song), 282-283
"Blues in the Dark" (song), 286n
Blues songs, 280-291
Bob Scobey Frisco Jazz Band, 291-292
Bodine, Alexis Ivanovitch (Sterling Noel), 269
Bohr, Niels, 193
Bois, J. Samuel, 91
Bolshakoff, S., 362n
Bolshevik party, 360
Bongiorno, Andrew, 300
Bonnard, Pierre, 226
Boodberg, Peter A., 336
Book of Changes, 309, 311
Brahms, Johannes, 279
Brandeis University, 201, 204
Breuer, Marcel, 233
Bridge, The, 229
Bridges, 229
British Sunbathing Association, 362
Brook Farm, 228
Brooklyn Bridge, New York, 229
Brosch, J., 359
Brown, George (Billy Hill), 284n
Brown, Nacio Herb, 281n

INDEX 389

Buck, Jack, 292
Buddhism, 312, 313, 321, 365
Bureau of Standards, U. S., 75
Burke, Kenneth, 289
Burns, Robert, 383
"Burnt Norten" (poem), 384
Burroughs, John, 380
Butler, Samuel, 343, 357

Cadillac, 237, 241
Cain, James M., 261
Campbell, Douglas G., 133-134
Cancer, 157
Canned activities, 170
Cantril, Hadley, 367, 368, 370
Carnap, Rudolf, 301, 322
Cars. See Automobiles
"Case of Identity, A," 263, 264
Casebook of Sherlock Holmes, 264
Catholicism, 314, 364
Causality, 313, 314, 315, 320
Causation, multiplicity of, 141
Cézanne, Paul, 234
"Chance philosophy," 190
Chandler, Raymond, 266, 267, 268
Chang Tung-sun, 299, 323
Change and individuality, 166-171
Chaplin, Charles, 268
Chase, Newell, 281n
Chassidism, 368
Chaudhri Zafrullah Khan, 71
Chester, George, 265
Chesterfield, Lord, 225, 226
Chesterton, Gerald K., 360
Chevrolet, 243, 244, 246
Chicago, Illinois, housing problems, 35-51; Negroes in, 35-51; Puerto Ricans in, 52-65
Chicago Commission on Human Relations, 38, 48-49
Chicago Daily News, 257
Children, psychology of, 126-132; and reading, 162; semantic play therapy for, 133-140
Children's Crusade, 358
Child's Conception of the World, The, 313
China, approach to knowledge, 299-323; ideographs, 335-337; influence of India on, 313, 321; religion in, 314-316
Chirico, Giorgio di, 221-223

Chisholm, Brock, 149
Choice, possibility of, 228, 381-382
Christ, 367
Christianity, 368
Christie, Agatha, 266
Chrysler, 239, 242
Chuang Tzu, 313
Ch'un-Ch'iu, 316
Churches, architecture, 230; authoritarianism in, 161; and self-defamation, 166-167; Cincinnati Social Hygiene Society, 290
Cinematographer, The (film), 248
City living, 169
Civic problems, 35-51
Clarke, Grant, 284n
Classics and Commercials, 258n
Client-Centered Therapy, 185, 204
Clockworks, as new principle of operation, 345-346, 349, 352
"Cold in Hand Blues" (song), 288n
Coleridge, Samuel Taylor, 192
Collected Poems, 1909-1935, T. S. Eliot, 233n, 384
Collins, Wilkie, 262
"Colonialism," 14
Comic books, 170
Committee on Mathematical Biology, U. of Chicago, 357
"Common qualities," 339
Commonwealth system, Puerto Rico, 55-64
Communication, in conferences, 103-110; international, 12-34; output and intake, 103-104; process in counseling, 143-151
Communications Workshop, San Francisco State College, 88
"Communist Underground Printing Facilities and Illegal Property," subcommittee on, 79
Communists and Communism, 24-25, 76-87, 157, 158, 269, 359-360, 361, 364, 366, 368, 369
Complete Poems of Robert Frost, 375
Composition in pictures, 249
"Compromise," verb, 22
Compton, C., 361
"Conceptual abstractions," 328, 336, 338, 339
Conceptual knowledge, 299-323
"Concrete" lauguage of China, 341

Conditioned stimulus, 348
Condon, Edward U., 75
Conference on Creativity, Granville, Ohio, 185
Conferences, communication in, 103-110
Conflicting Patterns of Thought, 18
Conformists and conformity, 172-173
Confucius and Confucianism, 307, 312, 316, 318, 365
"Connectibility," 325
Connotation and denotation, 14-15, 23-25
Connotations in pictures, 249
"Consciousness of abstracting," 112
Conservation areas, civic, 39
Constitutions, of Puerto Rican organizations, 56-58
"Constructions" and knowledge, 322
Consumer-motivation studies, 244n
Consumer Reports, 244n, 246
Continental Op, 267
"*Contribuable*" vs. "taxpayer," 14-15
Co-operation, social, 157
Cooke, Rose Terry, 375
Cooper Union, New York City, 201, 234, 386
Copernicus, 174
Correlation logic, 316
"Correspondence theories" of truth, 327
Corsini, Raymond J., 295, 298
Cosmogony, Chinese, 312-313, 319
Coulton, G. C., 366
Council of Geneva, 359
Counseling, 141-151
Counseling and Psychotherapy, 185
"Countertransference" in psychoanalysis, 120
Court of Inquiry into Punjab Disturbances of 1953, Report of, 69n, 71
Cowley, Malcolm, 376
Craigie house, Cambridge, Mass., 228
Crane, Hart, 229
Crane, Jimmy, 284n
"Creative person," 204
Creativity, 159, 169, 172-185, 194-199, 211-214; anxiety of separateness, 180; conditions fostering, 181-183; creative act and concomitants, 179-181; creative process, 173-175; definition of creative process, 174; empathic understanding, 182-183; Eureka feeling, 180; evaluation, 179-182, 184; extensionality, 178; fostering of, 184; hypotheses from theory of, 183-185; individual worth, 181-182; inner conditions of, 177-179, 184; motivation for, 175-177; and openness to experience, 178, 184; philosophy of, 190; playing ability, 179, 184; psychological safety, 181-184; social need for, 172-173; symbolic expression, 183
Crime stories, 256-271
Critique of Practical Reason, 321
Critique of Pure Reason, 321
Crowd Culture: an Examination of the American Way of Life, 257
Crucible, The, 365, 367
Cubism in art, 231
"Cultural pluralism," 64
Cultural problems and mental health, 196
Culture, as a whole, 323; authoritarianism in, 164; influence on language, 12-34; and judgment, 381
Culture and Personality, 74
Cybernetics, 344

Dante, 262
D'Artagnan, 262
Darwin, Charles, 304
Das Wesen der Heresie, 359
"Dating" statements, 151, 210
Dawn, Indian daily, 69
De Bergerac, Cyrano, 276
Decline of the West, The, 314
Defensiveness Scale, 144
Definition, in Western logic, 308
De Kooning, Willem, 108, 231
Democracy, meanings of, 52-65; and specialization, 156-159
Democracy in Jonesville, 67
Democratic ideals, 157-158
Denotation and connotation, 14-15, 23-25
De Rose, Peter, 284n
Descartes, 344, 346
Design as communication, 221-234
De Soto Adventurer, 239
Detective stories, 256-271
Dettering, Richard, 325-342
Deviationists, 358-370
Dewey, John, 75, 163-164

INDEX

Dialectic reasoning, 20
"Dialectical Materialism and General Semantics," 364
Diamond, Stanley, 88-102
Dianetics, 274-275
Dickens, Charles, 260, 262
Dickens, Dali and Others, 265
Dickerson, Roy E., 290-291
Dill, Robert W., 77, 81, 82, 87
"Discontinuity," 272-274, 277
Diversity of Creatures, A, 276
Divine Comedy, The, 262
DKW automobile, 246
Dodge, 246
Dogma and heresy, 365-366
Dogmatic propositions and deviations, 370
Donaldson, Walter, 283n
Down Beat, 286n
Doyle, Arthur Conan, 262, 264
Drawings, primitive, 332
Dufy, Raoul, 226
Dupin, 262
Dynamics of Groups at Work, The, 51

Eames, Charles, 233
Eastern thought, 198, 199, 299-323. *See also* China
"Easy as A.B.C.," 276
Eaton, Jimmy, 284n
Edsel automobile, 243, 245
Education and the Nature of Man, 171
Education of parents, 167
Education for What Is Real, 171
Egyptian ideographs, 334, 335
Einstein, Albert, 175, 193
Eisenhower, Dwight D., 12, 363
Ekstein, Rudolph, 238
Electronic computers, 353
Eliot, George, 386
Eliot, T. S., 223, 384
Ellsworth, Bob, 283n
"Embedded canalizations," 253
Embler, Weller, 221, 234n, 260-261, 270, 371, 386
Emerson, A. E., 149
Emerson, Ralph Waldo, 376
Emotional Dynamics and Group Culture, 51
"Emotive language," 304
Empathy, 106, 182-183
Empirical "verifiability," 326

Empiricism, 13, 17, 326, 327
"Empty words," Chinese, 305
Ends-means relationship, 212
English language, 338
Entropy, relation to information, 356
Entwistle, William, 329, 331
Environment, adaptation to, 173
Epictetus, 223
Equifinality of response, 348, 349
Erewhon, 343, 357
"Essence" and "being," 336, 339
Ethics, and sanity, 215; and value in psychology, 190
Euphrosyne, 226
"Eureka feeling," 180
European psychologists, 193
Evaluation, internal locus of, 179, 213
Evaluations, evaluating of, 151
Evans, J. L., 325
Exclusiveness, rule of, 308
Exercise of Choice in Speech and Behavior (chart), 145
Existentialism, 378
"Expanding economy," 16-17
Experience, openness to, 178, 208, 209, 211
"Experience with Languages," 294
Experiences, and modern psychology, 199
Experimental knowledge, 300, 301, 302
Expressive aspect of oral communication, 329
Extensionality, 99, 132, 178, 204, 210, 211, 247, 280, 340
External evaluation and creativity, 182
Extralinguistic facts and meaning, 326

Faber, Billy, 283n
Facts, learning of, 374-376; and truth, 383
Fame, 384
Family, authoritarianism in, 161
Fascism, 158
Faulkner, William, 376
Fears and rumors, 37
Fermi, Enrico, 193
Fessenden, Reginald, 260
Feudalism, in China, 316
Fiat automobile, 246
57th Street Meeting of Friends, Chicago, 38
Fine art vs. popular art, 258-259, 260

Fishman, Irving, 77, 78, 80-81, 87
Fite, Warner, 294
Flair, 227
Folk and Jazz Festival, Music Inn, Lenox, Mass. (1954), 292
Ford automobile, 241, 242, 244, 245, 246
Form and civilization, 225
"Form," in Western thought, 319
Forster, E. M., 276, 382
Fotine, Larry, 283n
"Fractional anticipatory reactions," 341
Frank, Philipp, 190
Freed, Arthur, 281n
"Freedom of criticism," 360
Freedom, notion of, 158; ordeal of, 159; requirements of, 159; and responsibility, 183
French Revolution, 322
Freud, Sigmund, 113, 115, 123, 124, 189-190, 193, 197, 235, 244
"Freud's ploy," 115
Friendliness, attitudes of, 39
"From Science-fiction to Fiction-science," 274n
Fromm, Erich, 190, 193
Fromm-Reichmann, Freida, 239
Frost, Robert, 375
Fuel, concept of, 346-347
Fully functioning personality, 202-216
Futurism in art, 231

Gaboriau, 262
Galileo, 174, 337
General Motors, 242
"Generalized other," 129
Genteel tradition, in America, 224-226; in modern painting, 226-227
George Washington Bridge, New York, 229
Gershwin, George, 281n
Gershwin, Ira, 281n
Gestalt psychology, 193, 200, 347, 348, 349, 354
"Get-Rich-Quick" Wallingford, 265
Ghyasuddin Pathan, 69
Gibson, J. J., 252
Gleason, Ralph, 286n
Glenn, Edmund S., 12, 34
Glock, Charles Y., 75-76
Goals in life, 128
Goethe, 23, 192

"Goin' to Chicago Blues" (song), 285n
Goldstein, Kurt, 193
"Good Man Is Hard to Find, A" (song), 287n
Good manners, ritual of, 225
Gostrey, Maria, 226
Graces, the, 226
"Grapevine" communication, 101
Gray's Manual of Botany, 372-373
Great Heresies, The, 359
Greece, ancient, grammar, 304, 306; mythology, 314, 315, 316; philosophers, 294
Green, Anna Katherine, 266
Green, Eddie, 287n
Greene, Graham, 256, 261
Gropius, Walter, 232
Growth-fostering techniques in psychology, 196-197
"Guernica" (mural), 232
"Guest's Impression of New England, A," 376
Guilt, sense of, 161

Haley, Jay, 113, 125
Hall, E. K., Jr., 370
Hallucinations, 127
Hamilton, Lady, 226
Hammett, Dashiell, 261, 266, 267, 268
Handy, W. C., 285n, 286n
"Harlem Blues" (song), 285
Harper's Bazaar, 227
Hart, Lorenz, 281n, 282n
"Have You Ever Been Lonely?" (song), 284n
Hayakawa, S. I., 88, 96, 102, 103, 110, 202, 217, 234, 235, 240, 241, 246, 274, 279, 291n, 304, 328, 337
Hayes, Clancy, 292
Health, mental, 187, 196, 201, 204, 216. See also Sanity
Heat engines, as new principle of operation, 346-347, 349, 353
Heaven, in Chinese thought, 315, 316
Hegel. See Marx-Hegel concepts
Heresy, crisis situations, 370; and dogma, 365-366; perceptual problem of, 367; psychology of, 358-370; sacred cows, 366-367; term, 359
Herrick, Robert, 287
Heterosexual reproduction, 153
Hidden Persuaders, The, 242n

Higuera, Fred, 292
Hillman automobile, 246
Hinduism, 313, 365
Hitchcock, Alfred, 261
Hitler, Adolf, 62, 158, 248
Hiwassee Dam, 229-230
Hodgson, Arthur, 362
Hoffman, Nicolas von, 53, 65
Hogben, Lancelot, 335
"Hollow Men, The," 223
Holmes, Oliver Wendell, 108
Holmes, Sherlock, 261-268
Homer, 223, 224, 380
Honigmann, John J., 66, 74
Horney, Karen, 190, 193, 236
Hornung, E. W., 265
Horsepower in cars, 237-238
Hortatory aspect of oral communication, 329
Hostility, attitudes of, 39
Hound of Heaven, The, 262
House and Garden, 227
Housing problems, Chicago, 35-51
Housman, A. E., 383
Howard, Dick, 283n
Hu Shih, Dr., 318
Hubbard, L. Ron, 274-275
Hull, Clark, 330, 341
Human beings, limited conception of, 195; as a symbolic class, 206
Human Dynamics Laboratory, U. of Chicago, 48
Human nature, philosophy of, 191
Humanism in psychology, 186-201
Hume, David, 325
Hunt, Lester C., Jr., 53, 65
Hyde, Douglas, 368
Hyde Park *Herald*, Chicago, 48
Hyde Park-Kenwood area, Chicago, 38
Hyde Park-Kenwood Conference, 51
Hyperbole, device of, 260
Hypothetical reasoning, 18

I Killed Stalin, 269
"I Need You Now" (song), 284n
IBM machines, 352
Ideals and design, 234
Ideas, choice of, 381-382
Identification, 147
Identity, idea of, 314-315; "law of," 306, 308, 310, 313, 316, 320
"Identity logic," 306

Identity and Reality, 315
Ideographic writing, 332-337
Ideological differences and heresy, 370
IFD disease, 280-291
"Ignorant Oil" (song), 289
"Il Trovatore" (painting), 221-224
Iliad, 380
"I'll Never Smile Again" (song), 284n
"I'm Alone Because I Love You" (song), 283n
"I'm Gonna Lock My Heart" (song), 284n
Impotence, fear of, 235-240, 244
"Indexing" statements, 151, 210, 253
India, influence on Chinese thought, 313, 321; intensional orientation in Pakistan, 66-74
Indifference, attitudes of, 39
Individuals and individualism, and change, 166-171; forces against, 160-165; uniqueness of, 152-171; worth of, 159, 181-182
Indo-European languages, 326, 335, 337, 340
Industrial Areas Foundation of Chicago, 65
Industrial Relations Center, U. of Chicago, 65
Industrial Revolutions, 344, 347
Inference, in Western thought, 317; checking, 149
Information theory, 343-357; in counseling, 143
Information and truth, 378-379
Ink blot tests, 144
Innovators in America, 194
Inquisition, 366
Institute of General Semantics, Chicago, 133
Institute for Motivational Research, 246
Institutions, authoritarianism in, 161
Intake, in communication, 103-104
Intellectuals and raw experience, 200
Intelligence, 160
"Intelligent machines," 343-357
Intensional orientation and national unity, 66-74
Intensionality, 280, 326
International communication, 12-34
International Design Conference, Aspen, Colorado, 110

394   INDEX

International Society for General Semantics, Chicago Chapter, 51, 217, 271n; St. Louis Chapter, 291
Interpretation, difficulties of, 12-34
"Interpretation," as knowledge group, 322
"Intervention," concepts of, 22-23
Intranational loyalties, 66
Introspection technique in psychology, 198
Intuitional reasoning, 20
Involuntary Speech and Behavior (chart), 145
Inwood Institute, 370
Irrationality and motivation research, 244
Islam in Pakistan, 68-74
"Isms" and heresies, 364
"It," word, 307

Jacobs, Al, 284n
Jaguar, 246
James, Henry, 225, 381
Japanese language, 335
Japanese science, 337n
Jaques, Howard W., 133, 140
Javert, 262
Jazz, 279-291
Jeep, 241
Jefferson, Thomas, 159
"Jet-Propelled Couch, The," 238
Johnson, Myra, 292
Johnson, Philip C., 233
Johnson, Wendell, 96, 102, 280-281, 283, 290
Jones, Raymond F., 272, 274, 277
Journal of Experimental Psychology, 197
Judaism, 363
Judgment and perception, 126-128
Judgments and truth, 380-381
Jukeboxes, 353
Jung, Carl G., 190, 193

Kallen, Kitty, 286n
Kant, Immanuel, 300, 313, 319, 321
Kelley, Earl C., 152, 171
Kendig, M., 133n
Khwaja Nazimuddin, 74
Kihss, Peter, 76-86
Kipling, Rudyard, 276

Klapper, Joseph T., 75-76
Knowledge, authoritarian concept of, 163; Chinese approach to, 299-323; groups, 322; operationalist theory of, 340; social nature of theoretical, 302, 303
Knowing and the Known, 75
Kobe, Japan, 239-240
Koestler, Arthur, 366, 368
Koffka, Kurt, 193
Korzybski, Alfred, 102, 108, 112, 127, 145, 203-204, 207, 210, 215, 307, 322, 325, 359
Ku Klux Klan, 358

Labels, 378
Laboratory for Study of Teaching and Learning Processes, U. of Chicago, 51
La Bruyère, Jean de, 126
Lammi, Dick, 292
"Language substitutes," 333
Language in Action, 110
Language, Meaning and Maturity, 110, 234n, 304
Language in Thought and Action, 110
Language, Truth and Logic, 307
Languages, "abstract" and "concrete," 341; as a logical system, 340; cultural influences on, 12-34; relation to truth, 371-386
Lao Tzu, 313
Latin script and English language, 338
Laughlin, Francis B., 87
Law, Vernon, 76
"Law of identity," 306, 308, 310, 313, 316, 320
Lawrence, D. H., 214-215
"Laws of parsimony," 340
Laws of science, 164
Laziness, effect on linguistics, 340
Le Vicomte de Bragellonne, 262
Leadership concept, Puerto Rican, 62
Leadership-training groups, 184
Learning, as passive process, 200
LeCoq, Inspector, 262
Lee, Irving J., 96, 102, 107
Lenin, 360, 364, 367
Lenzen, V. F., 301
Les grâces, 225, 226
Les Miserables, 262
Levels of talk, 147

INDEX 395

Lewin, Kurt, 193
Li An-che, 323
Liaquat Ali Khan, 68n
Life, 251, 254
Life, as goal-directed, 128
Lin Shao Ch'i, 361
Lindeman, Edith, 286n
Linder, Robert, 238
"Linguistic thinking," 302
Linguistics, effect of laziness on, 340
Lipgar, Robert, 180n
Listening, importance of, 103-106, 132
"Little Things Mean a Lot" (song), 286n
Living things, fundamentals of, 352
Livingston, Arthur, 300
Lobdell, Frank, 240n, 246n
Logic, of analogy, 317-318; Chinese, 299-303; correlation logic, 316; Eastern vs. Western, 300-323; identity logic, 306; and language, 341; mathematical, 305; nature of, 304; of opposition, 320; of sentiment, 301
"Logical positivism," 325
Logical Syntax of Language, The, 301
Logographic writing, 333, 334
"Looking at the World Thru Rose Colored Glasses" (song), 283n
Love, songs of, 280-291
Lowe, Ruth, 284n
Lowell, James Russell, 228
Lowie, Robert, 66

Mabley, Jack, 258, 259-260
McCarran, Senator, 83
McCarran Act, 78
McCoy, Joe, 286n
Mach, Ernst, 325, 340
"Machine Stops, The," 276
Machines, benefits of, 166; and human nervous system, 343-357; influence of, 164-165; learning to live with, 170-171; technological "phylums" of, 345-347
McIntire, Samuel, 227
Macrorie, Ken, 75, 86
Magic, essence of, 280-281
Malie, Tommy, 283n
Maloney, Martin, 256, 271n
"Man I Love, The" (song), 281n
Manipulative aspect of oral communication, 329, 330

Mao's China: Party Reform Documents 1942-1944, 361
Map-territory relations, 209, 210, 252, 254
"Marauder," 243
Marcantonio, Vito, 64
Marconi, 260
Marcus Aurelius, 192
Marlow, Philip, 268
Marriage counseling, 290-291
Marx-Hegel concepts, 13, 17, 20, 28, 30, 318, 320, 321
Maslow, A. H., 127, 186, 201, 204-210, 214, 215
Mass communication, 220
Mass education, 163
"Matching the action" in cinematography, 250
Materialism and Empirio-criticism, 364n
Materialistic thought, 314
Mathematical logic, 305
"Mathematical properties" of world, 322
Matisse, Henri, 226-227
Mau Mau, 358
Mead, George Herbert, 129n
Mead, Margaret, 13-14
Meadows, Fred, 283n
Meaning; extralinguistic facts, 326; intensional tests, 326; multiplicity, 141; phonetic writing, 325-342; picture writing, 331-333; search for a criterion, 325-328; speech, 329-331
Measuring Intelligence, 129n
Mechanistic science, 164
Mecklin, J. M., 366
Meeting of East and West, 336
"Mein Fuehrer," 62
"Memphis Blues, The," (song), 286n
Men Like Gods, 276
Mencius, 317, 320
Mencius on the Mind, 317
Mendelsohn, Eric, 233
Menninger, Karl, 236
Menninger Foundation, 238
Menotti, Gian-Carlo, 261
Mental health, see Health, mental
Mental Health Research Institute, U. of Michigan, 357
Mercury automobile, 239, 243
Merrill, Maud, 129n

Merrill-Palmer School, Detroit, 132
"Metaphor in Everyday Life," 234
"Metaphor and Social Belief," 234n
Metaphysics, Western, 321
MG automobile, 246
Mian Mumtaz Muhammad Khan Daultana, 73
Mielziner, Jo, 229
Mies van der Rohe, Ludwig, 233
Miles, Lizzie, 292
Milk, regulations concerning, 88-102
Miller, Arthur, 261, 365, 367
Milton, 384
Mind, Self and Society, 129n
Mind and Society, The, 300
Ming dynasty, 313
Ministry of Fear, The, 256
Minority groups, 35-51, 52-65
Miró, Joan, 207
Mirza Ghulam Ahmad, 71-72
Mr. Justice Raffles, 265
Modern architecture, straight line in, 231-232
Modern design, 221-234
"Modern Science of Mental Health," 274
Modifiability of verbal environment, 149
Mohammad, 69
Monet, Claude, 234
Monsieur Verdoux, 268
Moonstone, The, 262
Moorhouse, A. C., 331
"Moral" problems, 215
"Morality and the Novel," 214n
Morgan, Russ, 283n
Morris Minor automobile, 246
Morton, Jelly Roll, 287
Motion pictures, 248, 249, 250, 252-253, 262
Motivation and Personality, 201, 204
Motivational research, 241-246
Mount Suribachi, 251
"Mowing" (poem), 375
Mowrer, O. H., 177n
"Multiple therapy" in psychoanalysis, 122
Multiplicity of causation and meanings, 141
Murders in the Rue Morgue, The, 261
Music appreciation classes, 169
Muslims in Pakistan, 68-74

Mussolini, 158
Mutual Assistance Program, 15
"My Blue Heaven" (song), 283n
"My Heart Stood Still" (song), 281n
"My Ideal" (song), 281n
Myers, Russell, 287
Myerson, Emile, 315
Mystery of Edwin Drood, The, 262
Mystery of Marie Roget, The, 261
Mystery stories, 256-271
Myth of flight and pursuit, 262

Nacionalista party, Puerto Rico, 55
Names and naming, 318, 319, 326-327, 371-386
Napier, Bill, 292
"National character," 13
National Council of YMCA's, 290
National unity and intensional orientation, 66-74
Nationalism, 66-74
Nature, 153, 166, 234, 310, 314, 317
"Nature" (painting), 226
Nature of Physical Theory, The, 302
"Nature of Social Perception, The," 367
Nazism, 158, 278
Negative entropy, 344
"Negro blues," 280-291
Negroes in Chicago, 35-51
Neighborhood Finds Itself, A, 51
Neighborhoods, communication in, 35-51
Nepravilnoe, 13
Nervous system, technological models of, 343-357
"Neurotic patterns," 117
Neutra, Richard, 233
New England church architecture, 230
New England Journeys, 376
New Knowledge in Human Values, 201
New Orleans Memories, 287n
New York, Puerto Ricans in, 63
New York *Daily News*, 81
New York *Herald Tribune*, 81
New York *Journal-American*, 81
New York *Post*, 362
New York Times, The, 76-87, 363, 364
New Yorker, The, 251
Newman, Cardinal John Henry, 359
News reporting, 75-87
Newton, Marshall E., 76

INDEX 397

Newtonian physics, 301, 337
Niebuhr, Reinhold, 368
1984 (novel), 276, 277, 385
Nobel Prize winners, United States, 193
Noel, Sterling, 269, 270
Nominalism, 14, 18, 317
Nonconformists, 358-370
"Normal distribution curve" of degrees of sanity, 143
"Normal" people, 207-208
North Atlantic Treaty Organization (NATO), 14-15
Northrop, F. S. C., 336, 337
Northwestern University, 292
"Nothing-but" label, 347, 348
"Novel as Metaphor, The," 234n, 261n
"Nudist," term, 362

O. Henry, 265
Objectivity, 380
Objects as class members, 327
"Obligations," 58, 59, 158
"Observational order," 301
Odyssey, 262
Occam's razor, 340
Odd John, 276
Old Testament, 262
Oliver Wendell Holmes, 110
O'Malley, L. S., 365
O'Neill, Ray, 83
"On Abstracting," 322n
"One-upmanship," 113-114
Ontology in philosophy, 314
"Open Window in Nice" (painting), 226
Openness to experience, *see* Experience, openness to
Operational Philosophy, 357
Opportunism, 360
Opposites, relation of, 310
Oral communication, aspects of, 329
Organismic reasoning, 20, 193, 200
Organizations, Puerto Rican, in Chicago, 52-65
Oriental thought, *see* China; Eastern thought
Ortega y Gasset, José, 381
Orwell, George, 265, 276, 385
Otto, Max, 12
Outdoor Art Club, Mill Valley, California, 217

Output, in communication, 103
Overgeneralizing, 108

Packard, Vance, 242n, 243n
Pakistan, 66-74
Pakistan, Heart of Asia, 68n
Pao Hsi Shih, 311
"Paper Doll" (song), 284n
Parent education, 167
Pareto, Vilfredo, 300-301
"Parts of speech" vs. "parts of writing," 341
Passive entertainment, 172
Patterns of thought, 12-14; classification of, 17-25
Pavlov, 193
"Peak experiences," 199
Peasants' Revolt, 358
Pemberton, William H., 141, 151
People in Quandaries, 281
Perception, 126-128, 154, 368
"Perceptual abstractions," 327, 331, 332, 336, 339
Perceptual knowledge, 299
Personality, theories of, 202-216
Pevsner, Nikolaus, 232
Philosophy, controversy, 12-13; Eastern, 299-323; ontology in, 314; unconscious, 190
Phoenix: Posthumous Papers of D. H. Lawrence, 214n
Phonetic writing, 325-342
Photographs as abstractions, 250-251
Photography as communication, 247-255
Piaget, Jean, 128-129, 131, 313
Picasso, Pablo, 194, 232
"Pickling in brine fallacy," 108
"Picture theory" of language, 327, 328, 332
Picture writing, nature of meaning in, 331-333
Pictures, as communication, 247-255; facts and naming of, 374-375
Pioneers of Modern Design, 232
Plank, Robert, 238, 278
Plato and Platonism, 306, 312, 324, 325, 328, 339
Play therapy, 131, 133-140
Playboy, 245
Ploys in psychoanalysis, 115-125

398 INDEX

Plymouth automobile, 239, 241, 244, 245, 246
Pocket Atlantic, The, 266n
Poe, Edgar Allan, 260, 261
Poem, by a four-year-old, 131
Poetic aspect of oral communication, 329
Poetry as equipment for living, 289
Political ceremony, 67
Political thought, analogical thought in, 317-318
Pollock, Jackson, 108, 231
Popular art vs. fine art, 258-259, 260
Popular songs, 279-291
Porter, Katherine Anne, 373
Portrait of a Lady, 381
Possibility and children, 126-132
Pragmatism, 13, 17
Predictability in maladjusted individuals, 146-147
Pribram, Karl, 13, 17, 20
"Primary process" in psychoanalysis, 198
Primrose, Joe, 286n
"Principle of economy," 340
"Principle of least effort," 340
Principles of Abnormal Psychology, 201
Problem-centered psychology, 194-195
Problem-solving, 169, 184
"Programs" and "goals," in information theory, 353-354
Project for the Study of Schizophrenic Communication, Veterans Administration Hospital, Palo Alto, Cal., 125
Projecting, 151
Propagandistic aspect of oral communication, 329
Psychoanalysis, 113-125, 187
Psychological Abstracts, 133
Psychology, of children, 126-132; conception of human beings, 195; end experiences, 199; freedom and creativity, 183; growth-fostering techniques, 196-197; humanistic, 186-201; importance of, 186-187; of individual, 159; introspection, 198; means and methods in, 194-195; philosophy of, 192; rodentomorphization of, 198; safety and creativity, 181-183; semantics in, 133-140
Psychotherapy and Personality Change, 185

Psychotherapy—Theory and Research Methods, 177n
Psychotics, ploys of, 121-123
Public Arts, The, 220
Public schools, *see* Schools
Puerto Ricans in Chicago, 52-65
Puerto Rico, history, 54-55
Punning (rebus-making), 334
Purdue University, 292
Puritanism, 58, 226, 230, 375
Purloined Letter, The, 261
Purposeful behavior, 153, 349, 352

Quaid-i-Azam Muhammad Ali Jinnah, 69
Quakers, 366
"Quantity of organization" concept, 344
Questions, Chinese vs. Western, 316-317
"Questions of uniqueness," 107
Quine, Willard V. O., 326

Raffles, 265, 268
"Raffles and Miss Blandish," 265n
Railroads, French, 19-20
Randolph, Jack, 83-84
Rank, Otto, 193
Rapoport, Anatol, 102, 343, 357, 364, 367
Reading and children, 162
Reality and children, 126-132
Reality principle and motivational research, 241-246
Rebus-making, 334
Reciprocity, idea of, 313, 314
"Rectification of names," 318, 319
Reed, Carol, 261
"Referential language," 304
Reflex theory of behavior, 348
"Reichian resistance" ploys, 124
Religion, authoritarianism in, 166-167; Chinese, 314-316; and mysticism, 167; and science, 314; Western, 314
Renault automobile, 246
Report of Court of Inquiry into Punjab Disturbances, 69n, 71
"Research Teams" in counseling, 151
"Residues" and "derivations," 320-321
"Resistance ploys" in psychoanalysis, 124
"Responsibility," 58, 59, 183

Return of Sherlock Holmes, The, 264
Reverse-angle shots, in motion pictures, 250
Richards, I. A., 317
"Rights," 58, 59
Rinehart, Mary Roberts, 266
Ritual of good manners, 225
Robey House, 104, 106
Robin, Leo, 281n
"Rock Pile Blues" (song), 289
Rodentomorphization of human psychology, 198
Rodgers, Richard, 281n, 282n
Roebling, John, 229
Roebling, Washington, 229
Rogers, Carl R., 172, 177n, 185, 204-213, 214, 215, 216
"Role-playing," 378
Roman Church, 366
Romney, George, 226
Rorschach test, 193
Rose, Wally, 292
Rossellini, Roberto, 261
Rousseau, 193, 322
"Rugged individualism," 157
Rumors, 37, 39
Rushing, Jimmy, 285n, 286n, 292
Russell, Betrand, 305, 322
Russian language, 13, 15-17, 26-33
Russian Nonconformity, 362
Russian Orthodox Church, 360, 362
Russian Treason Trials, 360
Russo, Salvatore, 133, 140
Ryle, Gilbert, 341

"St. James Infirmary" (song), 286n
Salomon, Louis B., 3, 11
Sammy Price Trio, 292
San Francisco *News*, 286n
Sanctuary, 260
Sanity, 205, 215, 271, 277; definition of, 203-204; degrees of, 143
Schools, authoritarianism in, 162-163; and living in modern society, 169; modification of, 167; subject matter in, 168
Schwartz, Harry, 85
Science, abstractions of, 336-337; information, 379-380; laws of, 164; as method, 195; philosophy of, 190-191; and religion, 314; terminology of, 105

Science of Culture, The, 2
Science and the Goals of Man, 357
Science and Sanity, 112, 203, 307, 359
Science fiction and communication, 272-278
Scientific American, The, 75
Scientific aspect of oral communication, 329
Scientific information, 379-380
Scientific Conference on Interpreting and Intercultural Barriers of Communication, (1956), 34
Scobey, Bob, 292
Second American Congress on General Semantics, 133
Second Conference on General Semantics, (1954), 34, 151, 291
Secretariat building, U. N., 233
Security, concepts of, 202-203
Seldes, Gilbert, 220
Selections from Science and Sanity, 359
"Self-actualizing person," 204-213
"Self-concepts," 207
Self-defamation and churches, 166-167
"Self-fulfilling prophecies," 101
Self-insight, 216
Self-knowledge, 209-210
Semantic dimensions of pictures, 250-251
Semantic play therapy, 133-140
"Semiclassic" music, 279-280
Semitic-speaking people, and Egyptian writing, 335
Senior, Clarence, 64
"Sensa" and knowledge, 322
"Sense," word, 318-319
Sentence-gestalt, 341
Servetus, 359, 360
Servo-mechanisms, 343-357
Seventh National Hi-Y-Tri-Hy-Y Congress, 290
Sex, and automobiles, 235-240, 241, 244; in schools, 163
"Sexual Fantasy and the 1957 Car," 235-240, 241
Shakespeare, 193
Shand, Terry, 284n
Shang Shu, 316
Sherlock Holmes, 261-268
Shuo Wen, 309, 310
"Sign of Four, The," 263
"Sign-writing" and "sound-writing,"

335-340
Simca, 246
Simon, Maurice, 368
"Simple Art of Murder, The," 266n
Slavery, 159
Slums, 35-51, 169-170
Smillie, David, 126, 132
Smith, Bessie, 287, 288, 291
Sniper, The, 268
Social co-operation, 157
Social Democracy, 360
Social development, 162
Social disorganization, 36-38
Social movements, psychology of, 358-370
Social Research, Inc., 246
Sociological World, 323
Socrates, 177, 209
"Some of the Directions and End Points of Therapy," 177n
"Somebody Else Is Taking My Place" (song), 283n
Songs, popular, 279-291
Sonnet, Matthew Arnold, 222
Sophocles, 223, 224
Sorcerer's Apprentice, legend of, 345n
Southeast Chicago Commission, 51
Soviet Union (publication), 77
Space, Time and Deity, 302
Spanish language, 53-62
Specialization and democracy, 156-159
Speech, meaning in, 329-331; relation of writing to, 328-335
Spengler, Oswald, 314
Spillane, Mickey, 257, 259, 261, 268, 270
Spinoza, 192
S—R psychology, *see* Stimulus-Response psychology
Stag parties, 235-236
Stalin, Joseph, 158, 269, 361
Standardization, 165
Stanley Theater, New York City, 81-82
Stapledon, Olaf, 276
Steadfast, 375
Steiger, Jimmy, 283n
Stein, Gertrude, 384
Stella, Joseph, 229
Stimulus-response psychology, 199, 347
Storing and transmitting of information, 343-357
Story of American Dissent, The, 366

Straight line in modern architecture, 231-232
Strand Magazine, 262
Structural Differential, 145-149
Studebaker, 242
"Study in Scarlet, A," 262, 263
Stutz, Carl, 286n
Subject matter in schools, 163, 168
Substance, idea of, 305, 306, 307, 312-315, 321
Subways, Paris vs. New York, 19-20
Sung dynasty, 313
Syllabic symbols principle, 334-335
Syllogistic thinking, 317
Symbol-fixation, 206-207
Symbolic expression, freedom of, 183
Synoptic thinkers, 193
Syntax of photography, 249-250

Talmudic Scholars, 368
Tao in Chinese thought, 310
Taoism, 365
Taste, 234, 381
Taylor, Edmond, 365
Taylor, George A., 298
Teachers, authoritarian, 168
Teaching, of subject matter, 163
Telemachus, 262
Teleology and vitalism, 349
Telepathy, 276, 277
"Telephone switchboard" model of nervous system, 347-348
"Telescreen," 276
Television, 170, 245, 248, 249, 257, 266
Tempest, The, 378
Terman, Lewis M., 129
Terminological tangles, 104-105
Terminology of sciences, 105
Thackeray, William Makepeace, 260
Thalia, 226
Thelen, Herbert A., 35, 51
"They-feeling" vs. "We-feeling," 363
Thief in the Night, A, 265
"Thinking" as defense, 149
Thompson, Francis, 262
Thoreau, Henry, 228, 229, 376
"Thought, Language and Culture," 323
"Threatening" language behavior, 145
Time, 243
"Tired" (song), 289n
"To be" and "to do," 20-23, 306-308

INDEX 401

Toch, Hans H., 358, 370
Tools, 345, 349, 374
Tot-lots, civic, 43, 46
Toward a Theory of Creativity, 172-185, 211
Transactional psychology, 76-77
Transactions of the New York Academy of Science, 367
"Transfer of learning," 331
"Transference" in psychoanalysis, 120
Translation, difficulties of, 12-34
Translations, U.N. Secretariat, 25
Transportation, French vs. American, 18-20
Treasury of the Blues, A, 285n, 286n, 289n
Trees in art, 229
Trevisa, John, 338
"Trial by Newspaper," 75
Triumph, 246
Triumph of the Alphabet, The, 331-332
Trotsky, Leon, 360
Trotskyism, 364
Truth, relation to language, 371-386; word, 382
Tsien, T. H., 324
Tyrants, 158-159, 178

Ulama, Muslim theologians, in Pakistan, 71-74
Un-American Activities, House Committee on, 75
Unconscious mind, 197
Unconscious processes, 113
Uniformity, 165
Uniforms in schools, 163
Uniqueness of individuals, 152-171, 200-201, 214
United Nations, buildings, New York, 233; Secretariat translations, 25, 33; Security Council, 25-33
United Press, 80, 81
United States, High Commission in Germany, 364; Nobel Prize winners from, 193; Office of Information, 250
Universalistic reasoning, 18
"Universals," recognition of, 348
University of Chicago, 48, 51, 292
Urban congestion, 289
Urban living, 169
Utopian fiction, 275-276

Validity, problem of, 323
Valjean, Jean, 262
Values, 190, 196, 302, 380-381
Van Gogh, Vincent, 214
Variety in nature, 153
Vassal, Gabrielle, 365
Vendryes, J., 332, 334
Verbal environment, modifiability of, 149
Verbs "to be" and "to do," 20-23, 306-308
Veterans Administration Mental Hygiene Clinic, Cleveland, Ohio, 278
Viereck, Peter, 256
Violence, literature of, 256-271
Visual aids, 252-253
Vitalism, 347, 349, 352
Vocabulary of art criticism, 104-105
Vogue, 227
Volkswagen, 237, 246
Voltaire, 262
Volvo, 246
Von Mises, Richard, 325
Voting, concepts of, 60
Voyage dans le Soleil, 276

Walden, 228
Walden Pond, 228-229
Wall Street Journal, The, 246
Walsh, Raoul, 261
Warner, W. Lloyd, 67
Watson, 261, 263
Welker, Senator, 76-87
Wells, H. G., 276
Wendt, Paul R., 247, 255n
Wertheimer, Max, 193
Western thought, categories of, 315
"What I Believe," 382
"What Is Meant by Aristotelian Structure of Language?" 304
"What's in a Picture," 251-252
White, Leslie A., 2
Whitehead, Alfred North, 301, 314
Whiting, George, 283n
Whiting, Richard, 281n
"Who Cares Who Killed Roger Ackroyd?" 258n
"Why Don't You Do Right?" (song), 286n
Wichita Guidance Center, Wichita, Kansas, 135-140
Wieboldt Foundation, 48

Wiener, Norbert, 344, 356
Wilde, Oscar, 234
Wilder, Billy, 261
Williams, Spencer, 289n
Williams, Tennessee, 261
Wilson, Edmund, 257-258, 260, 261
Wilson, Woodrow, 266
"Winin' Boy Blues" (song), 287
Winterset, 229
Wittgenstein, Ludwig, 325
Woman in White, The, 262
"Worker-priest" controversy, in Catholic Church, 364
Workshop Way of Learning, The, 171
World, external, as "structure," 322
World outlook and facts, 192
World War I, and concepts of communication, 277
Wright, Frank Lloyd, 104, 106, 232

Wright, Tom, 38
Writing, relation of speech to, 328-335
Wylie, Philip, 236

Yang and *yin*, 310, 312
Yenching Journal of Social Studies, 323
"You Were Meant for Me" (song), 281n
"You Were Only Fooling" (song), 283n
Young, Joe, 283n
"Young Woman's Blues" (song), 288-289
"You've Been a Good Ole Wagon" (song), 287n

Zadig, 262
Zionism, 363, 364
Zipg, George K., 340

Etc., a review of general semantics.
Our language and our world; selections from Etc.: a review of general semantics, 1953–1958. Edited by S. I. Hayakawa. Illus., except as noted, by William H. Schneider. [1st ed.] New York, Harper [1959]

xii, 402 p. illus. 22 cm.

Bibliographical footnotes.

1. General semantics—Addresses, essays, lectures. 2. Language and languages. I. Hayakawa, Samuel Ichiyé, 1906– ed. II. Title.

B820.E83   149.94082   59–6324

Library of Congress